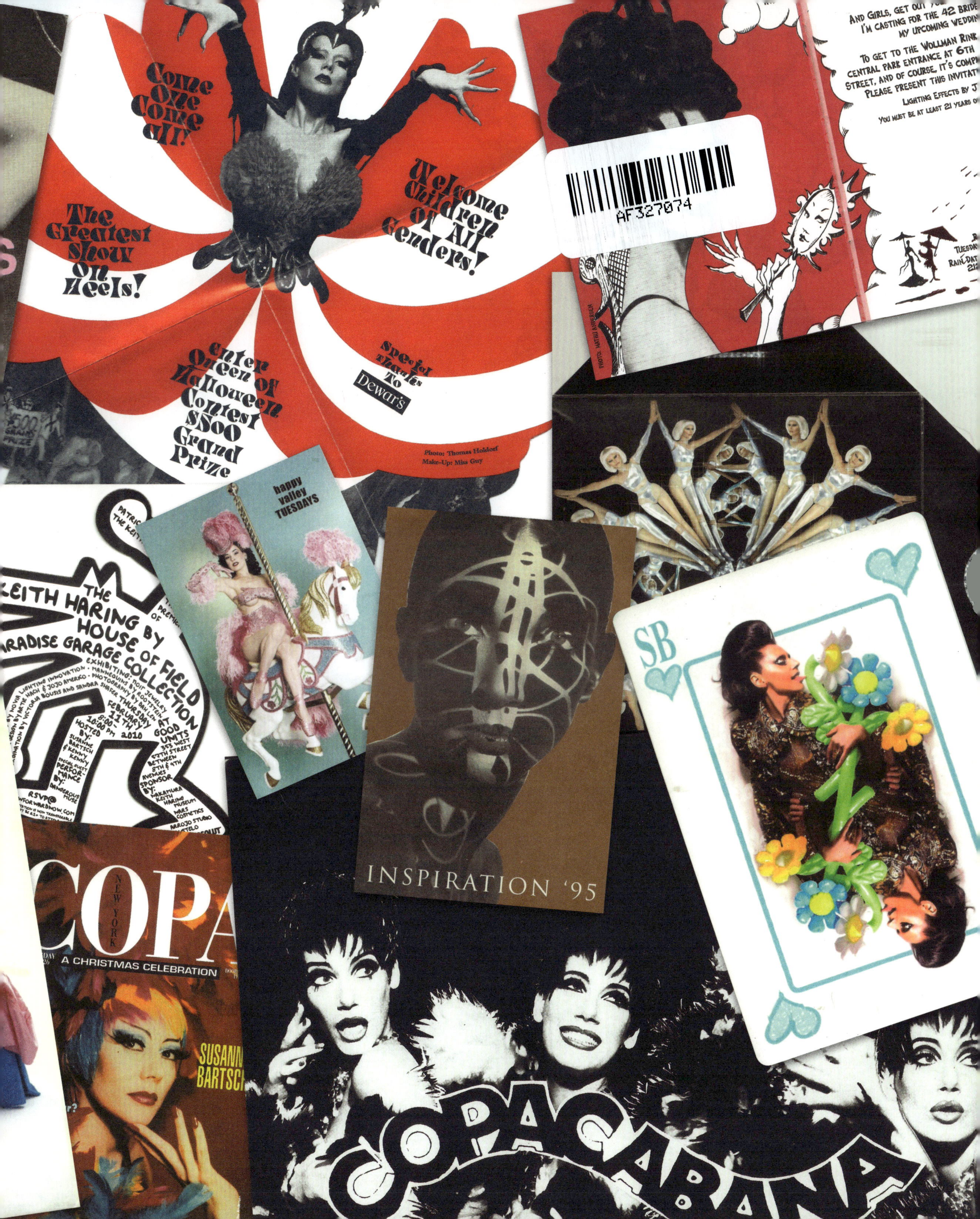
Come One Come All!
Welcome Children of All Genders!
The Greatest Show on Heels!
Enter Queen of Halloween Contest $500 Grand Prize
Special Thanks To Dewar's
Photo: Thomas Holdorf
Make-Up: Miss Guy
AND GIRLS, GET OUT YOUR
I'M CASTING FOR THE 42 BRID
MY UPCOMING WEDDIN
TO GET TO THE WOLLMAN RINK
CENTRAL PARK ENTRANCE AT 6TH
STREET, AND OF COURSE, IT'S COMPLI
PLEASE PRESENT THIS INVITAT
Lighting Effects by J
You must be at least 21 years o
AF327074
THE KEITH HARING
HOUSE OF FIELD
PARADISE GARAGE COLLECTION
happy valley TUESDAYS
GOOD UMITS
INSPIRATION '95
SB
COPA
NEW YORK
A CHRISTMAS CELEBRATION
SUSANNE BARTSCH
COPACABANA

Fashion Underground

The World of Susanne Bartsch

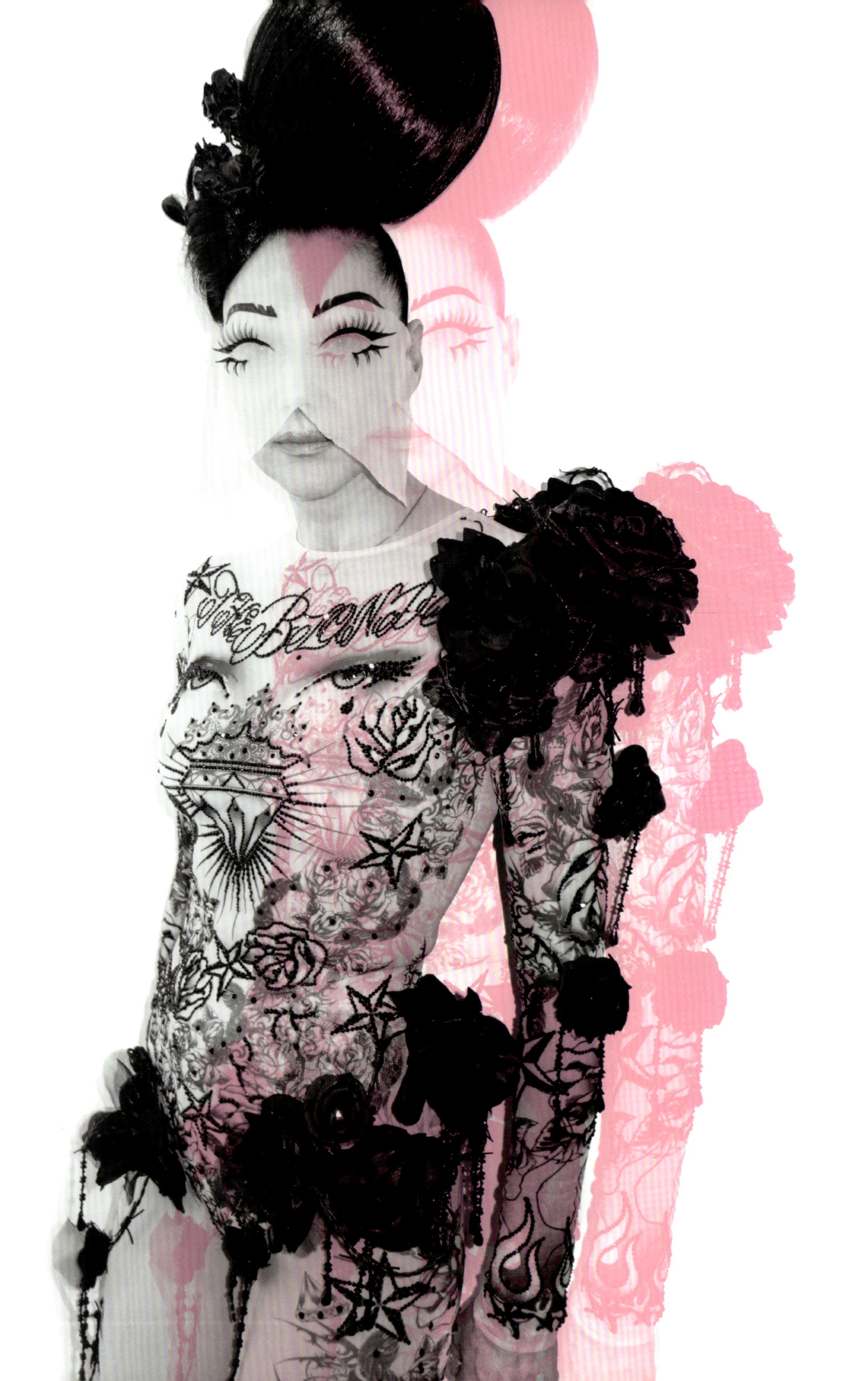

Yale University Press New Haven and London in association with
The Fashion Institute of Technology New York

Valerie Steele and Melissa Marra
with Susanne Bartsch and Waleed Khairzada

Fashion Underground

The World of Susanne Bartsch

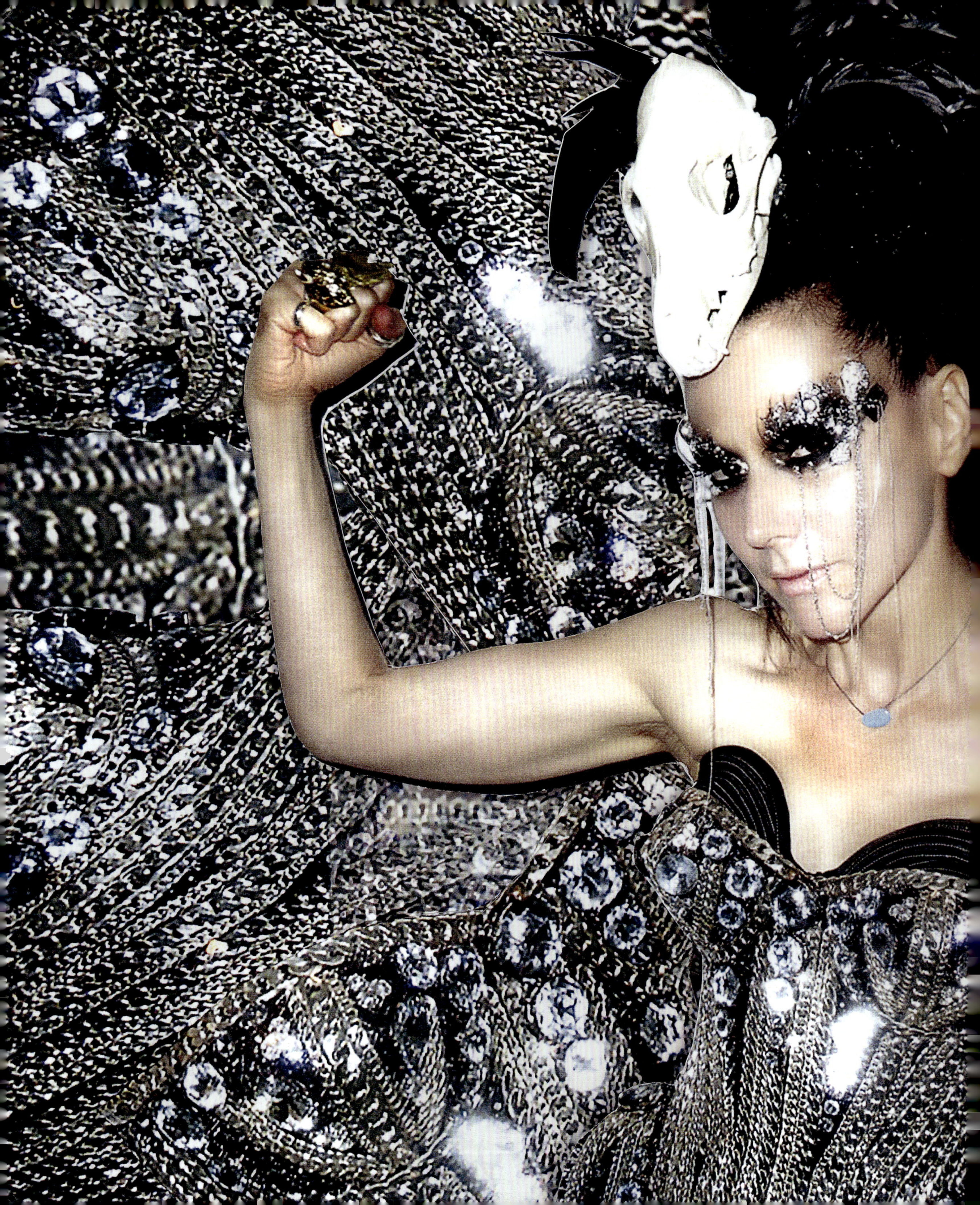

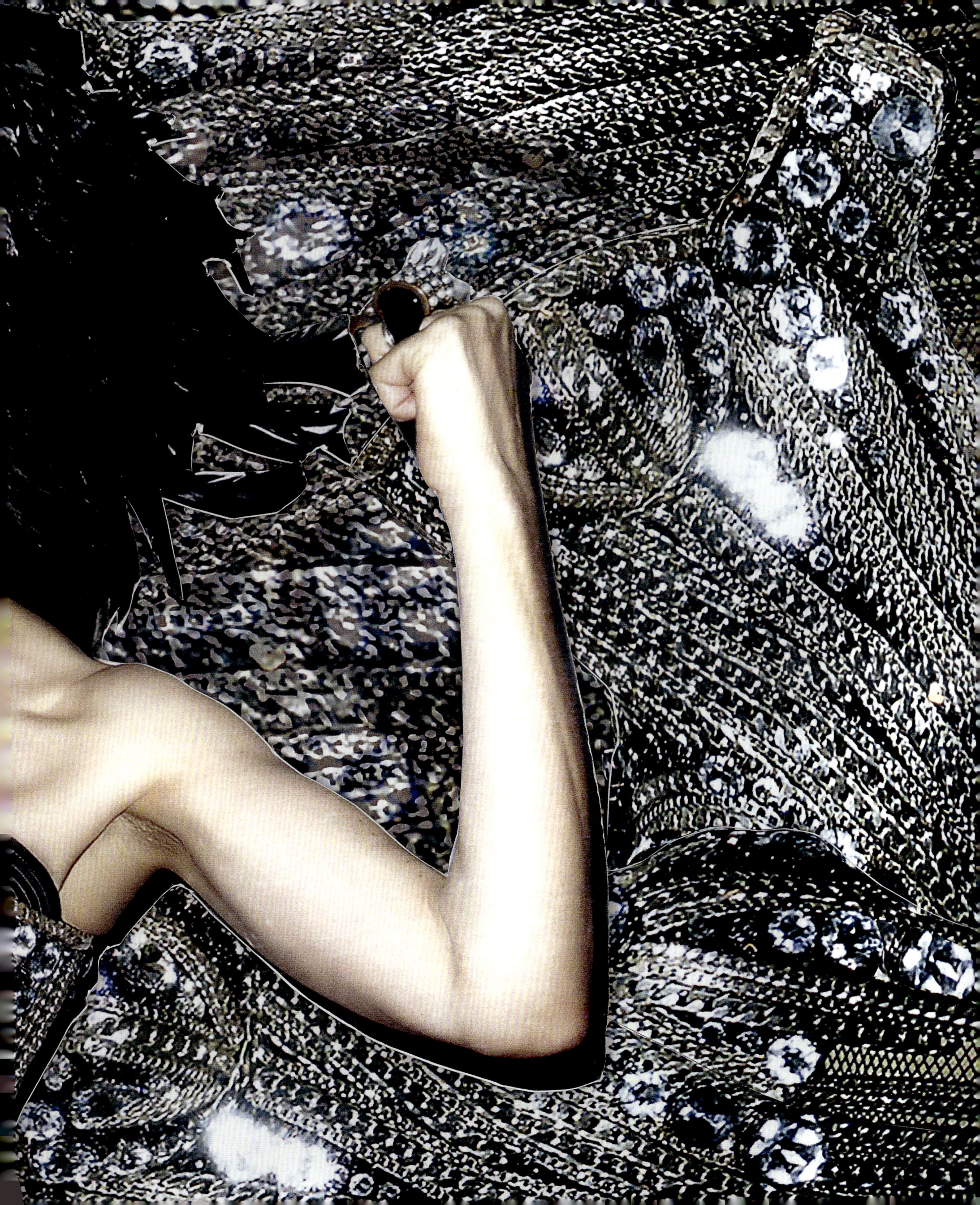

Designed by Paul Sloman / +SUBTRACT

Printed and bound in Italy by Conti Tipolcolor S.p.A.

Library of Congress Cataloging-in-Publication Data

Steele, Valerie, author.
  Fashion underground : the world of Susanne Bartsch / Valerie Steele.
    pages cm
  Includes bibliographical references.
  ISBN 978-0-300-21462-8 (cl : alk. paper)
 1. Bartsch, Susanne, 1951– –Influence.
 2. Fashion designers–United States–Biography. 3. Fashion design.
 4. Counterculture–New York (State)–New York.
 5. Special events–Planning. I. Title.
  TT505.B34S74 2015
  746.9'2092--dc23
  [B]
                          2015026151

A catalogue record for this book is available from
The British Library

Frontispiece: Susanne in bodysuit by
The Blonds. Blonds fashion show, February 2015.
Photo by Roxanne Lowit, adapted by Nick Shea.

Pages 4–5 and front cover: Portrait of Susanne Bartsch.
Photo: Marco Ovando, art: Maxwell N. Burnstein.

Back cover: Susanne at the opening night of her
Kunst parties, Verboten Club, Brooklyn, March 2013.
Photo by Oliver Correa.

Contents

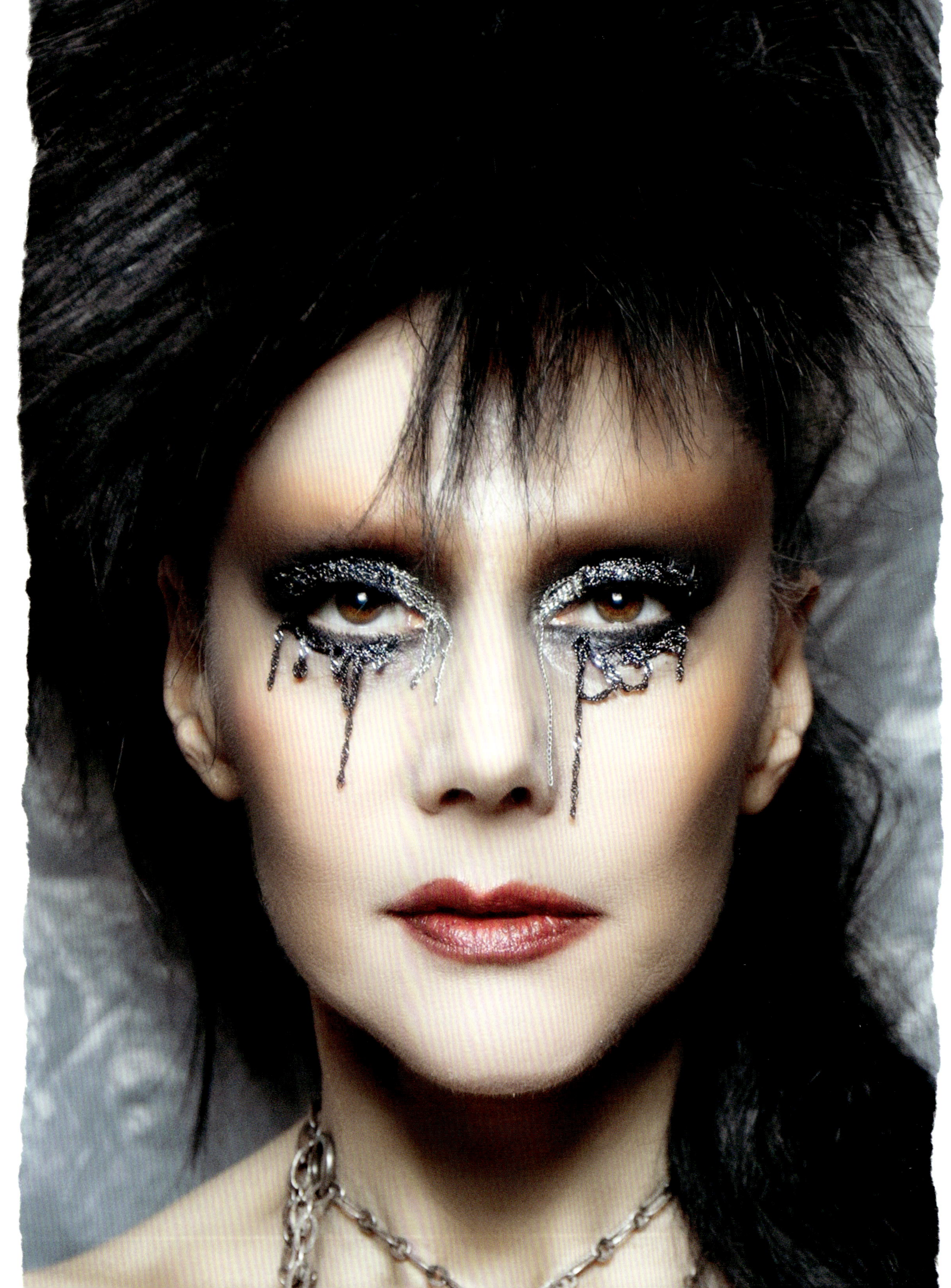

Fashion Underground
The World of Susanne Bartsch
By Valerie Steele

Born in Switzerland, Susanne Bartsch moved to London as a teenager and was part of the fashion scene there for more than a decade before arriving in New York City on February 14, 1981. Although she loved New York, Bartsch missed the flamboyant, post-Punk styles of London. So she opened her own boutique in SoHo and began importing avant-garde fashion by designers such as BodyMap and Vivienne Westwood. Bartsch also organized influential fashion shows like "New London in New York" and "London Goes to Tokyo," featuring designers such as Rachel Auburn, Leigh Bowery, and Stephen Jones. Channeling her ability to stage fashion spectacles, and inspired by the London club nights Blitz and Taboo, in 1986 she organized her first party at Savage, a club a few doors from the Chelsea Hotel, where she lived.

"It was about seeing and being seen," says Bartsch. She quickly became known for her spectacular events, which brought together uptown and downtown, gay and straight, people of all races, genders, and ages – united by a love of dressing up. "It was drag queens, strippers, muscle men, feathers," says Bartsch. "Later it became more androgynous." Many people created incredible one-of-a-kind looks. But life was not just a party. AIDS was devastating the gay community, and, in 1989 Bartsch organized the Love Ball, a pioneering AIDS benefit that married fashion and philanthropy.

Over the next twenty-five years of sartorial self-expression, Bartsch has been hailed as "the nightlife equivalent of a couture label."[2] Her Halloween and New Year's Eve parties and her Copacabana and Fashion Week events, in particular, have become legendary. Her penchant for extreme fashions by as-yet-unknown talents has helped launch the careers of people like the corsetiere Mr. Pearl and the designer Zaldy. As the editorial director of *Paper* magazine,

"Style is about expressing yourself. You can be whatever you want to be – a silver screen siren, a Marie Antoinette baroque creature, a Victorian punk. I love that about fashion and makeup!"[1]

"Makeup has become an essential if not major part of my looks."
Photo by Santiago Felipe.

Mickey Boardman puts it, "Susanne is a beacon of over-the-top fabulous, night-life-inspired, do-it-yourself fashion."[3]

But this book is not only about one woman, however extraordinary her personal style; it is about her entire world – a fashion underground of creative individuals, who have taken dressing up to the level of performance art. Fashion is a complex global system and a multi-billion-dollar industry, involving the production and consumption of commodities, images, and fantasies. Yet fashion is also an extremely personal, physical phenomenon – what scholars call an "embodied practice" – and, as such, it expresses ideas about identity, gender, and sexuality. The term "fashion underground" refers to a subculture comprised of diverse individuals who are not necessarily (yet) fashion professionals, but who devote considerable time and attention to fashioning their appearance. Their role in creating and influencing fashion has not been fully appreciated, but they have been crucial players in that world.

Creativity and Subcultural Capital

Creativity is a phenomenon whereby something new is created – be it an idea, a work of art, or an invention. Creativity is usually attributed primarily to an individual "genius," such as Pablo Picasso or Coco Chanel. But the world of Susanne Bartsch demonstrates what research has shown – that creativity "arises from the synergy of many sources and not only from the mind of a single person," as the psychologist Mihaly Csikszentmihaly puts it.[4] Especially relevant to the study of creativity is the concept of the "motley crew," an expression that refers to a group of people of diverse backgrounds, appearance, and personality, who have specialized skills and personal tastes. The fifteenth-century term "motley" signifies the multi-colored costume of the court jester. A motley crew is thus the opposite of a uniform, homogenous group.[5] The motley crew may also be compared with members of a "subculture" or an "underground," that is, a group of people that distinguishes itself from the larger, mainstream culture to which it belongs.

It is from this diversity and outsider-as-insider status that their creativity emerges. Everyone mentions the variety of Bartsch's milieu, and this is important because a creative milieu tends to be characterized by diversity, not homogeneity, and also by freedom, rather than hierarchy or rigidity.[6] Creativity is related closely to an intense interest in a particular domain, such as fashion, which, in turn, leads individuals to acquire a deep body of knowledge about relevant techniques and moments in fashion history. If creativity is to flourish, there must be a group of knowledgeable people who come together to share ideas. Bartsch and her friends comprise a motley crew of Club Kids, drag queens, performers, and creators, from a wide range of backgrounds. They are members of a subculture that unite around a deep interest in fashion, defined not in

1 Mr. Pearl. Photo by Josef Astor.

2 Susanne with her Adel Rootstein mannequin on the tube in London. Outfits by Mathu and Zaldy. Originally appeared in *The Face*, December 1991. Photo by Norbert Schoerner.

3 Susanne at her home in the Chelsea Hotel, wearing a corset by Mr. Pearl, Early 1990s. © Michael James O'Brien.

4 Susanne wearing "penis corset" by Mr. Pearl, *Vanity Fair*, February 1989. Photo by Josef Astor.

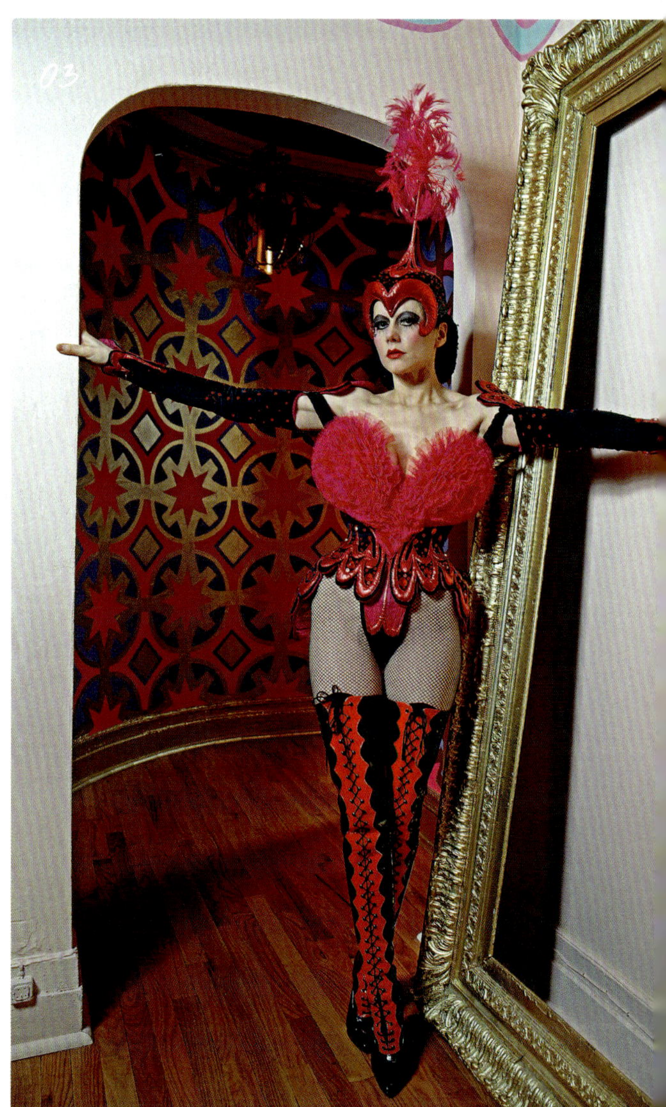

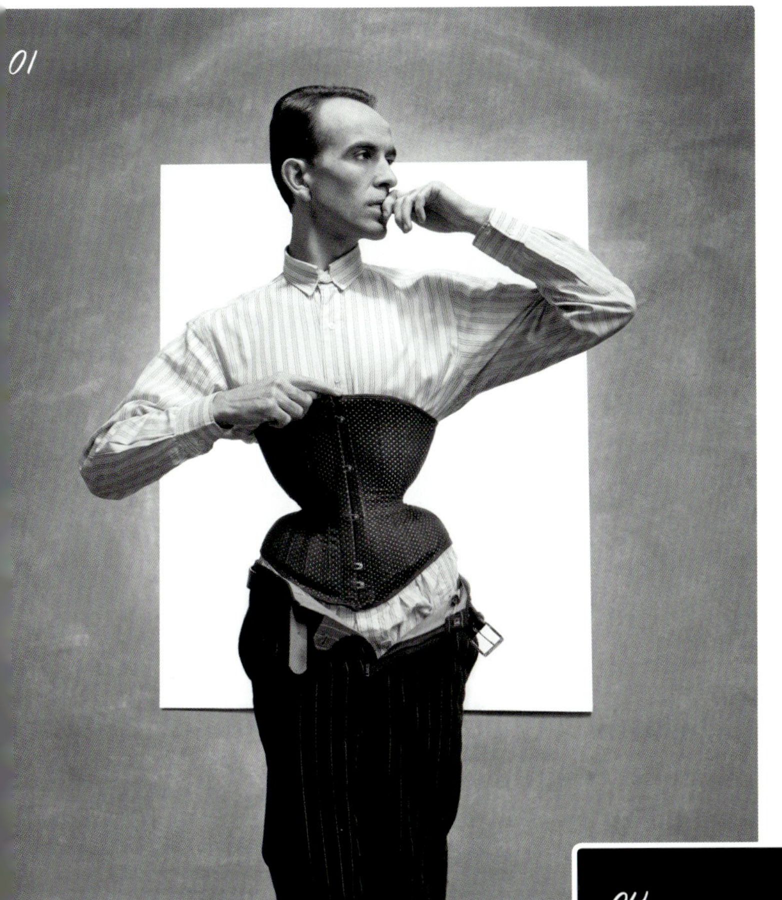

01

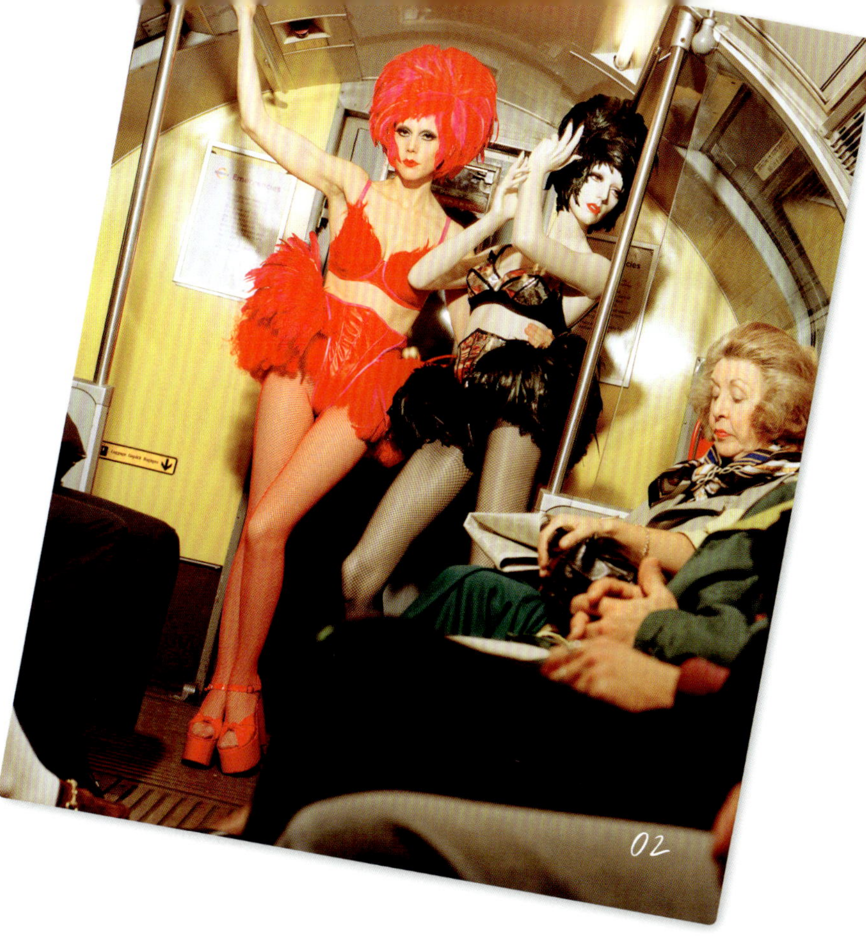

02

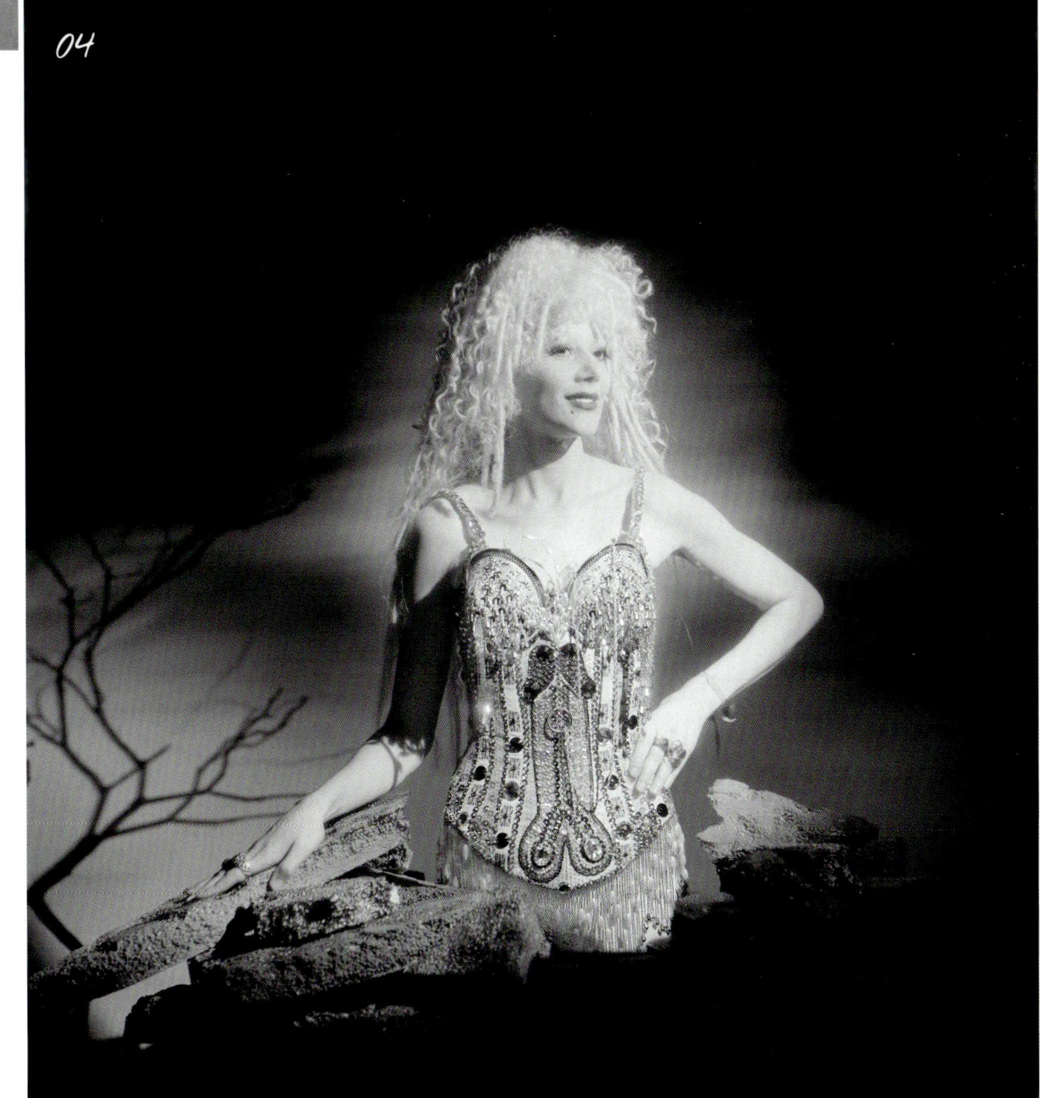

04

Wearing "penis Corset" by Mr Pearl

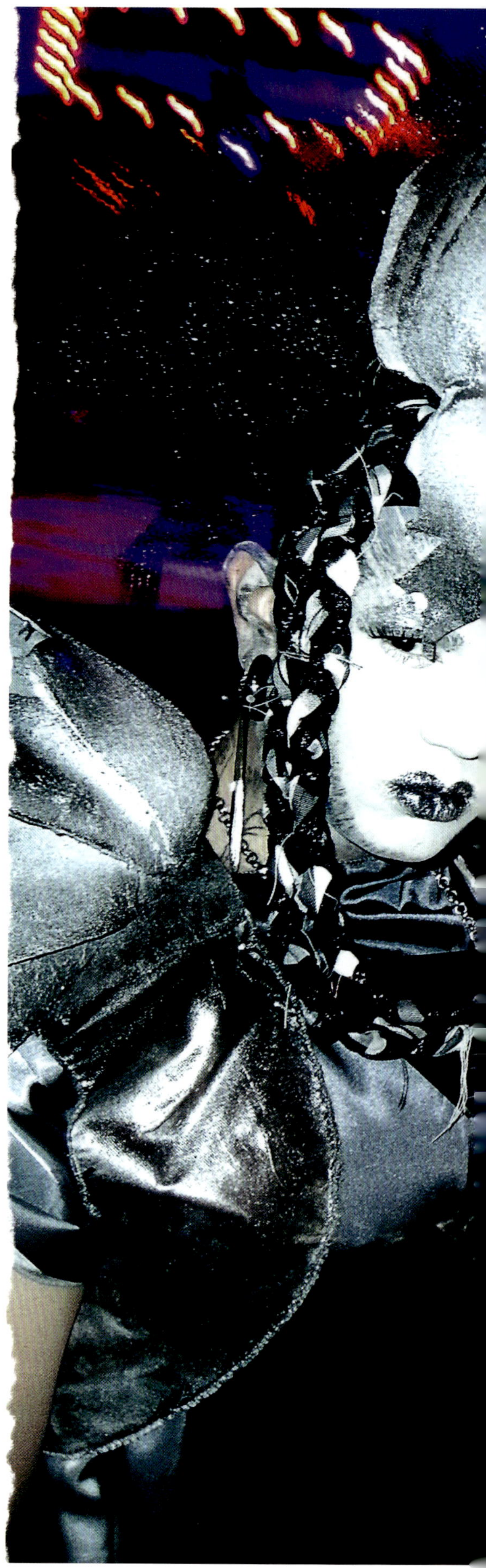

Susanne, Onehalf Nelson, and
Erickatoure Aviance at
Catwalk at Marquee, 2013.
Photo by Marco Ovando.

terms of seasonal trends, but by self-expression and transformation. Consider the following two stories:

"I was a Club Kid and Susanne asked if I would make her some clothes," says the Philippine-American costume and fashion designer Zaldy. "She never told me what to do. She knew that I understood she needs to command the room, be very sexy, and be able to walk around and dance all night long. She still wears things that I made for her ten years ago; she just restyles them a little and they look fresh. Susanne opened up the world for me – and for so many creative people. She took me to Paris and, all of a sudden, I'm in a Thierry Mugler fashion show, meeting all of my fashion icons."[7]

In Paris, Zaldy modeled as both a boy and a girl for designers such as Jean Paul Gaultier, Thierry Mugler, and Vivienne Westwood – and even did a controversial Levi's commercial that only aired after 9 pm. He also learned how to make corsets and "glamorous evening looks," and when he returned to the U.S., he made costumes for everyone from Michael Jackson to Lady Gaga. But it all started with making clothes for Susanne Bartsch: "I just love dressing her up," says Zaldy.[8]

"My then boyfriend Zaldy introduced me to Susanne in the late 1980s," recalls the artist Mathu Andersen. "We were Club Kids, not female impersonators, just doing what people did then – being fabulous. She became our muse. We started doing her costumes and make-up and I photographed her for her invitations. A lot of people today don't know how incredibly influential she has been. She was certainly instrumental in my life. When I came to New York, I was doing make-up, trying to get connections with the fashion industry, and my point of entry into fashion was a Halloween party that Susanne did at the Palladium. Steven Klein [the photographer] saw me doing make-up in the lobby and asked if I'd like to work with him. After that I moved quickly up the ranks."[9]

Designers and other fashion professionals constantly seek inspiration, and they often find it in youth, music, and sexual subcultures, where there exists a strong interest in issues of taste and style. "Club cultures are taste cultures," observes the sociologist Sarah Thornton, and the people who go to particular clubs share a taste for certain kinds of music and fashion.[10] Thornton draws on Pierre Bourdieu's ideas about economic, social, and cultural capital to develop a theory of subcultural capital. To simplify, economic capital involves what you own (property and income), social capital "who you know (and who knows you)," and cultural capital what you know "through upbringing and education which

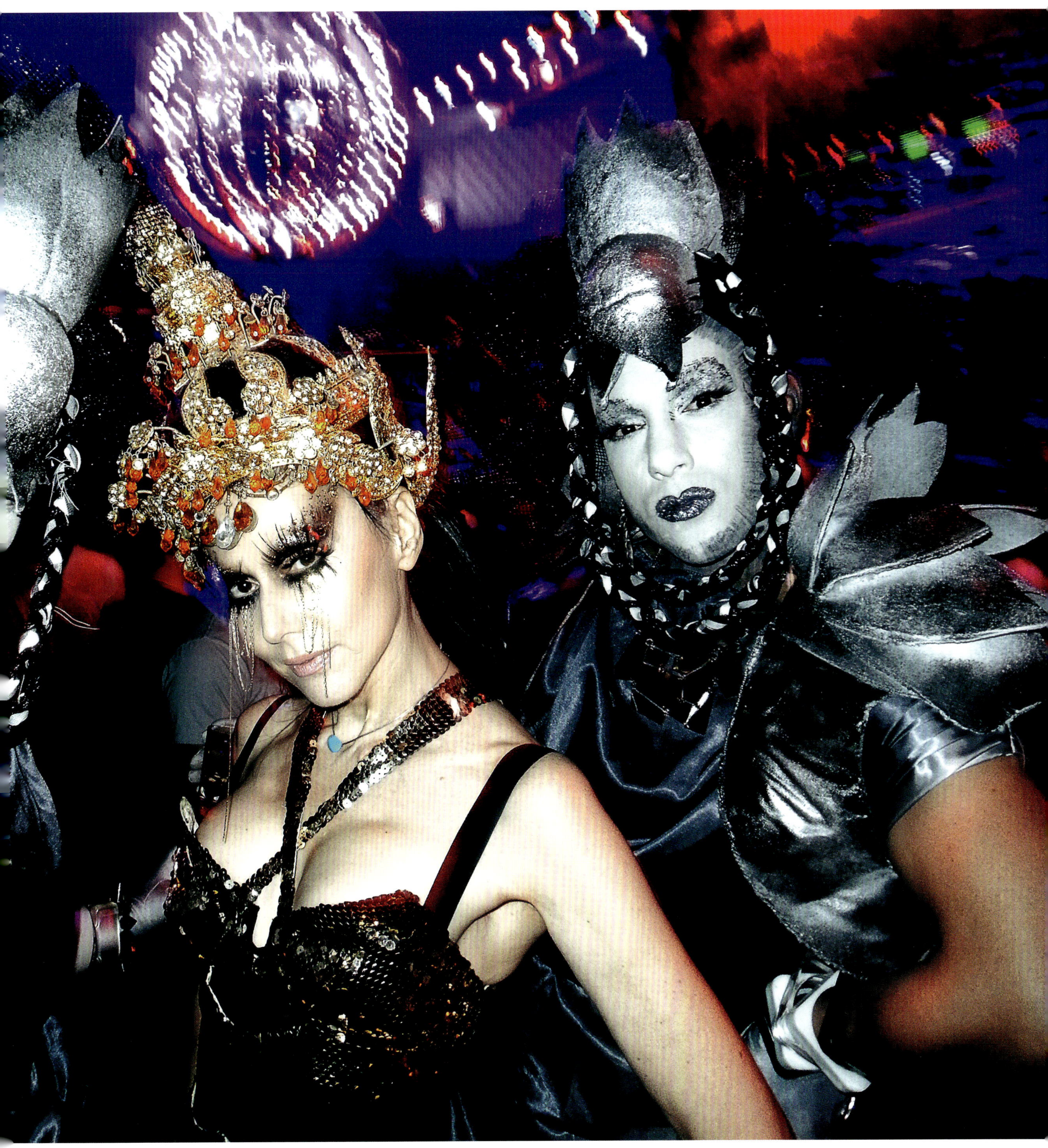

confers social status." By extension, subcultural capital involves knowing about things that are valued within a particular subculture. Just as the possession of books, an education, and good manners are forms of cultural capital, so fashionable hairstyles, a knowledge of the latest trends in music, and "hipness" or "coolness" are forms of subcultural capital.[11]

Creative places are those where creative, knowledgeable, energetic, enthusiastic, and diverse people congregate and put their ideas together, acquiring the ability to determine which ideas are best. The existence of such arenas also enables individuals to acquire allies and mentors, to make connections, and to gain reputations. Schools, laboratories, ateliers, and conferences can all be creative places, but history shows that less formal meeting places such as stores, clubs, and bars can also foster creativity. As Csikzentmihalyi states in his book, *Creativity*, "Centers of creativity tend to be at the intersections of different cultures, where beliefs, lifestyles, and knowledge mingle and allow individuals to see new combinations of ideas with greater ease."[12] Creativity also often involves "the crossing of boundaries of domains," as when the domain of fashion overlaps with domains such as music or dance or art.[13]

"Susanne is a ceaseless chameleon, whose transformations and reinventions have made her an unofficial muse and proselytizer for talent," says the *Vogue* editor Hamish Bowles. "She has been a catalyst for the cross-fertilization of ideas between creative people in a wide range of fields – artists, musicians, fashion designers."[14] "It doesn't get any better than creating something new," says Bartsch. "And when people appreciate it, it's fantastic." By exploring how Bartsch has created her various looks, in collaboration with a wide range of fashion designers and hair and make-up artists (both famous and unknown), it is possible to gain insight into the nature of the creative person, the significance of the places and spaces within which creativity flourishes, and the process of creativity as it manifests itself in the world of fashion.

The Swiss Miss

"We called her the Swiss Miss," say old friends from London. Bartsch's Swiss-German accent is still very pronounced – her friends imitate it constantly – and her English is smattered with Cockney slang and camp expressions. Many of her friends agree with her former assistant, Richie Rich, who thinks that "her Swiss-German upbringing gave her incredible discipline."[15] "She's a very serious business woman and a party girl at the same time, which don't usually go together," says the milliner Stephen Jones.[16] "She's very professional," confirms Mickey Boardman. "Susanne seems wild and crazy, but she's really focused, and when she wants to do something – like her AIDS benefit, the Love Ball – she gets everyone involved," says Robert Forrest, an executive fashion consultant.[17]

Top: Susanne with Zaldy, headpiece from Thailand, customized by Mr. Pearl, corset by Mr. Pearl. June 1991. Photo by Josef Astor.

Bottom: "A New Year's Eve Look," The Raleigh Hotel, Miami, 1990s. Photo by Andrea Barbiroli.

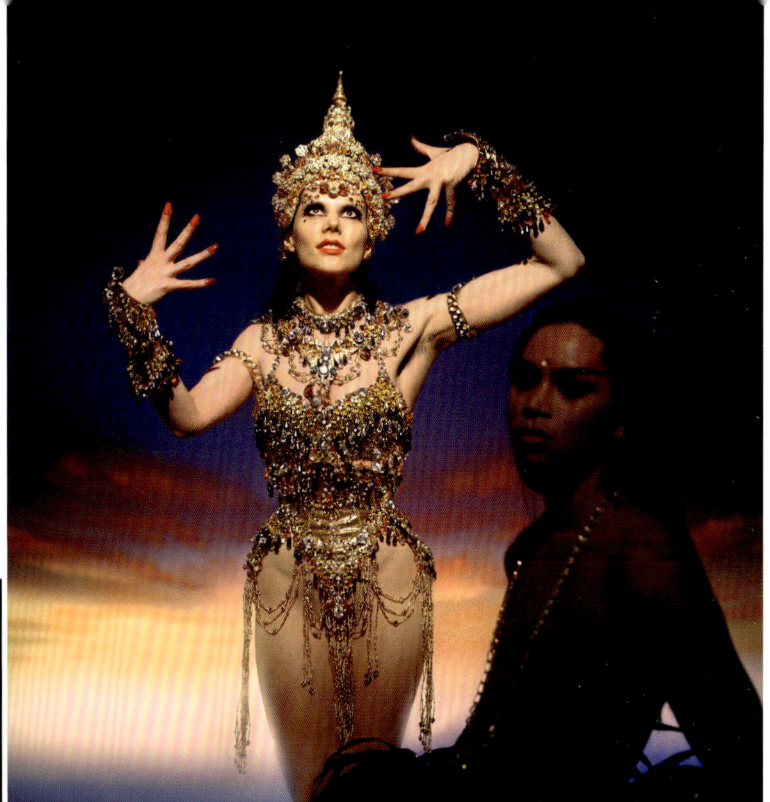

Suzanne with Zaldy

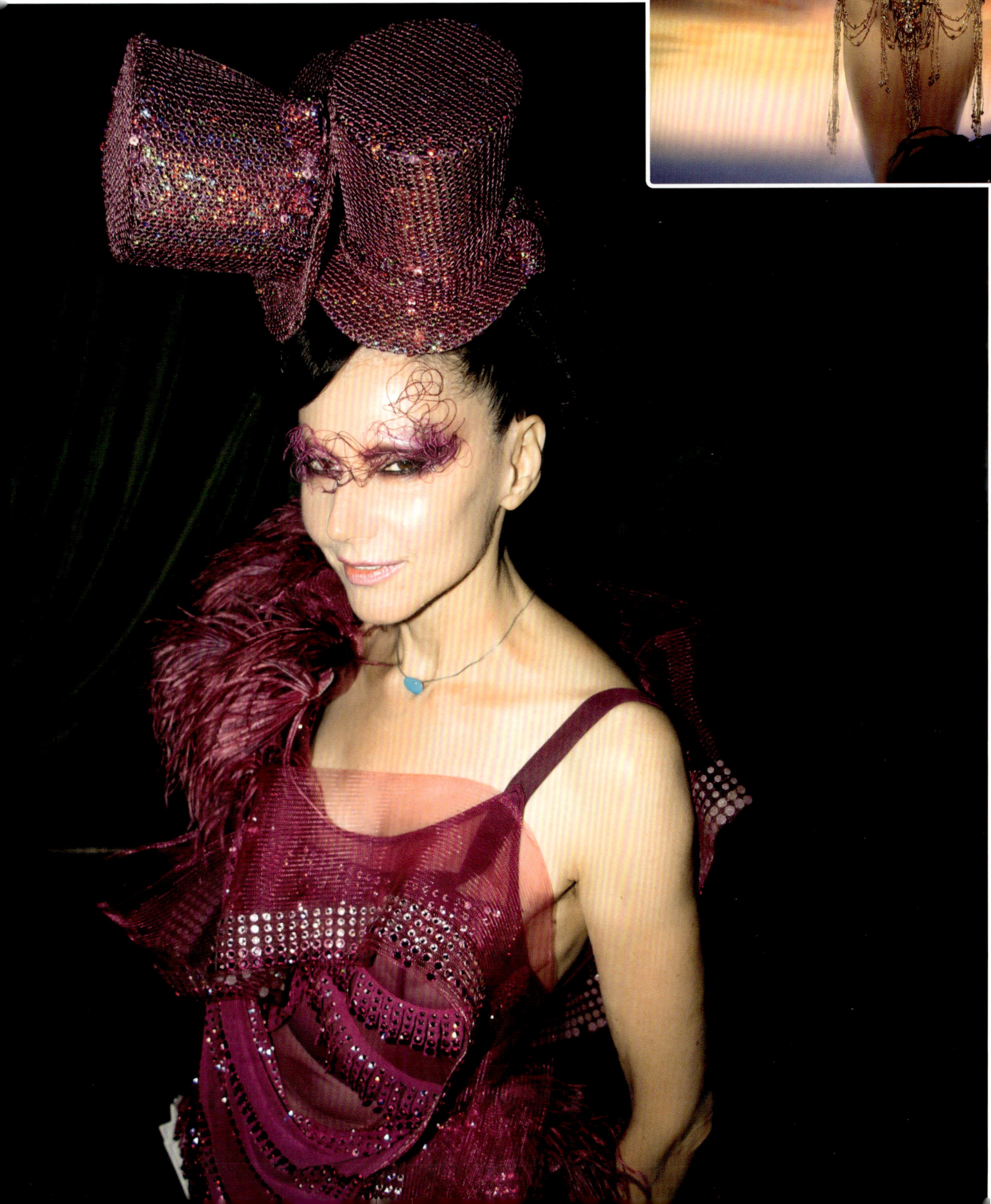

A New Year's Eve look

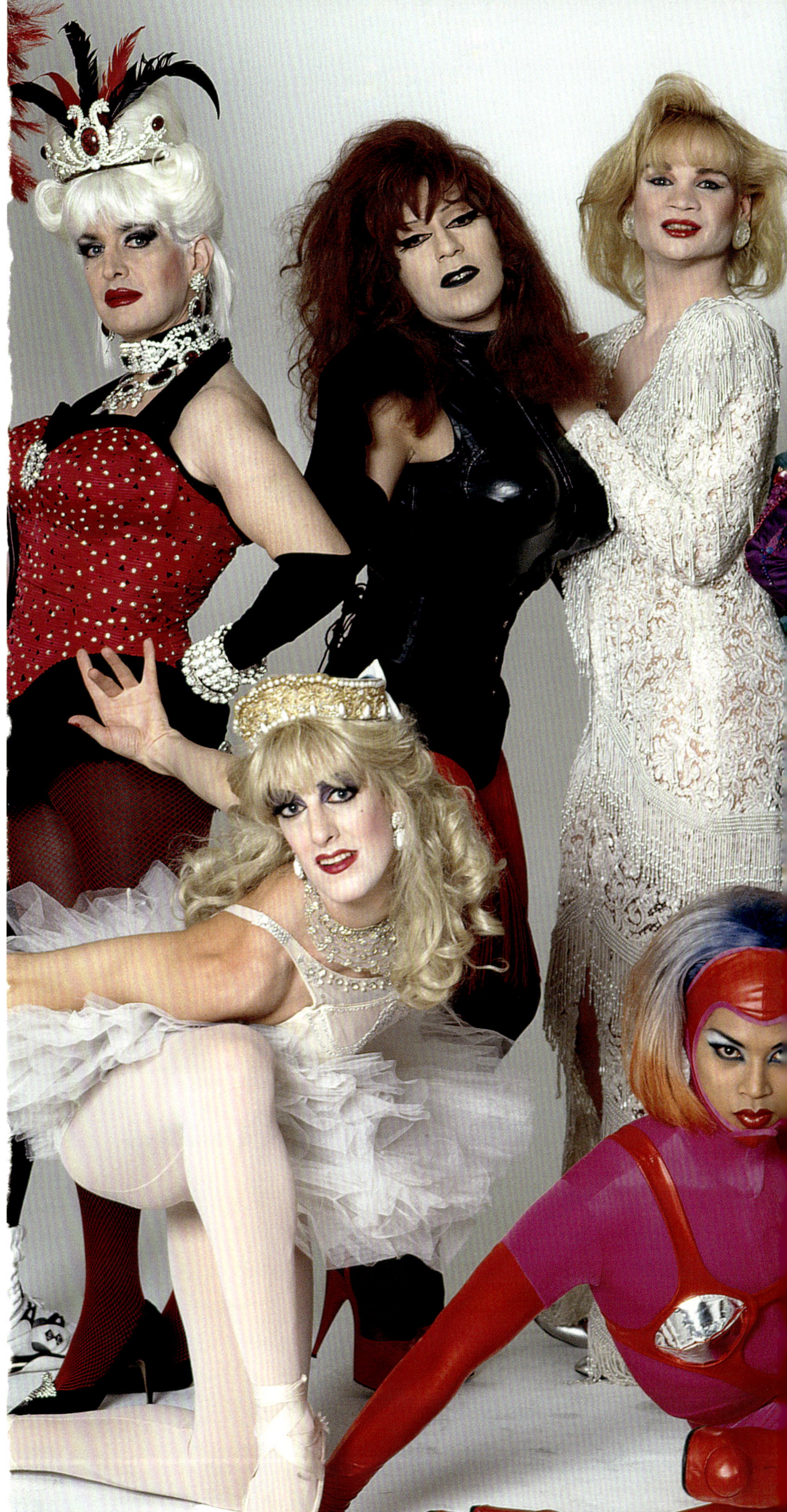

Susanne and her crew, 1991.
Susanne's outfit by Mr. Pearl.
© Michael James O'Brien.

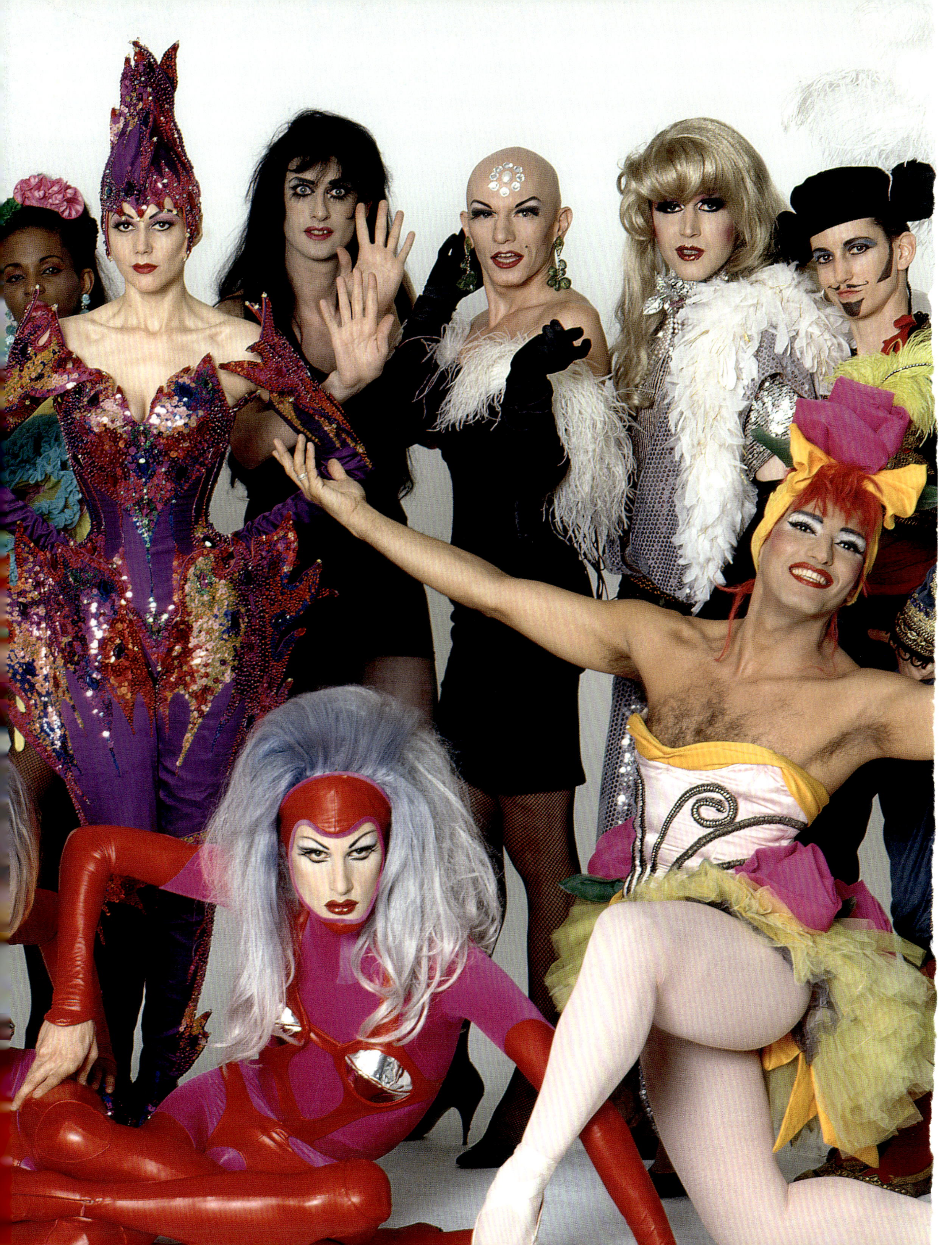

Looking back at her youth, Bartsch says: "Switzerland was a great base for me, very solid, very safe. My mother used to ski to school. My father made us a doll house. We grew our own vegetables. But Switzerland in those days was a bit narrow-minded, which made me rebel. I knew that I didn't want to just get married – I wanted more." Specifically, she wanted to go to London. "My excuse was to learn English. My parents hooked me up with an English family and I was supposed to go to school there." It didn't work out. "One day I just left." Her parents stopped sending money, and aged seventeen, she went to the Swiss Center in Piccadilly to get a visa. They put her to work at the cheese counter, selling Emmental. Characteristically, she remembers her uniform – "a red dress with a high neck and gold buttons on the boobs." Once she had her papers, she left to find a more interesting job.

The year was 1968 and London had emerged recently as a new fashion capital. Bartsch found a job at one of London's new boutiques, and was soon a member of the city's fashion and music scene – an experience that would have a profound effect on her entire life. If she had worried that staying in Switzerland would lead to a boring "hausfrau" existence, there was certainly no danger of that in London. She fell in love with the designer Paul Reeves, who helped launch the fashion for floral shirts and velvet pants for men, and began working at his boutique, Universal Witness. Bartsch recalls: "David Bowie used to come in, looking angelic in a flowing chiffon dress and a floppy hat."

One day she was sitting at the sales counter, knitting a sweater, when a woman said that she wanted to buy it. "So I said 'OK, give me three hundred quid' and she said 'I'll take it.'" So Bartsch got knitting machines, hired knitters, and started a small business. "Pop stars like Jimmy Page wore my sweaters. But I don't think I was ready for a business," she admits. She went on vacation to Italy with friends, fell in love with an Italian man, and stayed away so long that her business fell apart. Eventually, of course, she returned to England.

"We met her with her knitting needles under her arm," recalls Bartsch's friend the artist Michael Costiff.[18] Together with his wife, Gerlinde, Costiff ran the Terrace Café at the Chelsea Antiques Market. "Gerlinde was a super-cool German chick, a little older than Susanne and completely outrageous," says Simon Doonan, the fashion writer and creative ambassador for Barneys New York.[19] They became friends when Bartsch started selling vintage clothing and antique jewelry, first at Vern Lambert's shop and later on her own stall at the Antiques Market. She lived in a borrowed apartment over Manolo Blahnik's store. She

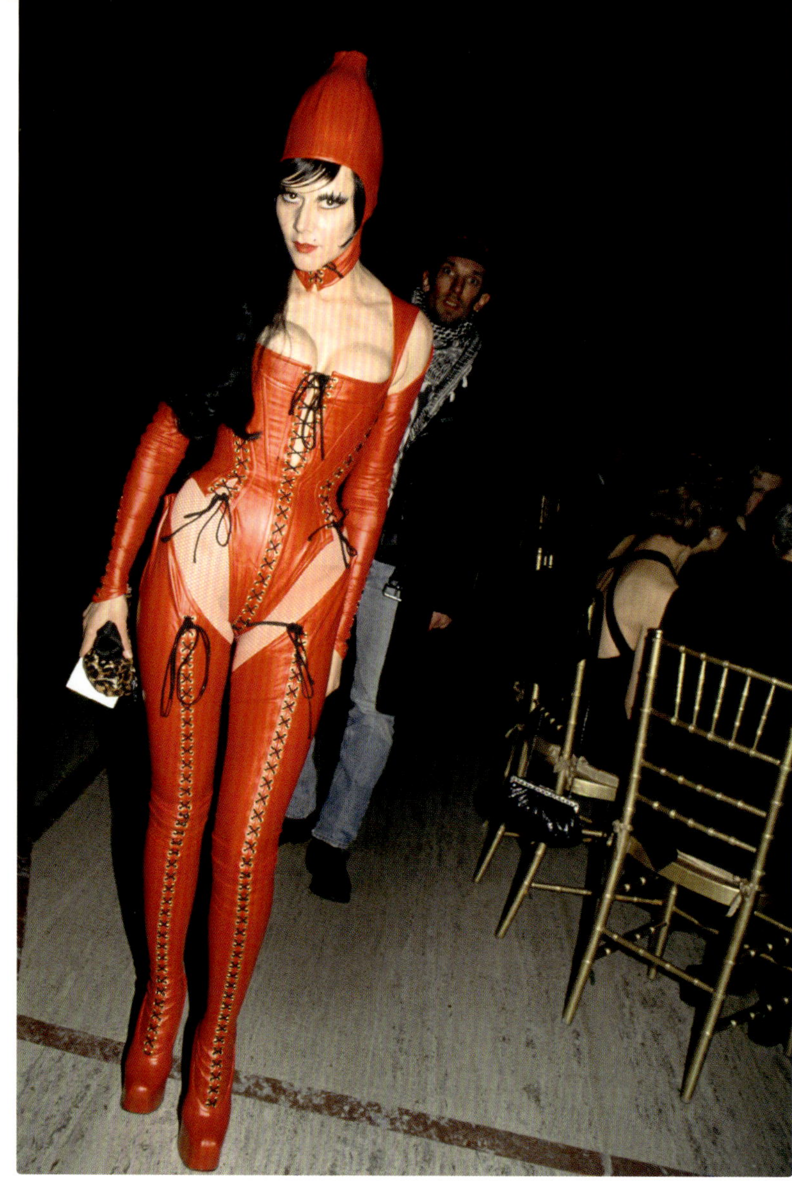

Above: Susanne wearing a Mathu and Zaldy outfit for the Council of Fashion Designers of America party in 1993. Photo by Roxanne Lowit.

Facing: Susanne at an Armani party, February 1993. Photo by Roxanne Lowit.

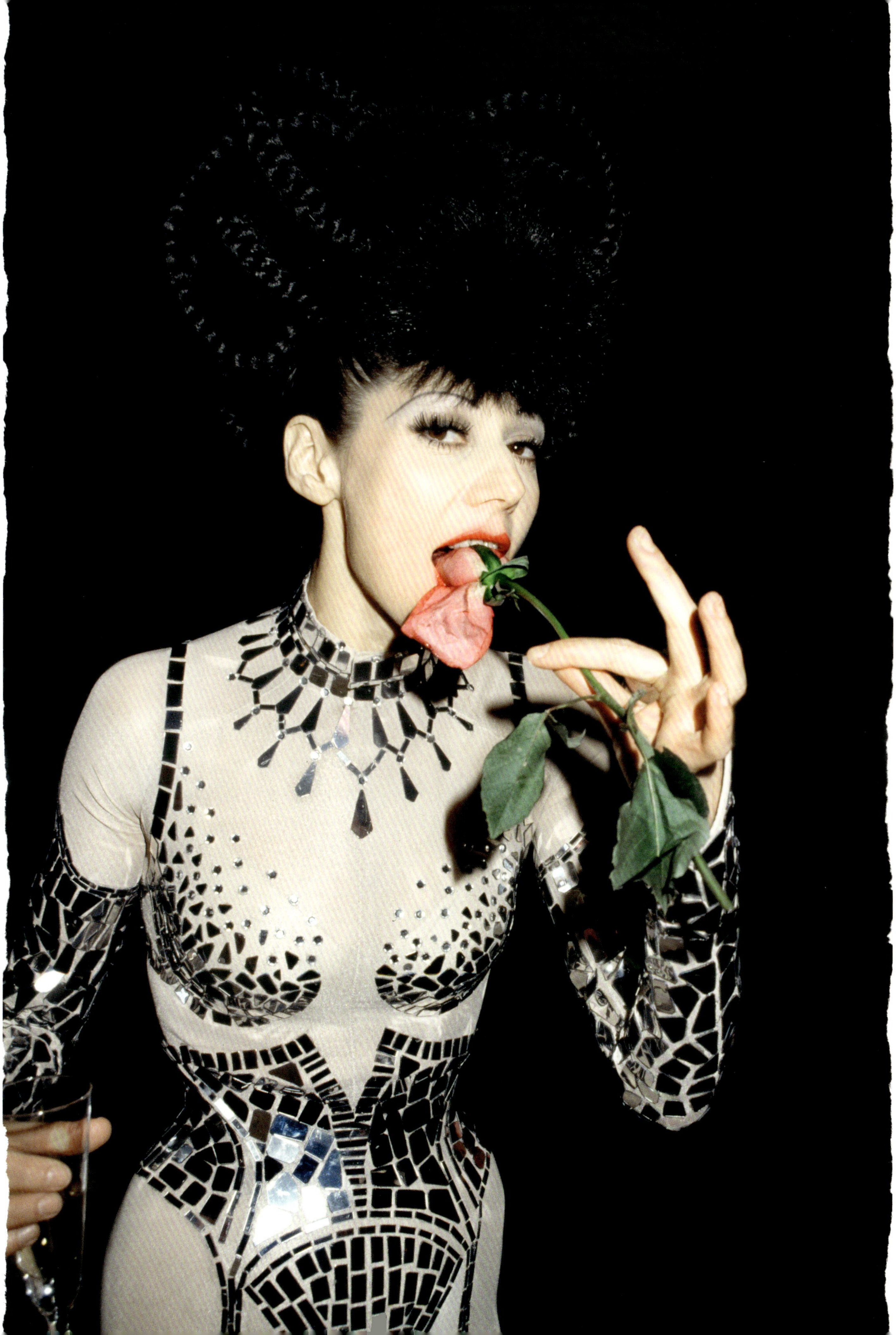

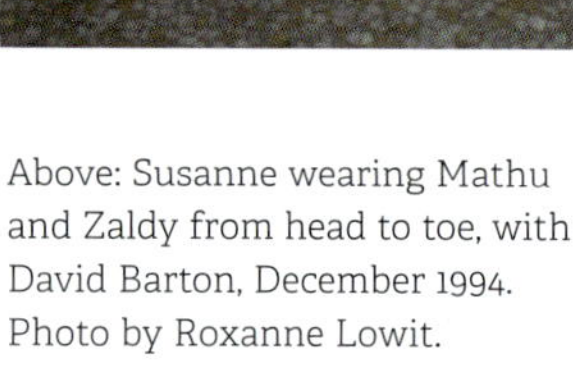

Above: Susanne wearing Mathu and Zaldy from head to toe, with David Barton, December 1994. Photo by Roxanne Lowit.

Below: Susanne in Mathu and Zaldy at the David LaChapelle party in New York City, mid-1990s. Photo by Roxanne Lowit.

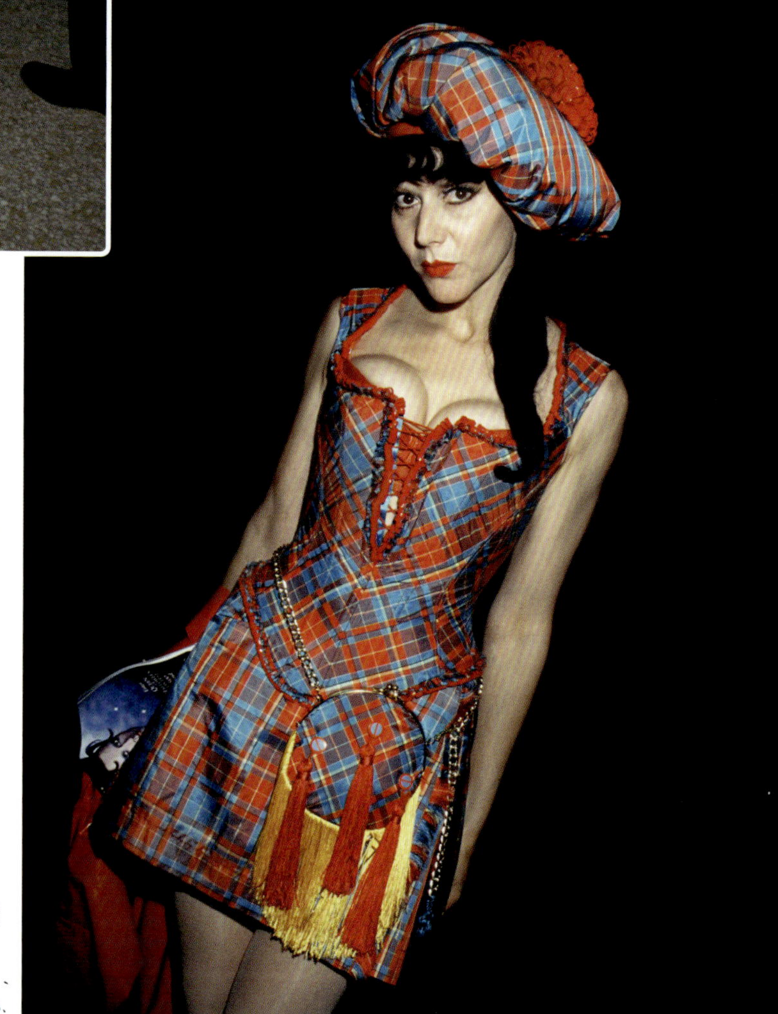

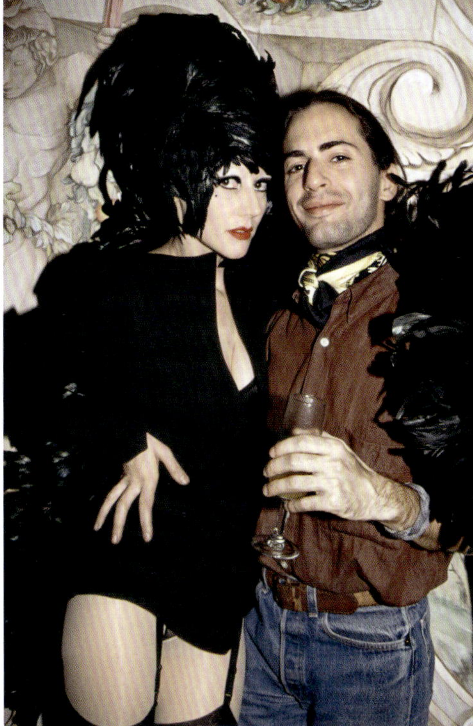

Susanne with Marc Jacobs, early in
the 1990s. Susanne is wearing
a Thierry Mugler jacket and
a Mathu and Zaldy feather hat.
Photo by Roxanne Lowit.

Below: Susanne is the Dancing Queen
in a design by Zaldy.
Photo by Citizen Chris.

Above: Susanne in a look by Mathu
and Zaldy, MAC Costmetics event,
1997. Photo by Roxanne Lowit.

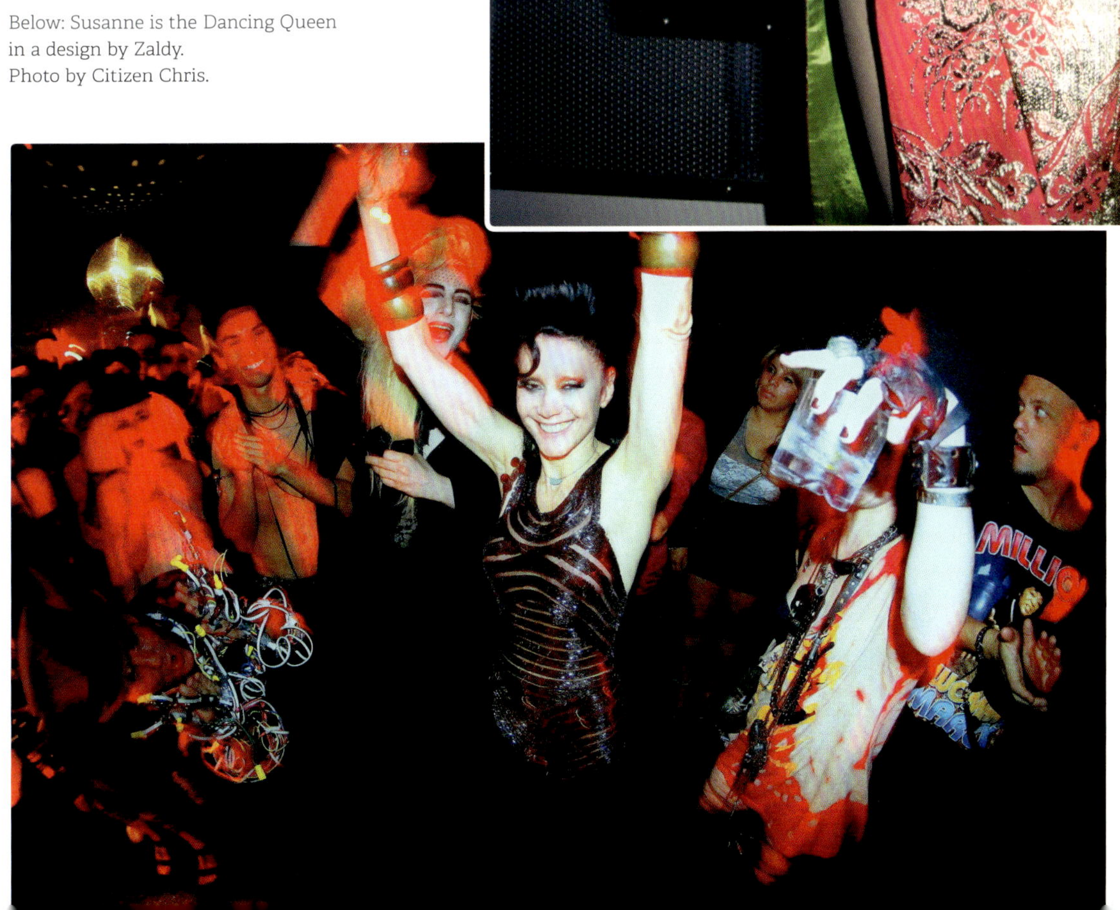

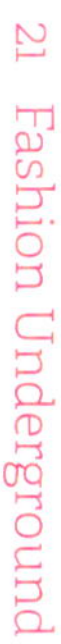

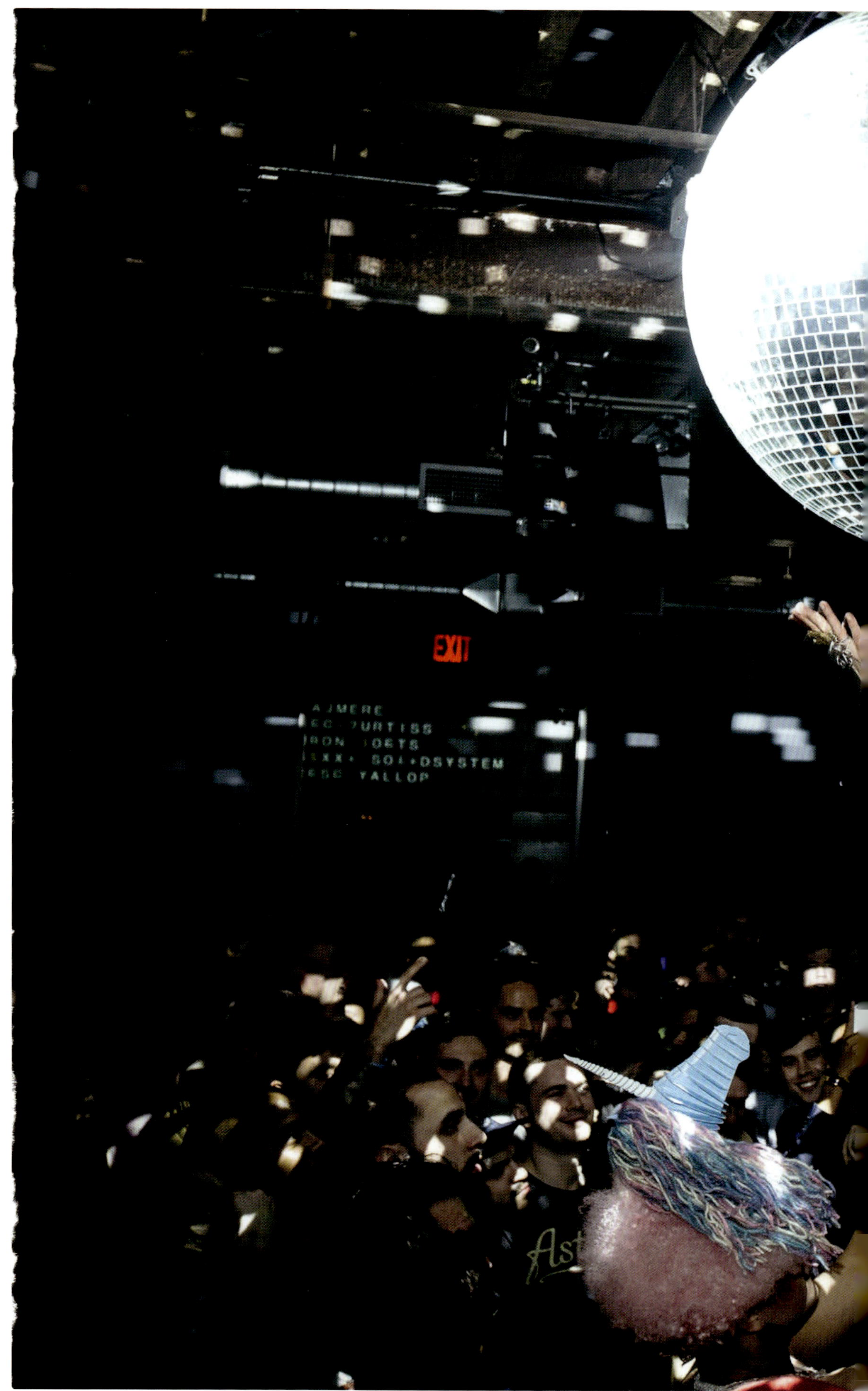

Susanne at the opening night of
her Kunst parties, Verboten Club,
Brooklyn, March 2013.
Photo by Oliver Correa.

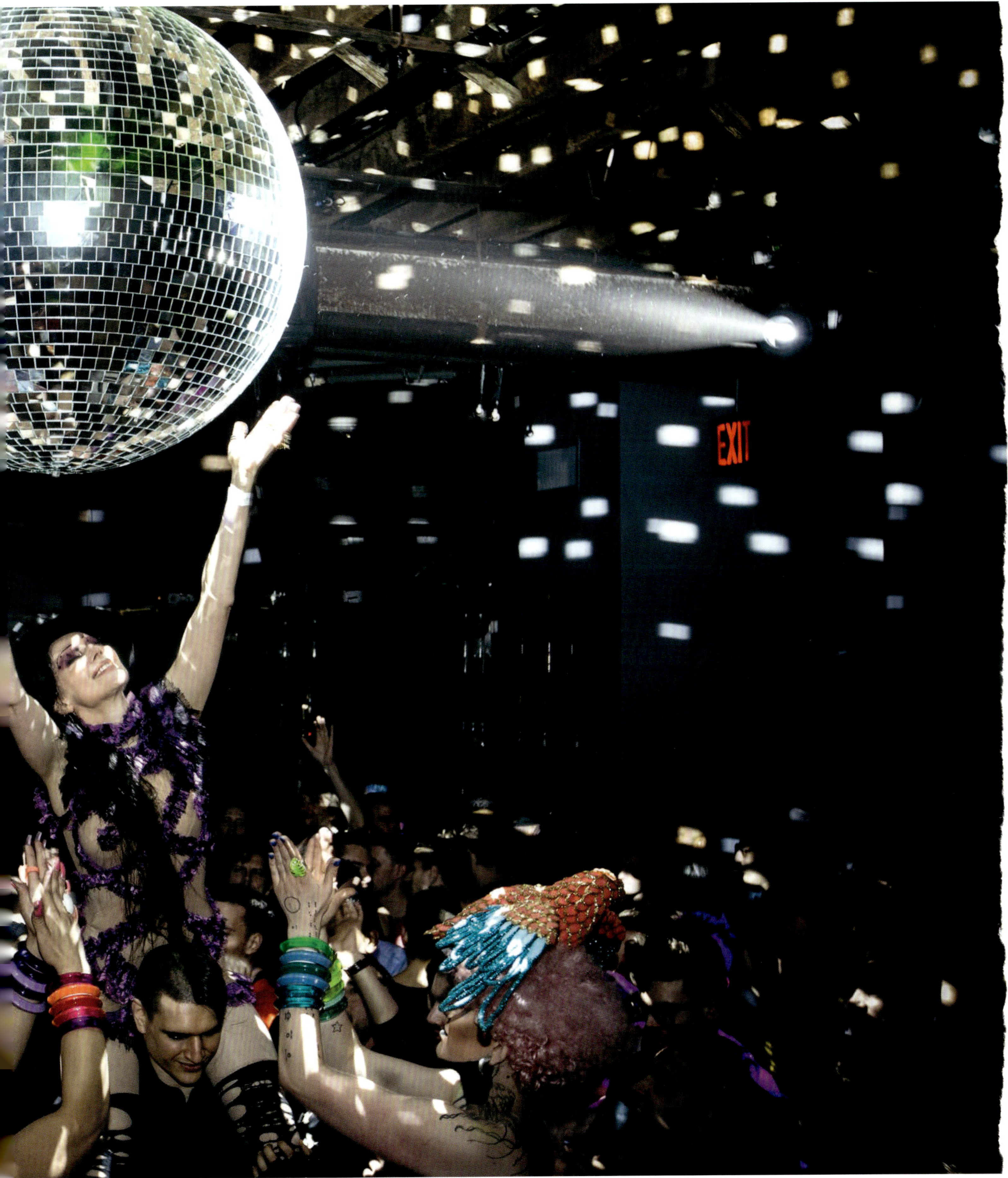
EXIT

recalls wearing Fortuny dresses, beaded frocks, and cloche hats from the 1920s, and bias-cut chiffon dresses from the 1930s. "We were all doing retro looks," says Costiff. "We all liked dressing up, and we developed our own styles."

Music, as well as fashion, was a big part of Bartsch's world. "When I first came to London, they had one-night-stand clubs, like reggae night," says Bartsch. "Once I was walking down the street in London and I saw a couple of guys go in a door and down some stairs, so I followed them, and it was a ska club down there." In 1979, Bartsch and her friends started going to the weekly Blitz club night in Covent Garden. Founded by Steve Strange and with George O'Dowd (the future Boy George) as the cloakroom attendant, the Blitz club was frequented by fashion students from Central Saint Martins, the Royal College of Art, and the London College of Fashion, including Rachel Auburn, Hamish Bowles, John Galliano, David Holah, Stephen Jones, and Stevie Stewart.

"During the 1980s, Susanne was an extraordinary ambassador for British fashion in New York and Tokyo. During the 1990s, she was a lone voice for flamboyance."

– Hamish Bowles

They wore eclectic, often bizarre, sometimes androgynous, highly stylized costumes and emphatic hair and make-up. To gain admission, guests needed to realize that Steve Strange wanted to populate his club with "people who created unique identities."[20] The style at Blitz was variously dubbed "New Dandy," "Romantic Rebel," and "Blitz Kid" before being labeled finally "New Romantic". "Everyone looked totally different every week," recalls Bartsch. "Blitz was a big influence. That was when I started to do looks that were head-to-toe: always a hat, jewelry: a certain look." Other clubs she frequented later included Taboo and Hell. "Blitz was about looks and style," she recalls. "Taboo was about decadence and the dress was more surreal."

London in the later years of the 1970s and during the 1980s was an especially vibrant period for independent creators of music, fashion, and design. There were new bands, designers, shops, and style magazines. "The club scene meant that people used to dress up," recalls the designer Wendy Dagworthy.[21] "It was that very flamboyant, post-punk generation," says Hamish Bowles. "I was a student at Central Saint Martins, going to clubs in London. Susanne was a key figure among the New Romantics, playing with gender ideas and her own self-presentation, which was stylized and dramatic. She has kept that torch alight through the decades, creating different personas through fashion, hair, and make-up. During the 1980s, she was an extraordinary ambassador for British fashion in New York and Tokyo. Later, during the 1990s, she was a lone voice for flamboyance. But it's all cyclical in fashion. Now there's a younger generation who look back to the eighties as a golden age of fashion and self-expression. Susanne is a continuing inspiration, as relevant now as she's ever been."[22]

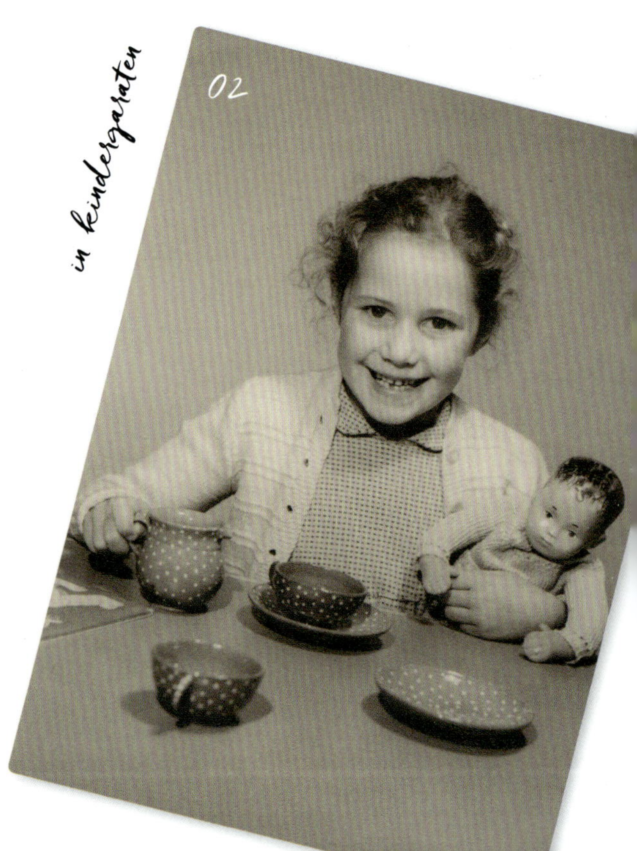

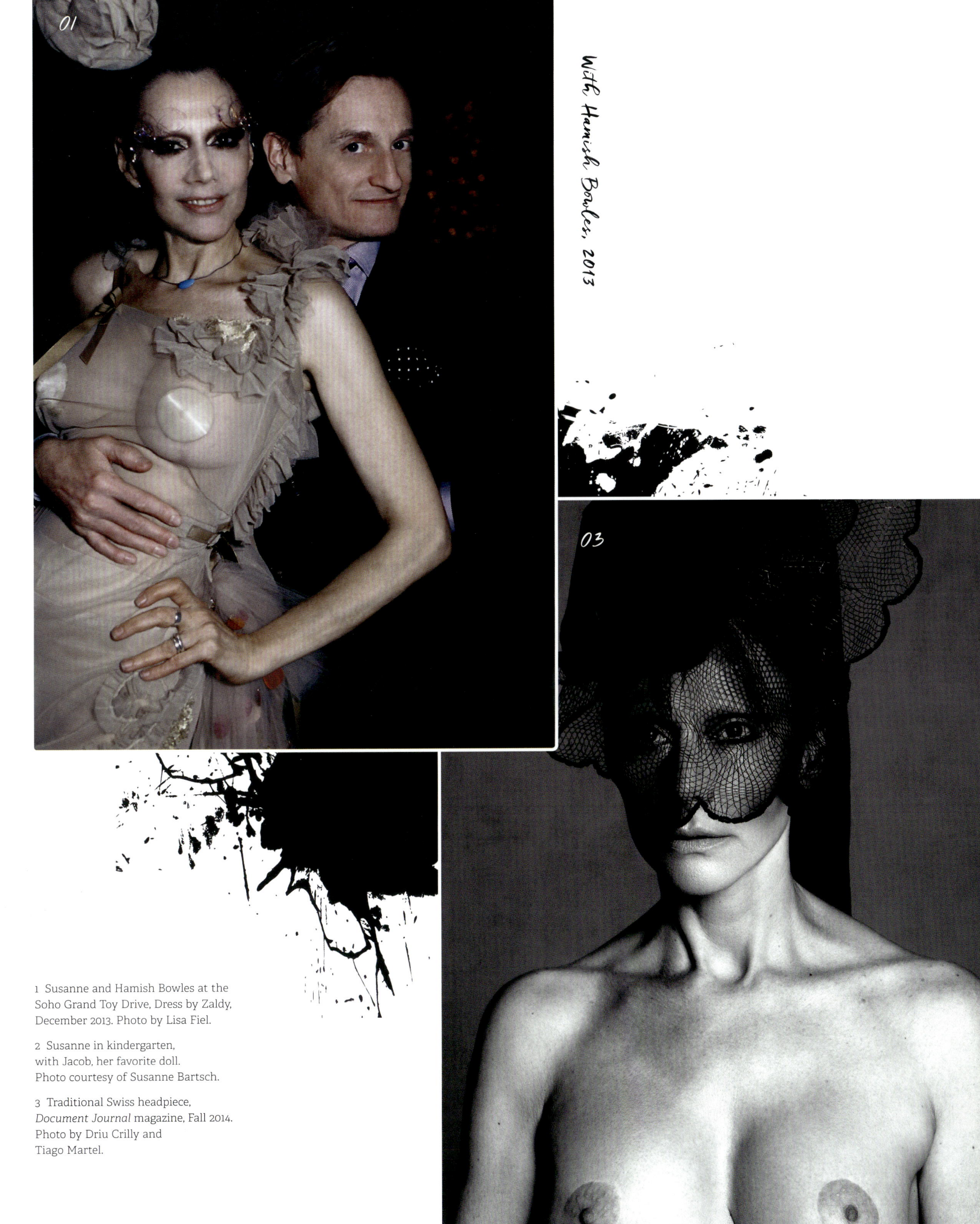

1 Susanne and Hamish Bowles at the
Soho Grand Toy Drive, Dress by Zaldy,
December 2013. Photo by Lisa Fiel.

2 Susanne in kindergarten,
with Jacob, her favorite doll.
Photo courtesy of Susanne Bartsch.

3 Traditional Swiss headpiece,
Document Journal magazine, Fall 2014.
Photo by Driu Crilly and
Tiago Martel.

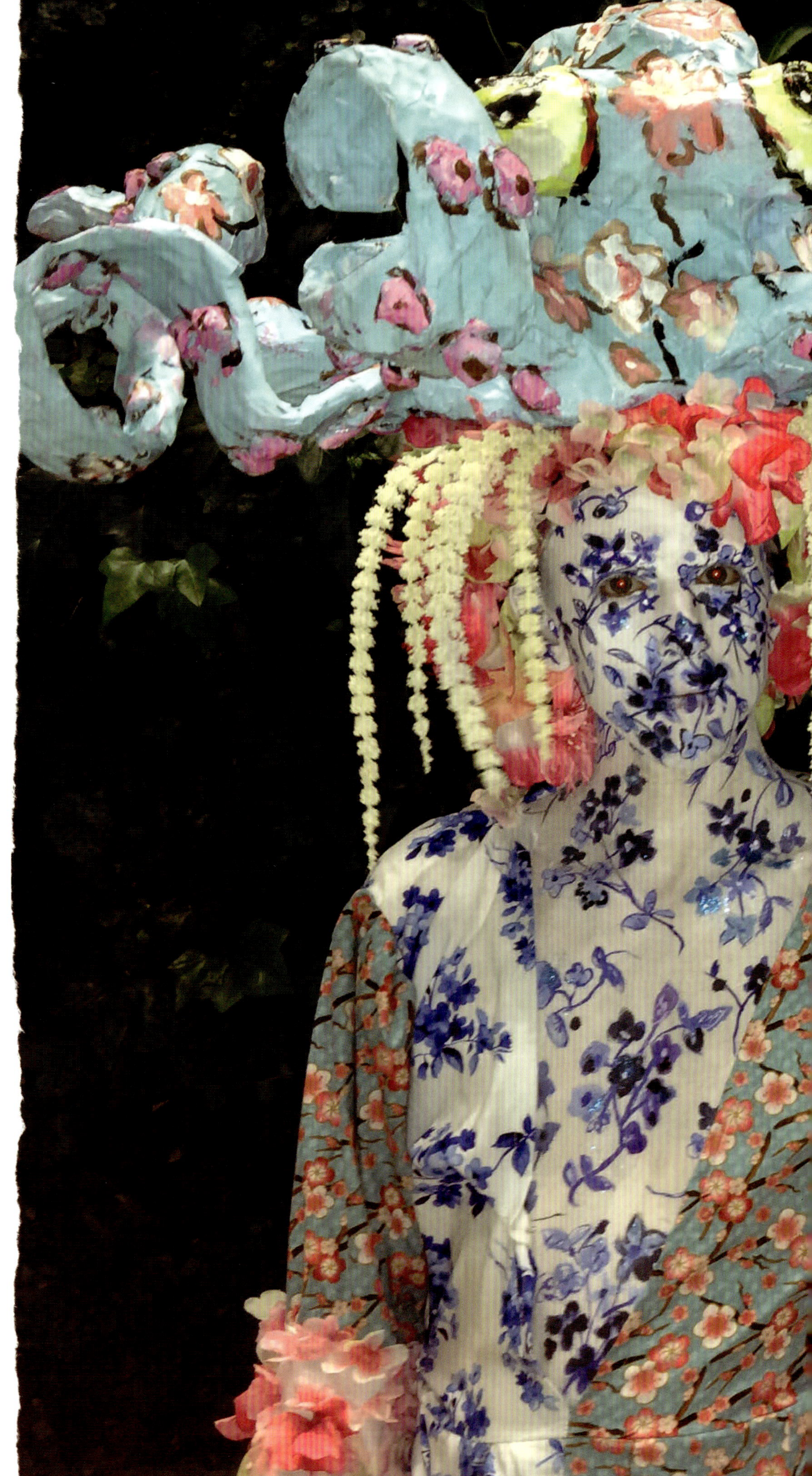

Adam VanBuren and Ryan Burke at
the *Art-à-Porter* surrealist picnic,
New York City, September 2014.
Photo courtesy of Susanne Bartsch.

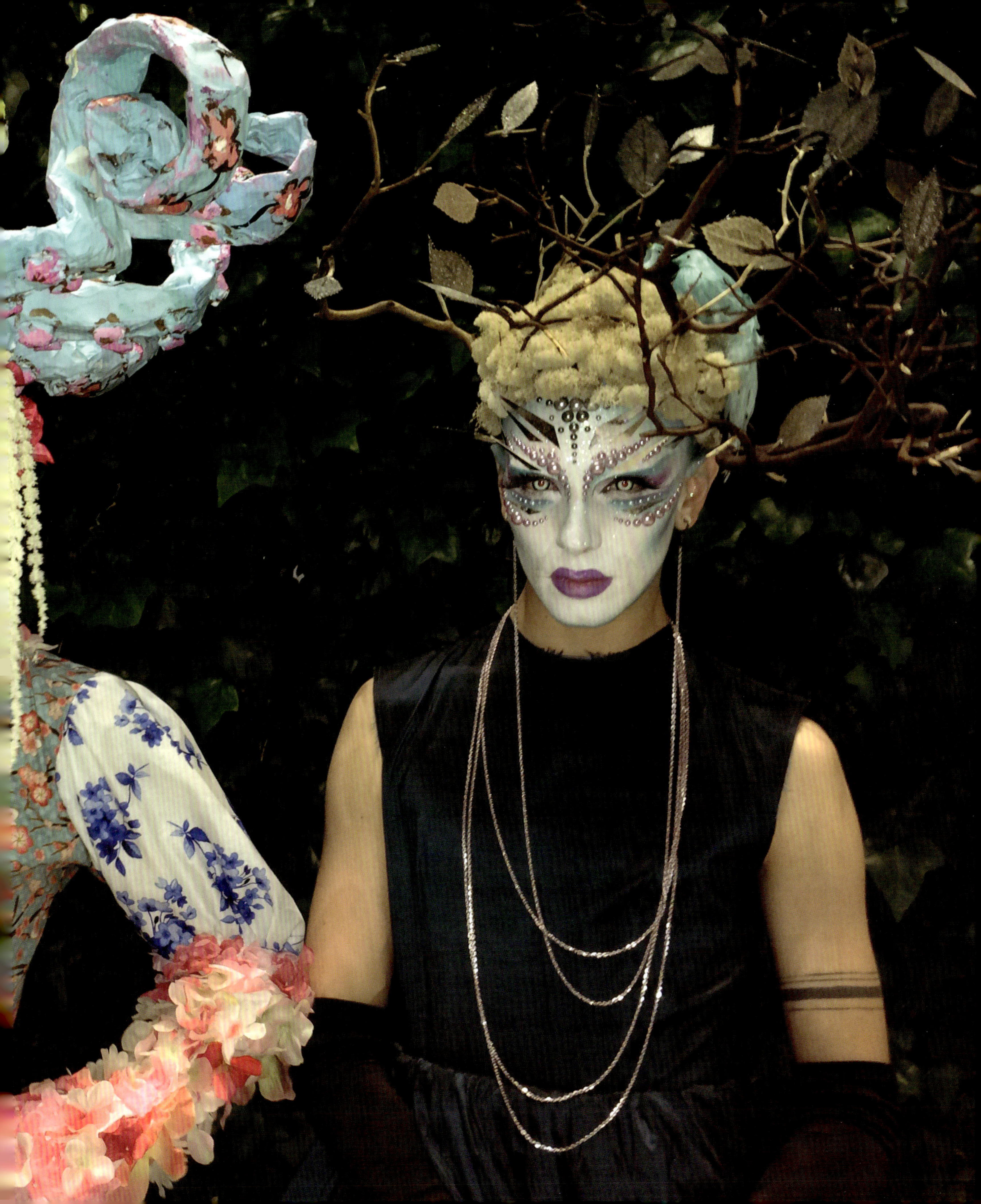

She Brought the English Scene to New York

On Valentine's Day, 1981, Bartsch arrived in New York City to live with her boyfriend, the artist Patrick Hughes, at the Chelsea Hotel. Eventually he moved out, but she continues to live in the Chelsea, in an apartment with two gilded Chinese beds, a mannequin of herself, and racks of clothing. "I fell in love with New York," she says, but the "boring," "straight" clothes she saw disheartened her, so she decided to import the more creative, individual styles she missed from the London fashion scene. "I decided to go to London and speak to some designers I liked to see if I could get things from them to sell in New York."

Still on a tourist visa, in September 1981, she opened her own eponymous boutique at 72 Thompson Street in SoHo. At this point in time, there were very few interesting stores in the neighborhood, but Bartsch saw its potential. "It looked like SoHo was up-and-coming. The landlord was supportive and I got the space very cheap. The shop was like a little hat box – tiny." Among the designers she chose to feature were David Holah (medieval-looking tunics with cowl necklines), Stephen Jones (sculptural hats), and Andrew Logan (broken-glass-and-mica jewelry). Most of them were very young, some still in art school. Bartsch's own antique jewelry was also on display.

Bartsch asked Michael Costiff to help design the shop. "First I had to demolish everything," he recalls. "Then I built it over three months of a very hot summer. I wanted it to look like an iceberg, all floaty and ethereal." The walls were painted glacial blue and overlaid with crumpled paper and muslin covered with plaster. The store was filled with surreal hat stands, as Bartsch was determined to make New Yorkers appreciate the joys of millinery. "The outside of the store is just as whimsical [as the interior]," wrote the *New York Times* style reporter John Duka, "with stalactites hanging over the windows, and huge rubberized garbardine banners in pink."[23] "Suddenly, we were a big sensation," recalls Costiff.

"Susanne really impacted New York fashion in the 1980s, when she brought the English scene to New York," recalls the art director of *Details* magazine, Ronnie Newhouse. "She brought back the idea of the spirited boutique, designers who were outside the system, and the merging of club life and boutique. Susanne was our first cover at *Details*. She was our poster child for downtown spirit. She also inspired the idea of the pull quote. That was our invention: We worked pull quotes into the design, because I loved the outrageous things she said."[24]

"My background was in clubs and parties," says the milliner Piers Atkinson. "I worked with Andrew Logan, who produced the Alternative Miss World contest. Susanne was the girl who brought my hats to America. I was so excited to be

"She is a fashion dream come to life, because she wants the extreme, show-piece version of what we like to do, not the commercial version."

– Piers Atkinson

Top: Susanne with her boyfriend Patrick Hughes two weeks after she arrived in New York City, February 1981. Photo by Bill Cunningham.

Bottom: Susanne at her stall at the Chelsea Antiques Market, London, late in the 1970s. Photo courtesy Susanne Bartsch.

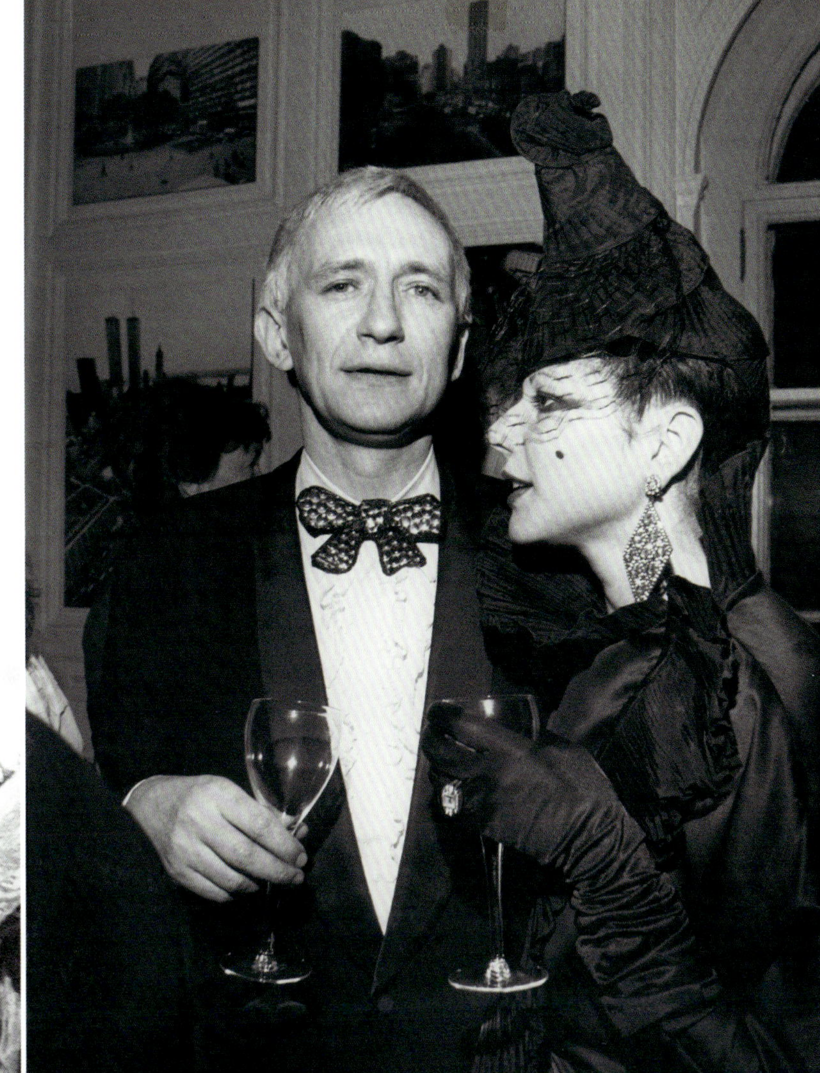

With Patrick Hughes, NY

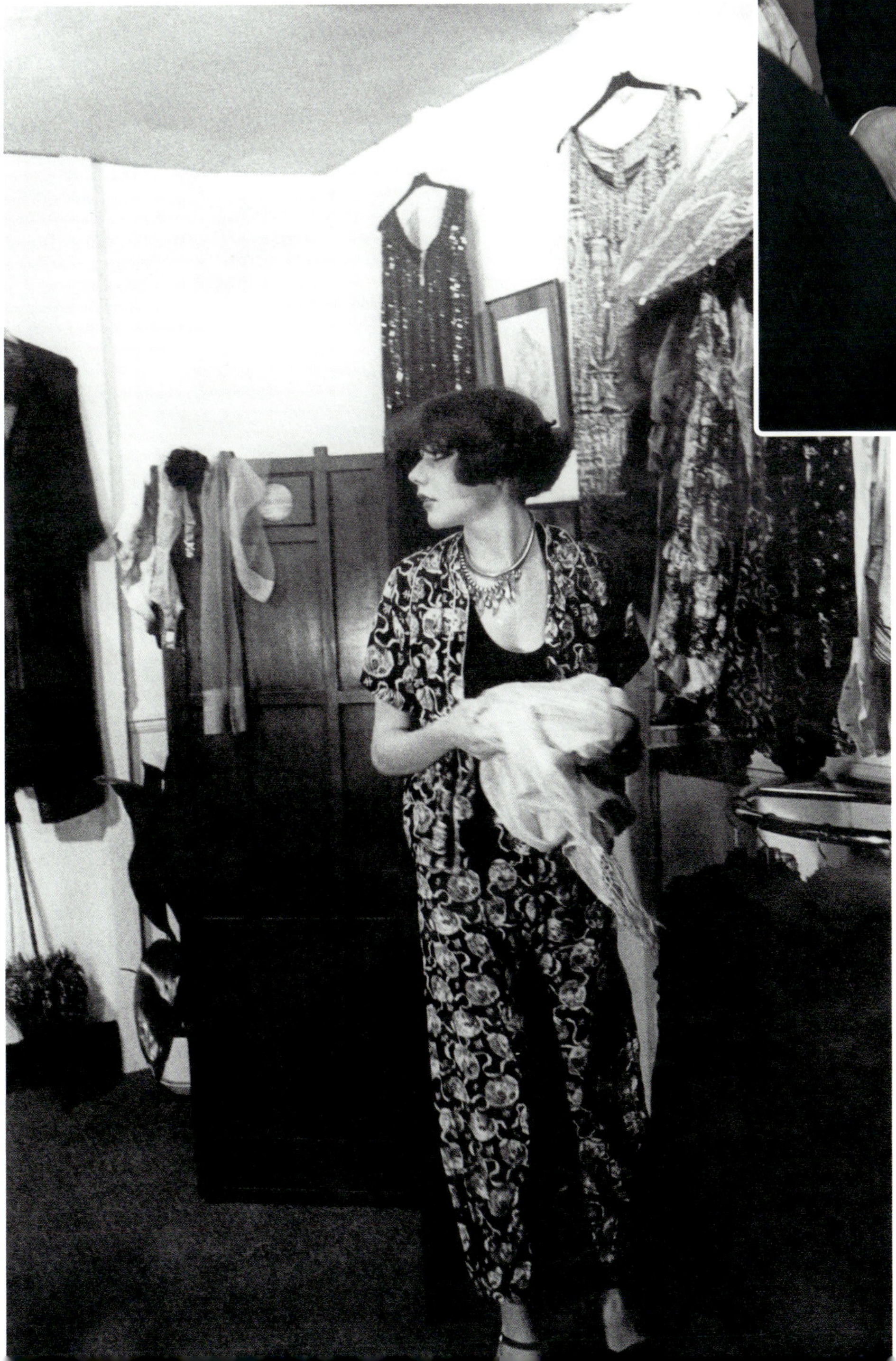

My stall at Chelsea Antiques Market

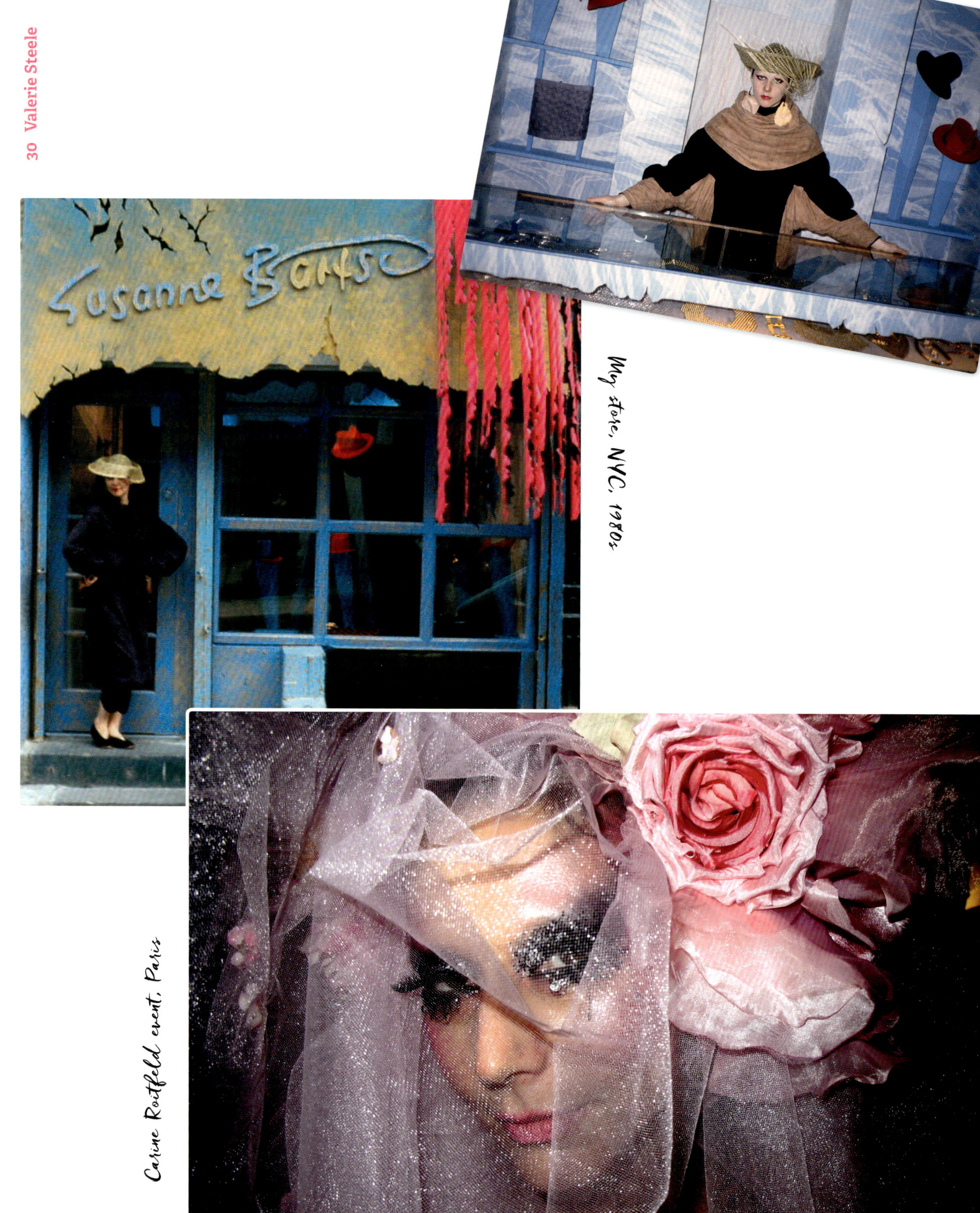

My store, NYC, 1980s

Carine Roitfeld event, Paris

working with her. I thought, 'It's *the* Susanne Bartsch!' We've worked together ever since. For me, as a designer, she is a fashion dream come to life, because she wants the extreme, show-piece version of what we like to do, not the commercial version. And she's one of the few people who can WEAR these show-piece hats. Sometimes she sees something of mine, like our famous hat worn by Rihanna, with a pair of huge red cherries, and Susanne says 'I want something bigger – I want a hat with a big, red apple, because New York is the Big Apple.' So we did the Big Apple hat. Other times, I make something and I think, this is perfect for Susanne, so I send it over. A lot of things we've created have been for her charity events. As a designer, you are often asked who is your ideal client? Susanne is mine, because she's a confident, intelligent, glamorous woman, a modern feminist."[25]

The African-American avant-garde fashion designer Andre Walker remembers meeting Bartsch in 1981 or 1982. "I was really young, maybe fifteen or sixteen. I went to a club and met some British people and learned there was a boutique opening up in SoHo. I ended up hanging out at her store all day. It was a great environment and I met everyone there, all the British designers I'd seen in *i-D* magazine. It was because of Susanne that I was invited to show my designs in Berlin. She was part of the pre-globalization of the fashion community. Susanne had such fabulosity with her accent and her hats. But that was just her incubating period. She hadn't even started bringing over hordes of British designers to show in clubs."[26]

New London in New York

Her boutique was successful, but tiny, so Bartsch decided to stage a fashion show for buyers and press, with the idea that she could wholesale clothes by a larger number of young designers. In 1983 she staged her first *New London in New York* fashion show at the Roxy Roller Rink. It took place during New York Fashion Week, but without financial backing. It was done on a shoestring with designers paying for their own flights to New York and sleeping four to a room in cheap hotels. Costiff built the set "with ropes and muslin, layers of white and blue." Featured were twenty mostly unknown English designers including Rachel Auburn, David Holah and Stevie Stewart of BodyMap, Leigh Bowery (the Australian-born performance artist, who also modeled the clothes), Sue Clowes (designer for English pop groups such as Culture Club), Greg Davis (then a designer), Stephen Jones, John Richmond, and Richard Torry.

"I had a little shop in Kensington Market selling clothes which I had designed and made,' recalls Auburn. "My best friend, Leigh Bowery, also had a shop there. One day Gerlinde [Costiff] brought Susanne to see my work, and she invited us to show at the Roxy. I remember looking at New Yorkers on the street with their big shoulder pads and working girl look, and thinking 'Oh my God, no one will

Top: Susanne in her shop on Thompson Street, décor by Michael Costiff, c. 1982. Susanne's hat by Stephen Jones and dress by David Holah. Courtesy of Susanne Bartsch.

Center: Susanne in front of her Thompson Street store designed by Michael Costiff, September 1981. Photo by Michael Costiff.

Bottom: Susanne at Carine Roitfeld event in Paris, wearing Piers Atkinson, 2012. Photo by Mao Padilha.

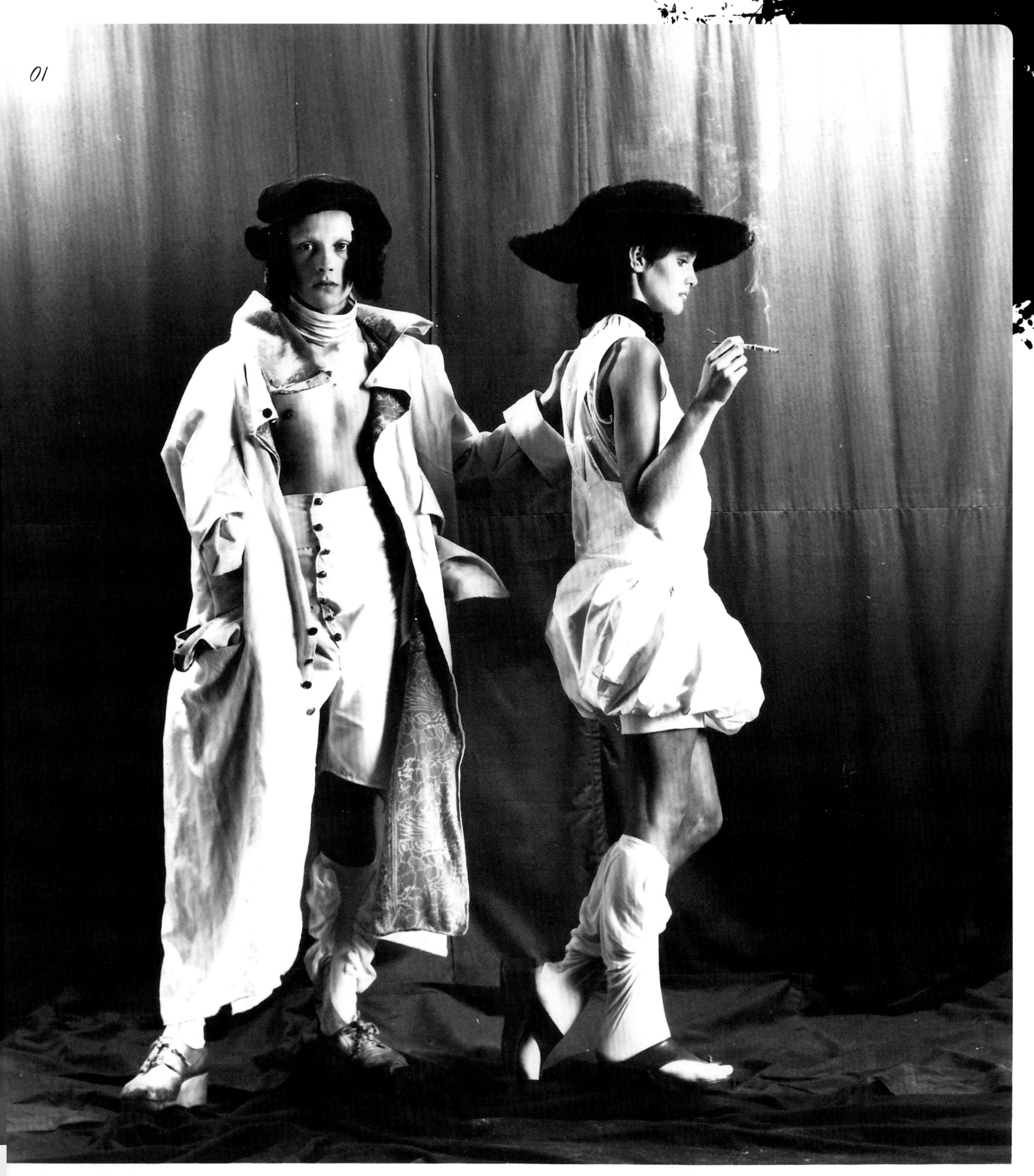

NEW LONDON IN NEW YORK - NOVEMBER 2, 1984
Designer: RACHEL AUBURN. Collection for men and women, Spring/Summer
1985. Avant-garde designs in a kaleidoscope of colors and shapes. Nylon
puckered socks, fake fur hats and other items in fake leather, nylon

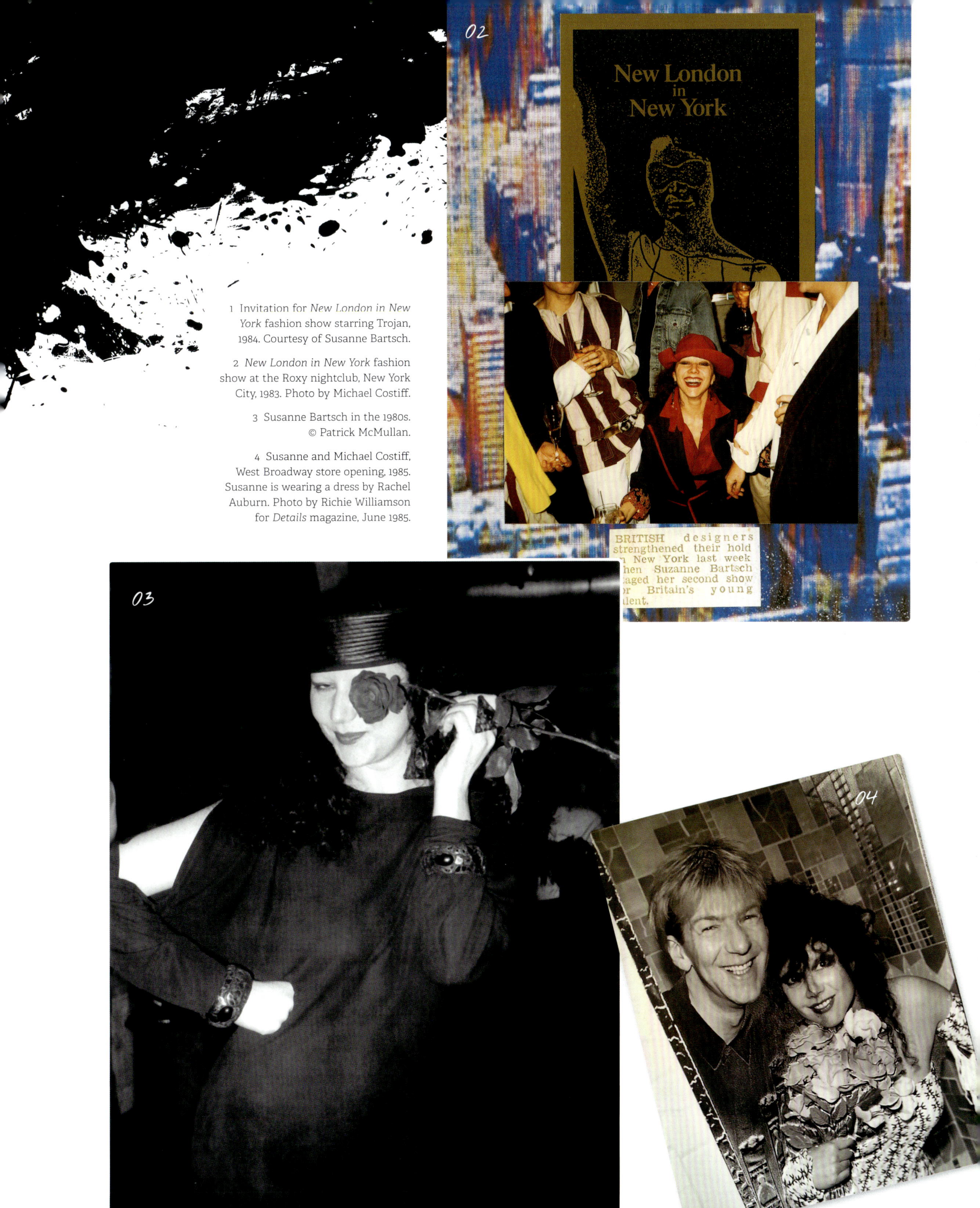

1 Invitation for *New London in New York* fashion show starring Trojan, 1984. Courtesy of Susanne Bartsch.

2 *New London in New York* fashion show at the Roxy nightclub, New York City, 1983. Photo by Michael Costiff.

3 Susanne Bartsch in the 1980s. © Patrick McMullan.

4 Susanne and Michael Costiff, West Broadway store opening, 1985. Susanne is wearing a dress by Rachel Auburn. Photo by Richie Williamson for *Details* magazine, June 1985.

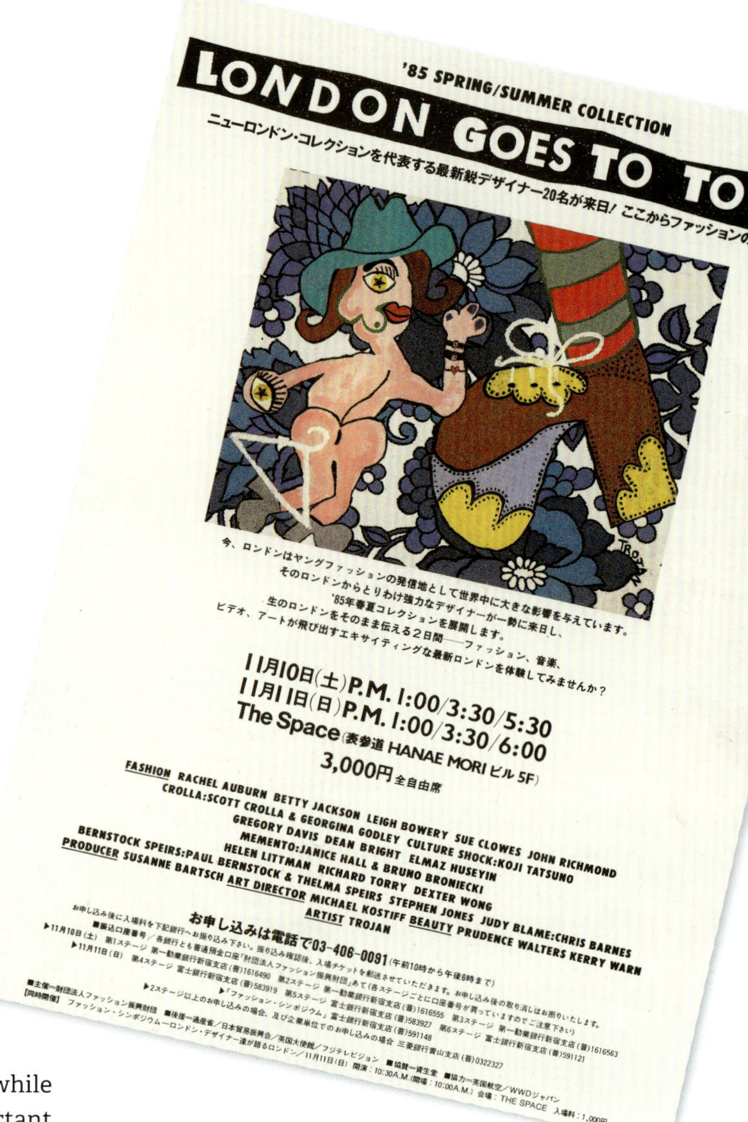

like our loose, ragamuffin style.' But Susanne had the energy and vision to bring this new style from London to New York, and she also decided to order my wacky knitwear made of recycled sweaters for her store."[27]

The first *London in New York* fashion show was well-attended by retailers from major stores such as Macy's, Bloomingdales, and Charivari, as well as by journalists and fashion groupies who were enthusiastic about the "hobo look" of patchwork, Edwardian coats, and high-waisted trousers. "Susanne always creates a great buzz," says the former designer Greg Davis, now a model agent, who participated in all three of Bartsch's *New London in New York* shows. "They were very exciting shows and an exciting period for London designers. There were queues of people wanting to come in. People were looking at what Susanne wore. She's a style icon, another Isabella Blow-type lady."[28]

Ellen Satzmann of Saks Fifth Avenue attended Bartsch's first show with her seventeen-year-old daughter and had "the best fun of the week," while Annie Flanders of *Details* pronounced it "so exhilarating and an important show. Everyone here is so scared by these economic problems they react by rushing back to safe values, and the English have done just the opposite."[29]

London Goes to Tokyo

Six months later, Bartsch organized another fashion show in New York at the Limelight nightclub, which *Women's Wear Daily* and Hanae Mori's Fashion Foundation then brought to Tokyo, where it had a powerful impact. "We'd just done the New York show, flew back to London, then to Tokyo," recalls Greg Davis. "Straight off the airplane, we were treated like rock stars. On the coach into Tokyo, we were filmed live on the TV, and they kept filming when we went to the center to review our clothes and see models."

"The 1984 *London Goes to Tokyo* fashion show was a huge turning point in Japanese fashion history, and a pivotal moment in my career," says Stephen Jones. "Hanae Mori's Fashion Foundation had always done a show in Tokyo highlighting the top fashion designers from Paris, so when they brought the London designers over, the Japanese thought this was the Next Big Thing in fashion. I got my license in Japan, because of the contacts I made there." Rachel Auburn and Leigh Bowery also traveled to Tokyo with Bartsch. "Thanks to the Tokyo trip, I got a design job for Isetan department Store and I also styled for Sheisedo," says Auburn. She would later turn from fashion to music, while Bowery would soon abandon fashion design per se, in favor of performance art, often within the context of club nights.

Above: *London Goes to Tokyo*, flyer, artwork by Trojan, 1984. Courtesy Michael Costiff.

Facing: *London Goes to Tokyo* fashion show, collage, 1984. Photo by Michael Costiff.

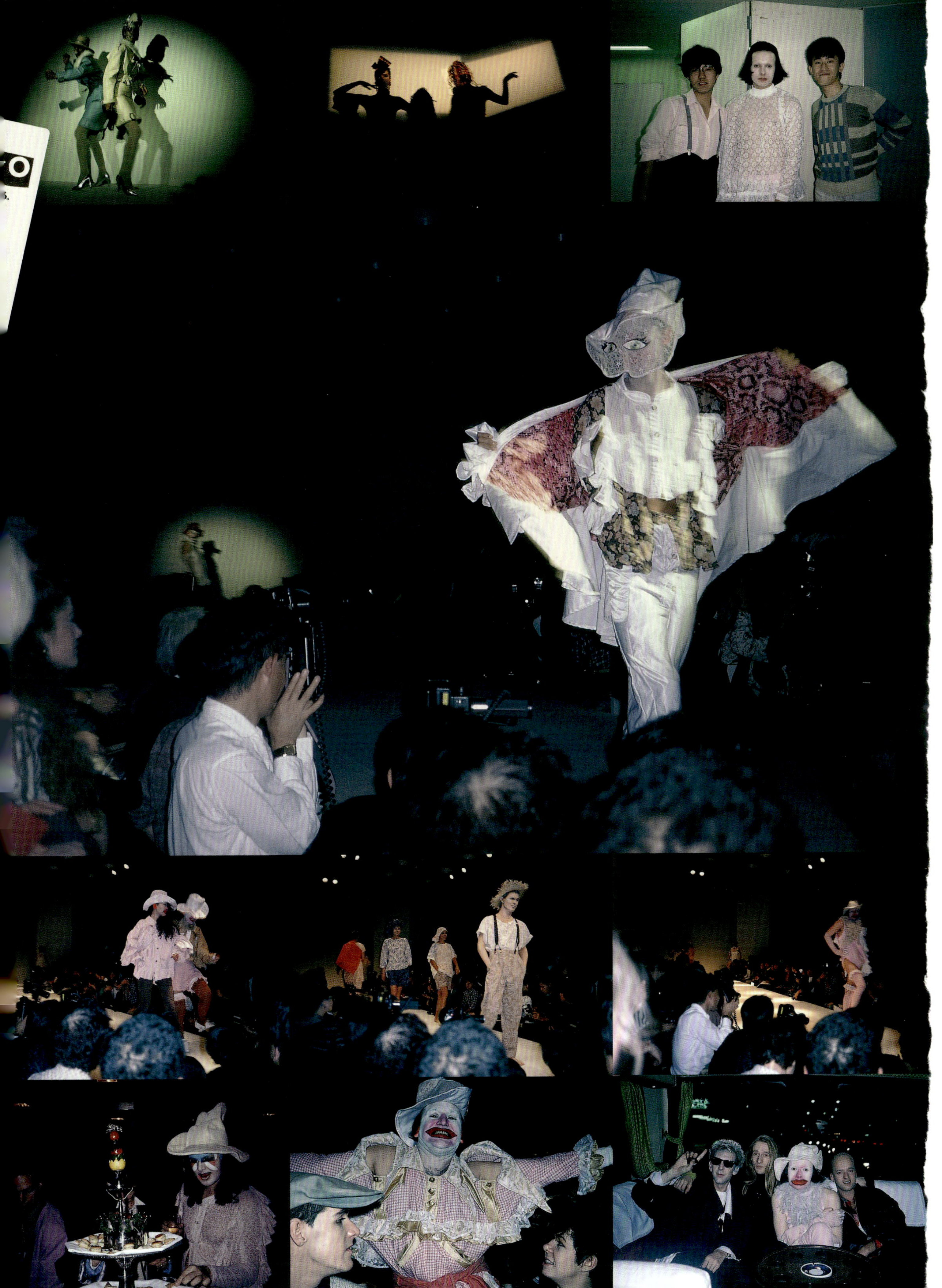

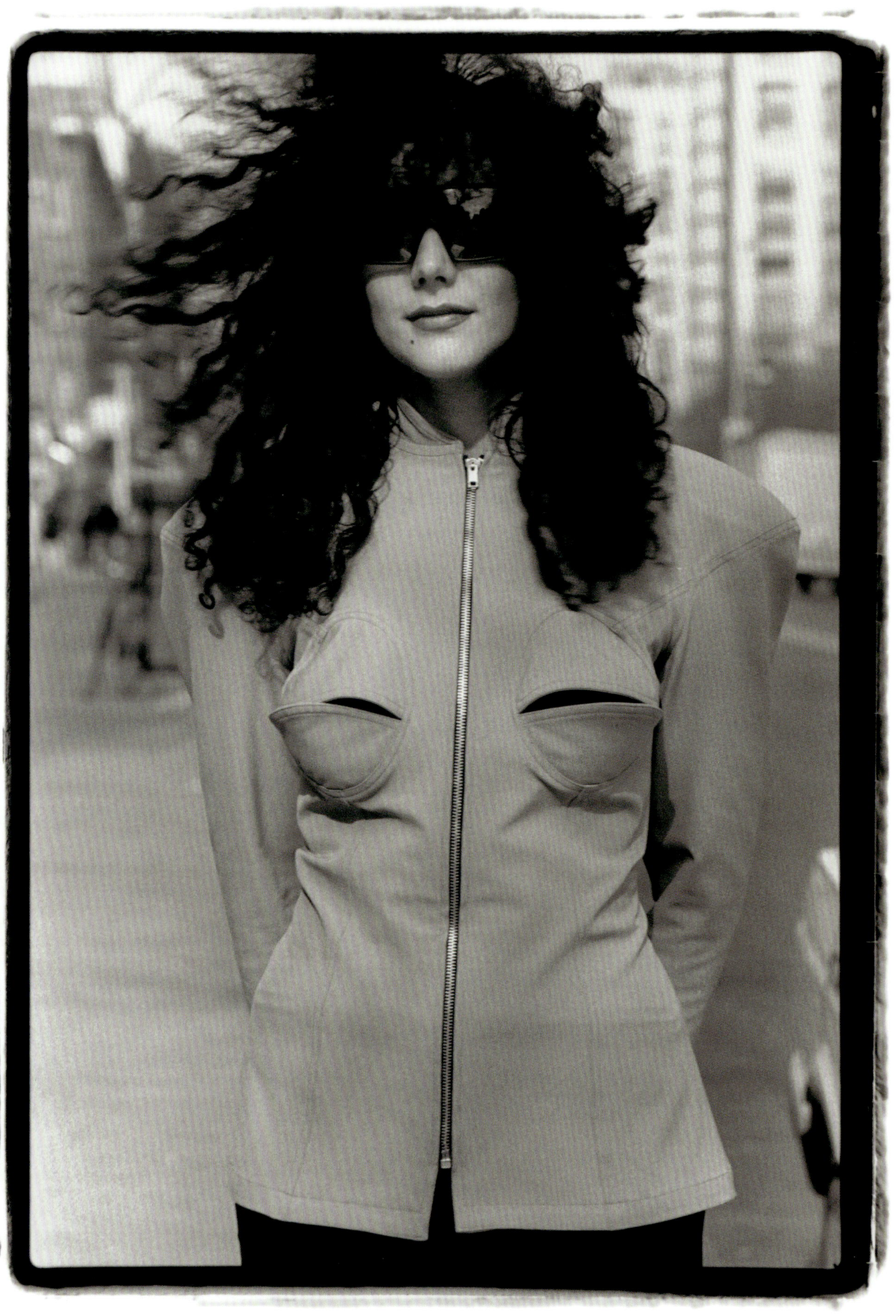

"Tits suit", 1987

Susanne Bartsch, "Tits Suit."
Day-drag outside the Soho Shop, 1987.
Photo © Amy Arbus.

A Disco Gothic Boutique

In 1985, Bartsch moved her eponymous boutique to larger premises at 456A West Broadway. Once again the store design by Michael Costiff was a striking architectural fantasy, with a glass-fronted Gothic entrance. Inside, Arabian-style arches and a red lacquer Japanese gateway punctuated the lavishly tiled, two-story interior. Also featured were a Chinese pagoda and an obelisk topped with a golden ship. "The store was like a castle made of broken tiles in beautiful sherbet colors," recalls Michael Leva, who worked there at the time and is now a fashion executive. Costiff called the style "disco gothic, wacky and unpredictable." Critics called it "light years ahead of other interiors, in terms of design, structure and merchandise."[30]

With this store, Bartsch became one of the first two retailers in New York to sell clothes by Vivienne Westwood. "She's the goddess of fashion – brilliant," Bartsch told journalists in 1985. "She's really changed the outlook and concept of fashion."[31] Along with Westwood, the store also sold clothing by Rachel Auburn, Leigh Bowery, John Galliano, Stephen Jones, and John Richmond, among others – mostly English, but also some young Japanese accessory designers and a few Americans, such as Gene Krell. Maria Cornejo was then living with John Richmond in London, where they had begun designing a collection together. She remembers when Bartsch came to look at their clothes: "She was a very eccentric, stylish woman, who took off all her clothes and started trying things on."[32]

Dressed like "a gypsy princess" in globe earrings, charm necklaces, and a leather corset, Bartsch told *Women's Wear Daily*, "When I first came here in 1981, I took one look at New Yorkers and decided I wanted to slap some style on their backs." Progress had been made. "Men and women are actually getting the nerve to wear our things. They don't need Halloween."[33]

"If you were into the art-fashion thing, there were two movements in the 1980s – Japan and London," says Michael Leva. "Susanne brought London fashion to New York and Diane B. brought the Japanese. It was one of the most important times in the history of fashion – a true upheaval. I first met John Galliano when I worked in the big store. I wore his burlap overalls with big pearl buttons to work. Susanne brought BodyMap to New York, and they brought a cool athleticism to fashion. It was a magical moment of creativity, so radically different from Seventh Avenue. We'd all go hang out at Susanne's stores – all the designers and musicians and people from London and Japan. Jasmin, the receptionist, was the most beautiful transgirl. Susanne was so ahead of her time."[34]

Seeing and Being Seen

After successfully staging fashion spectacles in New York and Tokyo, in 1987 Bartsch organized her first weekly Tuesday party at Savage, a club a few doors

1 Susanne in her West Broadway store with unknown guest (L) and the artist Andrew Logan (R), 1980s. © Patrick McMullan.

2 Susanne at her West Broadway store opening, 1985. Photo by Josef Astor.

3 West Broadway store exterior, New York City, 1985. Photo by Tim Street-Porter, courtesy of Michael Costiff.

4 Interior of West Broadway store, New York City, 1985. Courtesy of Susanne Bartsch.

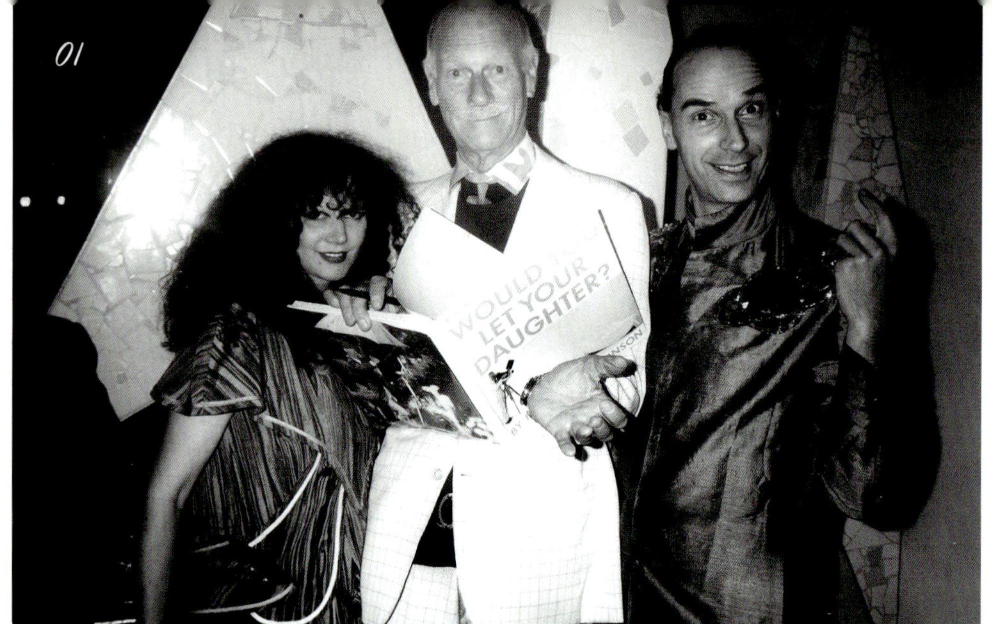

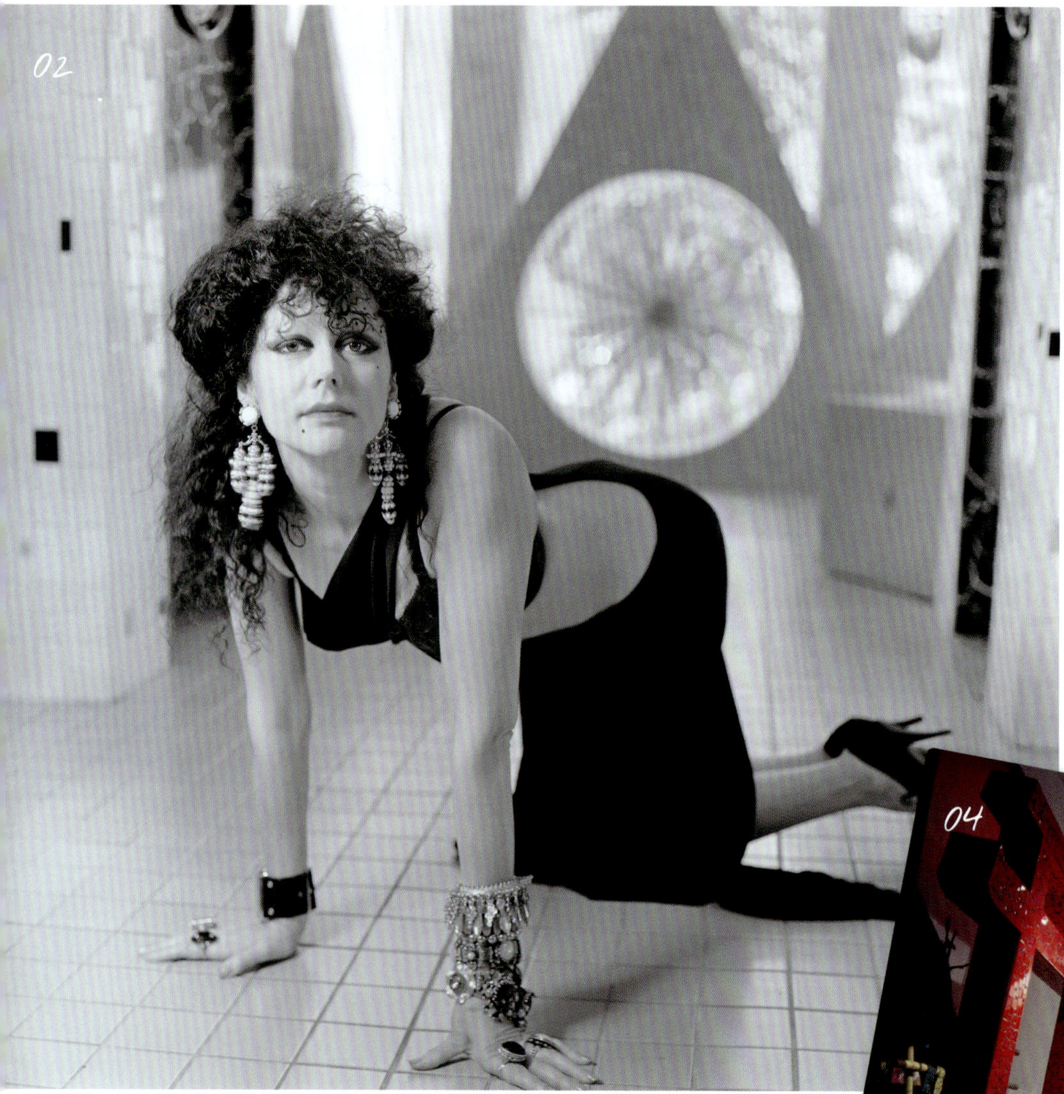

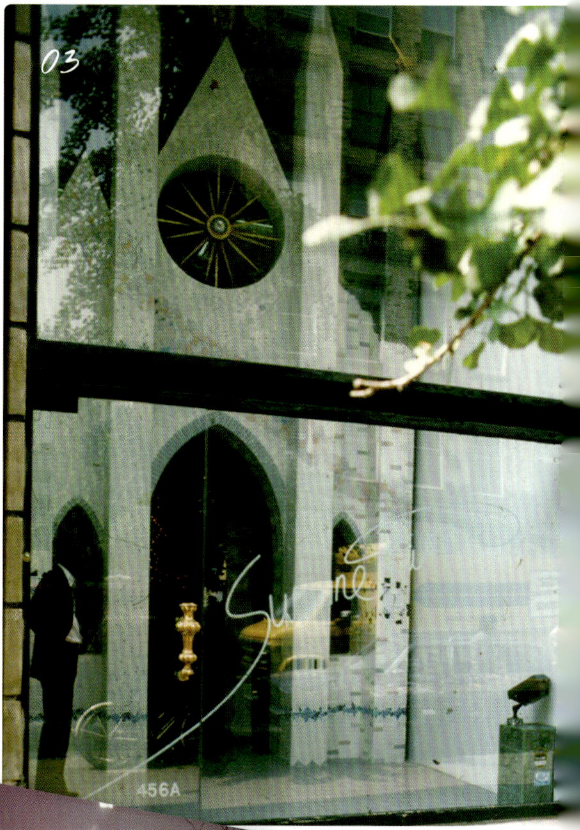

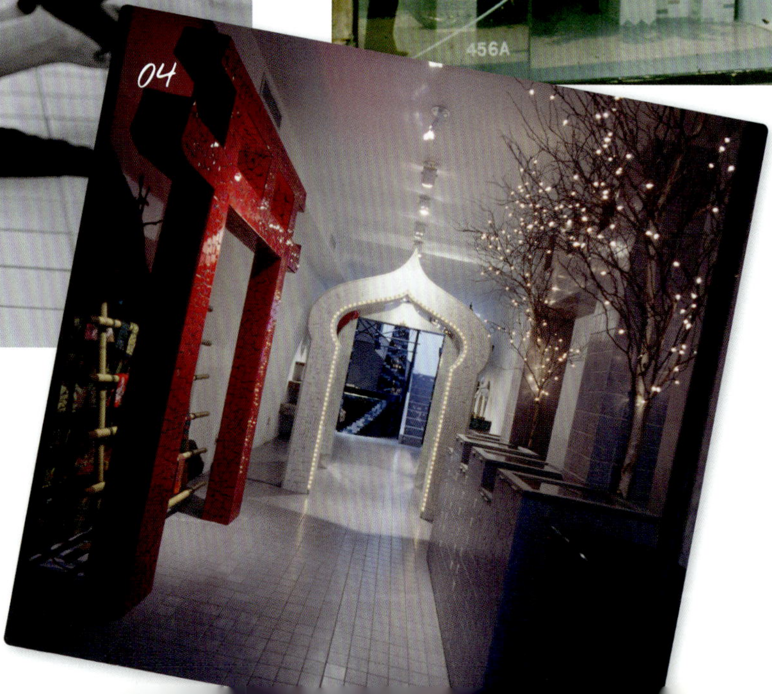

Facing: Upper-floor interior of Susanne's West Broadway store, New York City, 1985. Photo by Tim Street-Porter, courtesy of Michael Costiff.

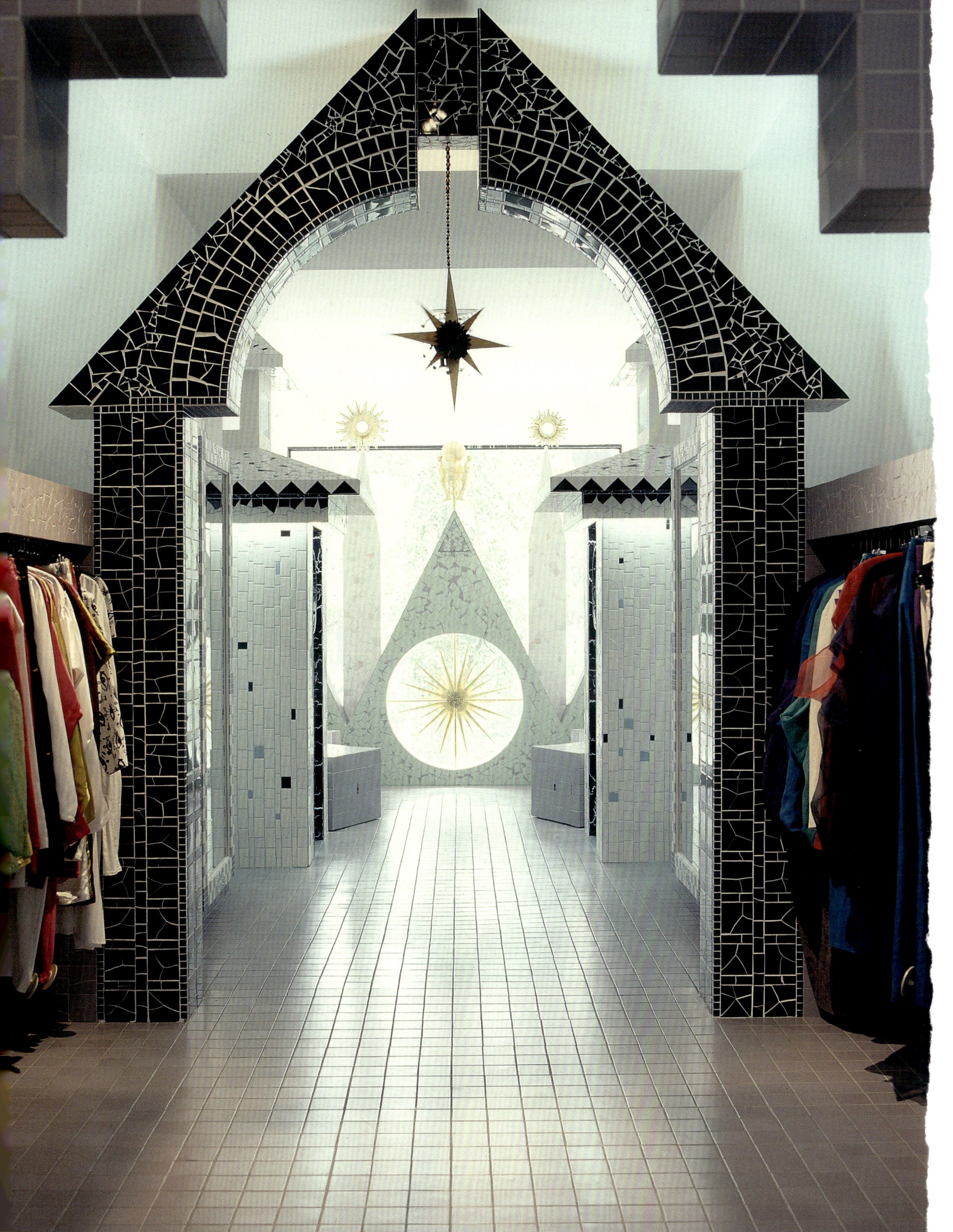

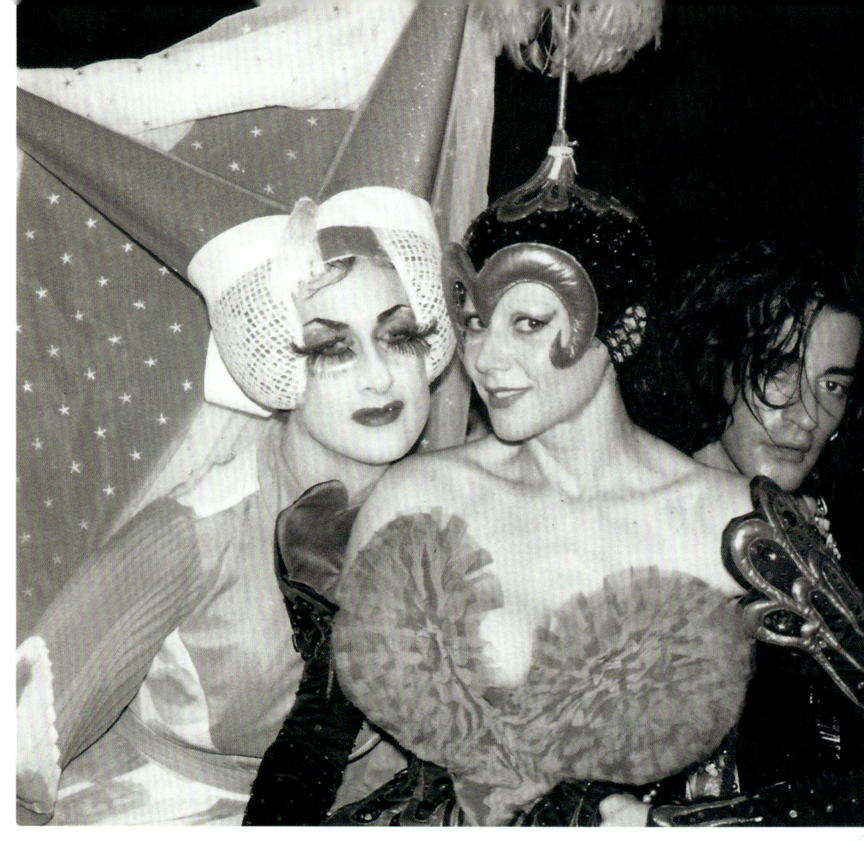

1 Susanne with the DJ Sister Dimension. Photo by Alexis Di Biasio.

2 Susanne as Virgo, sculpted by Adel Rootstein, zodiac window display, Barney's New York, Seventeenth Street, 1989. Photo © Barney's New York.

down from the Chelsea Hotel. The concept was to provide a space for people to dress up and express their creativity through their appearance. Savage was about "seeing and being seen," recalls Bartsch. "It was "very high-energy, very mixed: straight, gay, uptown, downtown, pier queens to trust funds. My mission was to get people to mix and dress up."

Leigh Bowery attended Bartsch's events whenever he came over from London. Once she threw him a surprise birthday party at the Bentley Hotel. "She had a cake made with a face and lightbulbs popping out of it all lit up," Bowery told *Paper*. "I love Susanne, she's got oomph!"[35] Bowery had started Taboo in 1985, when it quickly became "the wildest, most fashionable night in [London]. With his body-morphing costumes, a taste for the bizarre and a deep desire to shock, Bowery radically challenged the boundaries between figure, gender, fashion, beauty, and art."[36] With her club nights, "Susanne gave New Yorkers freedom of expression," says Maria Cornejo. "It was common in London, but not in New York. Leigh was a walking art installation, and Susanne's outfits were genius. She gave a lot of people a voice, especially transgender kids. She has mad outfits, but good values. She's always been very grounded and nurturing."

"Susanne hired me as a go-go dancer at a club called Savage," recalls RuPaul, later the star of *RuPaul's Drag Race*. "Midway through the evening, she came over to my go-go box and said 'You're a superstar.' She believed in me from day one, and continued to hire me as a performer and as an emcee. Back then Susanne was known as 'the Flo Zeigfeld of New York Nightlife.' She championed downtown performers and presented us to the world. The first time I saw Paris was during one of her famous cabaret tours. Same with Switzerland and Japan, she was my gateway to the world stage. Susanne is from the Andy Warhol school of thought, which is to create your own stardom, even if only to entertain yourself. She loves the unusual, the unique, and has always made room for the ones who dance to the beat of a different drummer."[37]

"I brought the drag queens into my clubs, because I liked the way they put on a look and transform themselves," says Bartsch. "Put on a dress and . . . showtime! I wanted them at my party, because they were a party already." Drag would become a very important part of Bartsch's world. She once jokingly told Simon Doonan that she had taken drag queens "out of the shadows; now they do fancy bar mitzvahs! That's all thanks to me! What a contribution to society!"[38]

"Susanne is a female drag queen," says RuPaul. "She has inspired women around the world to challenge the idea of demure." "'Drag' is an English expression for dressing up, doing a look," says Bartsch. "It's Cockney slang. It doesn't necessarily mean a man in a dress." She describes her own style in terms of day drag, semi-drag, and full drag.

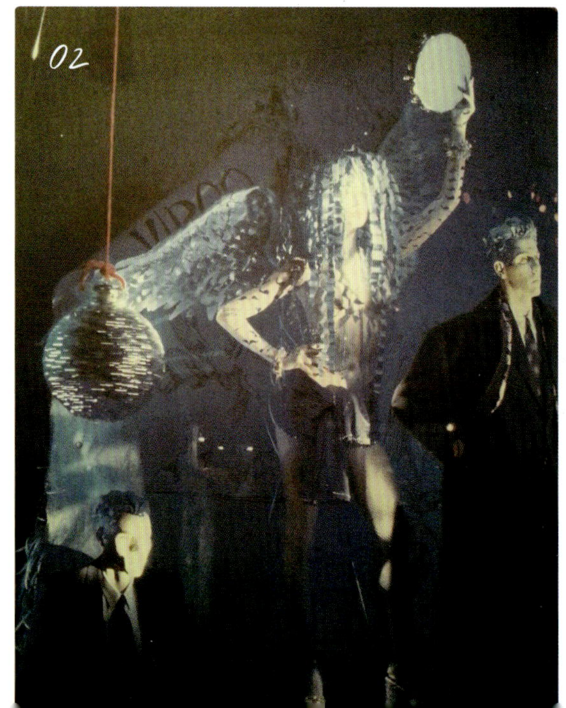

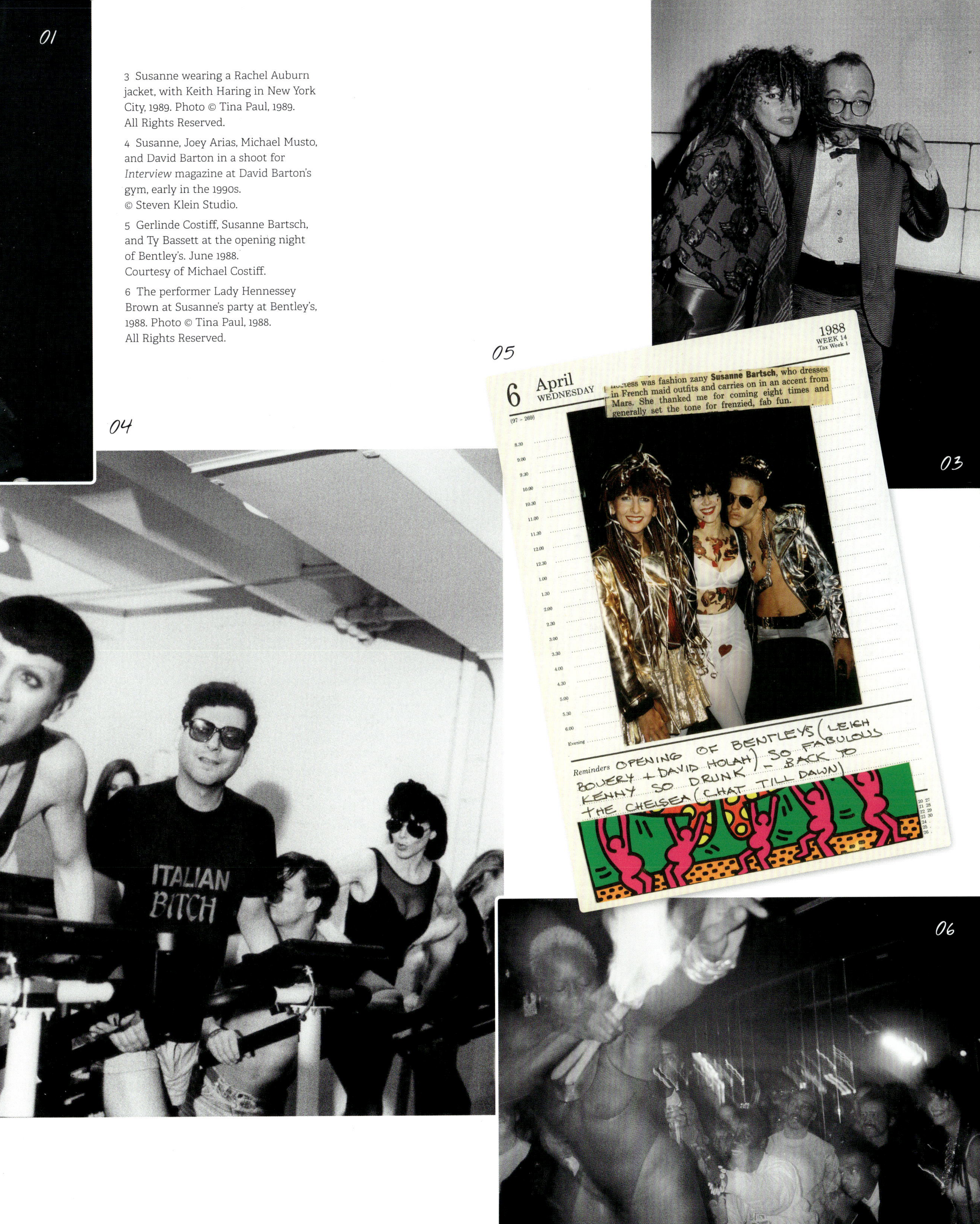

3 Susanne wearing a Rachel Auburn jacket, with Keith Haring in New York City, 1989. Photo © Tina Paul, 1989. All Rights Reserved.

4 Susanne, Joey Arias, Michael Musto, and David Barton in a shoot for *Interview* magazine at David Barton's gym, early in the 1990s. © Steven Klein Studio.

5 Gerlinde Costiff, Susanne Bartsch, and Ty Bassett at the opening night of Bentley's. June 1988. Courtesy of Michael Costiff.

6 The performer Lady Hennessey Brown at Susanne's party at Bentley's, 1988. Photo © Tina Paul, 1988. All Rights Reserved.

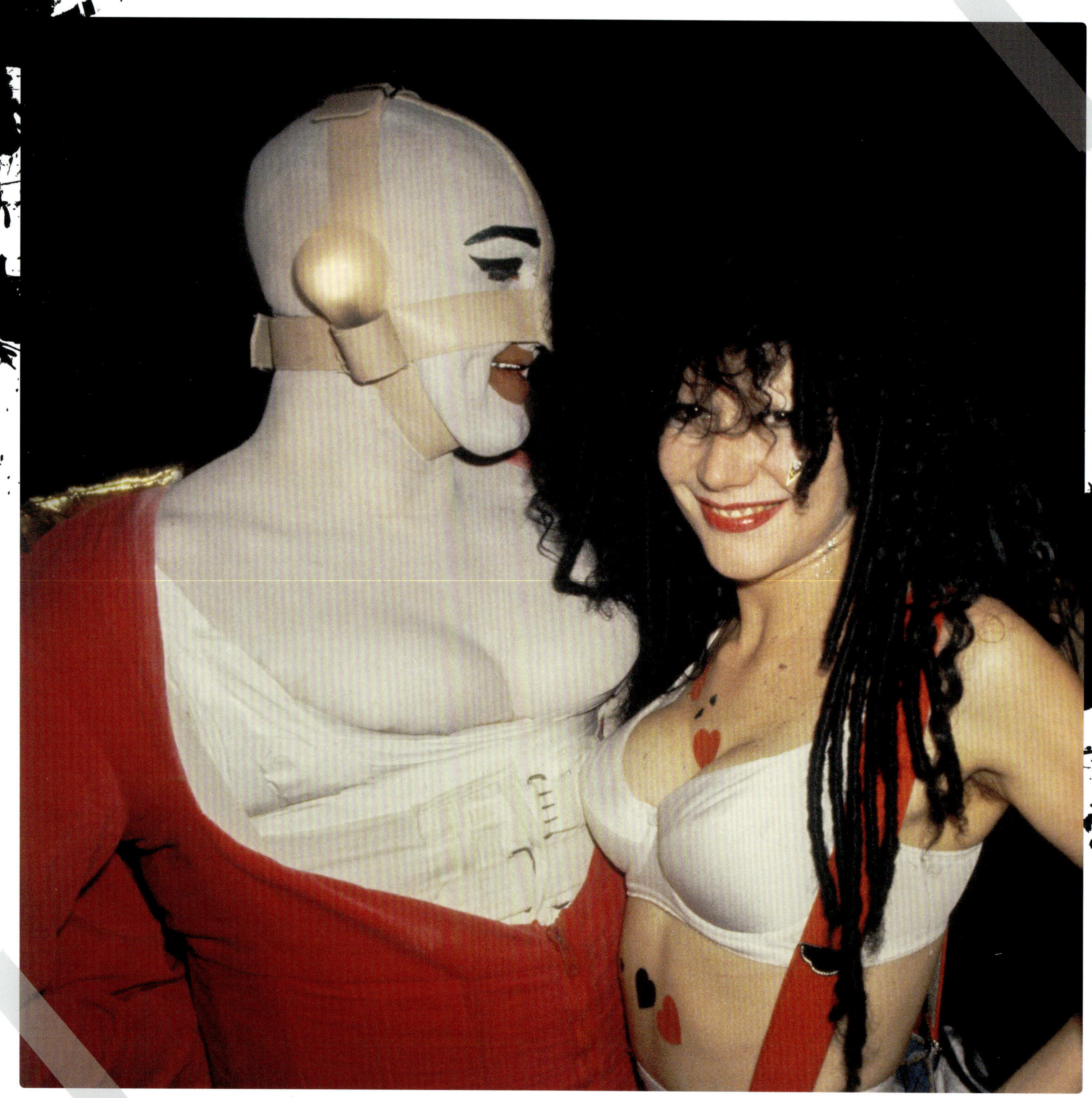

Susanne and Leigh Bowery at Savage in 1987. © Todd Eberle.

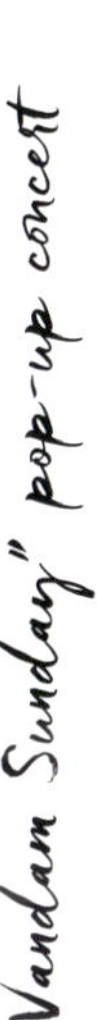

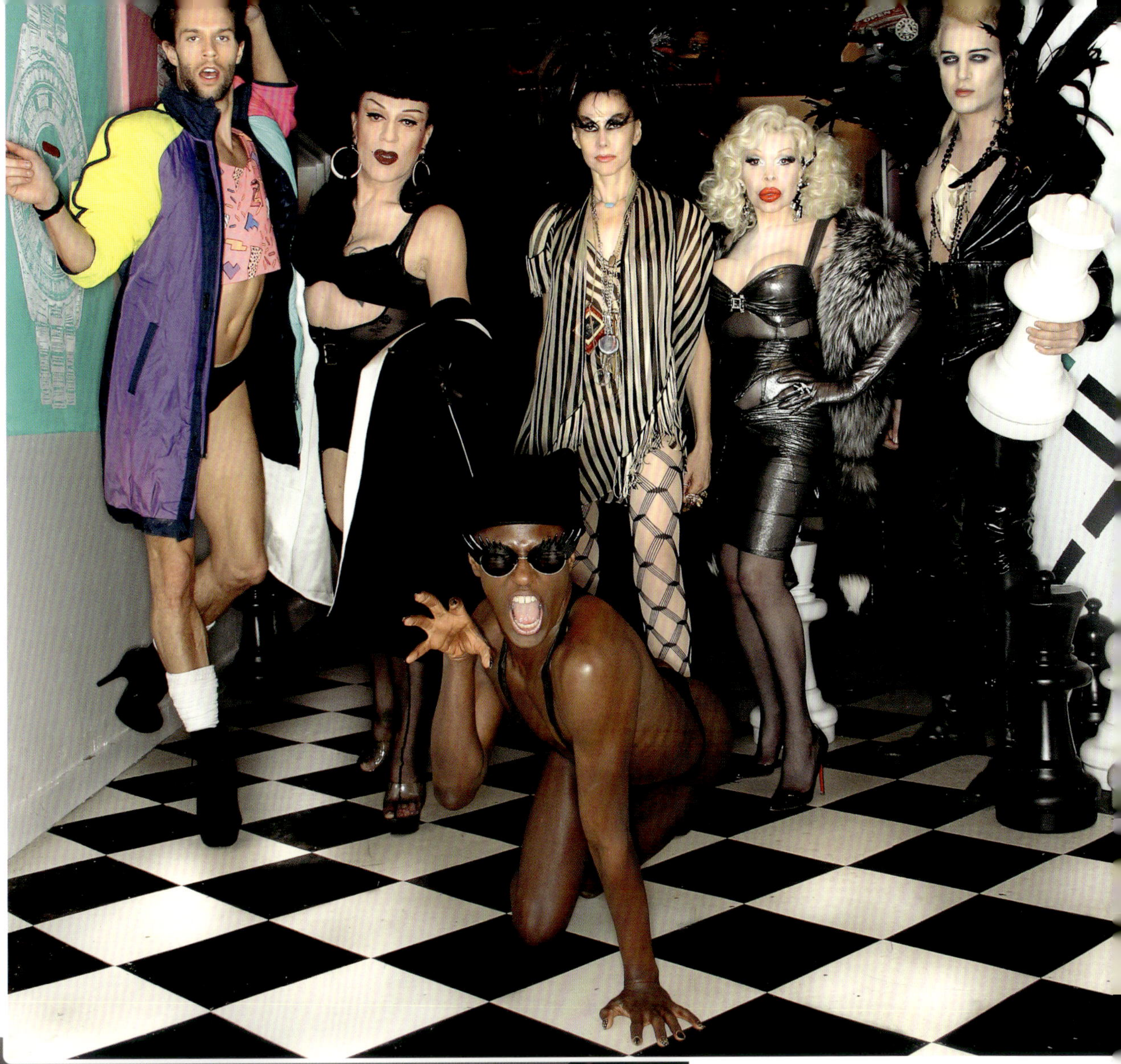

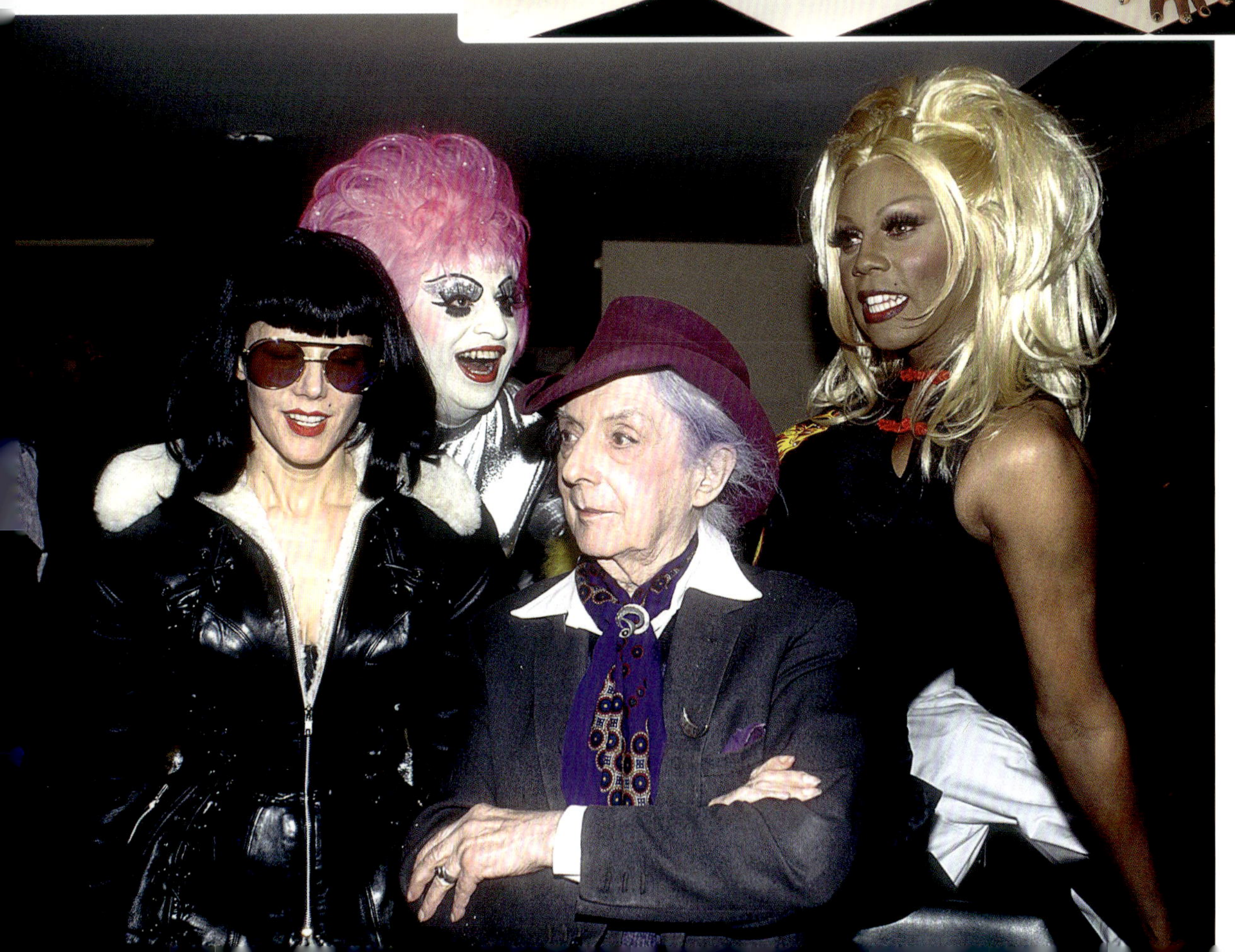

Above, from left to right: JB Dubbs, Joey Arias, Jonte, Susanne Bartsch, Amanda Lepore, and Kayvon at Vandam Sunday photoshoot. Pop-up concert at Revere Hotel, Boston. Photo by Marco Ovando.

Left: Susanne with Brandywine, Quentin Crisp, and RuPaul, 1995. © Patrick McMullan.

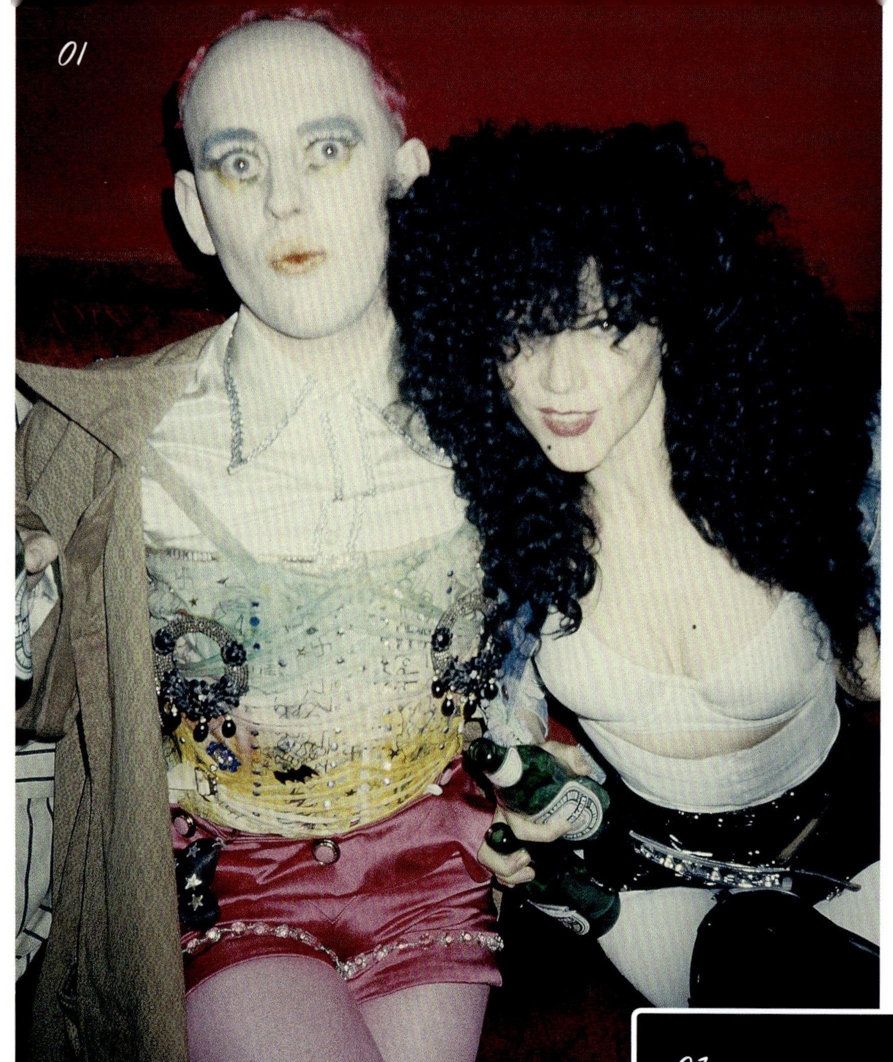

1 Kenny Kenny and Susanne at the door at Savage, New York City, 1987. Photo by Michael Costiff.

2 Susanne in an outfit by John Pezewski, late 1980s. © Patrick McMullan.

3 Susanne in a Savage/Bentley's era look, 1980s. Photo by Roxanne Lowit.

4 Susanne at Savage, 1987. Outfit by Betsey Johnson. Photo © Patrick McMullan.

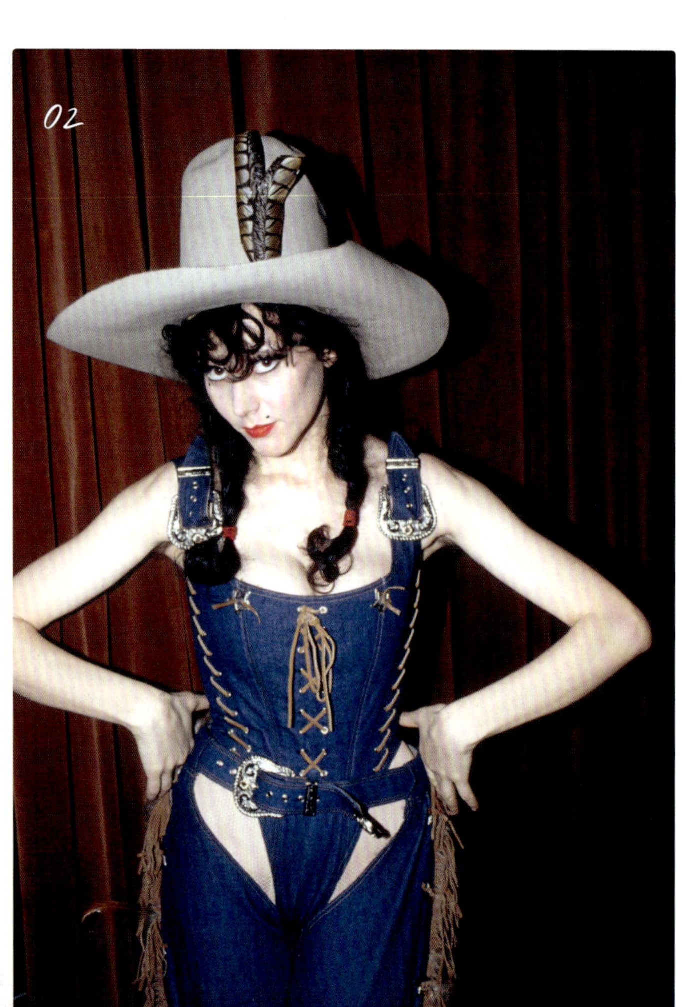

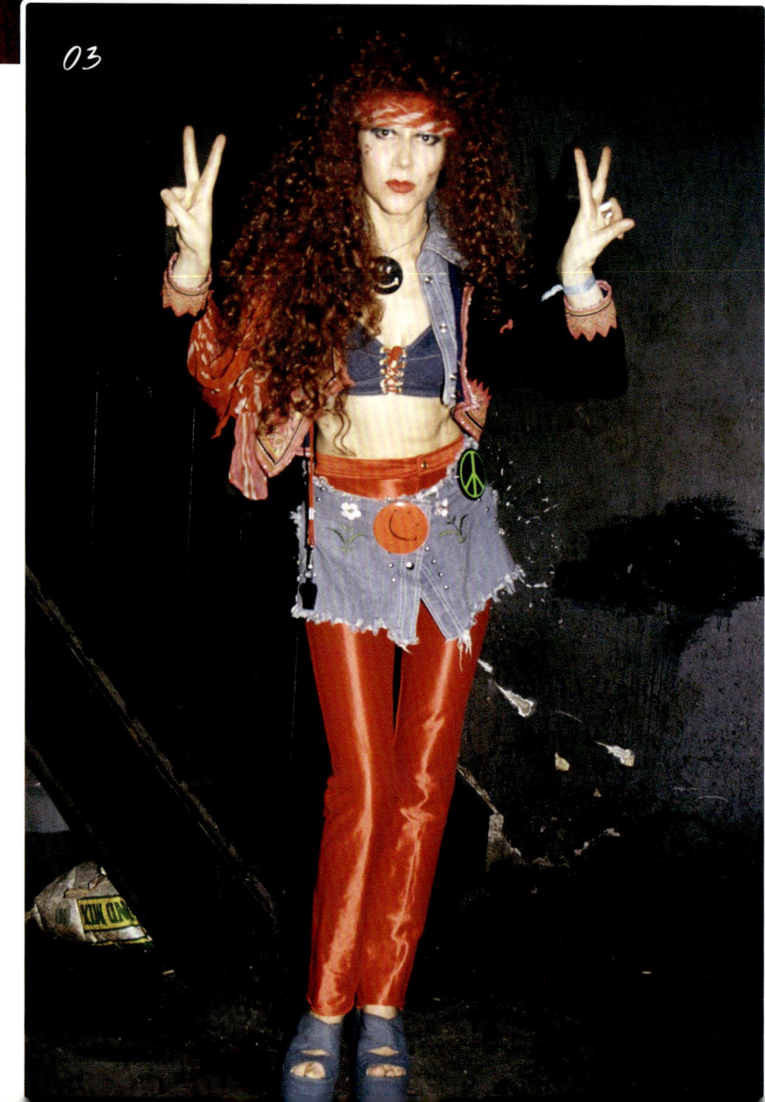

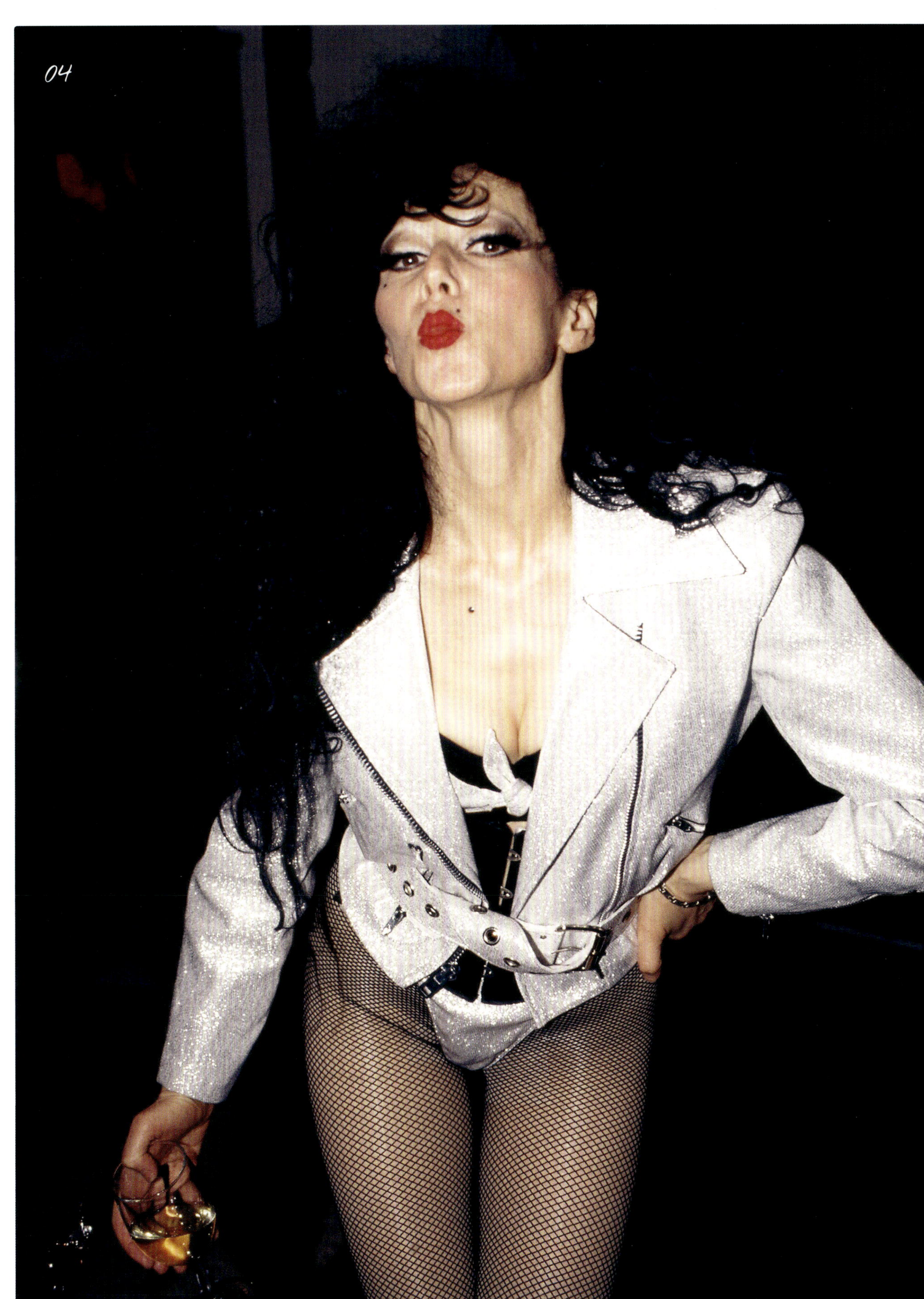

At Savage, 1987

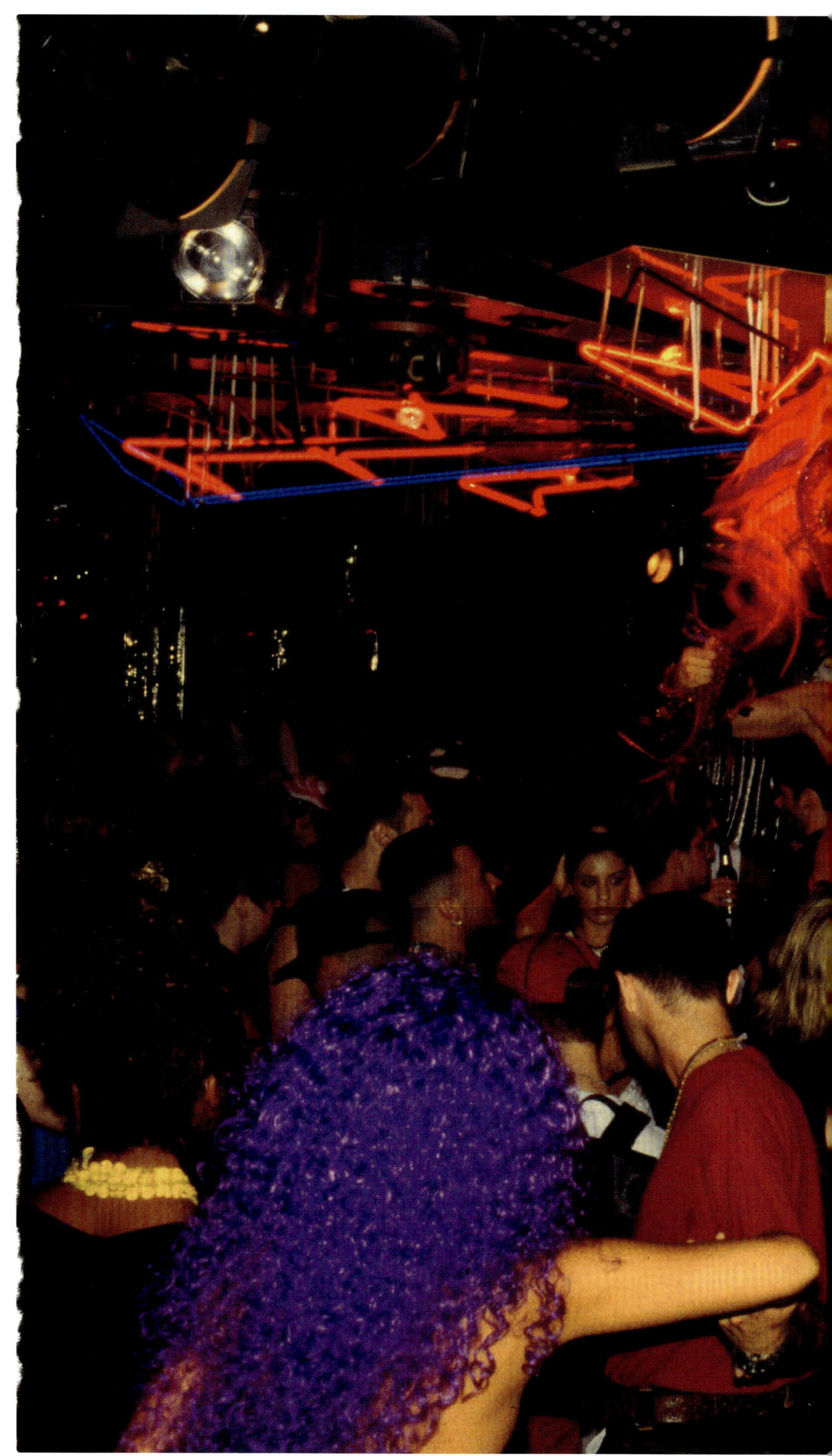

Susanne's last party at Copacabana, 1993. Photo © Tina Paul 1993. All Rights Reserved.

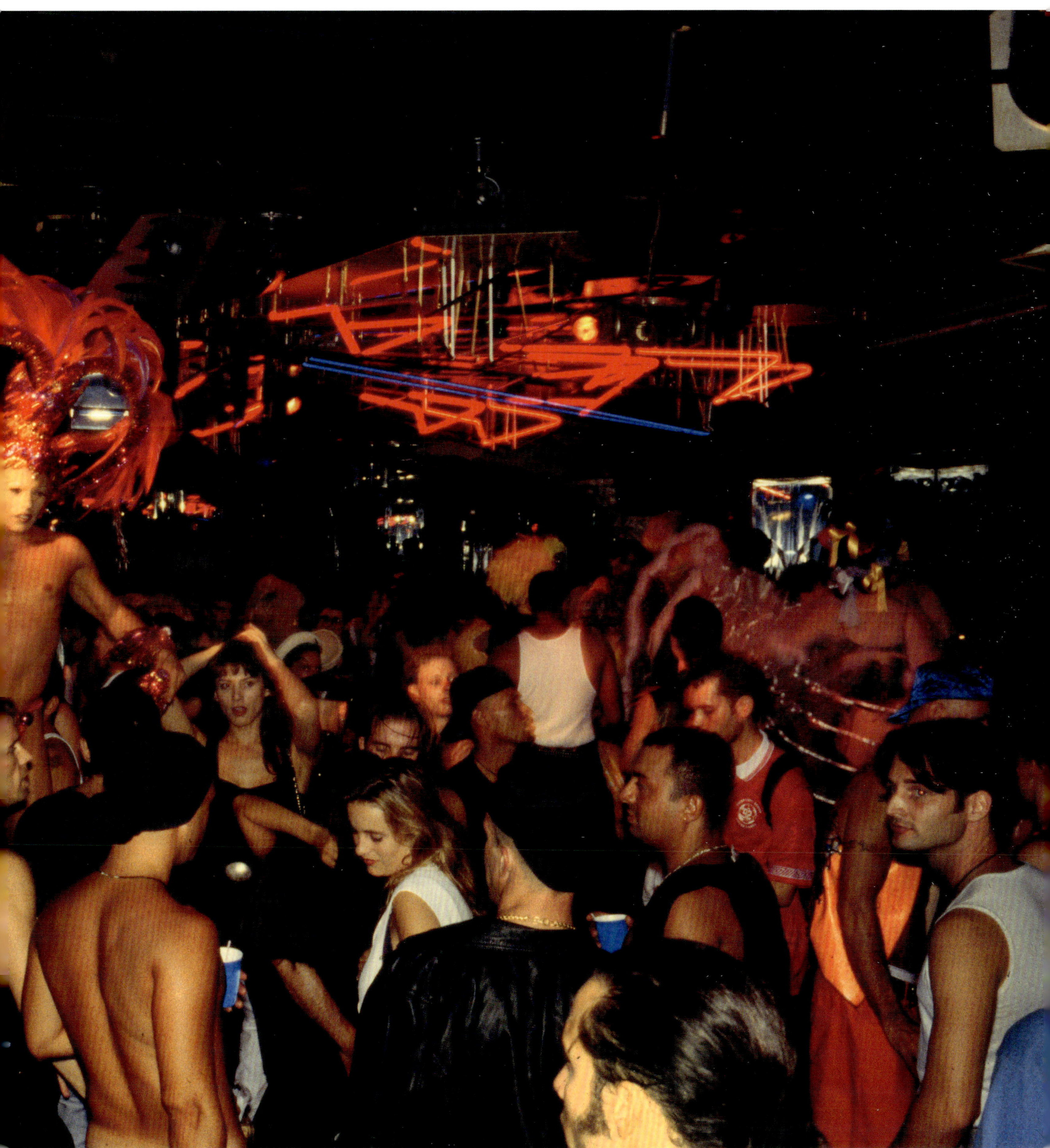

"The drag scene has a long history and has evolved over time," says the singer and performer Joey Arias. "In the past, queens dressed up as Betty Davis or Judy Garland, but that evolved into crazier looks. Susanne just started picking people she thought looked great, people who were not the norm. Before I really got into drag, I had a character called Justine, all latex and a fringed skirt, which embodied sensuality. Thierry Mugler saw it and said, 'This is a Russ Meyer look.' Now 'drag' means 'dress up.' The word has morphed."[39]

After differences with her business partner, Bartsch walked away from her store, and, moving on from Savage, she began a weekly Wednesday event at the Bentley Hotel in 1988: "She created a unique nightlife experience with a large dose of fashion," says Patricia Field, the retailer and television and film stylist. "These were unique looks, not commercial fashion, but fashion as art. Of course, this has an impact on commercial fashion."[40] "I love walking with Susanne into business meetings," says Arias. "She's a powerhouse, like a DV or an Anna Wintour. She's strong with her convictions."[41]

"There were two floors at Bentley's," says Bartsch. "Drag queens and disco downstairs, with Sister Dimension spinning, and upstairs we had house music and the art of the striptease." No one had ever presented strippers outside the context of a sex club, and in a mixed but heavily gay event like Bartsch's nights at Bentley's, their performances were less erotic than deliberately outrageous, a kind of "naïve decadence" that made some performers, notably Lady Hennessey Brown, into downtown stars. "Susanne was the first person to put porn in a fashion context," says Simon Doonan. "To Susanne, strippers were just interesting people, like when she went to Brazil and brought back a samba school."

Disco was also a fascinating choice, since it had had its heyday a decade before, when it was closely associated with gay nightlife in the pre-AIDS era. "There was such a gap between the disco era and the AIDS era – Susanne was like a bridge between the two generations," says the New York artist Scott Ewalt. "She brought back the sexy, fun thing in the middle of a very serious, grim era."[42] "You wrapped your 20-foot boa around me and brought me into your world and I never looked back," the transvestite Sister Dimension tells Bartsch.[43]

The journalist Michael Musto recalls that both Savage and Bentley's were "off-the-beaten-track places you would never go [that] transformed into places you had to go – Susanne's parties became the central place for all the fab freaks and off-beat celebrities of New York. I was immediately hooked and never missed a party. Sister Dimension was a drag performer who was a great DJ. But you couldn't say it was a gay party – it was the ultimate in a mixed crowd."[44]

Fashion Designers on the Dance Floor

Later in 1988 Bartsch launched a monthly event at the legendary Copacabana nightclub. "Copa was old school glamour," says Bartsch. "The fact that it was

1 Susanne and her Adel Rootstein mannequin, 1991. Photo by John Swannell, courtesy of Adel Rootstein.

2 Susanne, Marc Jacobs, and Scott at Copacabana, c. 1990. © Patrick McMullan.

3 Susanne in Rio Carnival costume, Copacabana, 1991. © Wouter Deruytter.

4 Susanne as cover girl for *Paper*, November 1988. Courtesy of *Paper* magazine.

5 Susanne with a couple of girl pals, New York City, Susanne's look by Mathu and Zaldy, *German Vogue*, 1992. Photo by Arthur Elgort.

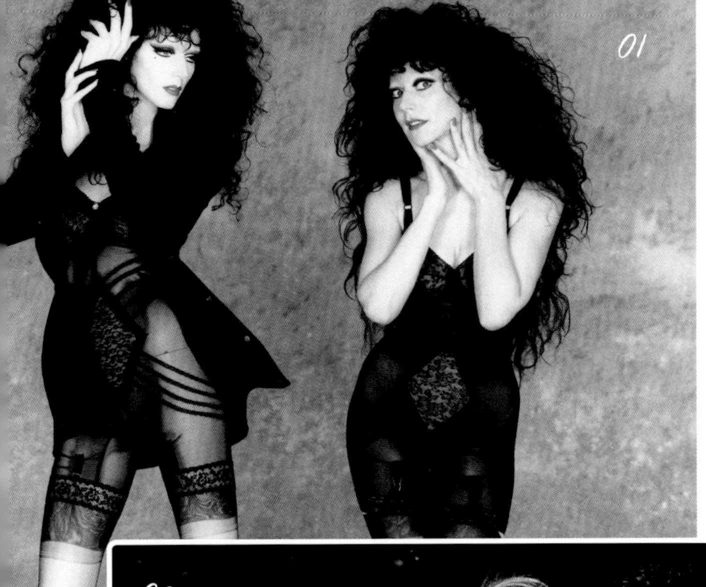

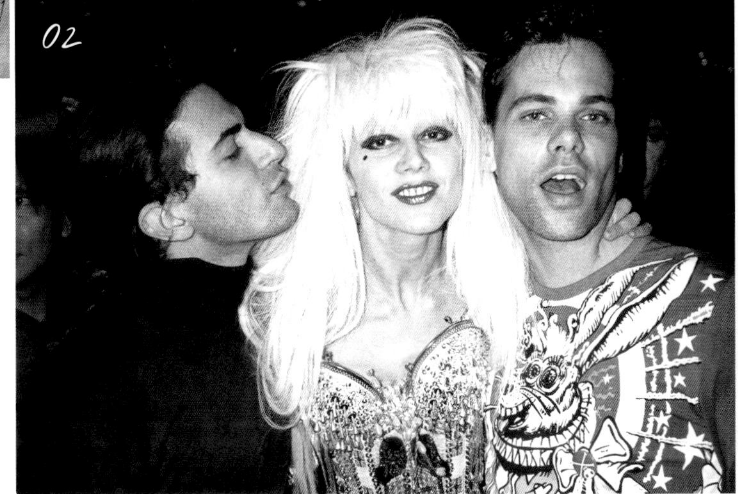

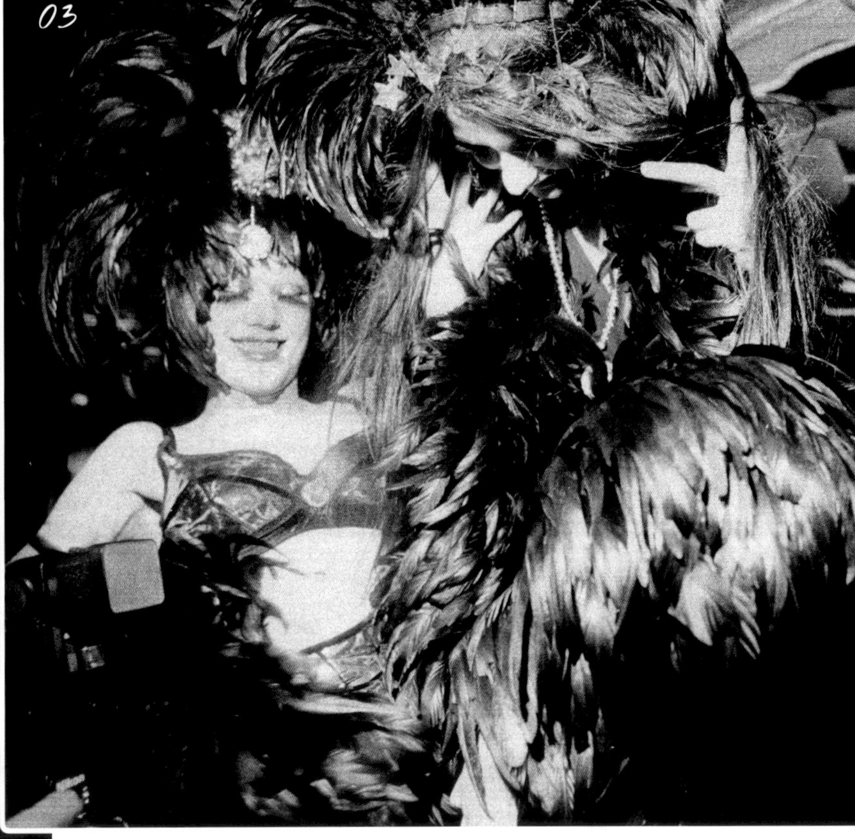

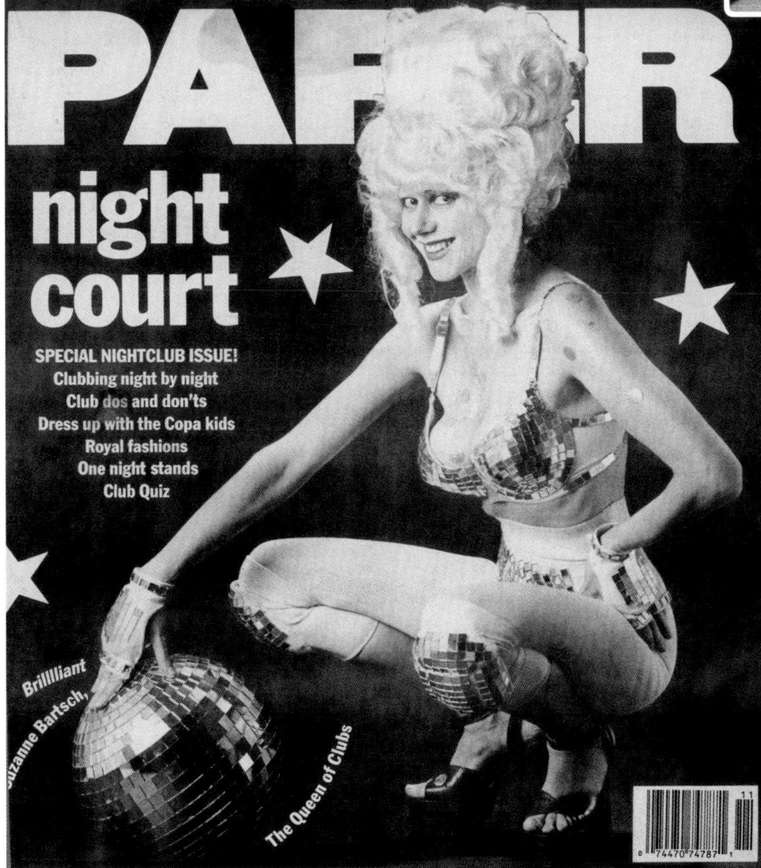
News: Politics and advertising
★ NEW YORK CITY ★ NOVEMBER 1988 ★ $1.95
PAPER
night court ★
SPECIAL NIGHTCLUB ISSUE!
Clubbing night by night
Club dos and don'ts
Dress up with the Copa kids
Royal fashions
One night stands
Club Quiz
Brillliant
Suzanne Bartsch,
The Queen of Clubs
NEWS ★ CLUBS ★ MUSIC ★ STYLE ★ MOVIES ★ PEOPLE

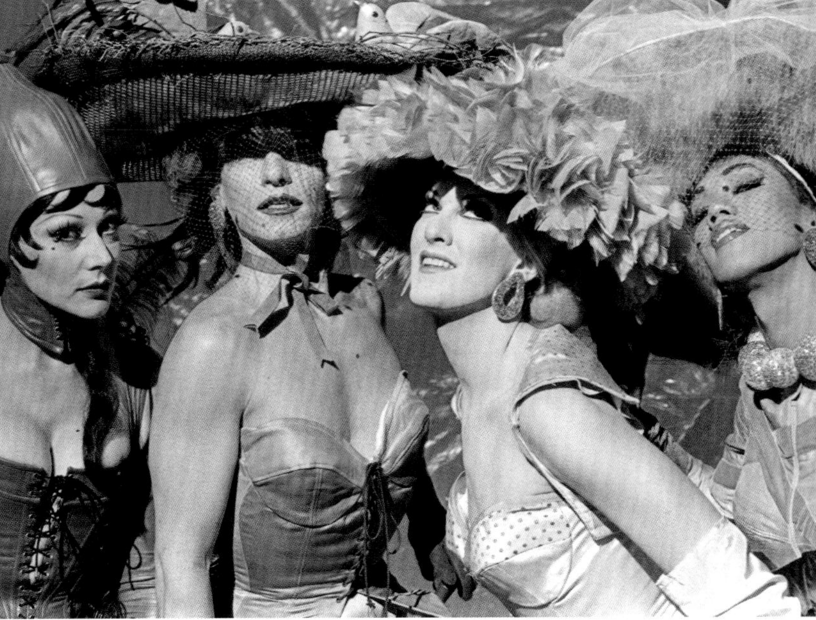

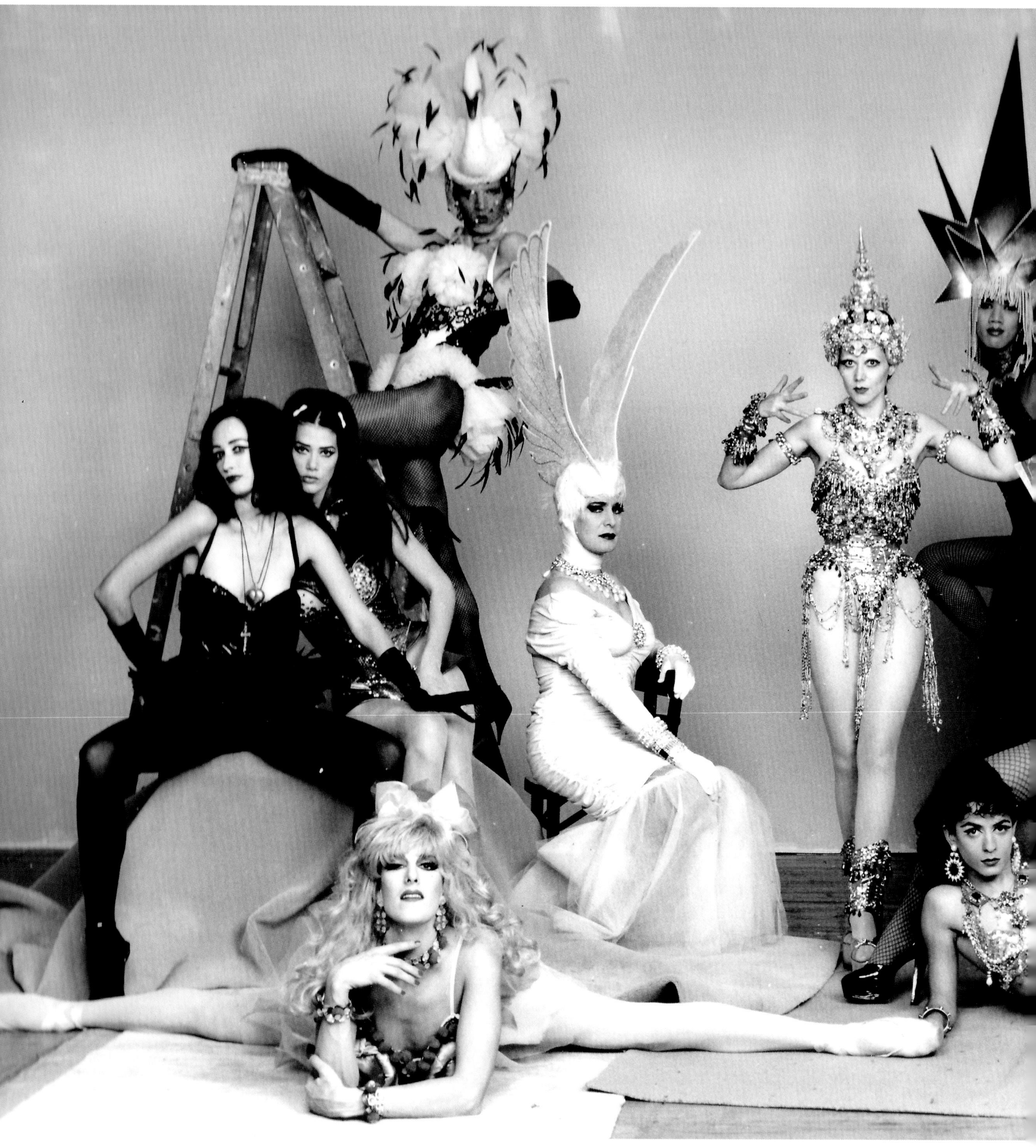

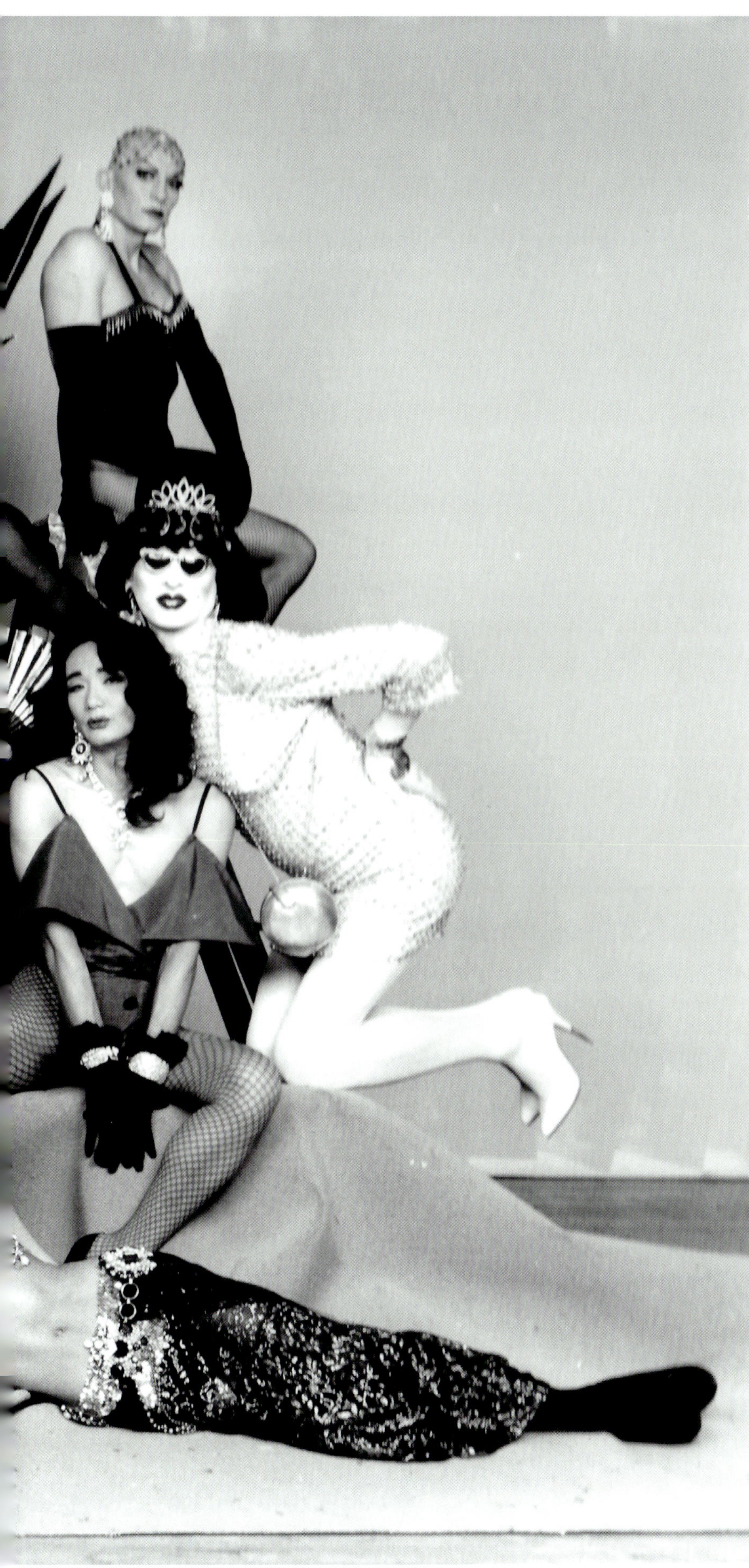

Susanne and crew, "The Final
Copacabana" invite photoshoot, 1993.
Photo by Jesse Frohman.

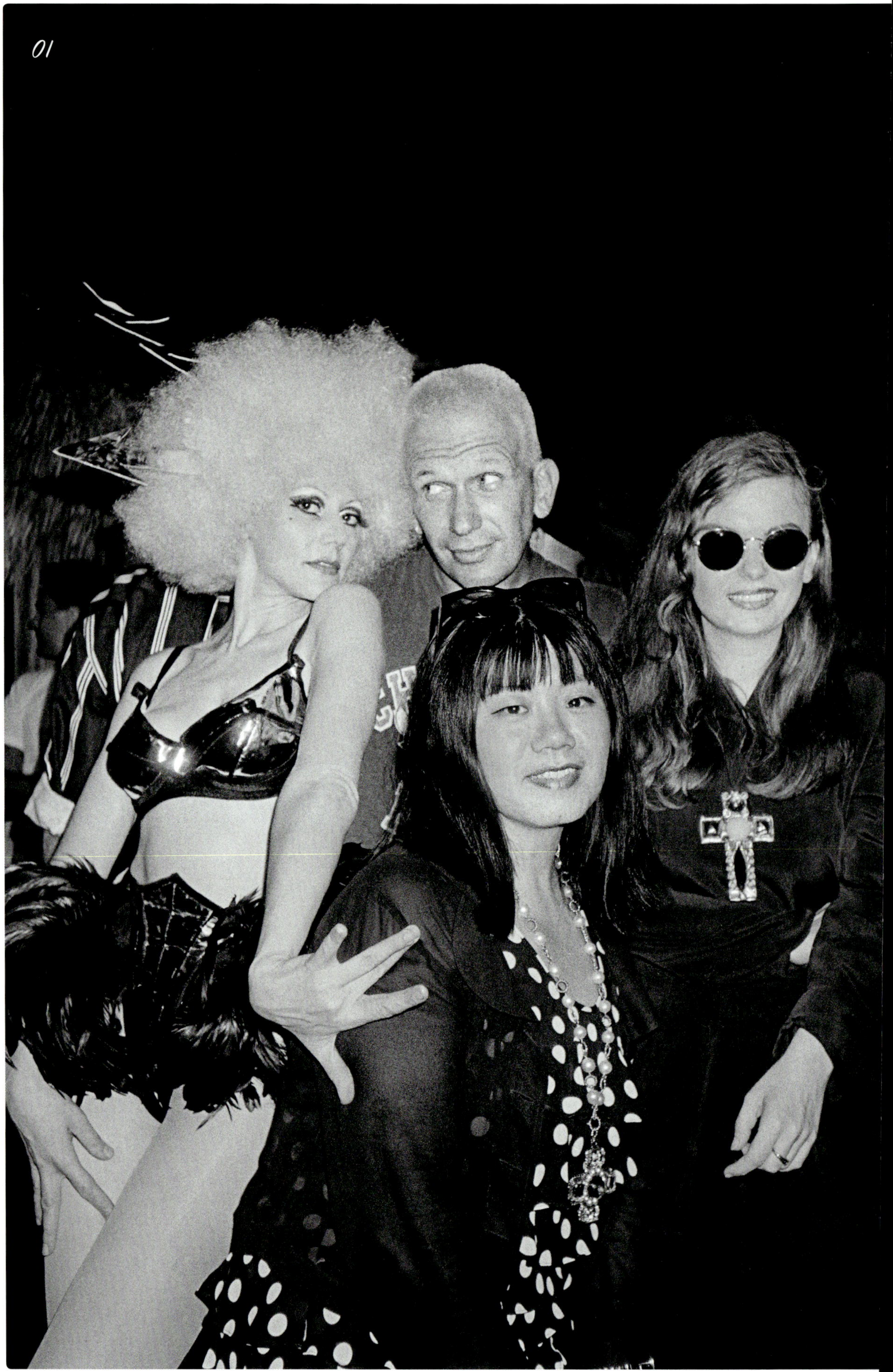

1 Susanne, Jean Paul Gaultier, Martine Sitbon, and Anna Sui at Amazon, 1991. Photo by Roxanne Lowit.

2 John Bartlett, Suzanne, and Richie Rich at Sweetie at Barney's, 2000. © Patrick McMullan.

3 Kabuki Starshine in pose at BMG post-Grammy celebration. The event was designed by Susanne, and took place at Barney's New York, 1998. Photo © Tina Paul, 1998. All Rights Reserved.

4 Susanne with Ty Bassett, late in the 1980s. Photo by Josef Astor.

5 Susanne with TY Basset at Copacabana, c. 1988. © Patrick McMullan.

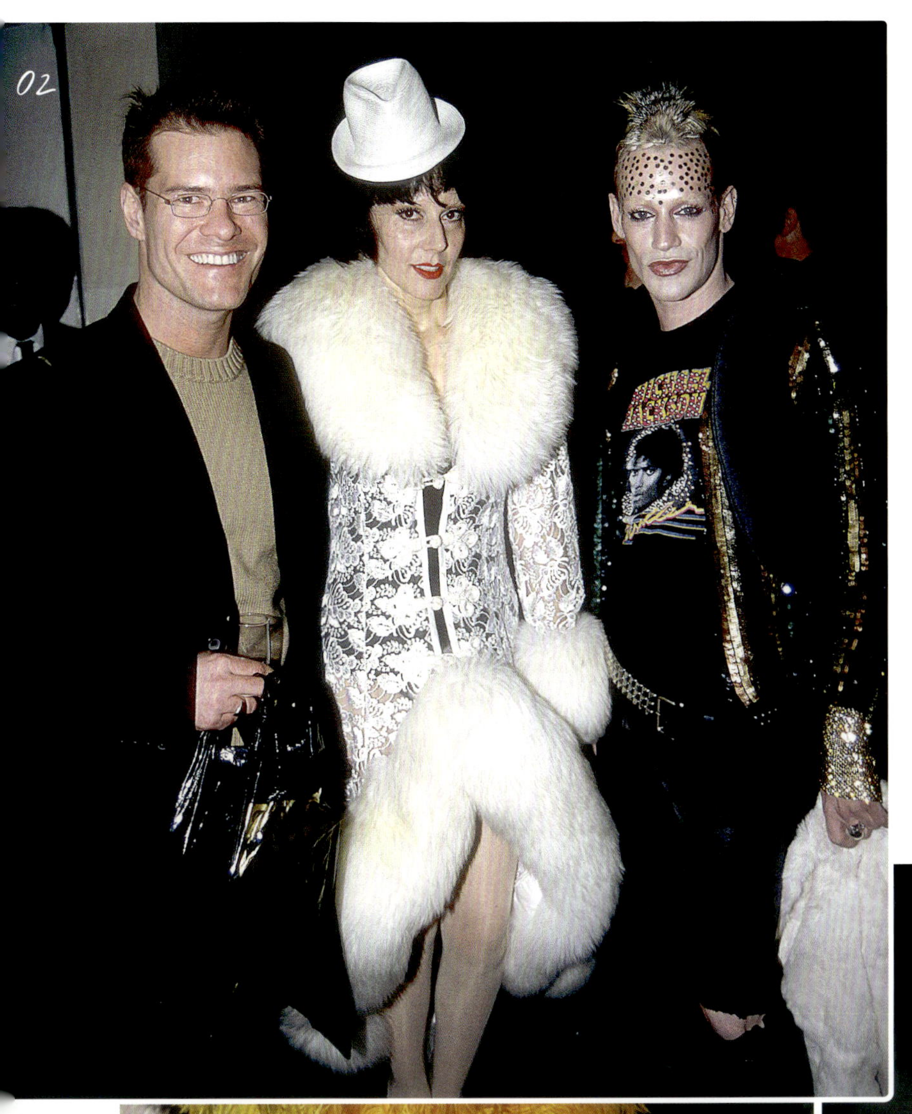

02

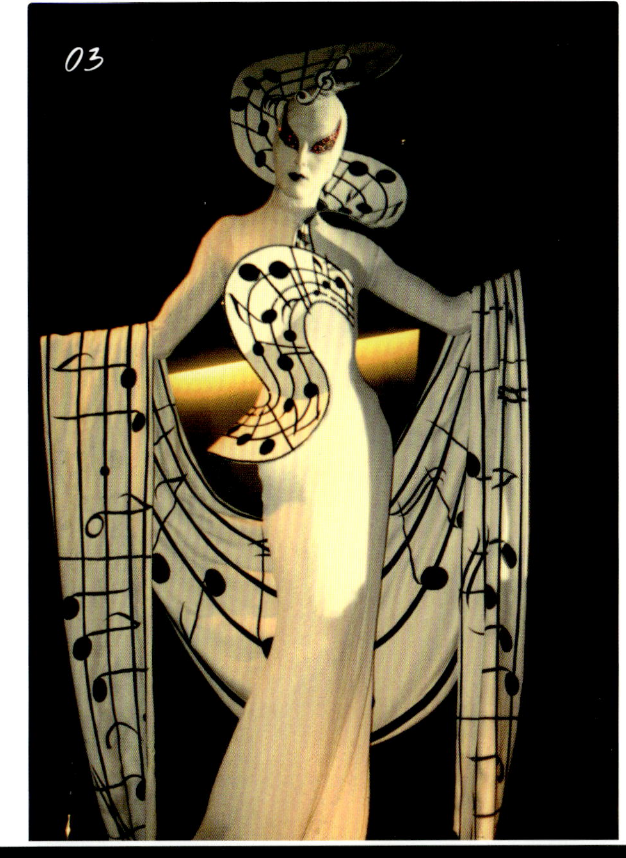

03

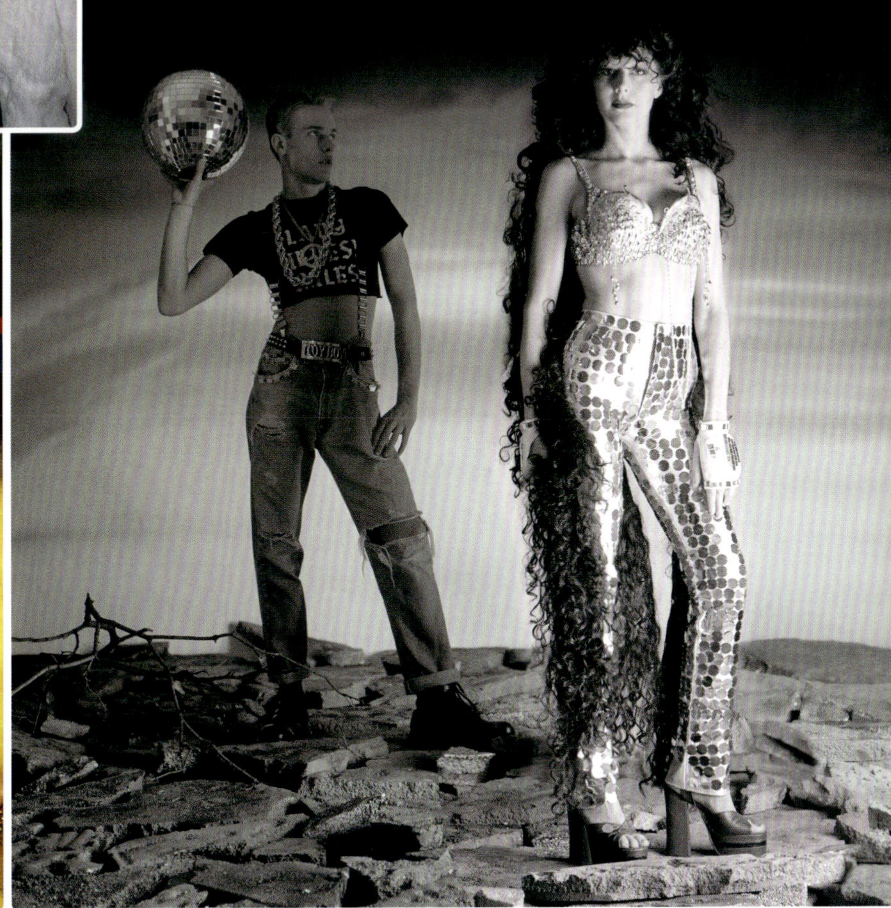

04

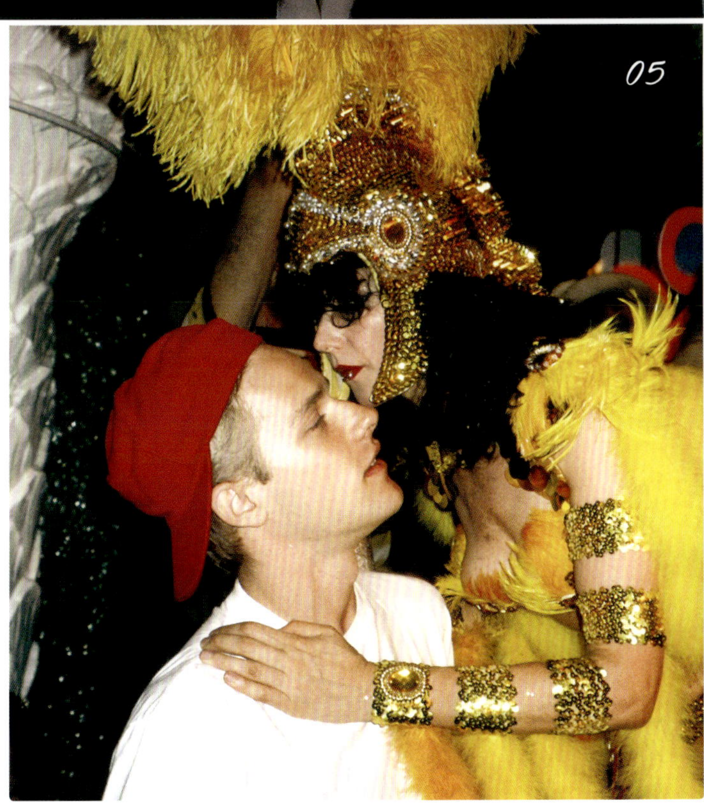

05

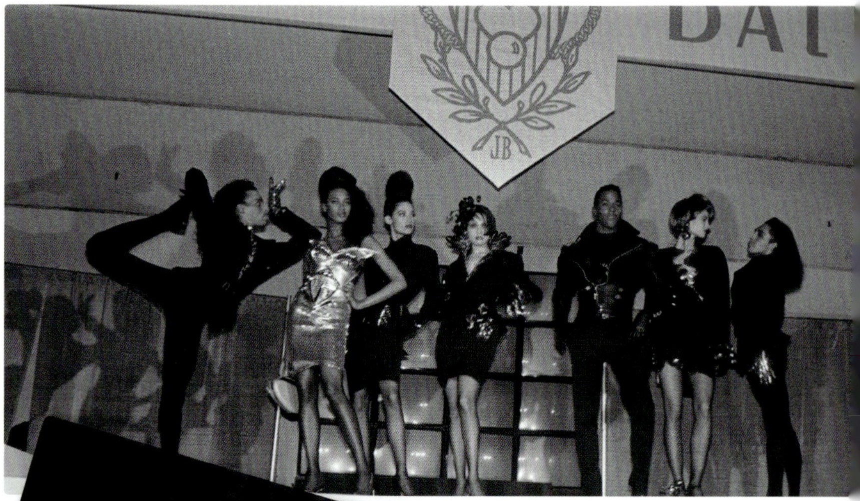

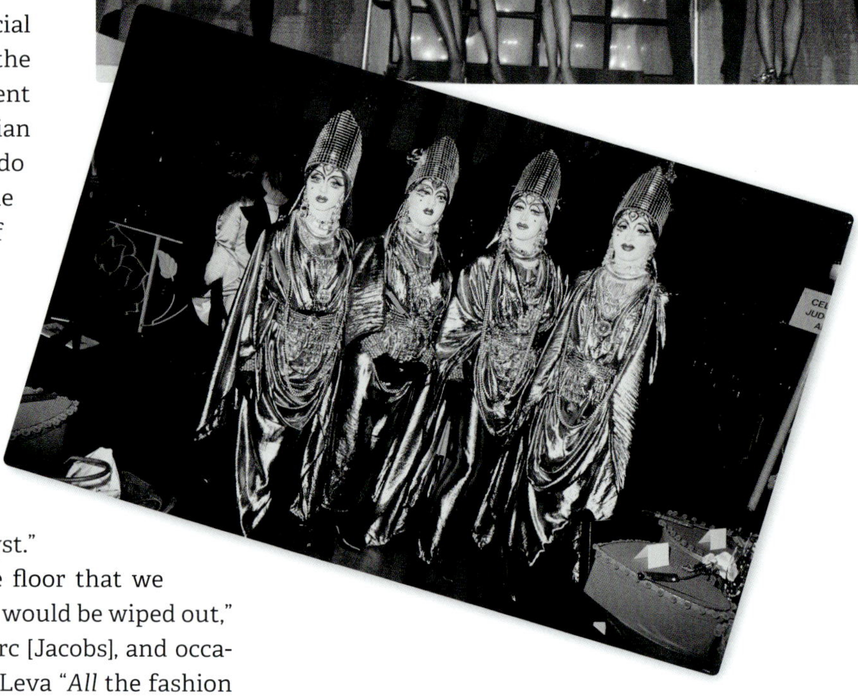

only once a month and uptown made it more of a special event. Every month there was a performance. We had the Village People at the opening and other disco relics. Different elements came together: uptown, downtown, Brazilian samba school carnival dancers, body builders, Renaldo Herrera and Michael Musto, trannies, sexy girls, the members of the Trockadero Ballet. We had a 'Copa Girl of the Month' party with audience participation, and we had Look Alikes, where four to six people would come in the same insane look."[45]

"Susanne has had an enormous impact in terms of propagating creativity," says Simon Doonan[46]. "It was fashion people who went to the Copacabana, and Susanne injected the world of fashion with life-enhancing effervescence. She's a Malcolm Gladwell-type connector, not a king-maker but an incredible catalyst."

"There were so many fashion designers on the dance floor that we used to say if a bomb went off, the entire design industry would be wiped out," says Scott Ewalt.[47] "Gaultier came there, and Mugler, Marc [Jacobs], and occasionally Calvin [Klein], and John Galliano," says Michael Leva "*All* the fashion kids in New York, and artists like Debbie Harry and Laurie Anderson, and older ladies in evening gowns. It was before all the evil Club Kids who were so druggy and nasty. Susanne has helped a lot of young designers with her love of the new and the artistic. And Copa wasn't segregated the way clubs can be. Susanne brought everyone together."[48]

"It was Fashion and Art, Uptown and Downtown," says Robert Forrest.[49] "And multi-racial," adds Ewalt. "A lot of other clubs just wanted the New York rich look. But Susanne's doormen welcomed Latin and Black guests, any age, any race. Just have a fantastic look."[50] In her 1991 essay on Bartsch for the *New Yorker*, Holly Brubach interviewed many Copacabana fans, including Marc Jacobs, who never missed a night. Other clubs were filled with "people with fake titles," said Jacobs. "If Susanne is running around with some drag queen with a fake title, it's *deliberately* fake, not trying to be something that it's not."[51]

"At first I was a little intimidated to go to Susanne's parties," recalls the make-up artist Kabuki. "They were like a Fellini movie. But Michael Musto said 'Go to Susanne's party and we'll photograph you for the *Village Voice*.' I saw her enveloped in a cloud of feathers. It was a really Marlene Dietrich moment. Then one night I did a Marie Antoinette meets *Alice in Wonderland* look, and Susanne came up to me and said, 'We've got to hire you.' Just getting welcomed by Susanne, I felt like I'd already made it. With Susanne, there was an understanding of gender and fashion and art. She chose people with a genuine artistic gift.

Top: Voguing legend Willi Ninja striking a pose on stage at the *Love Ball*, Roseland Ballroom, 1989. Photo © Tina Paul, 1989. All Rights Reserved.

Above: The Copacabana girls, Queenius Quadruplets, at the first *Love Ball*, 1989. Courtesy of Susanne Bartsch.

Facing: Susanne with the *Love Ball* trophy, 1989. Costume by Mr. Pearl. Photo by Roxanne Lowit.

The fashion people all went to her parties and were inspired
by them. Working with Susanne gave you credibility and led to
my doing runway work with Thierry Mugler."[52]

Richie Rich, who later became a co-designer of the fashion
house Heatherette along with Traver Rains, was a Club Kid
when Bartsch asked him to be her assistant. "She said, 'You're
going to learn so much' – and, boy, did I! She is very organized.
She taught me how to do everything from the invitation to the
guest list, clipboards, head counts, making sure hotels are
booked, every little detail. Her motto was 'Everybody is a star'
and she always said, 'Without energy, there is no party.'"[53]
"Susanne has inspired so many people to fly the fashion freak
flag," says the designer John Bartlett. "Many of my favorite
personal fashion moments revolve around her Copacabana
first Thursdays of the month."[54]

In 1988, Bartsch married Ty Bassett. She recalls, "I told Gerlinde 'I need a boyfriend' and she said, 'I know a really cute boy.'
We were together for five years. He customized a few corsets
for me and designed invitations, but mostly he ran the back of
the house at Copa."

The Love Ball, Love Ball 2, and the Balade de l'Amour

Tragically, life in 1980s New York was not just a party. "All our
friends started dying very quickly and horribly," says Simon
Doonan.[55] "AIDS was like the end of the world, a Holocaust," recalls Stephen Jones.
"By 1988, AIDS had taken half my rolodex," a tearful Bartsch told Doonan: "Gary, Julio.
Peter and Mark [. . .] I survived this period by becoming a fundraiser."[56] Her idea was
to take the energy of her Copa nights and the inspiration of the Harlem house balls,
to organize costume competitions with celebrity judges and raise money for DIFFA
(Design Industry Foundation Fighting AIDS).

In 1989 Bartsch organized the Love Ball, one of the first and most important AIDS
benefits. "The Love Ball was Susanne's idea," says the advertising executive Marc
Balet. "She approached me and Simon Doonan and others and we began to organize
it."[57] Doonan recalls, "Susanne and I had felt helpless and then she got galvanized –
and she reinvented the fundraiser. She said, 'We get everything free, everything
donated.' That way she got *all* of the money for DIFFA. The committee met every
Monday night – and *worked*. Susanne was the taskmaster and ringleader."[58] Bartsch
enlisted corporations from Armani to Sara Lee to support the event, which was held
at the Roseland Ballroom in New York City.

'Voguing,' a highly stylized form of modern house dance, originating from ballroom, was still an obscure phenomenon when Bartsch featured Harlem voguers at

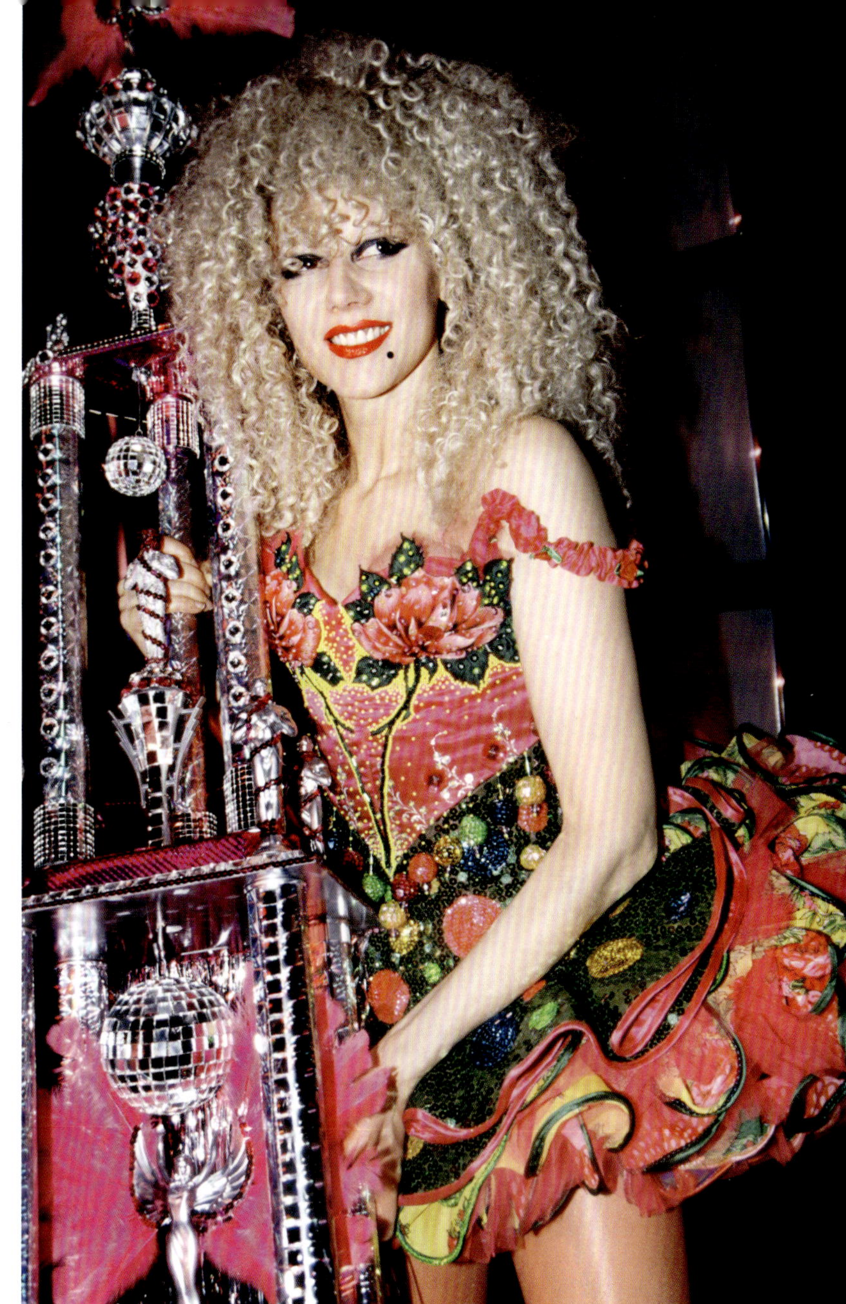

the Love Ball. "Madonna's eyes were on sticks – she was galvanized," recalls Doonan.[59] "Cut to a year and a half later, and she recruited voguers from the House of Extravaganza to perform with her." The voguers were also extremely interested in the fashion scene. "You can't imagine how excited the Harlem house stars were to be competing on the same stage as the House of Mugler," says Scott Ewalt. "When Iman walked out, they went crazy."[60]

"I got very involved with the Love Ball and that's when I started working with Thierry Mugler," recalls the hairstylist Danilo. "I'd known Susanne for years: I was a hairdresser in SoHo and she had her shop a block away. When we did the Love Ball, Thierry needed hair and Susanne said 'I'll give you my hairdresser' and he liked what I did. It was so crowded that I had to do all the models' hair in the men's room. I thought 'If I can do hair in the toilet, I can do it anywhere.' I ended up working ten years at Mugler."[61]

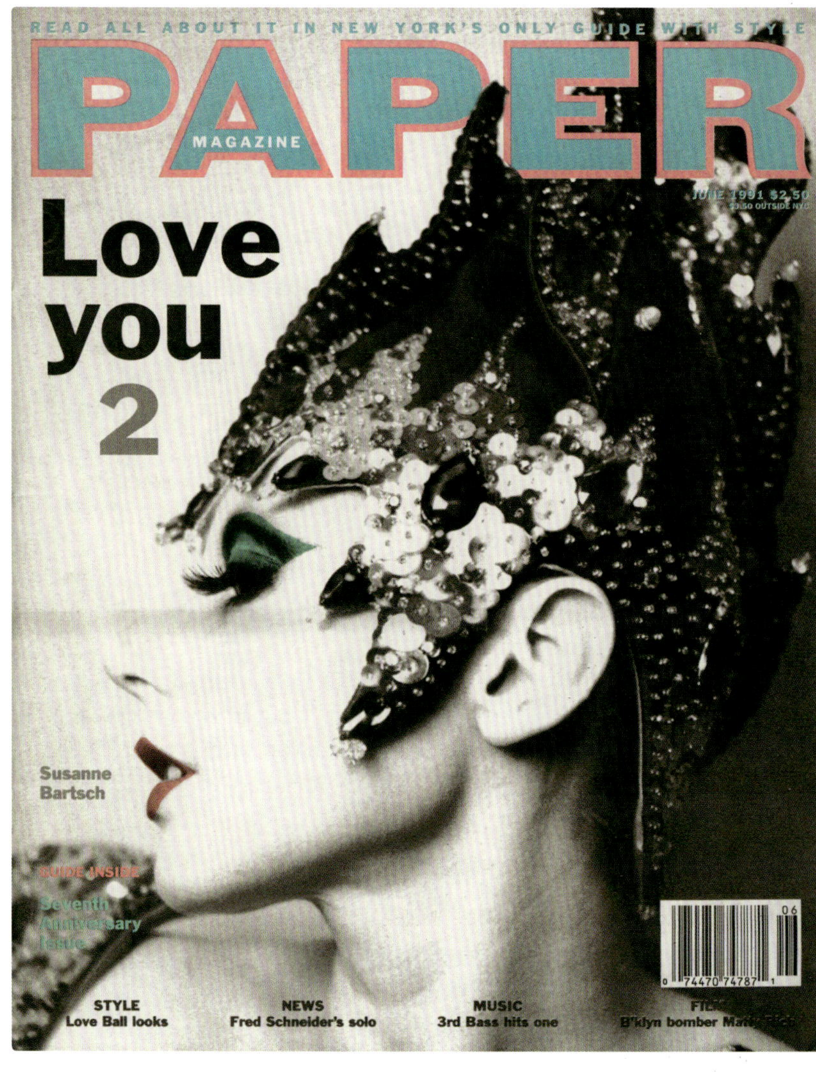

The Roseland Ballroom inspired Bartsch's costume for the event, which was created for her by Mr. Pearl, the South African born corsetiere and tight-lacer. Mr. Pearl created many of Bartsch's looks in the 1980s and in the early years of the 1990s. "I really liked the restrictive feeling of corsets," Bartsch recalls, hugging herself. "It's bondage, but comfortable bondage. And corsets are like high heels – they just do the trick." A letter from Mr. Pearl, dated November 27, 1989, details his ideas for a new outfit for Bartsch: a bodysuit overlaid with metallic gold kid leather and worked with jewels, along with the costs: 1,500 British pounds, a substantial figure at that time. By the final years of the 1990s, Mr. Pearl was working for many of the top fashion designers in Paris, including Lagerfeld at Chanel, Galliano at Dior, Christian Lacroix, and Mugler. By 2000, he was world-famous, at least in fashion circles, for his extraordinary couture corsets.

The Love Ball was the apotheosis of New York events," says Doonan. "Malcolm Forbes and Judy Peabody were there, but also every drag queen on earth." "In an age of AIDS, Susanne created parties that brought everyone together to dress up and have fun," says Joey Arias. "Everyone came: Wall Street, drag queens, Upper East Side ladies."[62] Kim Hastreiter, the publisher of *Paper* magazine, recalls inviting designers such as Geoffrey Beene, Andre Walker, Angel Estrada, and Isabel Toledo to make dresses out of copies of *Paper*.[63] Guests included the dancer and choreographer Karole Armitage, David Byrne of the new wave band Talking heads, the artist Keith Haring, the drag queen and DJ Lady Miss Bunny,

Above: "Under the direction of Susanne Bartsch, Love Ball 2 goes over the top." *Paper*, June, 1991. Photo by Cavid Hershkovits, courtesy of *Paper* magazine.

1 House of Armani on stage at Love Ball 2 with glamorous onlookers, Roseland Ballroom, 1991. Photo © Tina Paul, 1991. All Rights Reserved.

2 Simon Doonan and Lypsinka at Love Ball 2, 1991. Photo courtesy of Simon Doonan.

3 Susanne on stage at the first Love Ball, Roseland Ballroom, 1989. Photo © Patrick McMullan.

4 Susanne with Donna Karan, Mathu and Zaldy at Love Ball 2 in 1991. Susanne's costume by Mr. Pearl. Photo by Roxanne Lowit.

5 Brooke Shields at Love Ball 2, 1991. Photo courtesy of Simon Doonan.

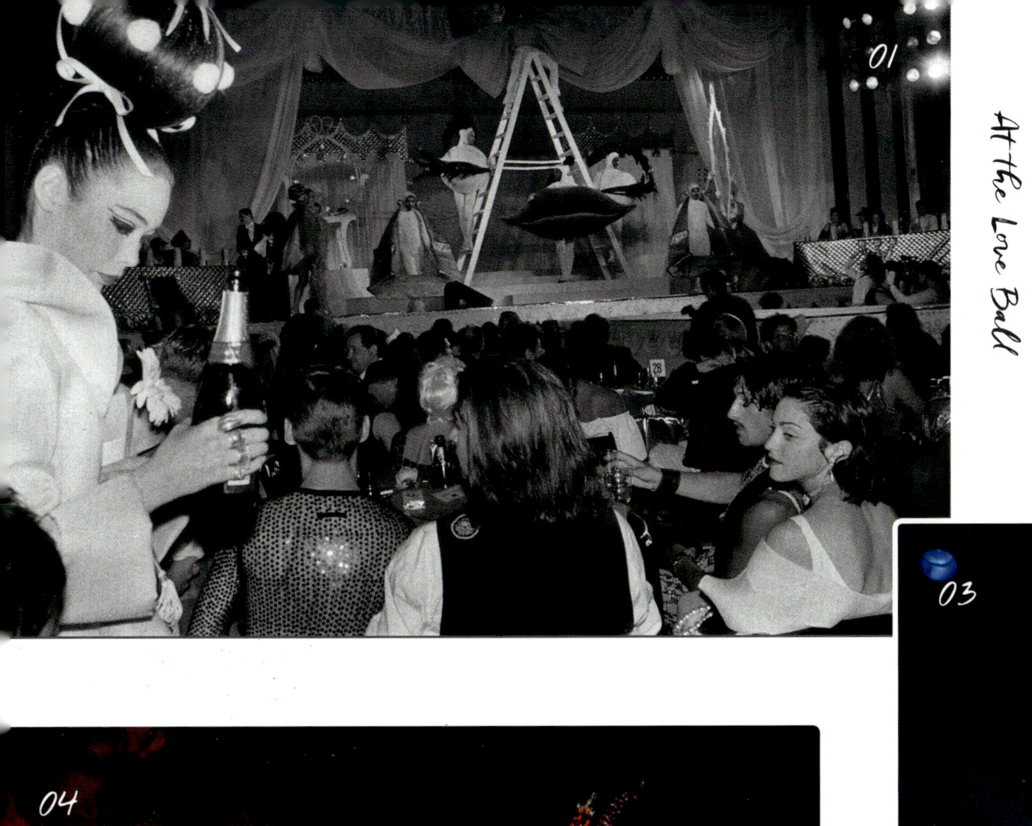

At the Love Ball

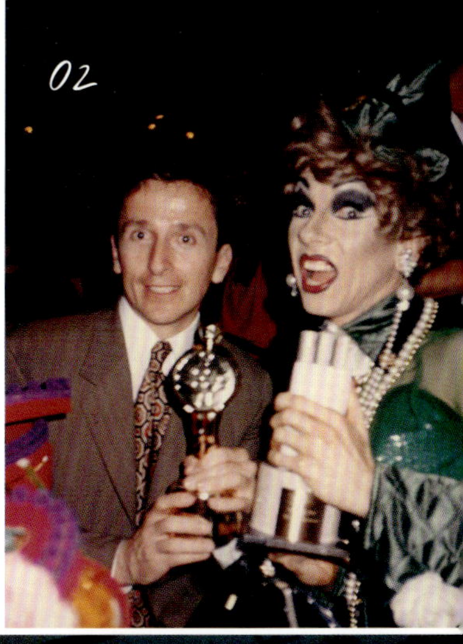

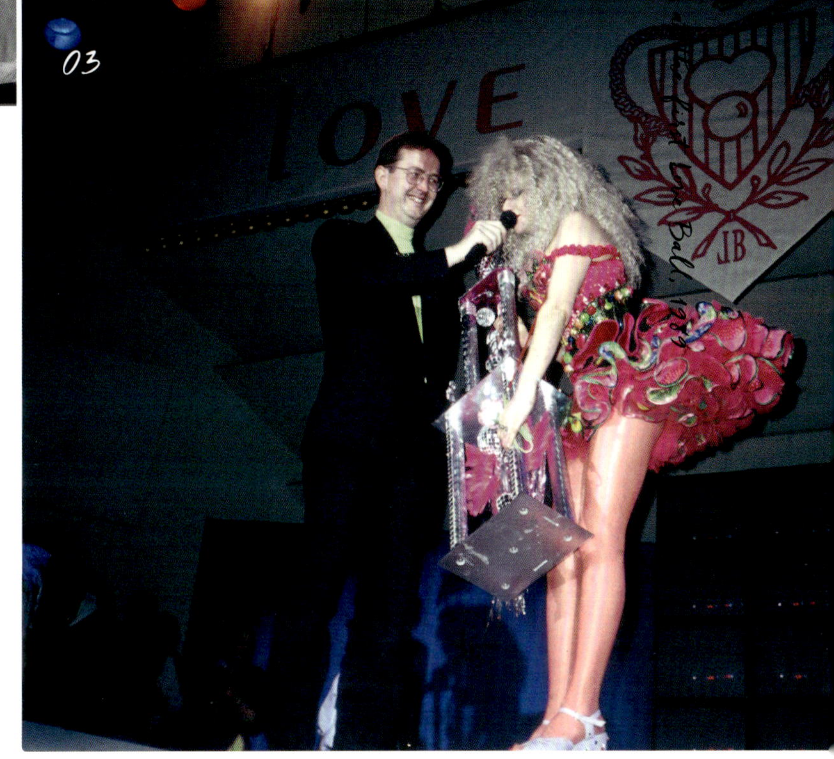

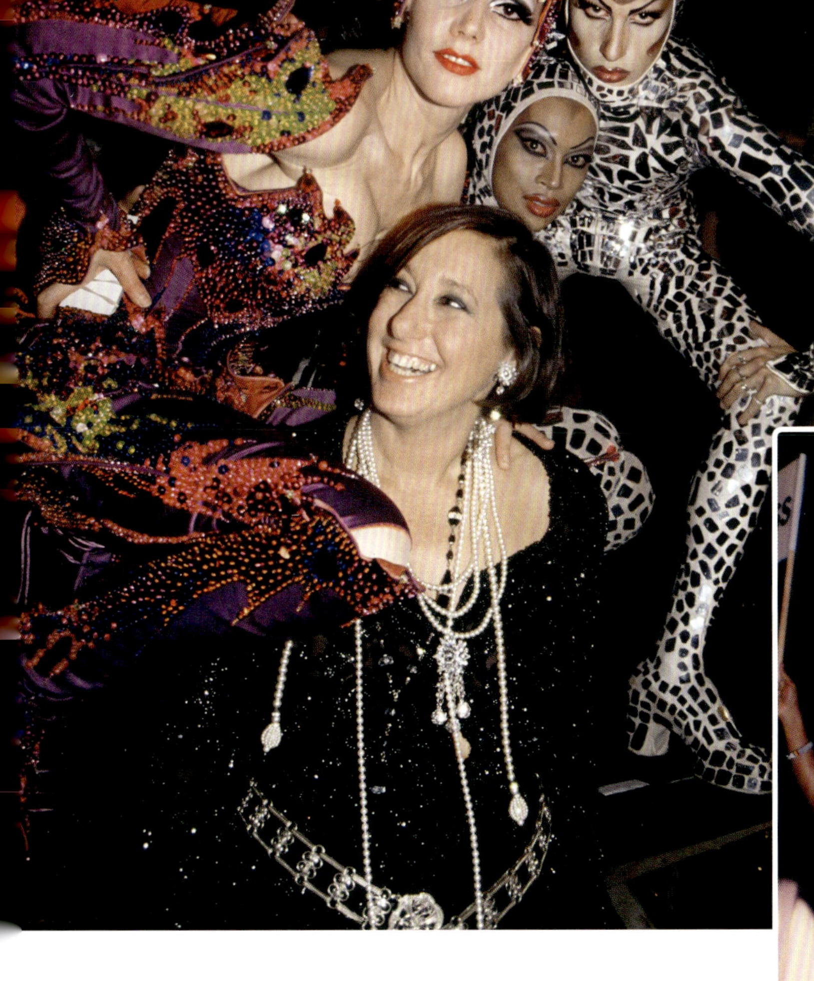

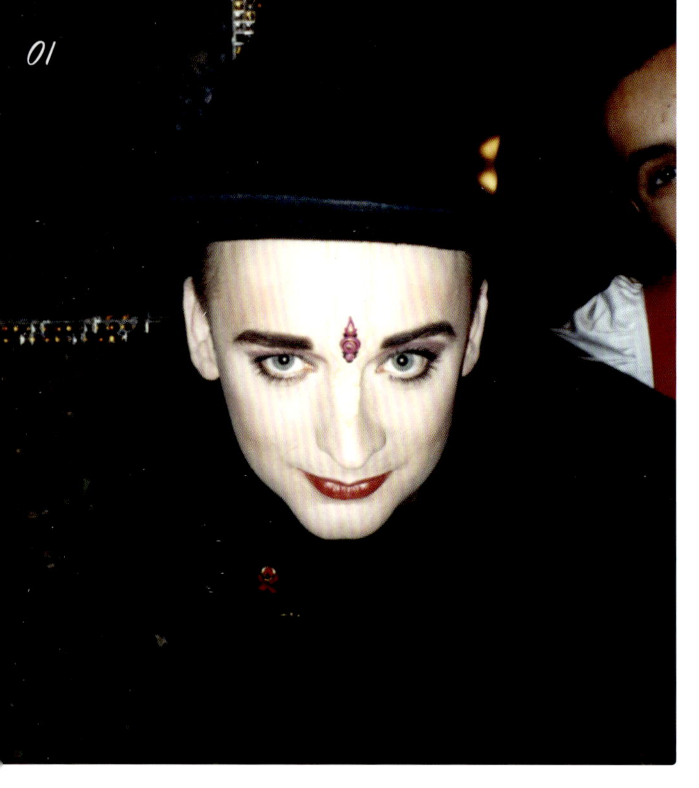

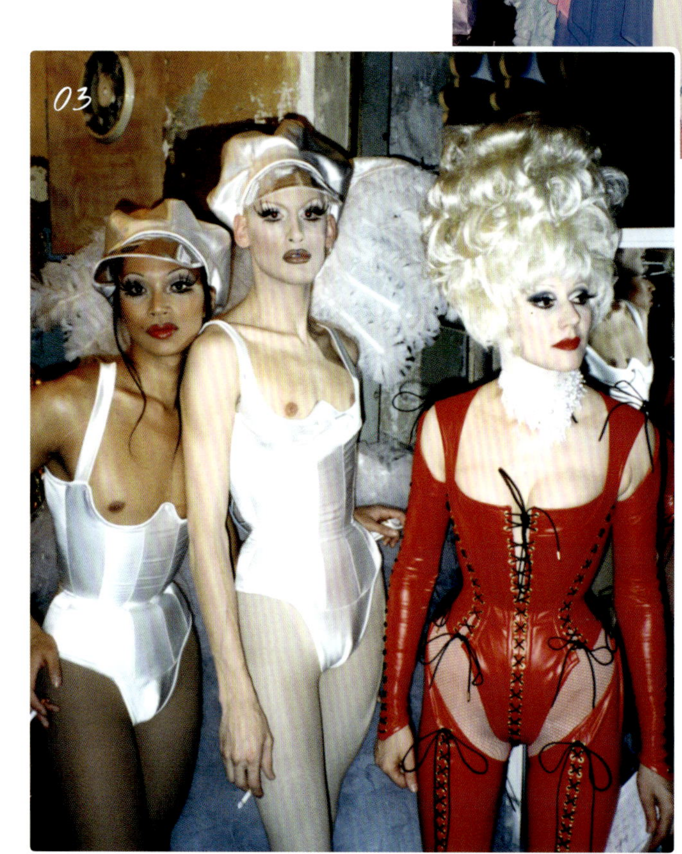

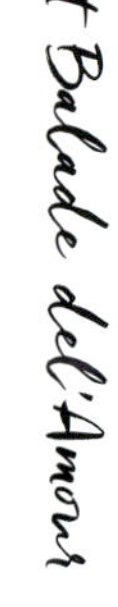
At Balade dell'Amore

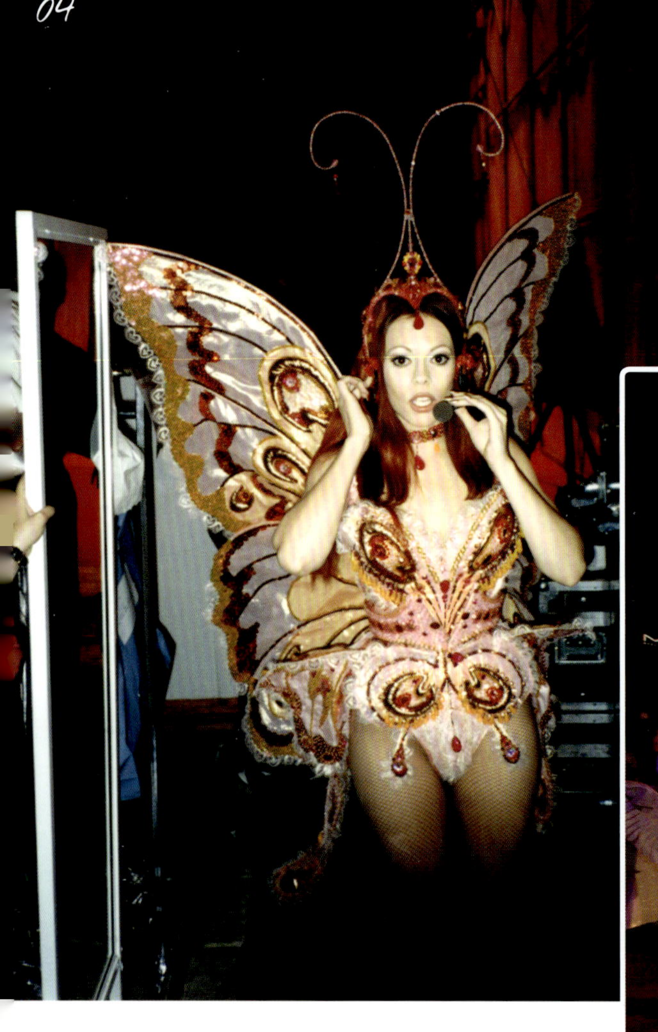

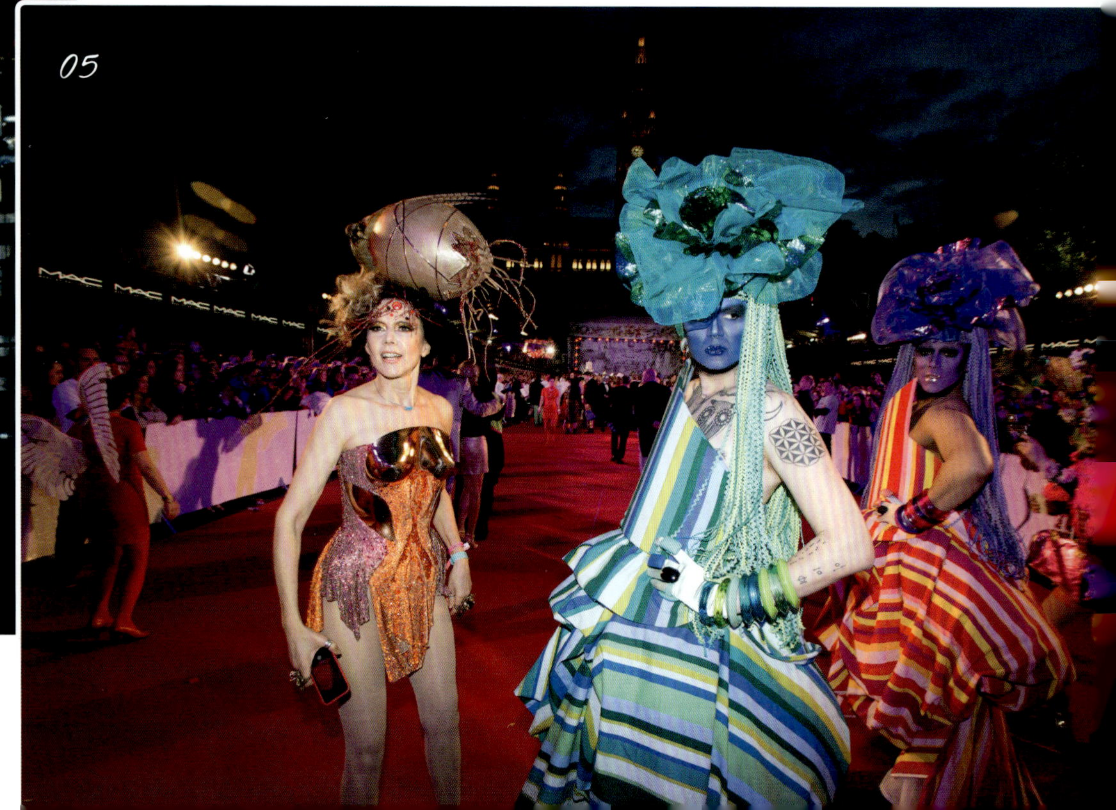

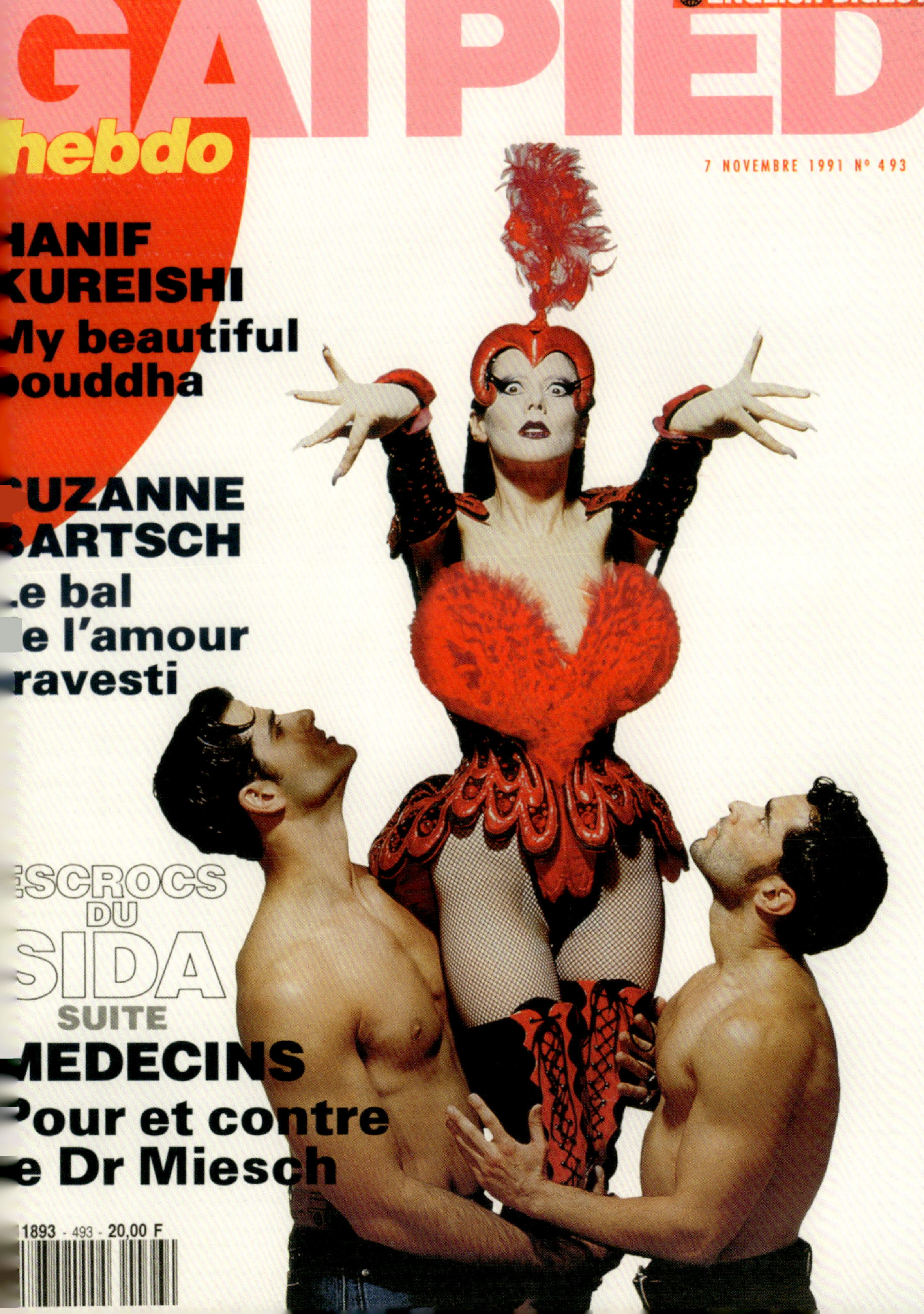

06

1 Boy George at Balade de l'Amour, Paris, 1992. Photography by Tim Palen.

2 Lady Miss Bunny at Love Ball 2, 1991. Photo courtesy of Simon Doonan.

3 Zaldy Goco, Mathu Andersen, and Susanne, at Balade de l'Amour, October 1992. Photography by Tim Palen.

4 Lady Kier from Deee-Lite during Balade de l'Amour, 1992. Photography by Tim Palen.

5 Susanne with Onehalf Nelson and Erickatoure Avianceat the Life Ball Red Carpet, Vienna, 2014. Susanne's corset by The Blonds. Headpiece by Garo Sparo. Photo by Rebecca Smeyne.

6 The Love Ball goes to Paris as Balade de l'Amour. *Gai Pied*, November 1991. Photo courtesy of Gayvox.fr, in charge of archives and assets of the Gaipied Group.

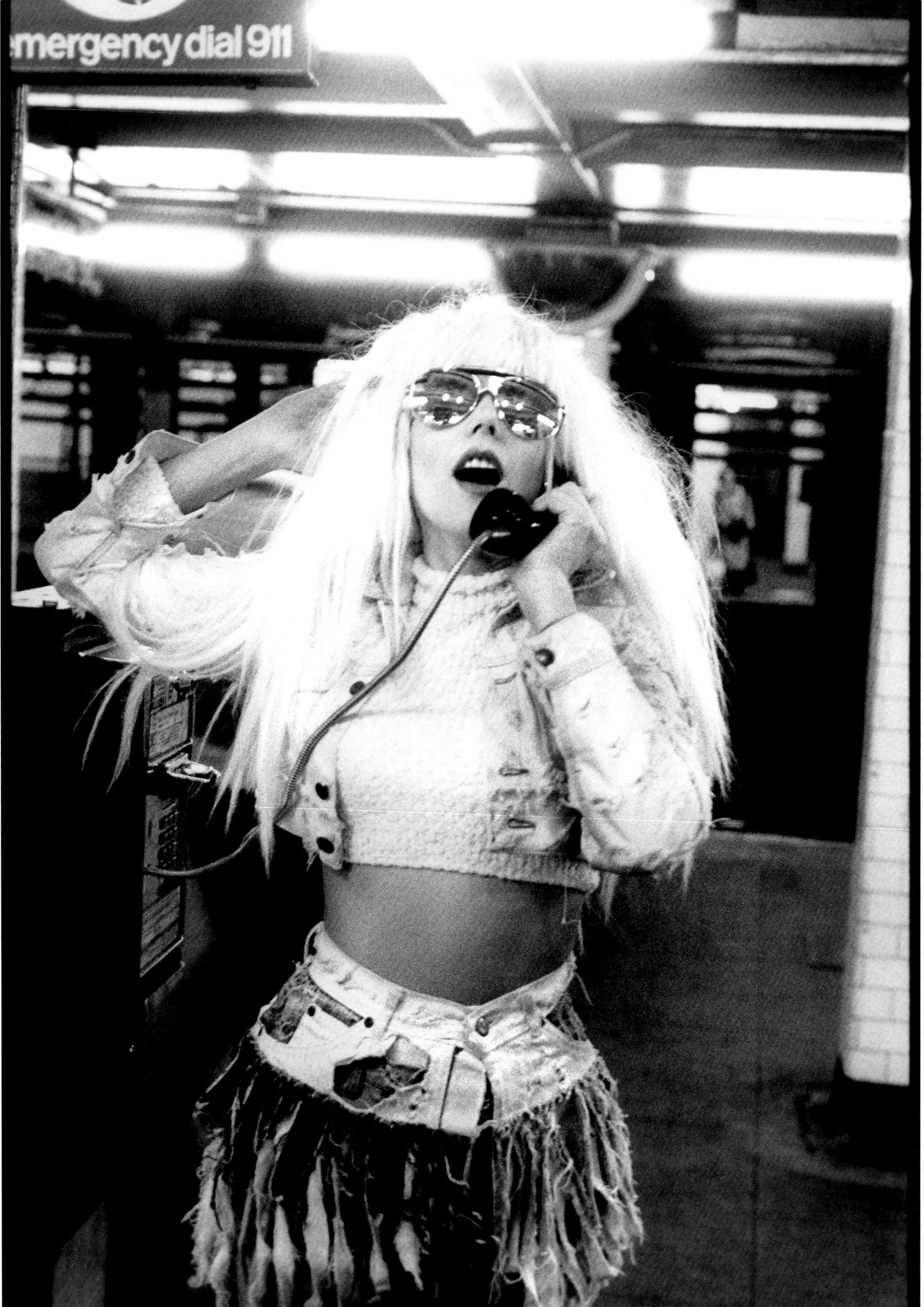

emergency dial 911

Facing: Susanne on the phone
in the subway, New York City,
1989. © David LaChapelle.

Below: Susanne and friends in
Coney Island, New York, 1989.
© David LaChapelle.

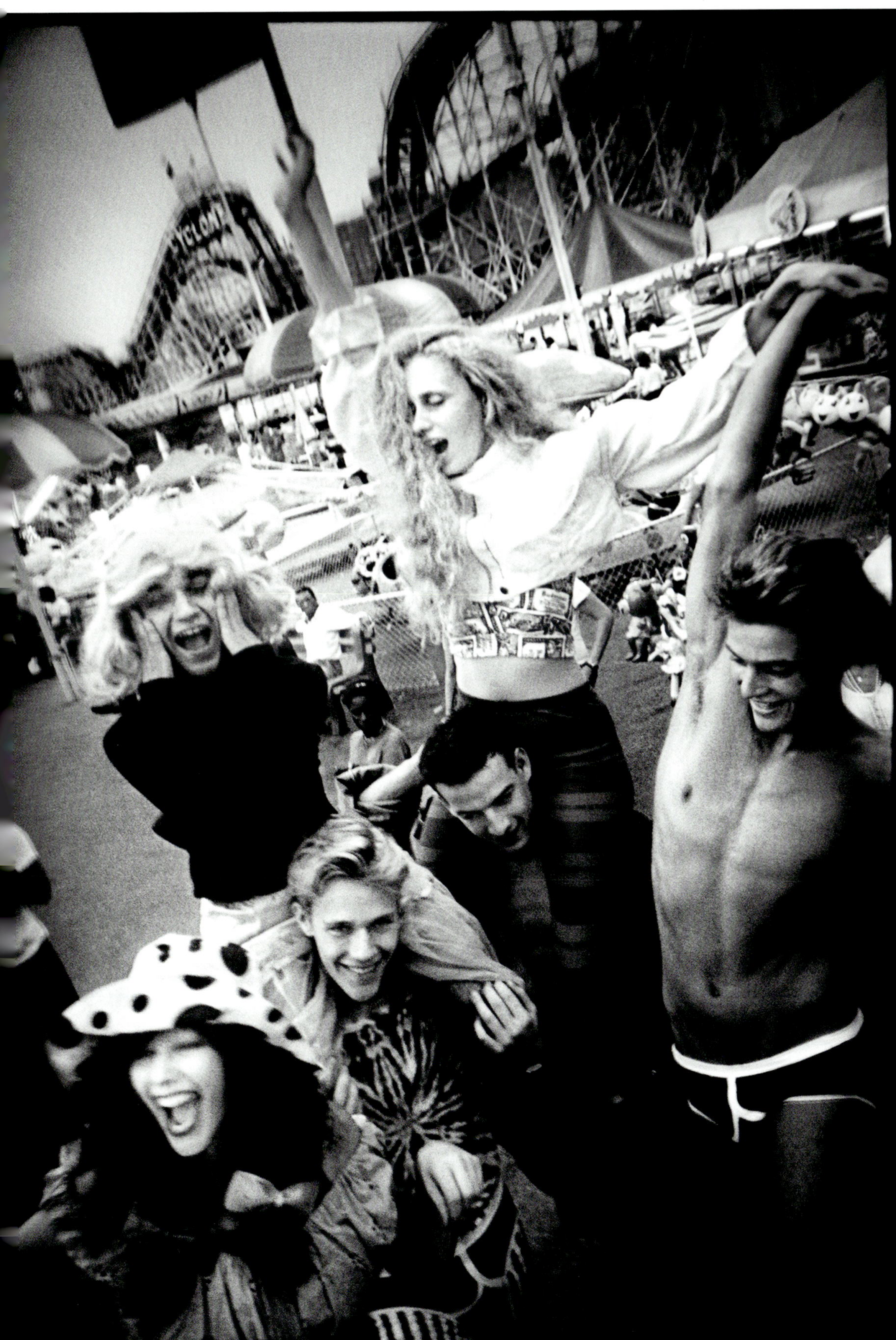

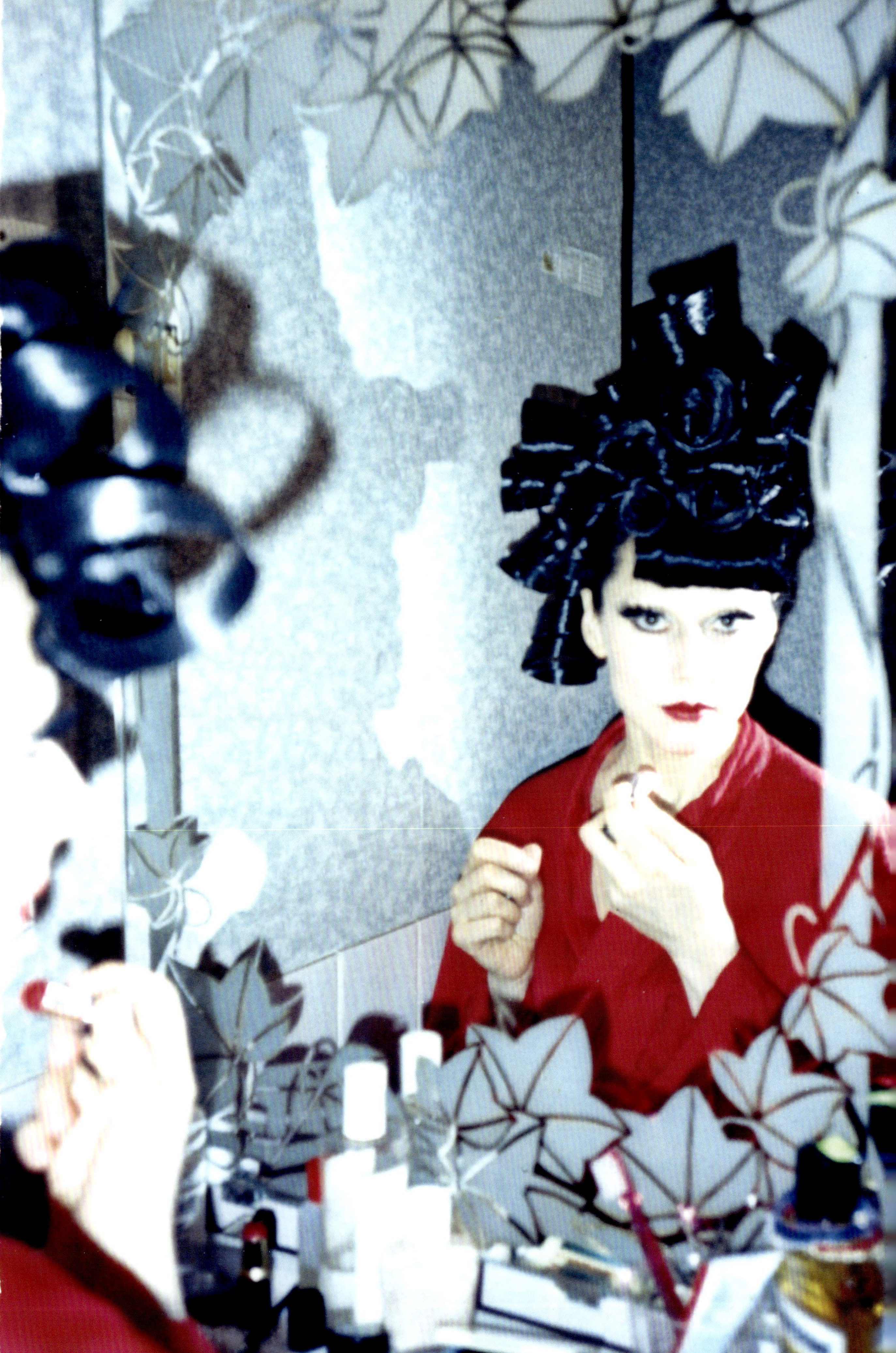

at Balade del'Amour, 1992

the singer Lady Miss Kier, the drag performer Lypsinka (John Epperson), Steve
Rubell, the co-owner of the famous nightclub Studio 54, Andre Leon Tally from
Vogue, and the actress and dancer Gwen Verdon.

"Then Susanne did Love Ball 2: The Crowning Glory," recalls Doonan. "It was
all about queens and crowns. Susanne threw herself body and soul into these
events. I've never forgotten her passion and commitment."[64] Once more, the
event took place at the Roseland Ballroom, and there were competing teams
and trophies designed by well-known artists. Leigh Bowery was one of the
Masters of Ceremonies. The photographer David LaChapelle worked with the
House of Armani. Doonan recalls: "The House of Barneys had Lypsinka wearing
a huge red dress, together with four young women from Dance Theater of
Harlem dressed as young men, because in those days Barneys did mostly mens-
wear."[65] At *Paper*, "we had to up our game," recalls Hastreiter, "so we came up
with the idea of doing famous women in history: Joey Arias was Wonder Woman
and Brooke Shields dressed as a (male) chauffeur."[66] Once again Mr. Pearl
designed Bartsch's look. The second Love Ball raised even more money for
DIFFA than the first.

Bartsch went on to organize other AIDS benefits, of which the most famous
was the Balade de l'Amour at the cabaret venue the Folies Bergère. "After doing
the Love Ball, Susanne decided to do the same thing in Paris," says Diane Pernet,
a fashion blogger and critic. The Balade de l'Amour turned out to be "an amazing
event," but it was "so difficult" to organize a benefit in France – much more difficult than in the United States. "People didn't want to be associated with AIDS,"
says Pernet. A core group of about a dozen people worked really hard for six
months, and as the event got closer, more and more people became involved. It
was crucially important that Bartsch had excellent connections in the Paris
fashion world, particularly with designers such as Jean Paul Gaultier, Thierry
Mugler, and Azzedine Alaïa. On the night of the event, hundreds of people vol-
unteered to work, for free. Boy George sang, RuPaul was the Master of Ceremonies, Jonathan Newhouse of Condé Nast published the catalogue, Nick Knight
did the cover photograph. "Pedro Almodovar, Roman Polanski, Mario Testino –
they all dressed up and performed. *Everyone* in fashion was involved."[67]

Ultimately, Bartsch raised a total of $2.5 million for AIDS advocacy from the
Love Balls and related benefits. She also inspired other events, like the annual
Life Ball in Vienna, which continues to this day. "There are thousands of people
at the Life Ball, and a labyrinth of rooms at the Vienna City Hall," says Theodora
Sopko, who worked as Bartsch's assistant from 2002 to 2005. "Susanne flies in
and hosts one of the rooms. She and her people dress up and perform. I remember one year she wanted an egg on her head, and it took three hours to put the
headpiece together. We had to sew the egg on top of her wig. Then Susanne is
on stage, spreading love."[68]

Susanne backstage before Balade
de l'Amour, 1992. Hair by Mathu.
Photography by Tim Palen.

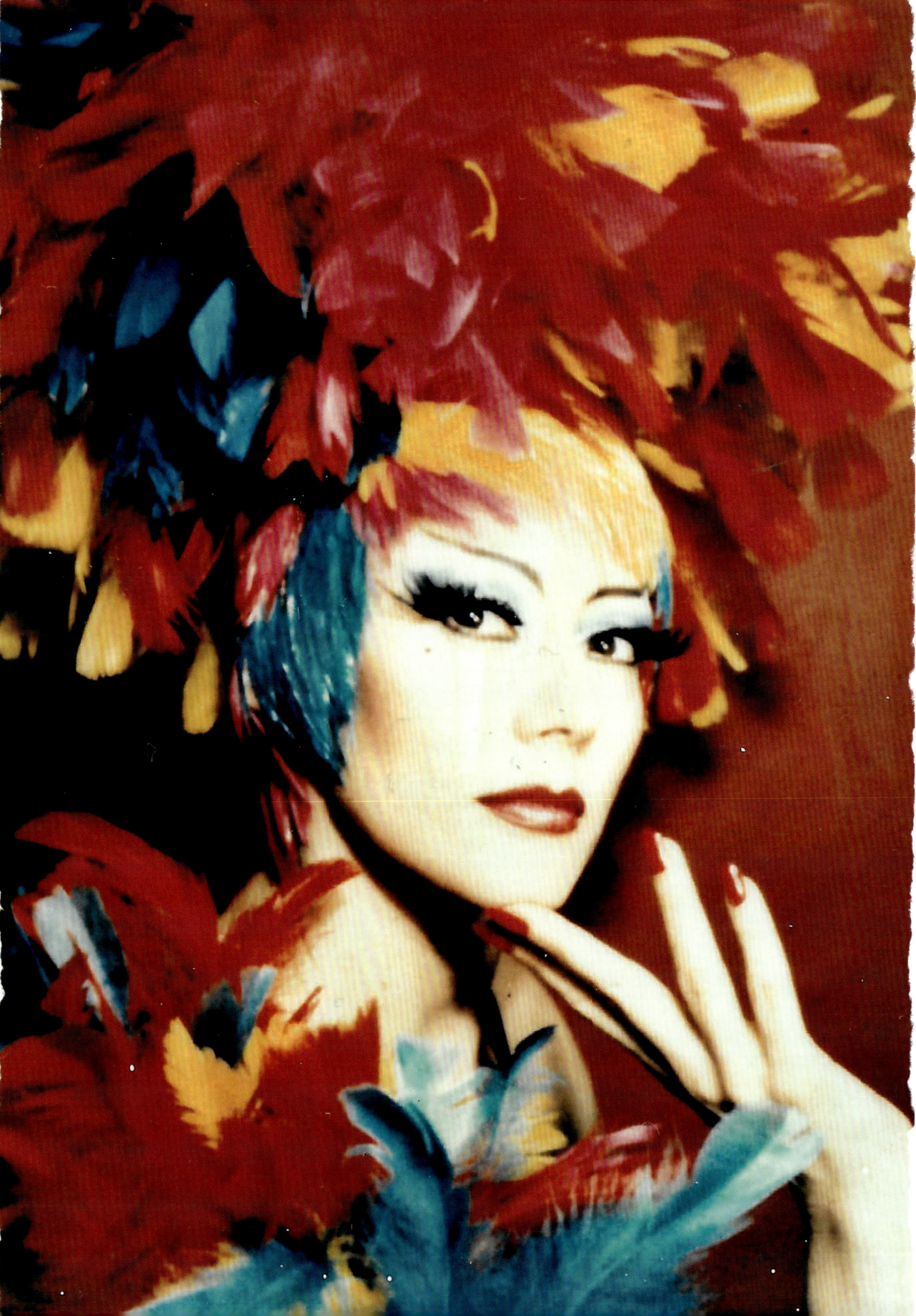

"Feathers are us." Look by Mathu
and Zaldy, 1990s.
Photo by Mathu Andersen.

The Life of the Party

Over the years, Bartsch has also been invited to organize parties and events in Paris, Milan, New York (often in connection with Fashion Week), South Beach (Miami), Los Angeles, and Tokyo. She has created parties for Armani, Adidas, Diesel, Dolce & Gabbana, Ian Schrager Hotels, the Council of Fashion Designers of America, and many others. She is a very desirable guest at fashion parties, because of her unique style. "As a photographer, I like people who make an effort to look cool," says Patrick McMullan. "I could do a whole book on Susanne's parties."[69]

"People who go to her parties *love* them," says David Barton, a fitness impresario and Bartsch's husband from 1995 to 2010. "She creates a scene. When I met her and we started hanging out, there were trannies, roller skaters, Club Kids, and she would be invited to throw a party, say, for Armani in Milan for Fashion Week, and somehow, all these people would be crowded onto a plane. I had not lived until I traveled with this group. We did an AIDS benefit, the Hoppening, at the Playboy Mansion in Los Angeles. We thought the Playboy Mansion would be the epicenter of the sexual revolution, but they were freaked out by the New York downtown scenesters and trannies."

"Her Halloween parties were always so fun," continues Barton. "She just *owns* Halloween. We'd hold the party after the parade, back before it was so commercial. Everyone was dressed up and dancing. It was like a Fellini movie! I was just a helper. It was work. Once, in the beginning, I was at a party, greeting people, and someone came and said 'Susanne needs you' so I went backstage – 'You need me?' – 'Yes! Get a garbage bag and clean up all the cups people have left around.' I was responsible for picking up all the garbage."

According to Barton, Bartsch's Miami New Year's Eve parties were also incredible: "Someone recently told me that one of them was the best party in his entire life."[70] "The Mugler collective would always do New Year's Eve in Miami," says Danilo. "One year the theme was Fashion Icons. Susanne and I went as Mathu and Zaldy."[71] Back in the Copa years, Bartsch had sometimes hired Mathu Anderson and Zaldy to dress as Look Alikes – and some of their looks became iconic.

Mauricio Padilha, the co-owner of MAO Public Relations, has been going to Bartsch's events since the Copa years. "I remember an event at the Planetarium to launch New York Fashion Week. It was chic and nice, but then the music got crazy and the globe opened up and out came these creatures and suddenly, Susanne comes out like the Queen Mother Alien that just came out of the spaceship. And suddenly it was an amazing party."[72]

Padilha insists that Bartsch remains the life of the party. "Not long ago, I was at Carine Roitfeld's party in Paris. Karl Lagerfeld was there." "Every designer from Alaïa to Valentino was there," says Roger Padilha, Mauricio's brother and the other co-owner of MAO PR. "Everyone was just standing around drinking

Page 66 clockwise from top left:
Susanne with Thierry Mugler at Indochine, 1989. Ensemble by Jo Dean. Photo by Roxanne Lowit.

Cartoon from the *New Yorker*, March 29, 1993. Drawing by Lee Lorenz. Lorenz / The New Yorker Collection / www.cartoonbank.com

Susanne and David Barton at the Delano Hotel, New Year's Eve party, 1998. Outfit by Mathu and Zaldy. © Patrick McMullan.

Susanne all legs up at the *Visionaire* party, 2000. © Patrick McMullan.

Susanne with the ballet star Jack Soto. © Patrick McMullan.

Susanne and David Barton. Susanne's outfit by Mathu and Zaldy. © Patrick McMullan.

Page 67 clockwise from top left:
Susanne at the Giorgio Armani Benefit for Women in Need, February 1993. This photograph was the inspiration for the 1993 *New Yorker* cartoon. Photo by Bill Cunnningham © *The New York Times*, February 1993.

Susanne wearing Mr. Pearl, 1992. © Patrick McMullan.

Susanne and François Sagat in Switzerland hosting an AIDS benefit. Dress by Mathu and Zaldy, 2011. © Patrick Mettraux and Lukas Beyeler.

Susanne and David Barton. © Patrick McMullan.

Susanne with David Barton and Kim Hastretter, 1994. © Patrick McMullan.

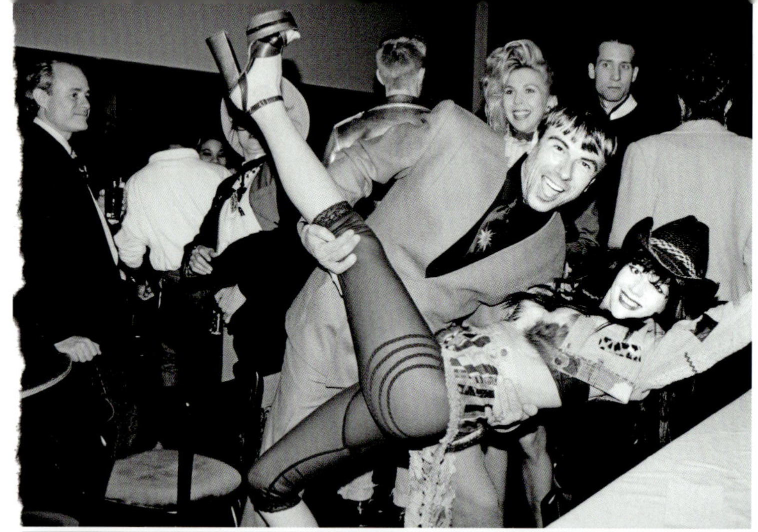

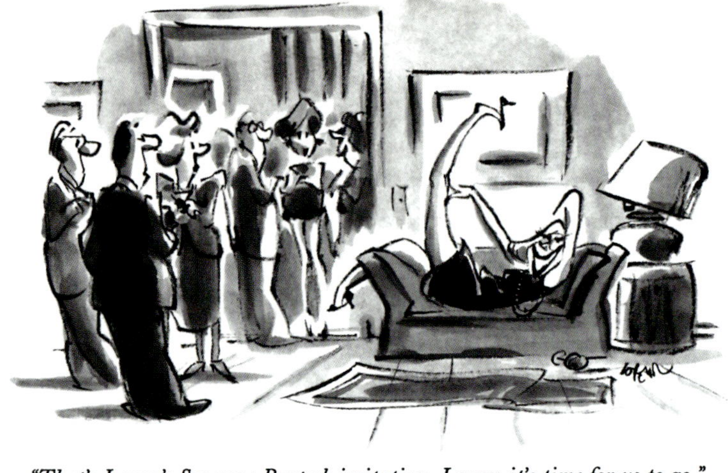

"That's Laura's Susanne Bartsch imitation. I guess it's time for us to go."

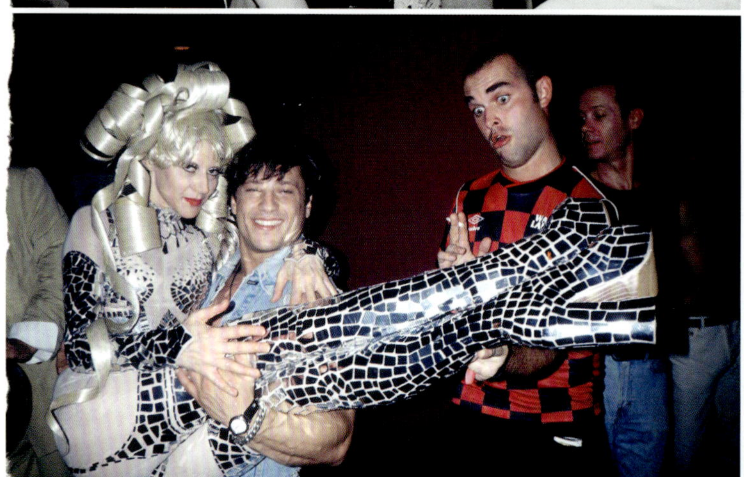

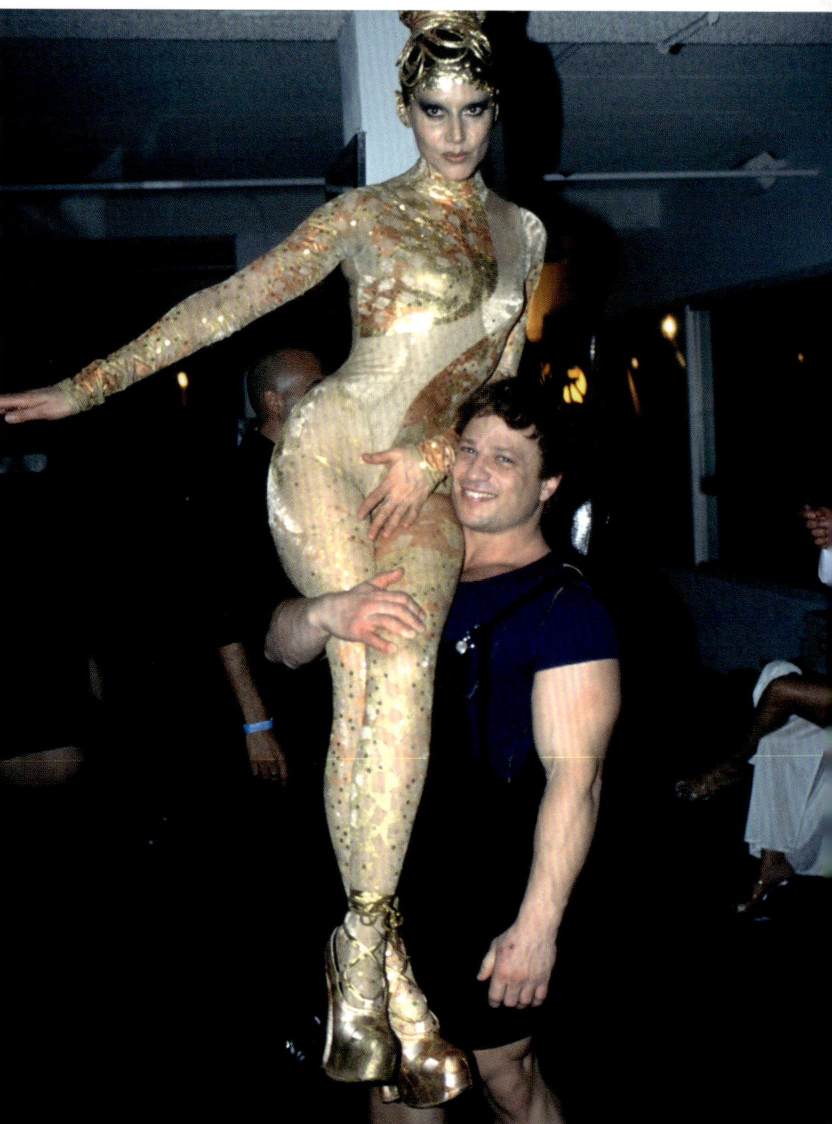

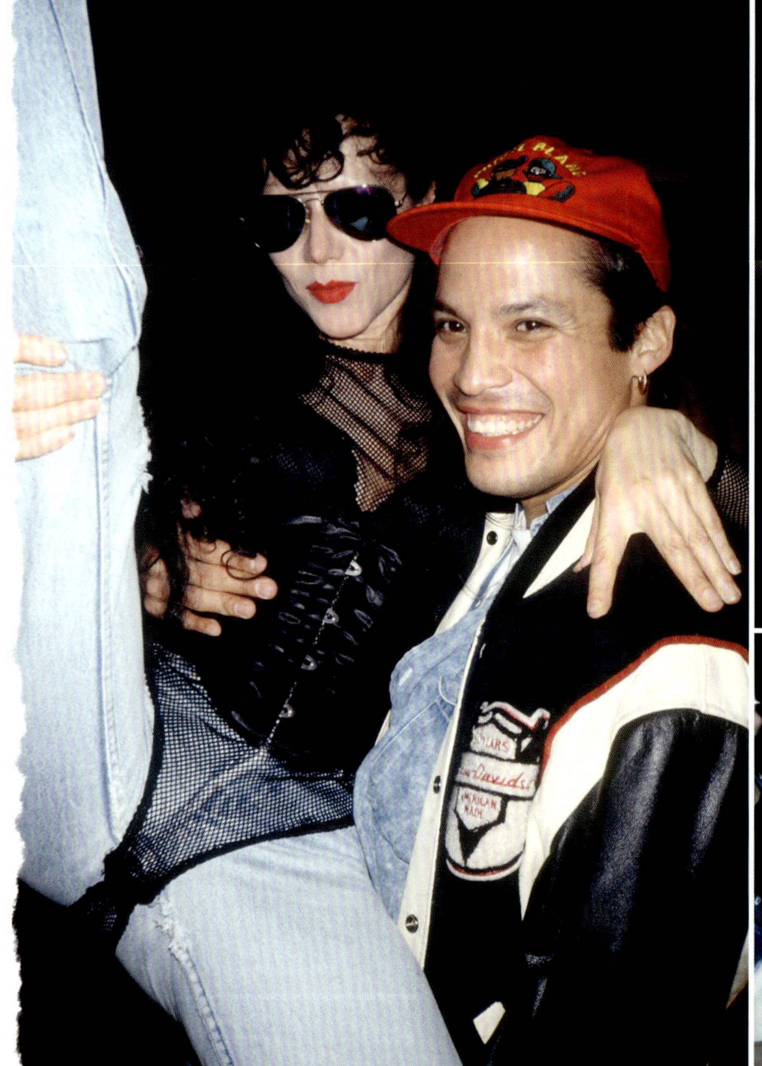

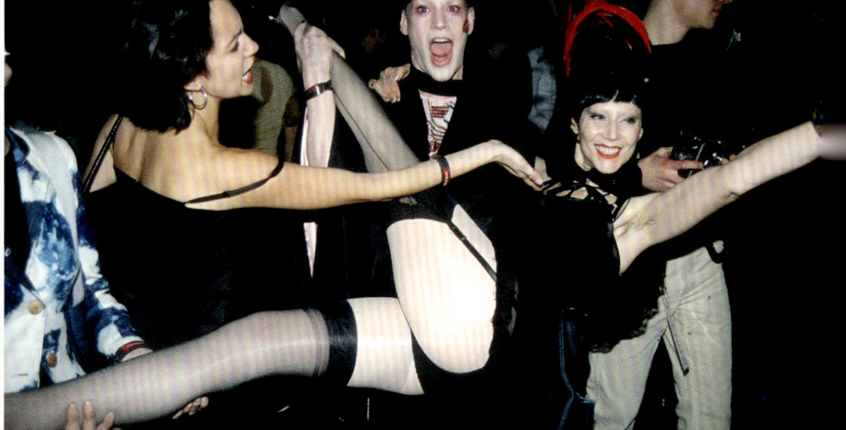

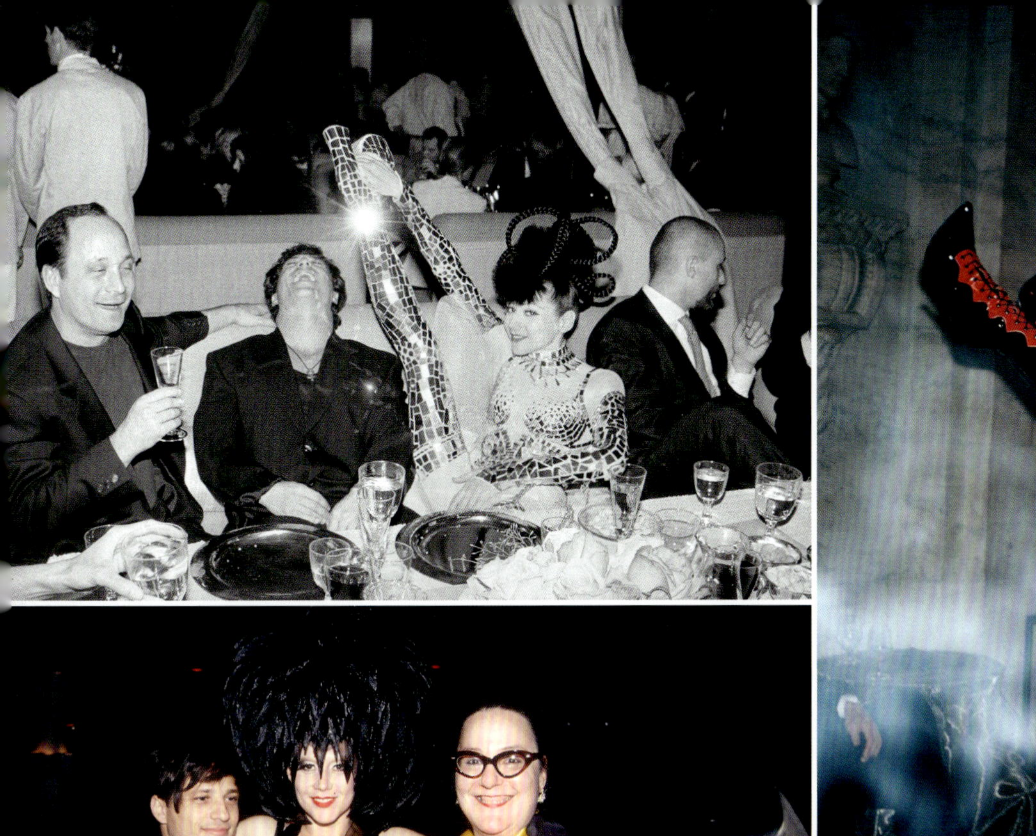
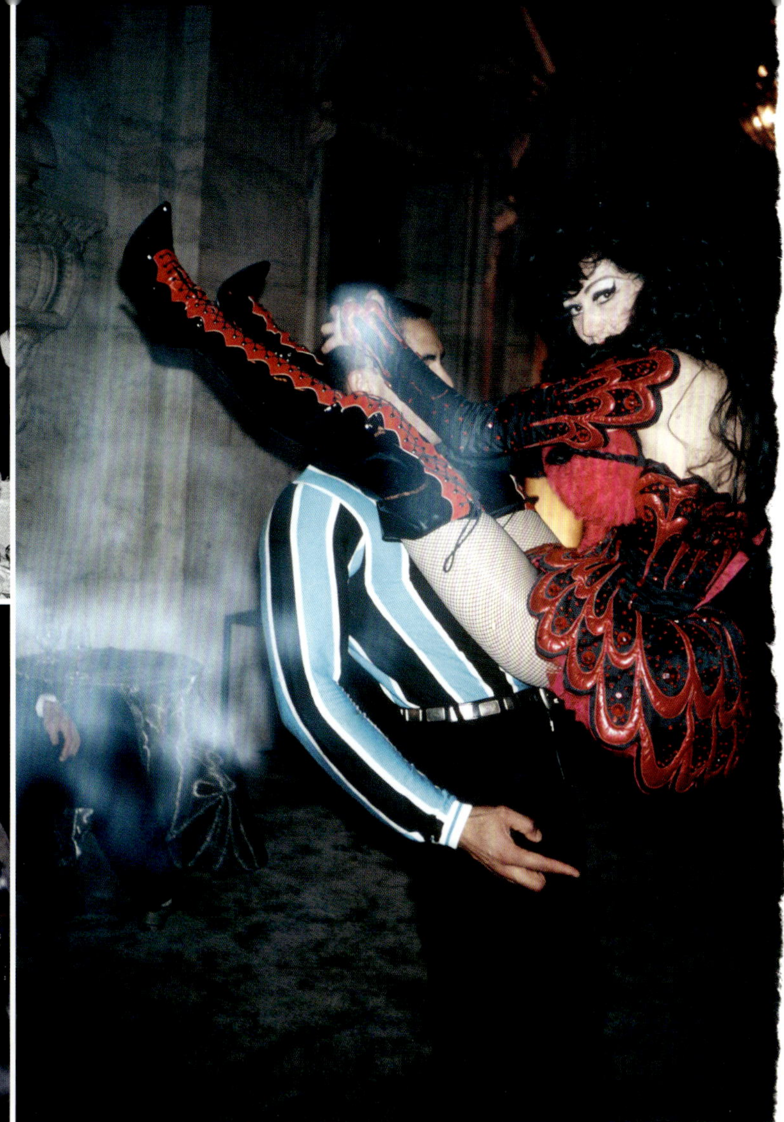
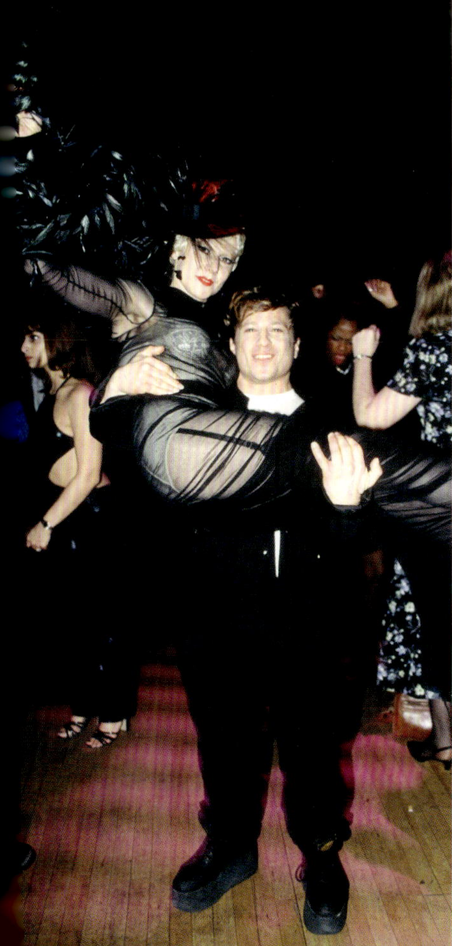
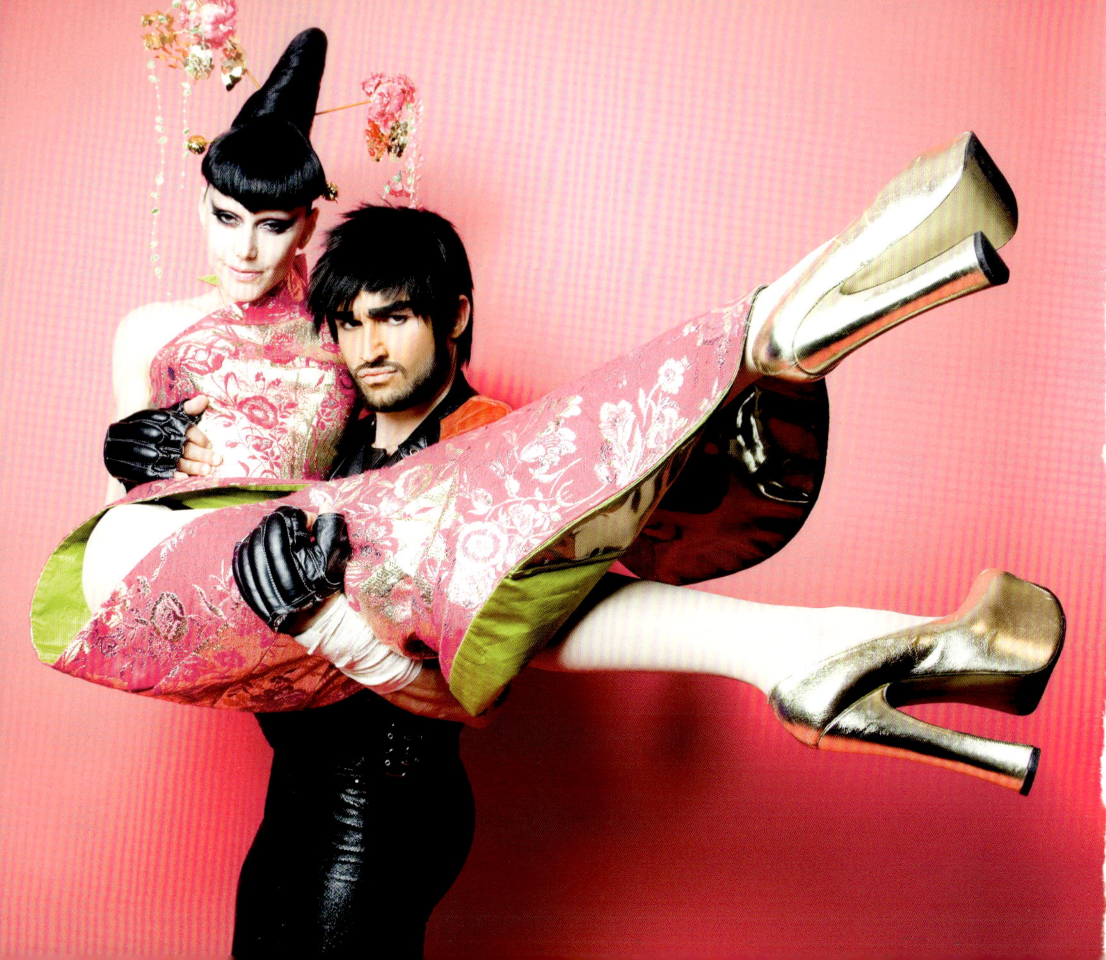

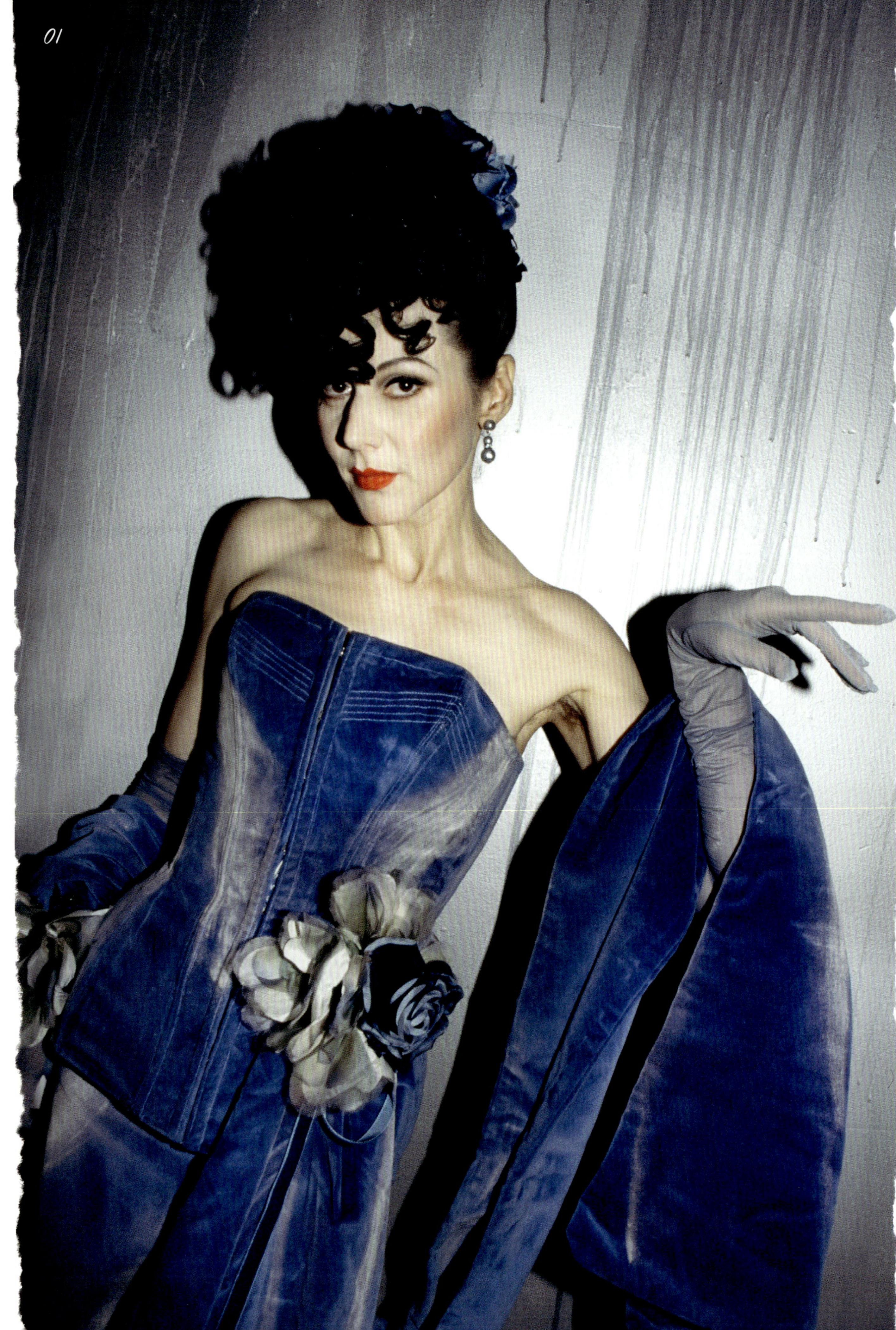

1 Susanne rocking an ensemble by John Galliano, 1997. Photo by Roxanne Lowit.

2 Susanne at her New Year's Eve party at the Delano Hotel in Miami Beach, Florida, 2000. Photo © Tina Paul, 2000. All Rights reserved.

3 Susanne in an Abel Villarreal coat. © Steven Klein Studio.

4 Susanne in Halloween look by Mathu and Zaldy, early in the 2000s. Photo by Roxanne Lowit.

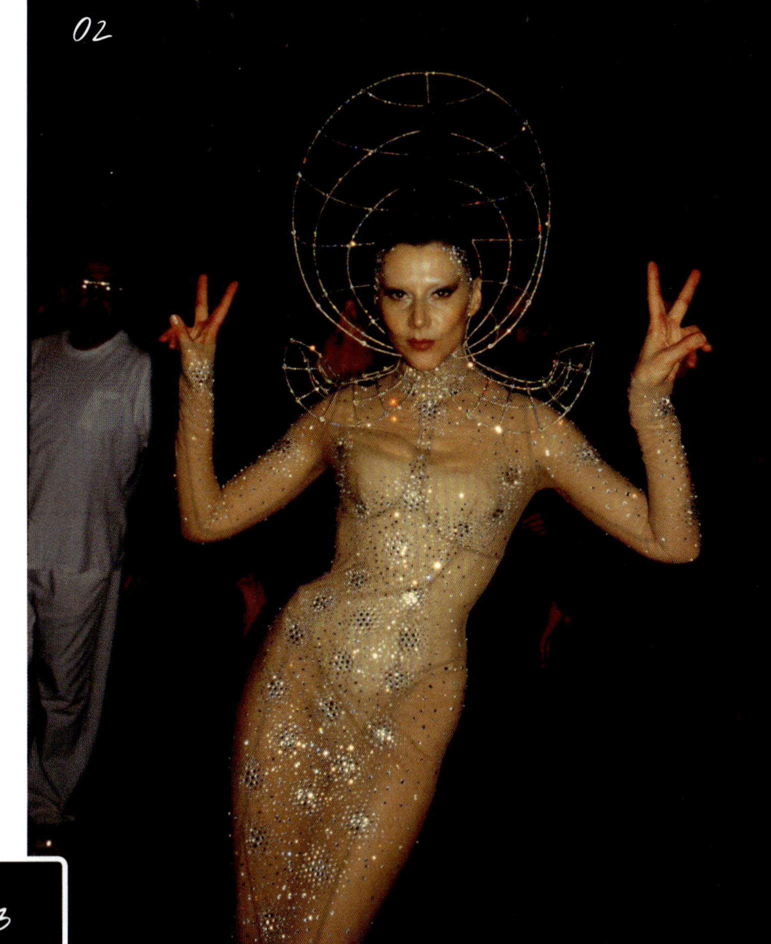

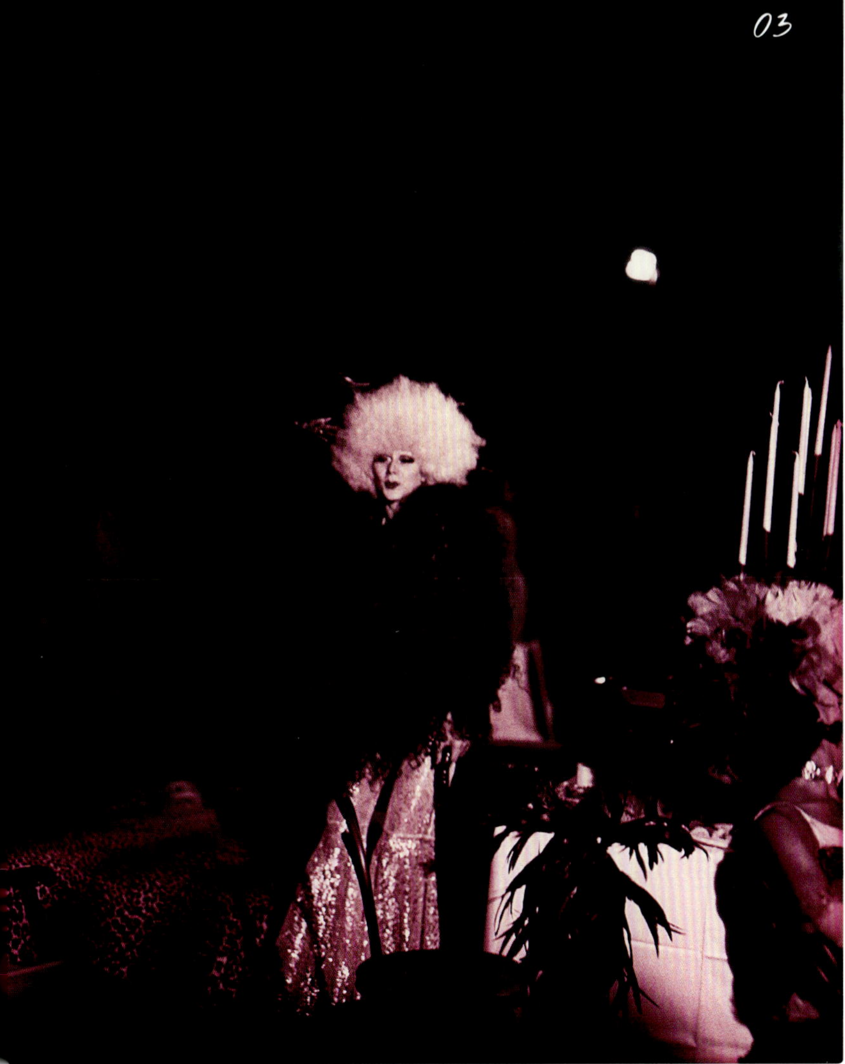

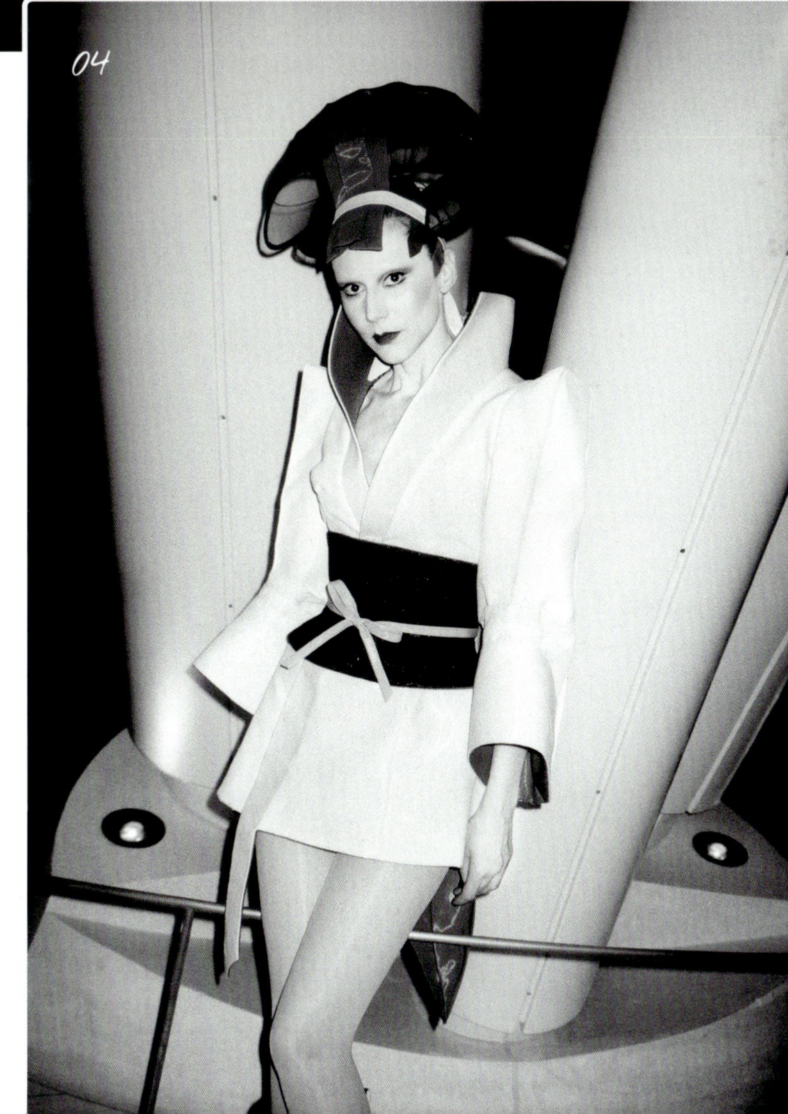

1 Susanne with downtown P.R. guru Mauricio Padilha, in Paris at Anna Dello Russo event, wearing a dress by Thierry Mugler, circa 2013. Photo by Mao Padilha.

2 Susanne with Giorgio Armani and David Barton, 1993. Susanne's costume by Mathu and Zaldy. Photo by Roxanne Lowit.

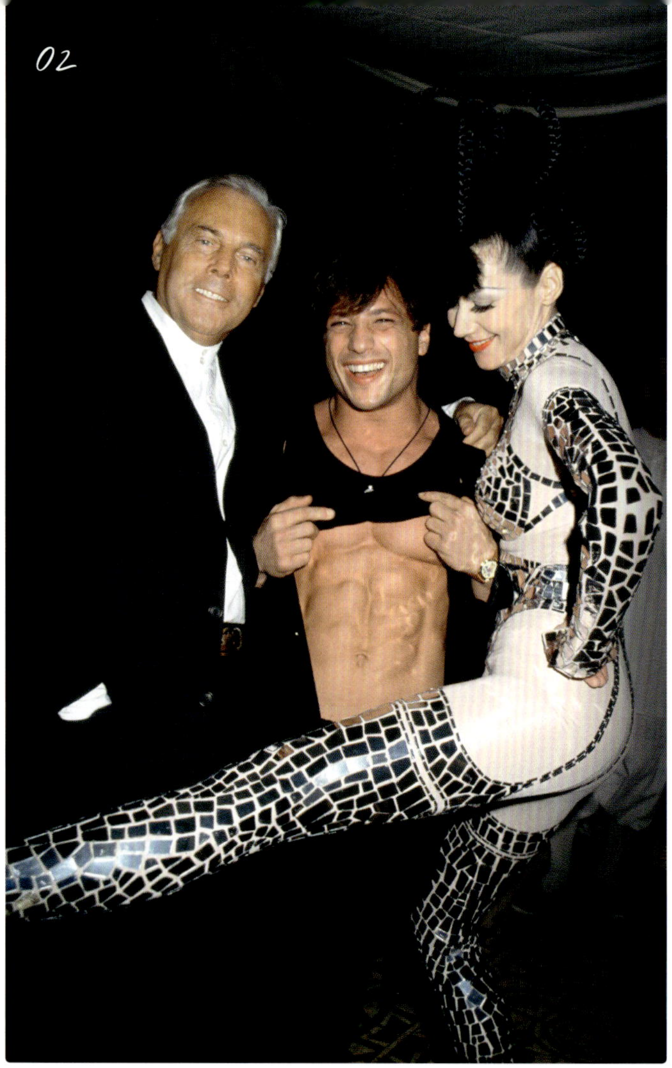

3 Susanne, Linda Evangelista, and an unknown guest, at a Chanel Party, September 1991. Photo by Roxanne Lowit.

4 Susanne in semi-drag afternoon look. Jeans painted by Kenny Scharf, jacket by Jo Dean. © Patrick McMullan.

5 Susanne with Lady Miss Kier and Dimitry of Deee-Lite. Photo © Roxanne Lowit.

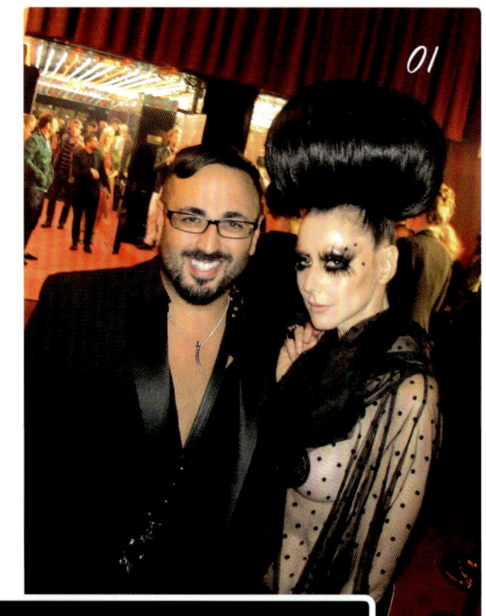

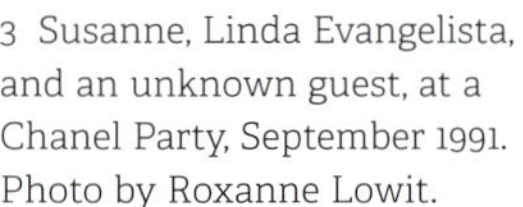

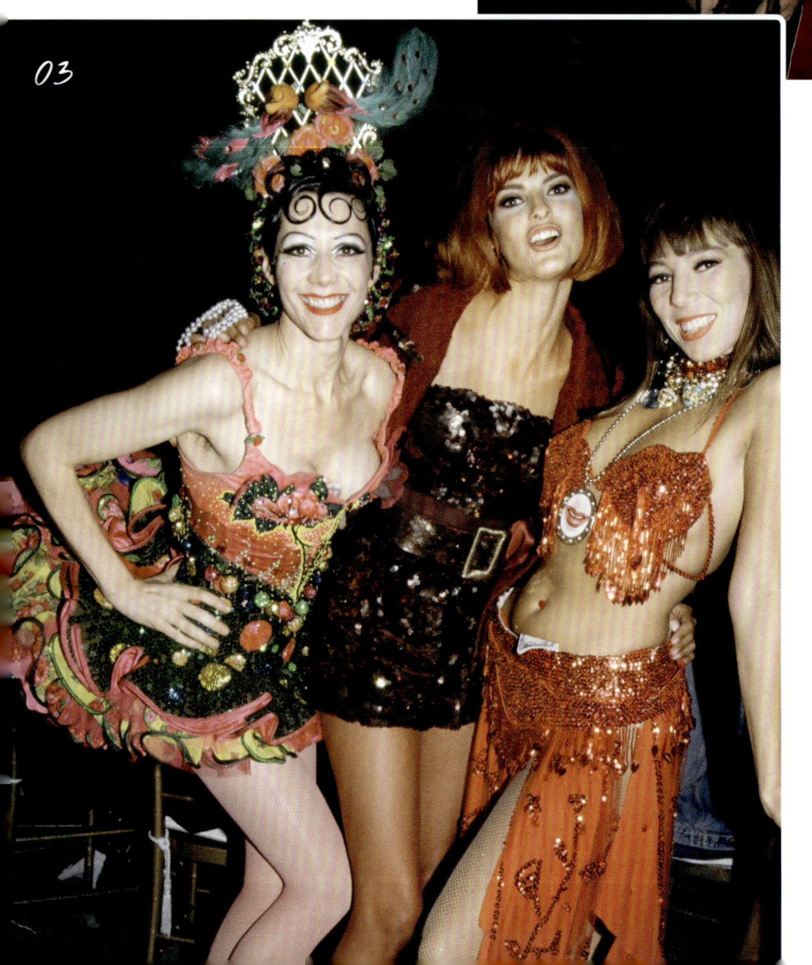

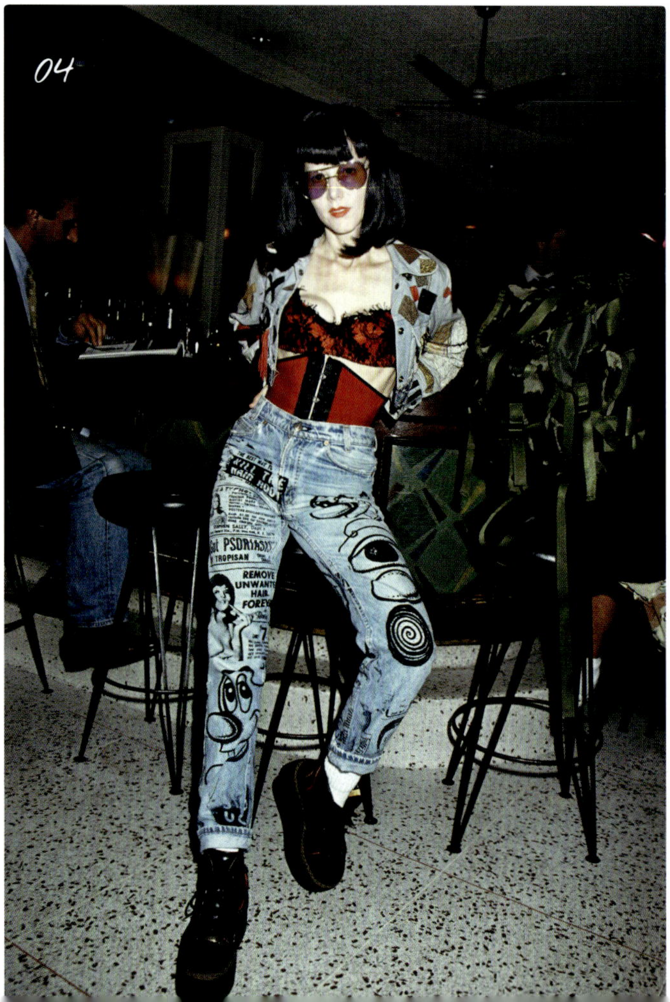

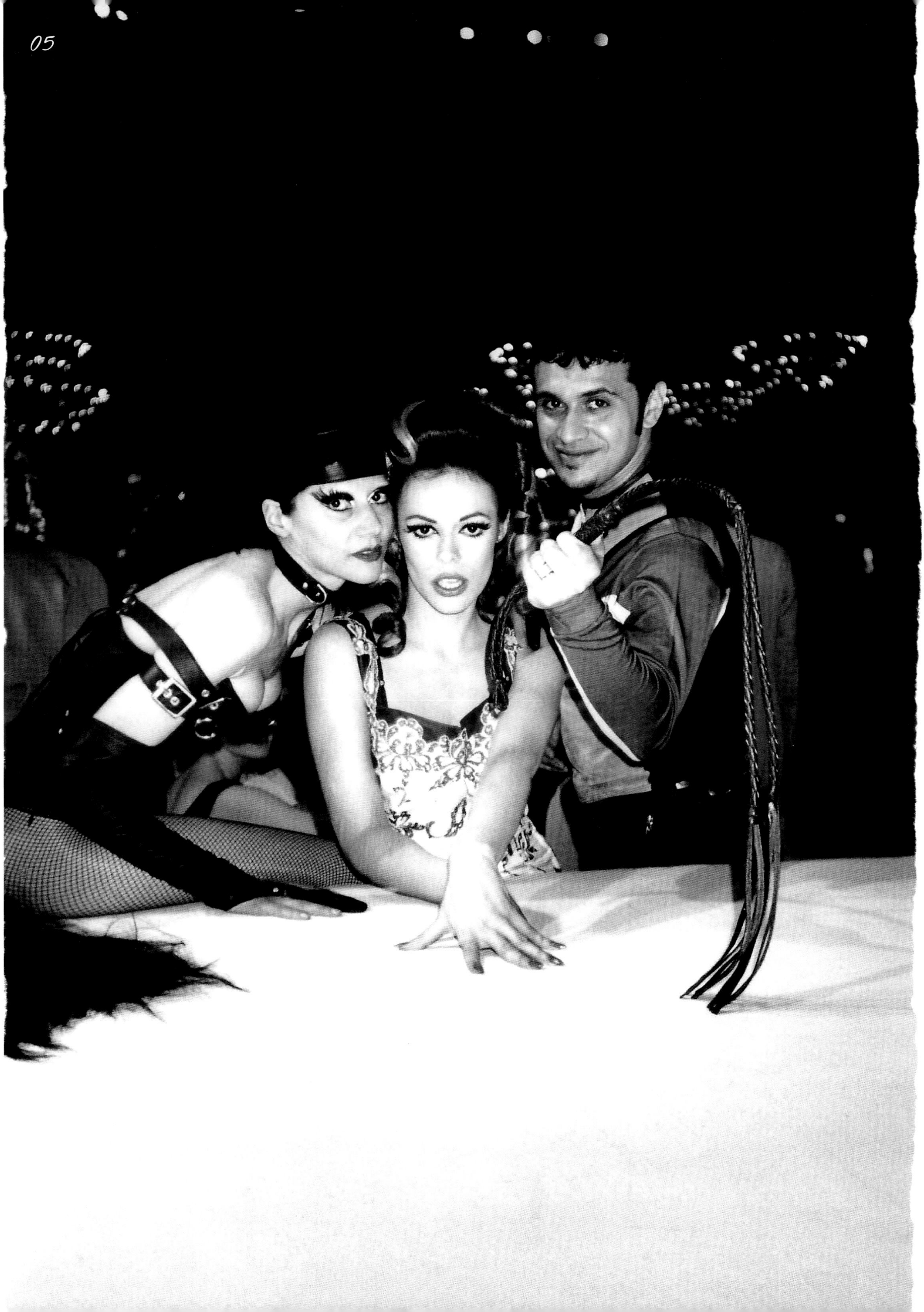

Below: Invitation for annual
Halloween ball at Palladium,
c. 1990. Photo by Mathu Andersen.

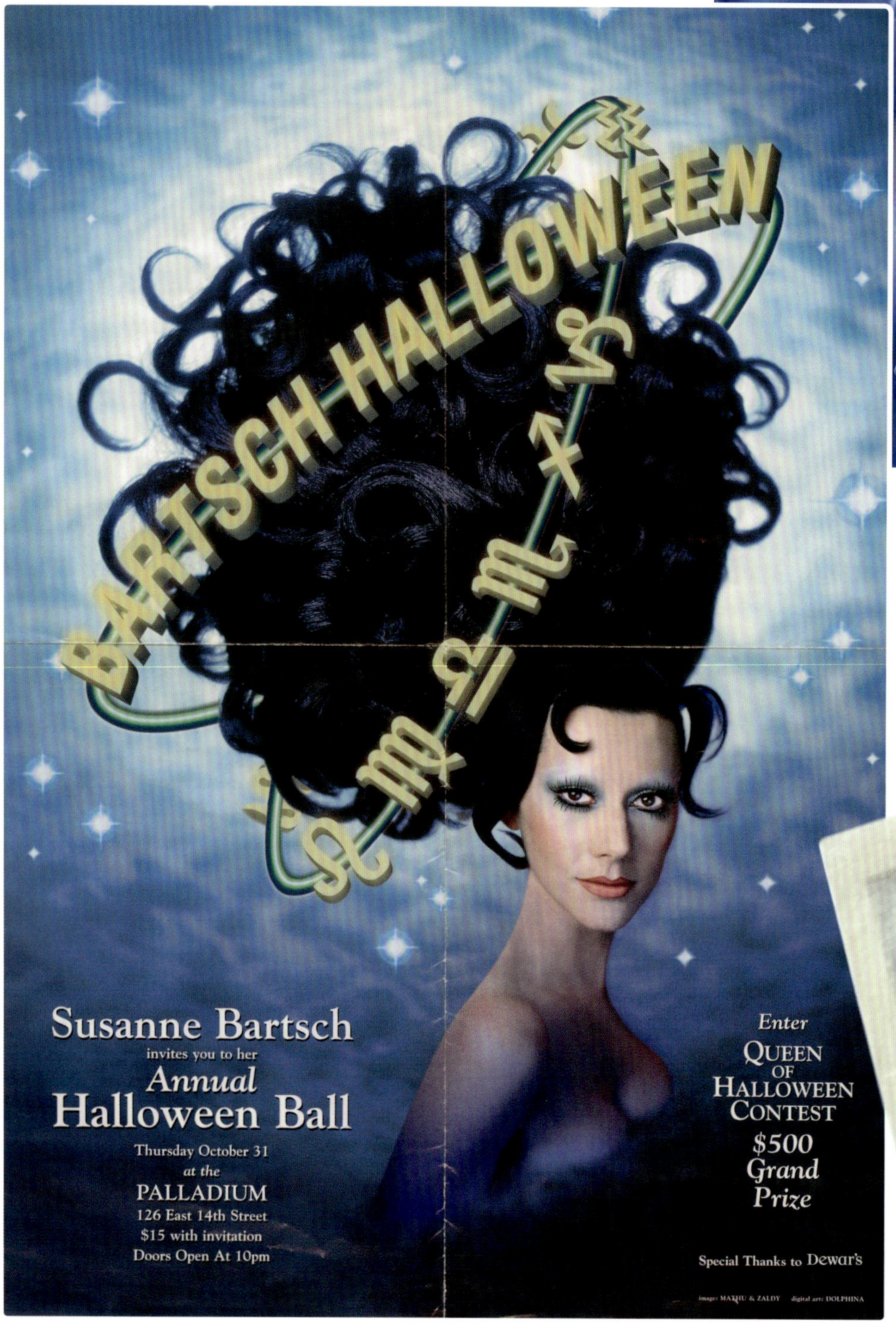

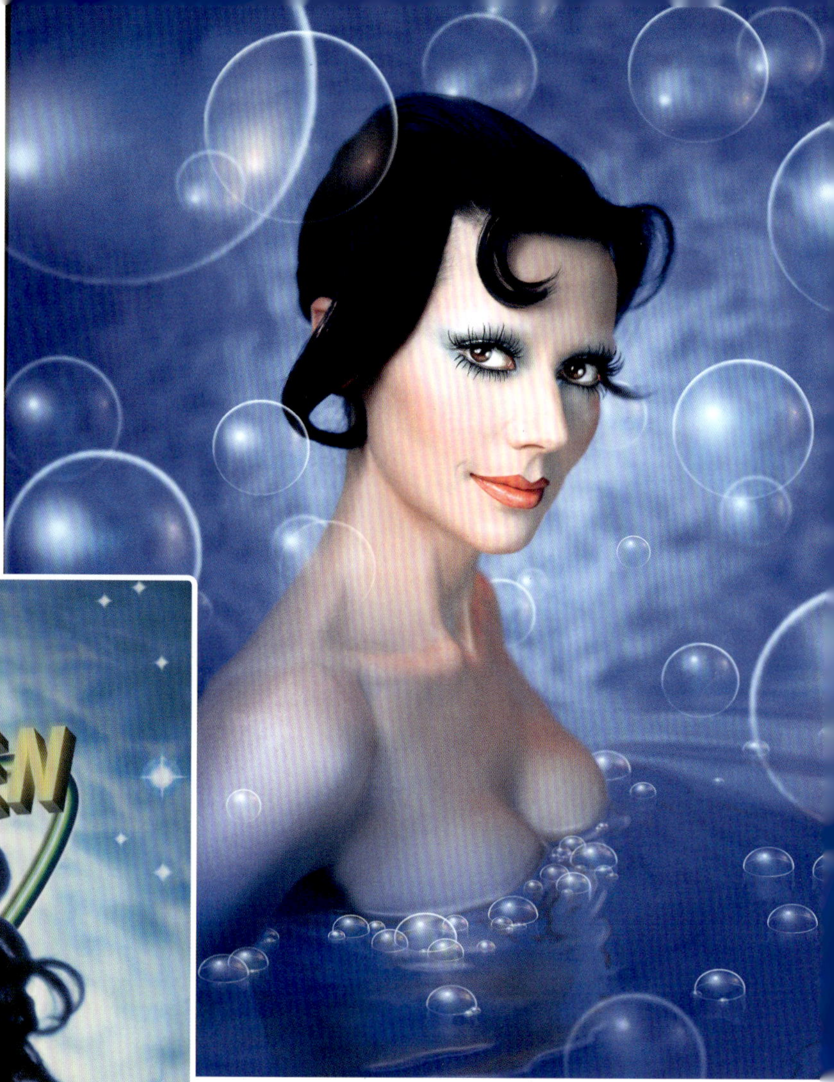

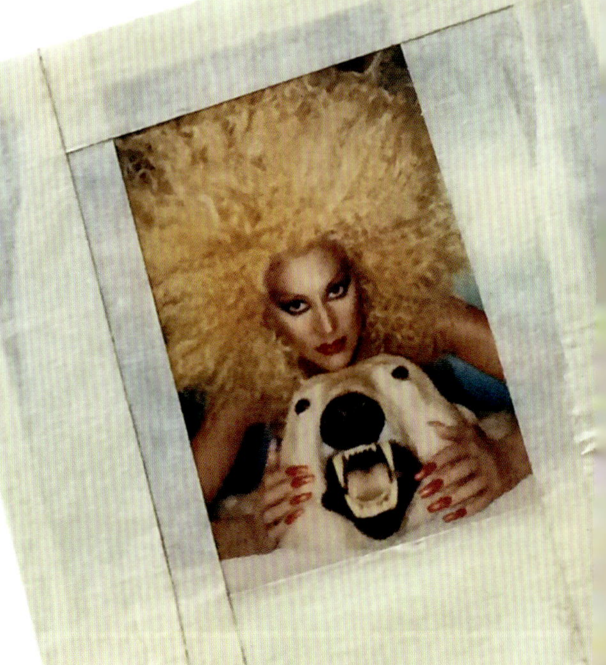

Above: Raleigh Hotel New Year's
Eve invitation photoshoot, 2003.
Photo by Mathu Andersen.

Facing: Invitation for a New Year's
Eve party, 1997. Artwork by Scott
Ewalt. Photography by
Mathu Andersen.

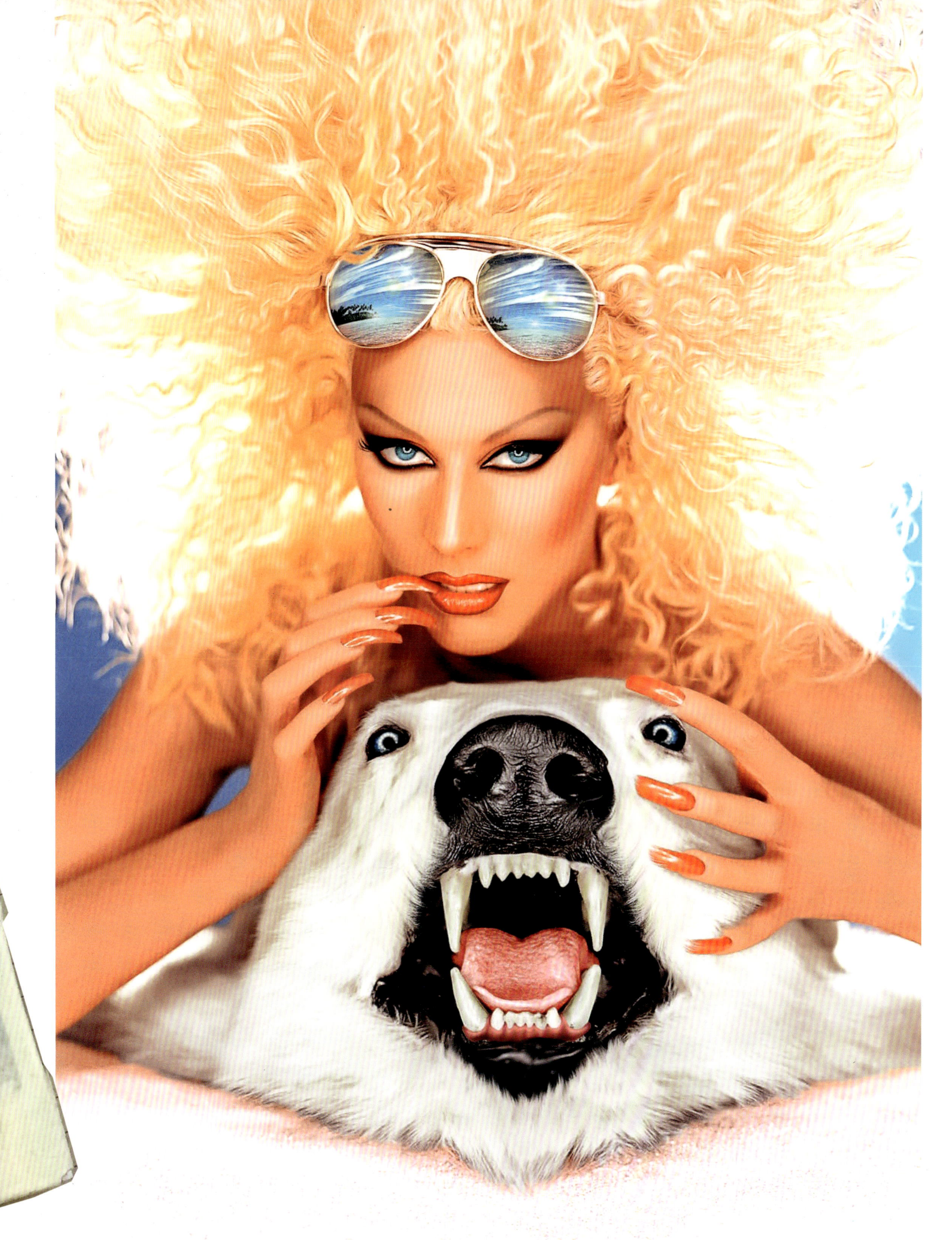

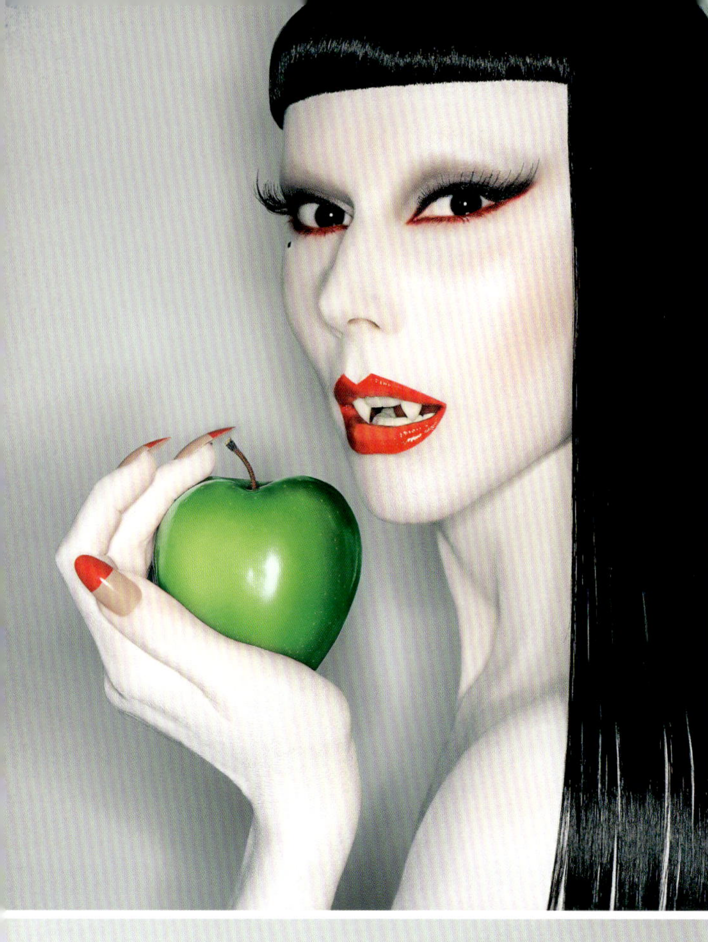

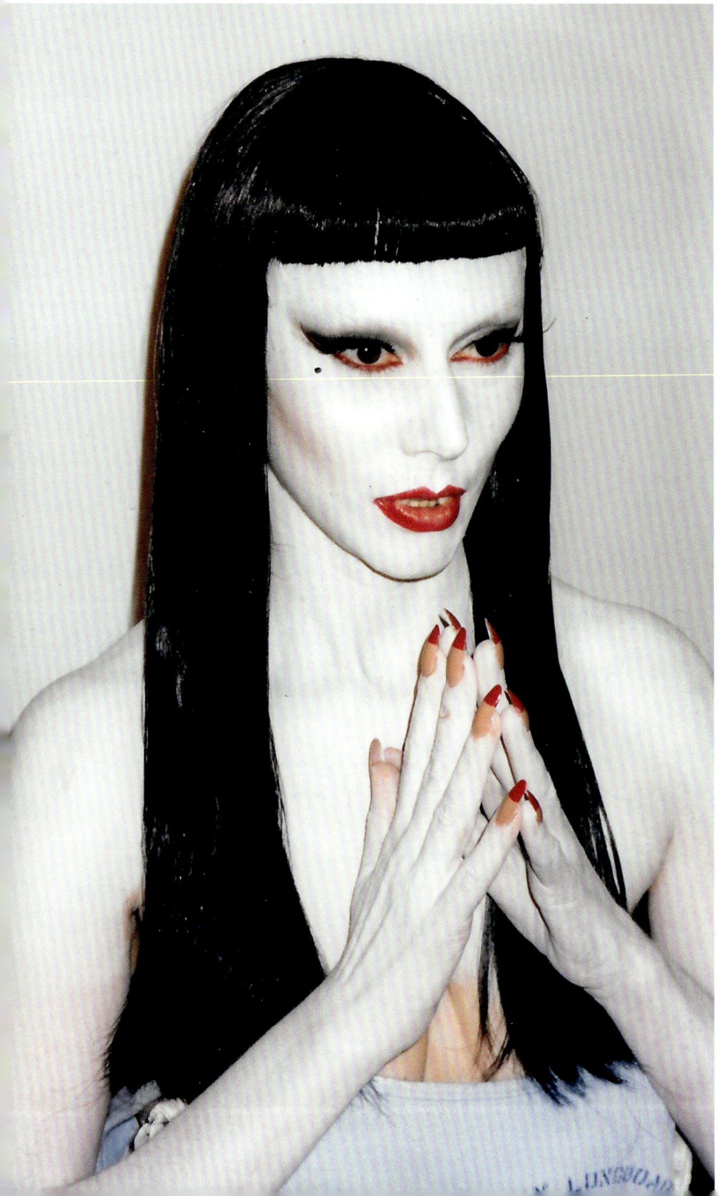

Left: "Poison Apple," Halloween Invitation, late 1990s. Photo by Mathu Andersen.

Below left: Backstage prepping for Poison Apple Halloween invitation photoshoot. Photo by Mathu Andersen.

Right: Invitation for the New Years Eve party at the Delano Hotel in Miami Beach, 1997. Artwork by Scott Ewalt, outfit by Zaldy. Photo by Mathu Andersen.

Below right: Invitation for annual Halloween ball at Palladium, October 31, 1994. Artwork by Scott Ewalt. Photo by Mathu Andersen.

Facing: Susanne in a Halloween invitation. Art by Scott Ewalt. Photo by Mathu Andersen.

The "Poison Apple" invitation photoshoot

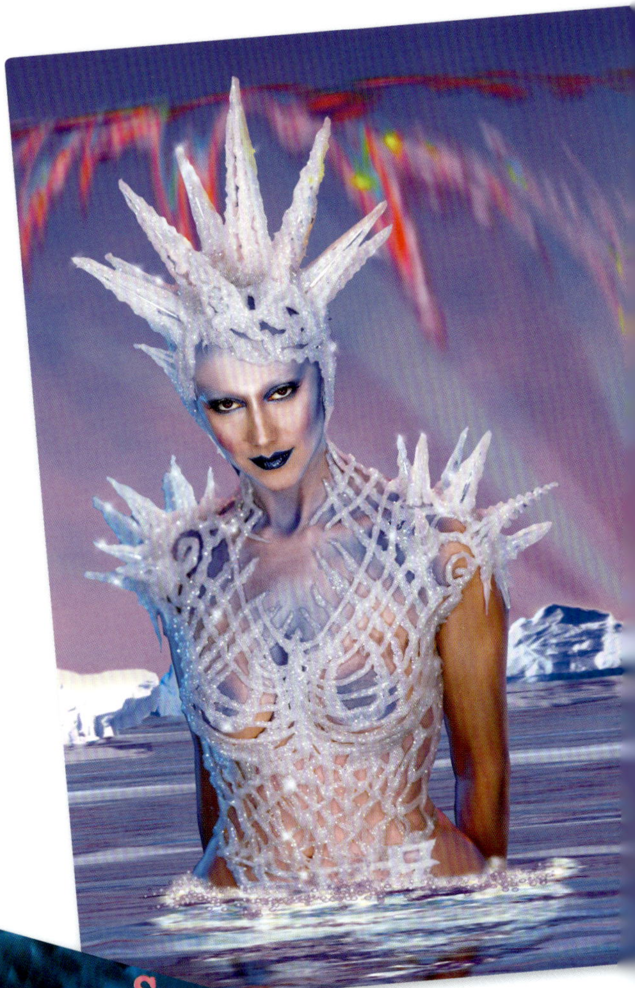

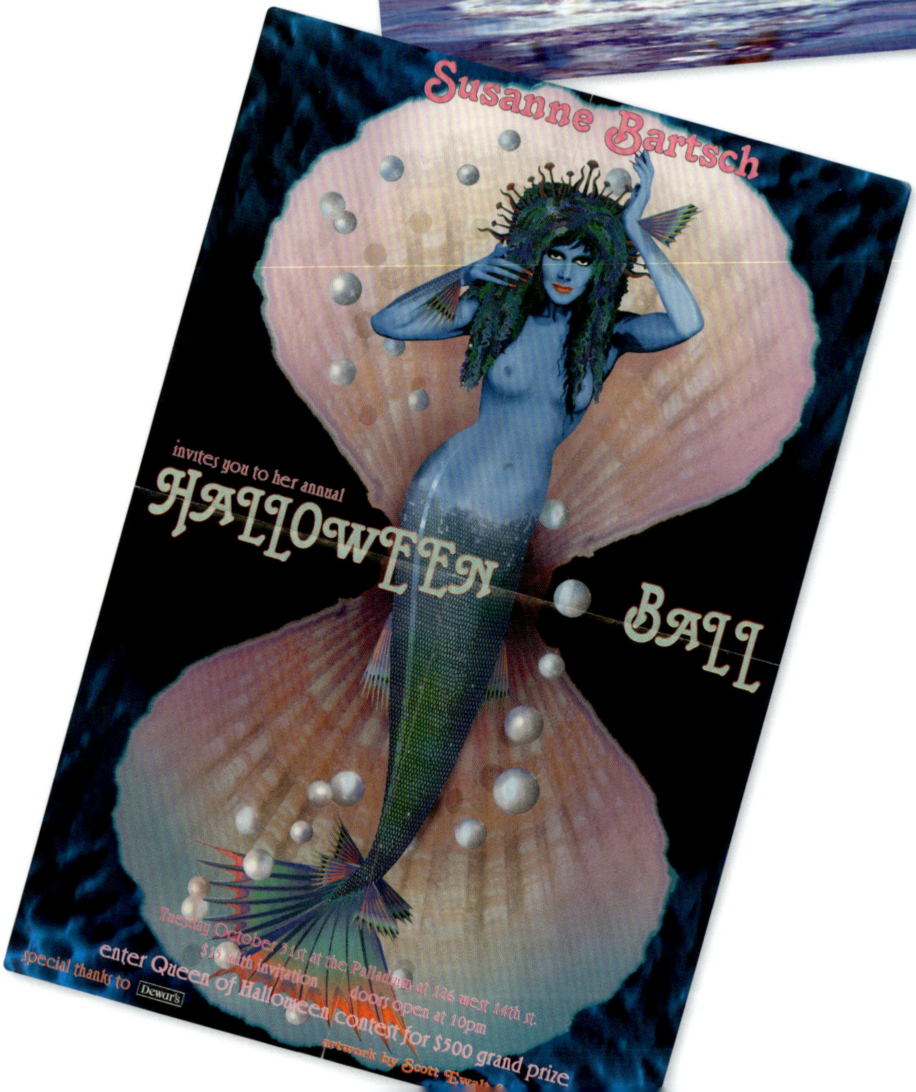

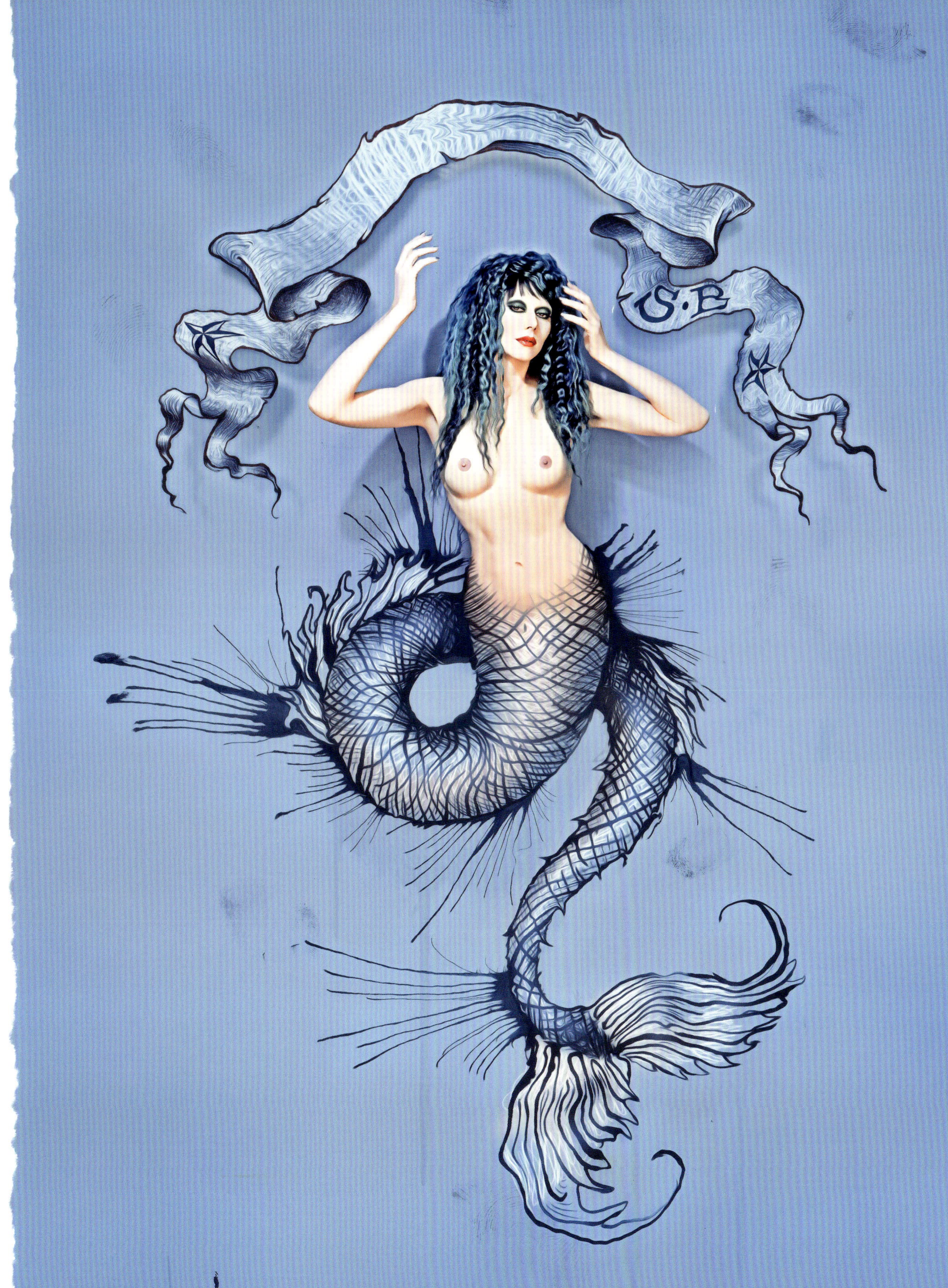

S·P

Right: Susanne Bartsch, 1999.
Photo by Rob Moritz.

Below left: Josephine Baker
photoshoot for Susanne's
Le Palace party, Paris, late 1990s.
The first time Susanne ever wore
full body paint.
Photo by Mathu Andersen.

Below right: Susanne swings.
Outfit by Mathu and Zaldy.
Photo by Michel Haddi
@Michel Haddi Studio.

Facing: Image for Halloween
Invitation, early-2000s.
Photo by Mathu Andersen.

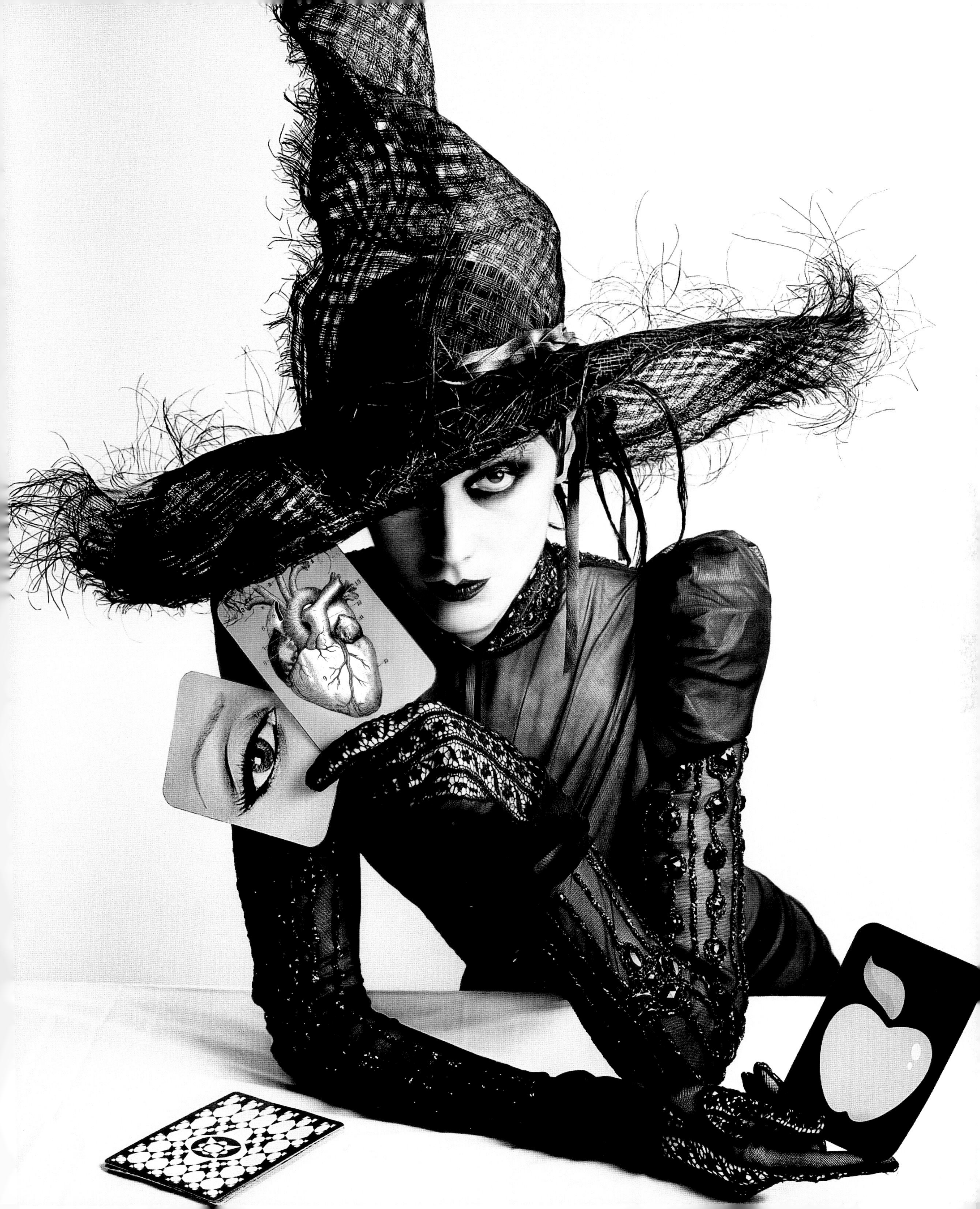

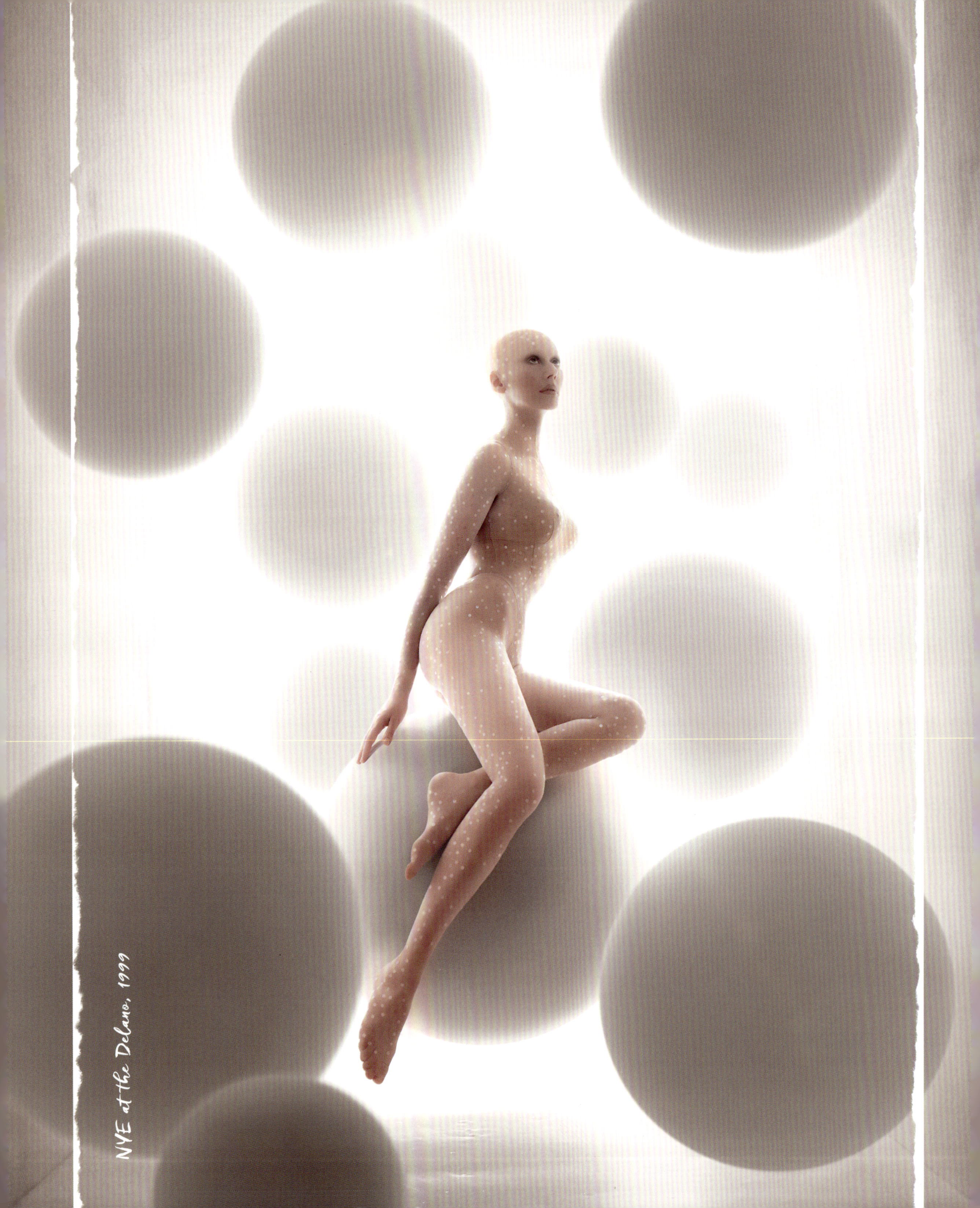

NYE at the Delano, 1999

Facing: Back of an invitation to the
Penultimate New Year's Eve party at
the Delano Hotel in Miami Beach,
1999. Invitation Mathu and Zaldy
Productions.

Below: Invitation for New Year's Eve,
2000, Ice Palace, Miami.
Photo by Mathu Andersen.

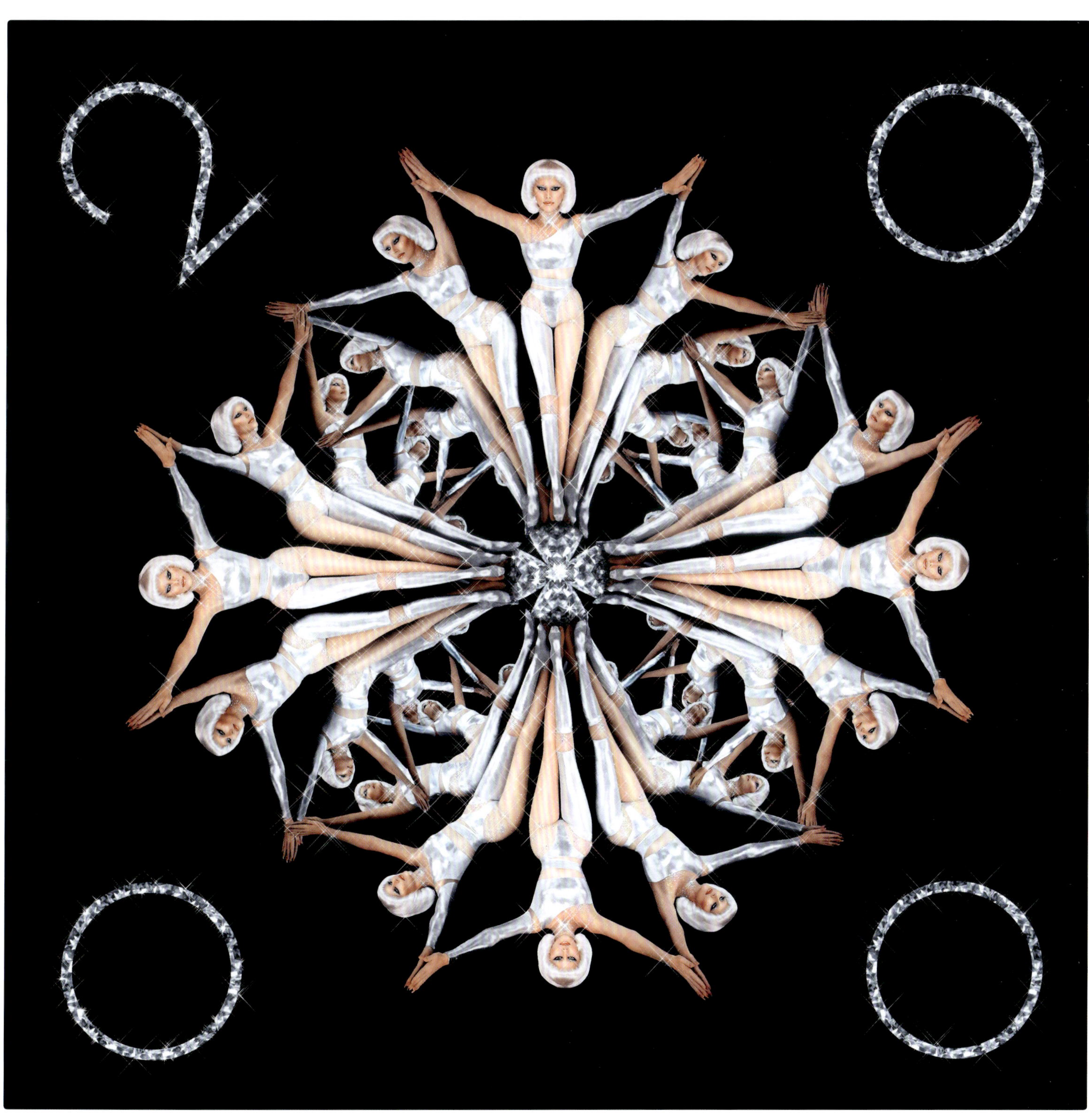

champagne."[73] "All these fashion people were wearing black when Susanne walks in, wearing a corset and carrying a pink veil all bunched up under her arm," continues Mauricio. "She got on a table and, suddenly, we were all dancing under this pink veil. It was no longer a stodgy French fashion party, it was a very cool, very New York party – and everyone was having so much fun."

Mugler, Marriage, and Motherhood

Once when Bartsch was in Los Angeles for an AIDS benefit honoring the French fashion designer Thierry Mugler, "she asked me to make something for her," says the former fashion designer Abel Villareal. The result was a "leather horse outfit with hoof-like shoes. Thierry loved it and later I worked with him on his leather pieces."[74] Joey Arias recalls, "Susanne has had so many amazing looks, but my favorite was her fetish horse outfit by Abel Villareal . . . I thought 'You are a creature of fantasy beyond fashion!' Even Leigh Bowery said, 'I can't believe this.' And Leigh's costumes – you didn't know what you were looking at, but he was coming towards you!"[75] "Susanne's outfits were shocking and challenging, but there was always an art and elegance about them," says Michael Leva. "Even when it was raunchy, it was performance art."[76]

We have already seen how many of Bartsch's friends – including Zaldy, Mathu Andersen, Danilo, and Mr Pearl – met Thiery Mugler through her events: "Susanne hired Pearl before he did for Mugler," says Scott Ewalt. "Mugler met Pearl and Abel [Villareal] through Susanne. Mugler was building a dream team from around the world. It was very unusual, because the Paris couture is usually so closed."[77]

"Susanne was an inspiration to designers like Mugler," says Simon Doonan. "Thierry is always inspired by a strong woman, a beauty, and an individual," says Danilo. Bartsch admits that she may have "inspired him because I'm not afraid of what people would say and he likes that... I'm theater and he's theater. He came to my parties in New York and I introduced people to him. I had trannies and sex changes around me and he put people like that in his shows. He asked me who worked in leather and I said Abel. He wanted a larger-than-life guy and I introduced him to Scott Ewalt. He saw me in a corset and met Mr. Pearl. Thierry asked me to model for him once. I was a bad model. I fell down. The shoes were impossible!"

"What designers like Mugler got from Susanne was a really daring woman who isn't afraid of not looking 'pretty,'" says Roger Padilha. "Her motive for dressing is different. It's not to look 'pretty' and find a husband, it's not about being photographed, it's obviously not to keep warm, since she's always half-

"Suzanne's motive for dressing is different. It's not about 'looking pretty'. It's about taking chances. She's not dressing for herself, she's dressing for all of us."

– Roger Padilha

Susanne in Abel Villarreal's leather horse look, April 1992. Photo by Albert Sanchez.

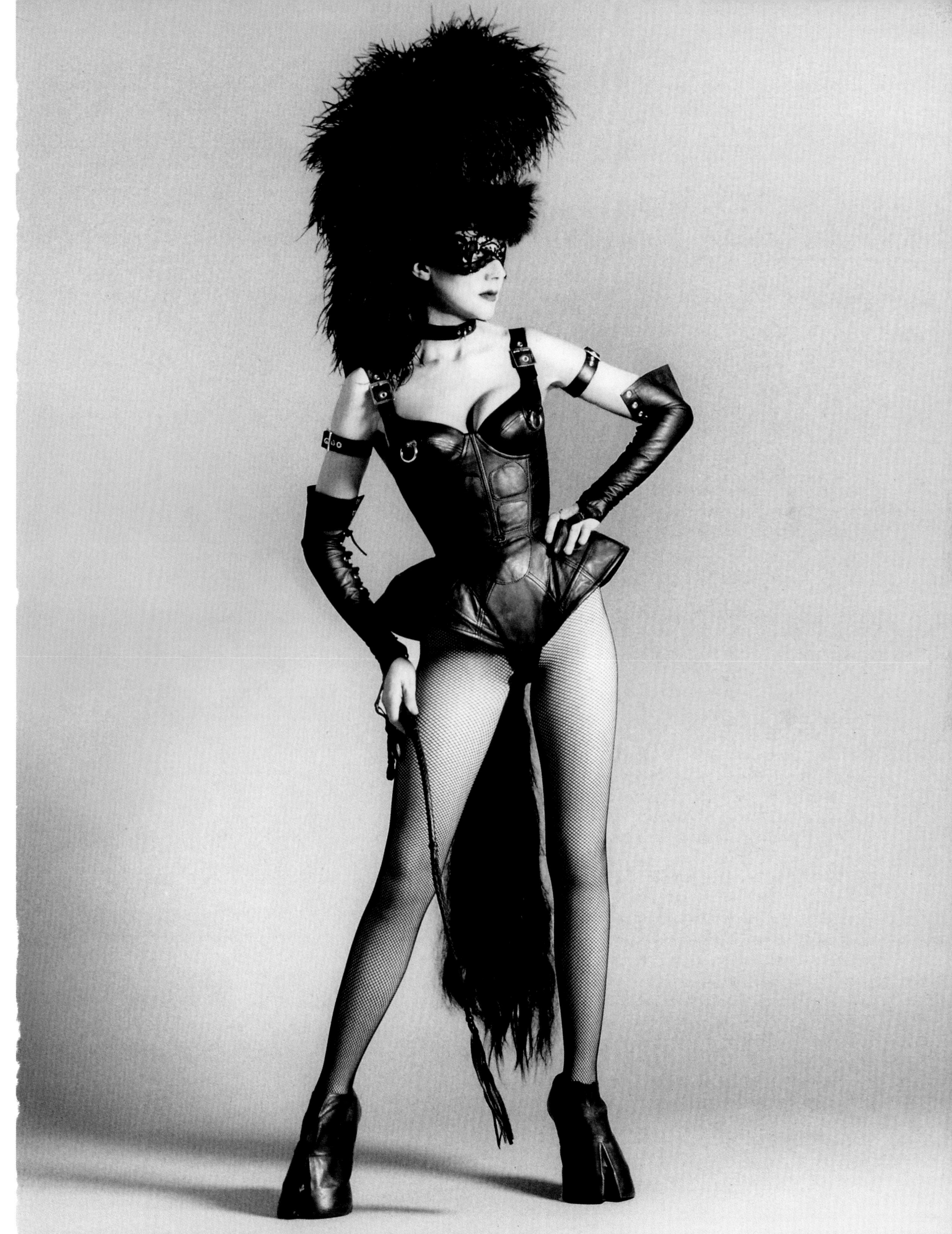

naked – it's about taking chances. She's not just dressing for herself, she's dressing for all of us, for our visual experience, enriching all of our lives."[78]

"Designers are sponges for all kinds of visual information," says *Vogue*'s Hamish Bowles. Mugler, of course, is far from being the only designer to gravitate to nightclubs to find inspiration. "Many designers have gone to clubs – Marc Jacobs, Jonathan Anderson, Christopher Kane . . ." Individuals like Susanne Bartsch would be "inspiring to any visual artist or creator," he adds, "by virtue of their self-presentation."

In 1995, Bartsch married again, this time to David Barton, the owner of a chain of gyms. Their one-year-old son, Bailey, attended, accompanied by his Godmother/Godfather, a drag queen known as The Baroness. Barton remembers, "Susanne wore that fantastic leather bodysuit [made by Villareal] and an egg veil that Thierry designed for her. I just wore a leather thong. Our son wore a little, tiny three-piece white suit. We didn't tell anyone that we were getting married. We organized a fashion event, *Inspirations*, and at the end, when the bride appeared, we came out. It was hard to find a person of the cloth to perform the ceremony. Eventually we found a cool gay priest from a Unitarian church in Brooklyn. He wore white robes. Susanne had forty-three bridesmaids – cool women and a couple of guys. RuPaul and Thierry Mugler were my best men. Playboy sponsored the wedding. I don't think Playboy sponsors weddings as a rule."[79] "We didn't know it was for real until the minister came out," says Roxanne Lowit, who was one of the bridesmaids. [80]

"I was lucky enough to be around when Bailey was little, and I watched Susanne juggle motherhood and business," says Richie Rich. "There was a nanny, but Susanne was very hands-on with everything. I remember her saying, 'I'm not going to the Met party, Bailey has a cold.' She was that kind of mom." The fashion journalist Lynn Yaeger recalls seeing Bartsch once at an event, wearing hot pants and thigh-high boots with huge platforms, talking to her son on the telephone, asking "real mommy questions," like "Do you have your gloves?" and "When are you coming home?"[81]

Paula Greif describes herself as "Susanne's friend from motherland." They first met in the 1980s, when Greif was the art director at *Elle* magazine. "Then around 1995, I ran into her at the Baby Gap. We both had kids – Anne, my daughter, and Bailey – who ended up going to school together from ages two to eighteen. Bailey's home life was full of drag queens and make-up and costumes, but in other ways he had an old-fashioned, proper, European childhood. Susanne and David looked far-out, but they were very solid parents. Susanne really put Bailey first and it was only as Bailey got older that she started going out again." Today Bailey is a student at Brown University. "He's not square, but he's not wild and crazy," says Greif. "He's charming and smart, with gorgeous manners."[82]

"I am theater and Mugler is theater."
– Susanne Bartsch

Top: Susanne wearing Thierry Mugler at the cabaret event she produced for Giorgio Armani, Milan. Courtesy of Susanne Bartsch.

Center: Susanne Bartsch wearing a Thierry Mugler hat and jacket, Miami, FL, 1996. Photo ©Bruce Weber.

Bottom: Susanne in an ensemble by Thierry Mugler, March 1992. Photo by Roxanne Lowit.

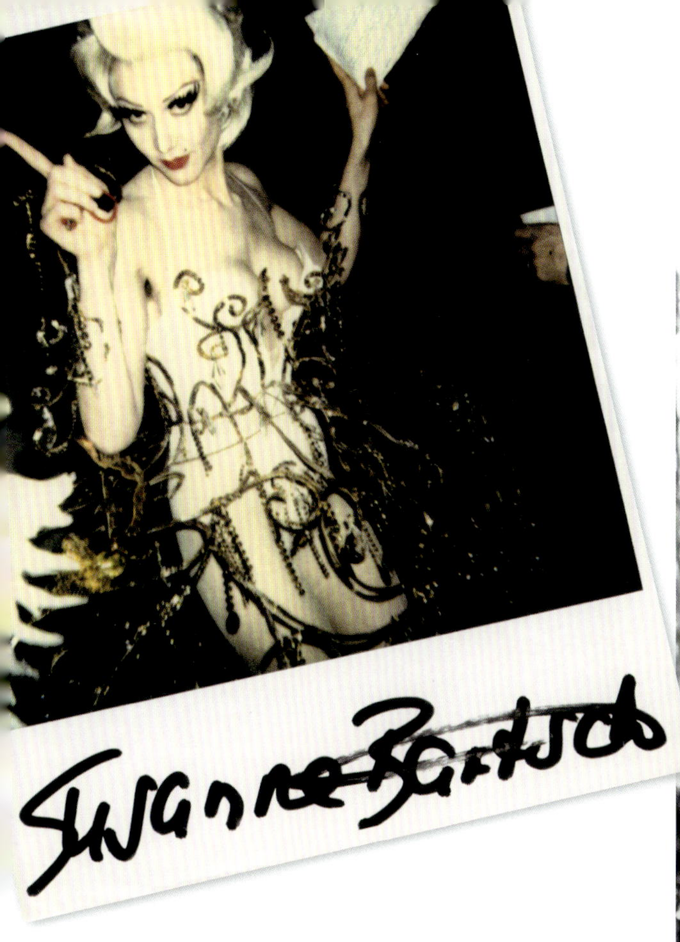
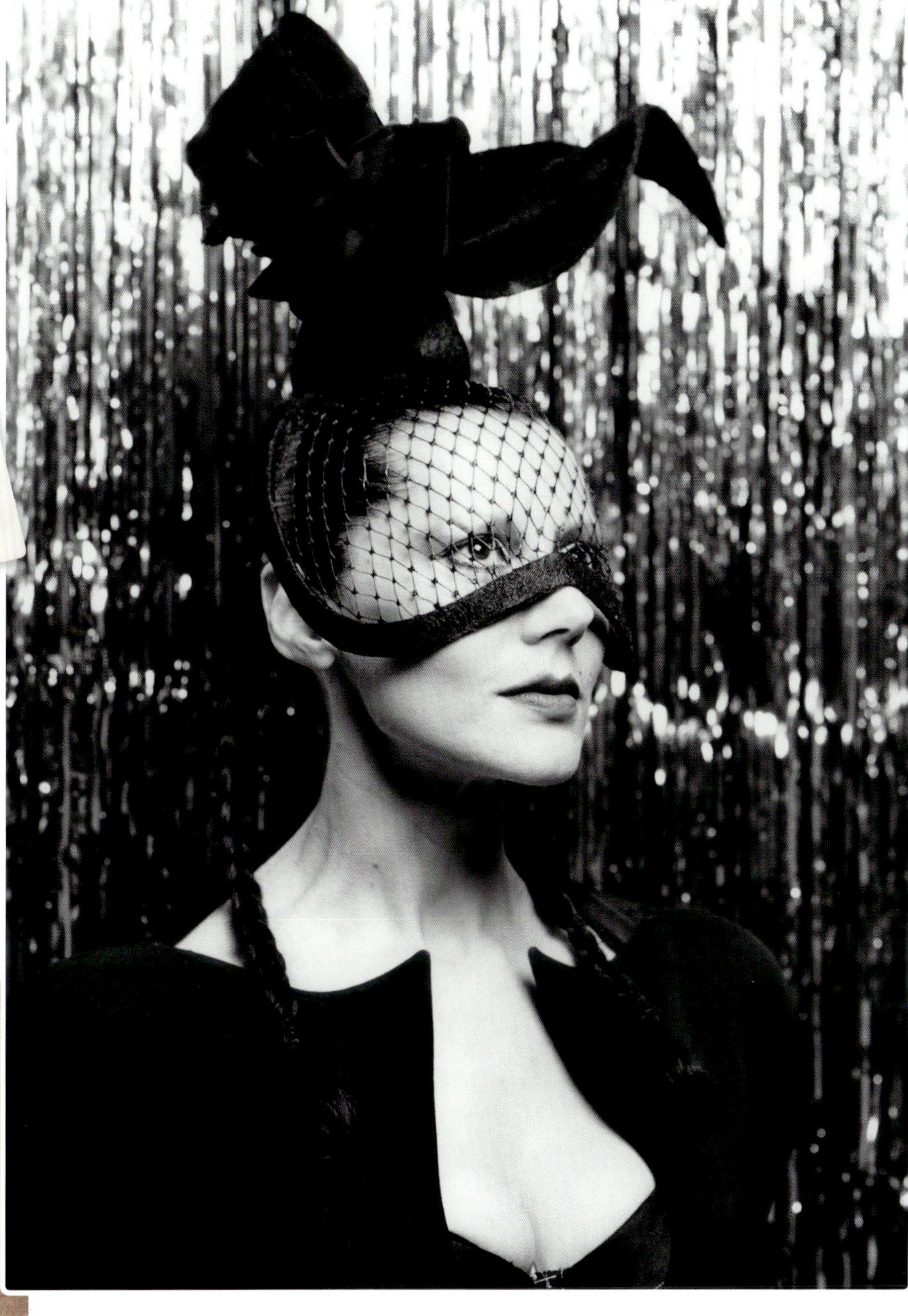
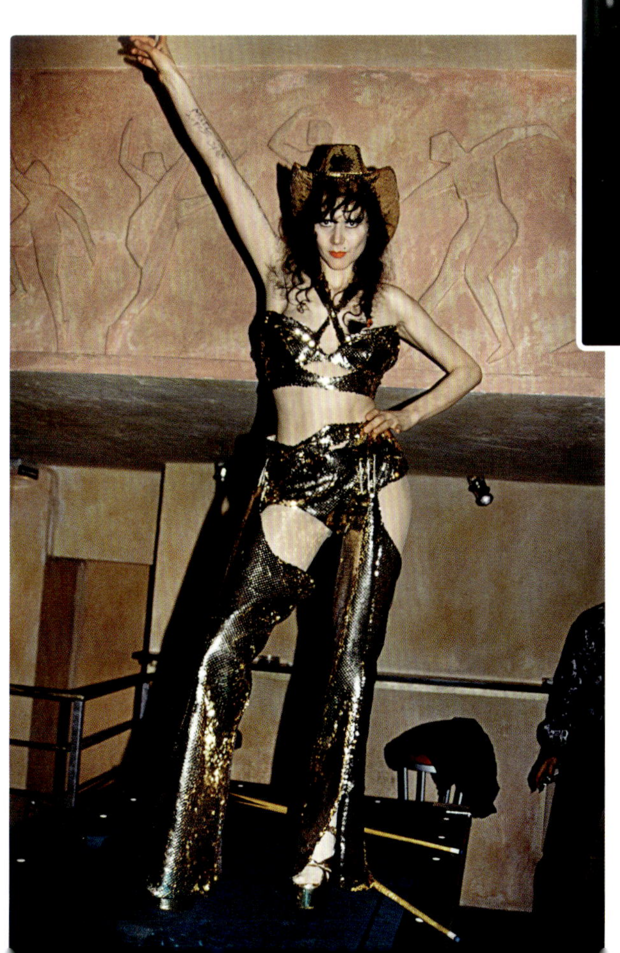

1 Susanne on her wedding day, wearing Thierry Mugler. *Inspiration* fashion show, May 1995. Photo by Roxanne Lowit. With sketch (right) for Susanne's wedding veil by Thierry Mugler. Courtesy of Susanne Bartsch.

2 Susanne and Stephen Sprouse at her wedding reception at David Barton's gym, May 1995. Photo by Roxanne Lowit.

3 Susanne and David on their wedding day, holding baby Bailey, May 1995. Photo by Roxanne Lowit.

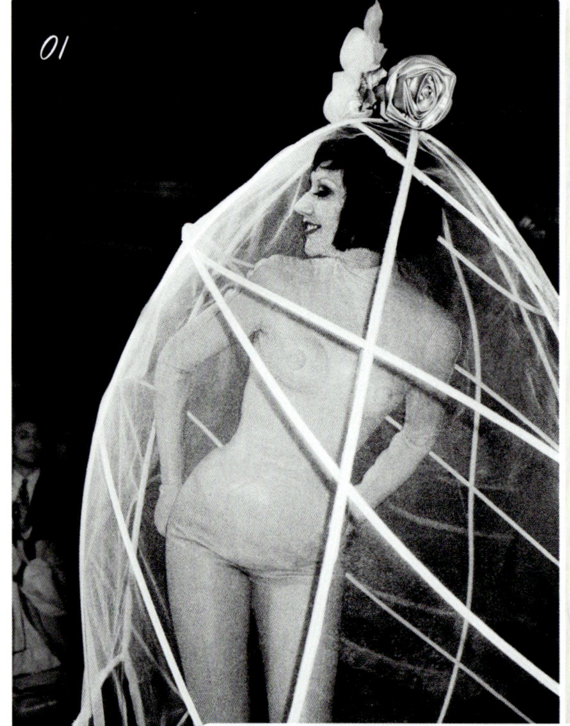

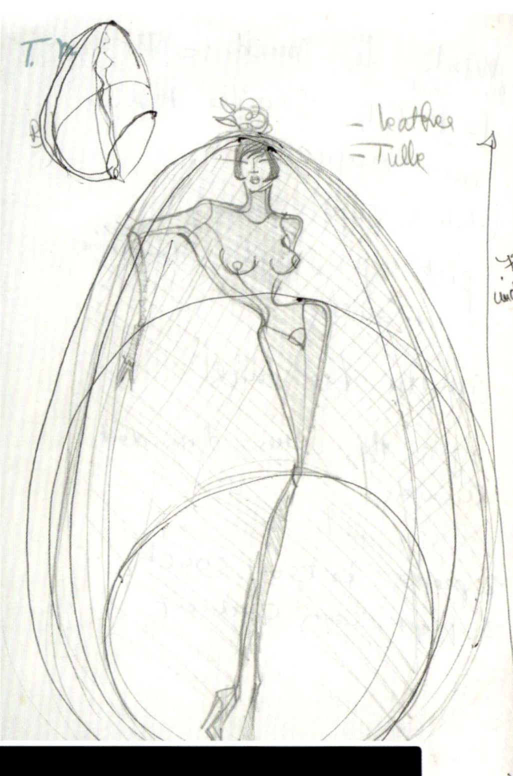

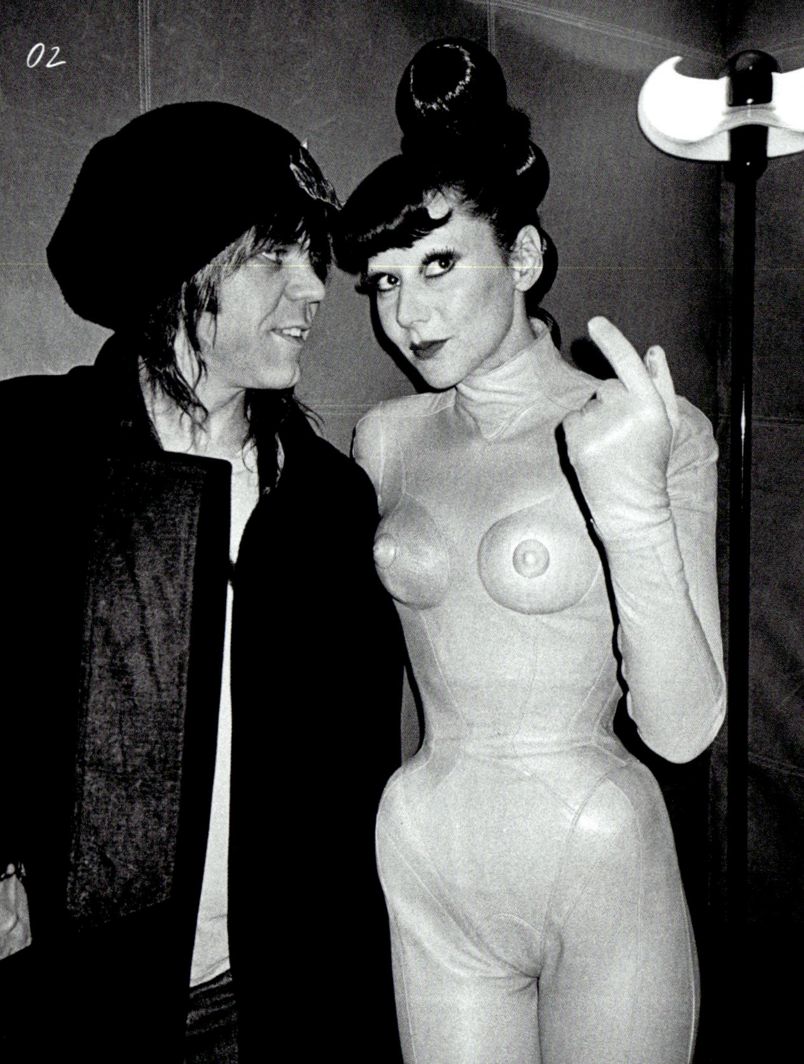

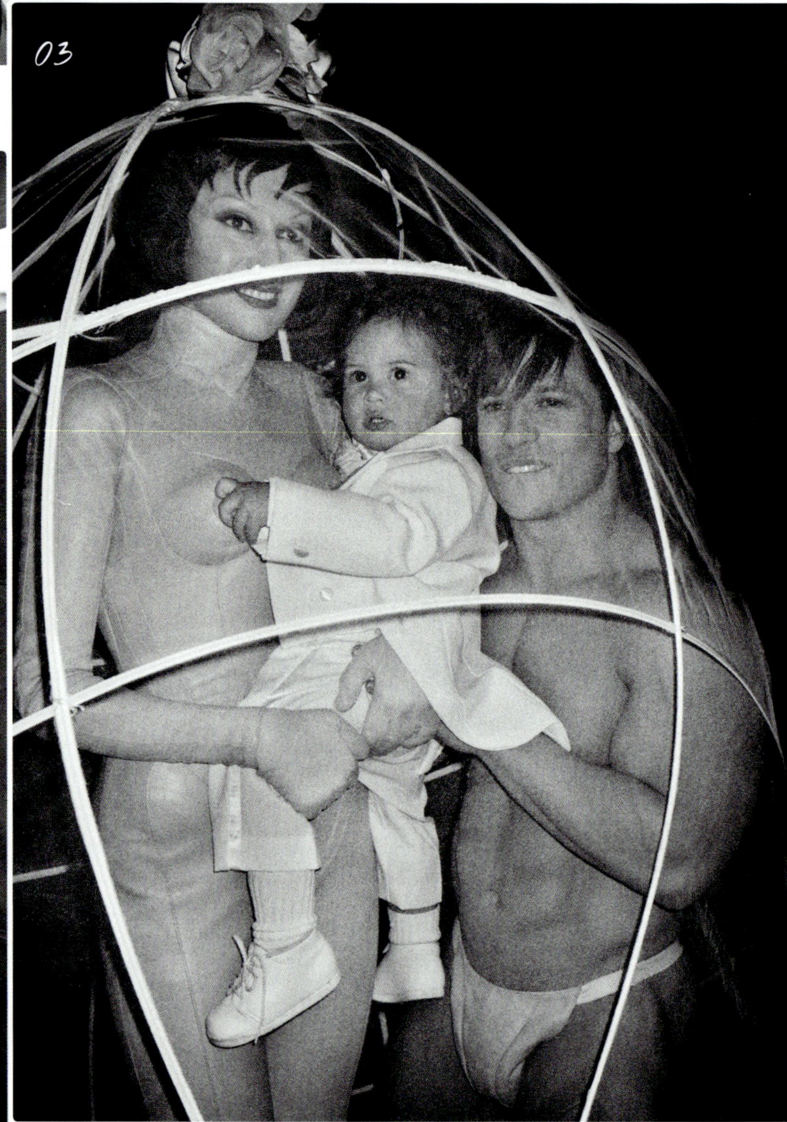

4 Susanne at the *Inspiration* fashion
show. Susanne was the bride at the
show's finale, May 1995. Photography
by Tim Palen.

5 Susanne backstage, getting ready
for the *Inspiration* fashion show,
which also served as her wedding
ceremony, 1995. © Patrick McMullan.

6 Susanne walking down the aisle
with David Barton, *Inspiration*
fashion show, May 1995.
© Patrick McMullan.

7 Thierry Mugler, Baroness,
Susanne, and David at their wedding
at Manhattan Center, May 1995.
Photography by Tim Palen.

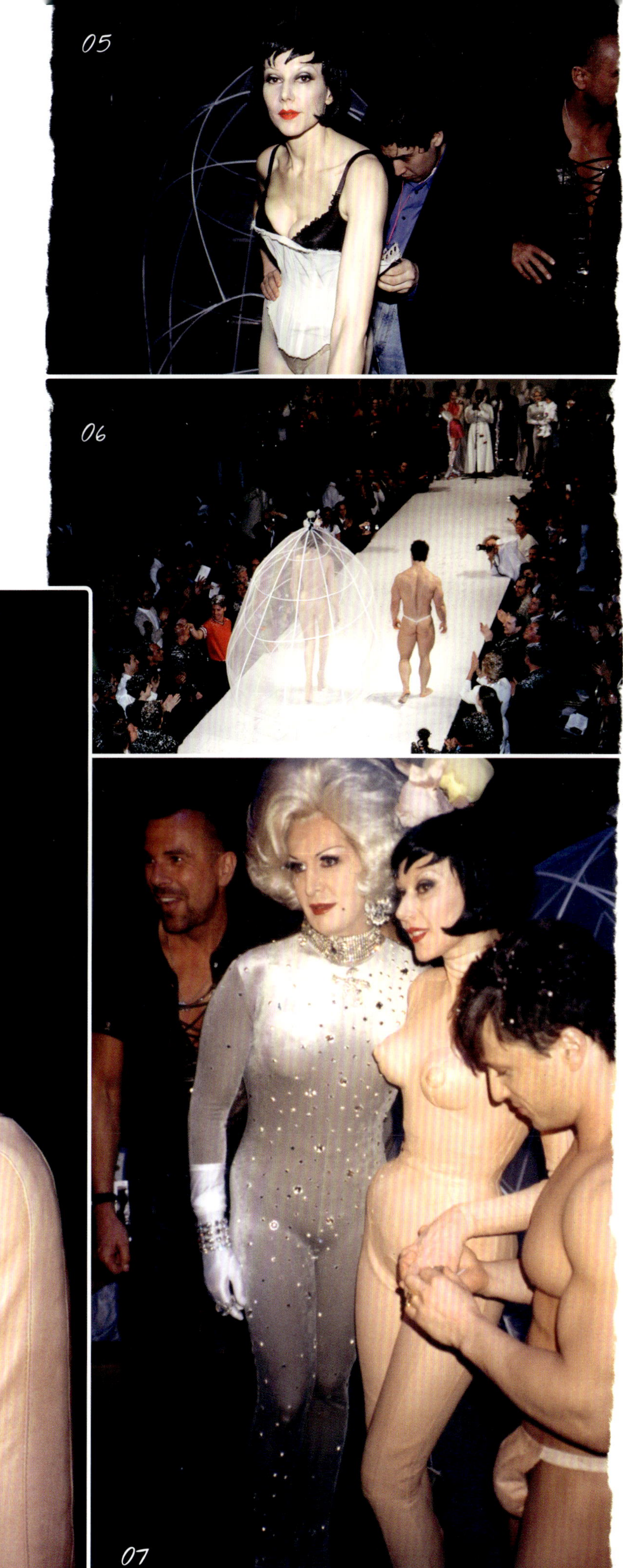

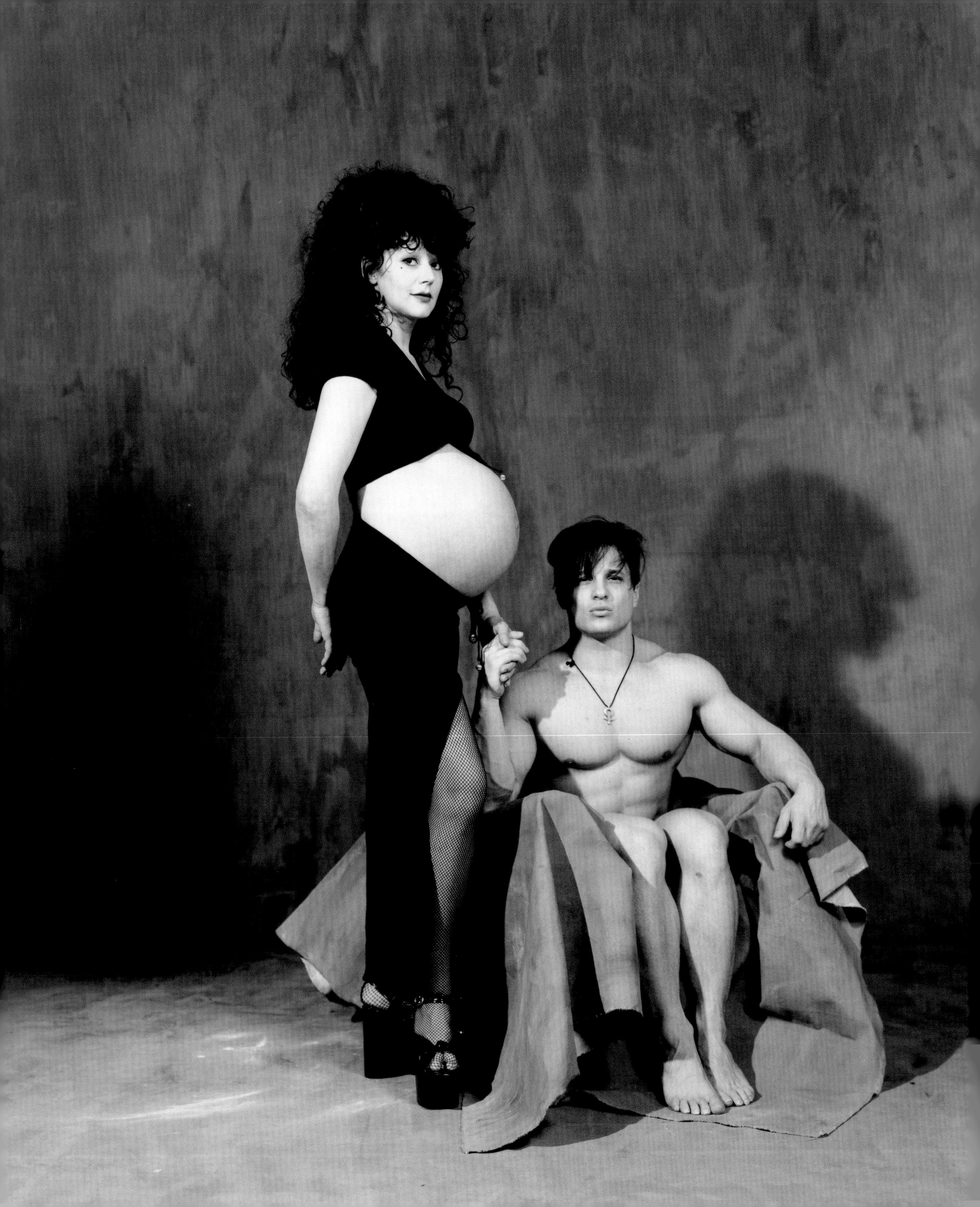

Facing: Susanne wearing Todd
Oldham with baby Bailey bump and
David Barton, taken the day before
Susanne gave birth, March 2, 1994.
Photo by Len Prince.

Below: Susanne and David Barton,
photoshoot for *Interview* magazine
at David Barton's gym.
Photo © Steven Klein Studio.

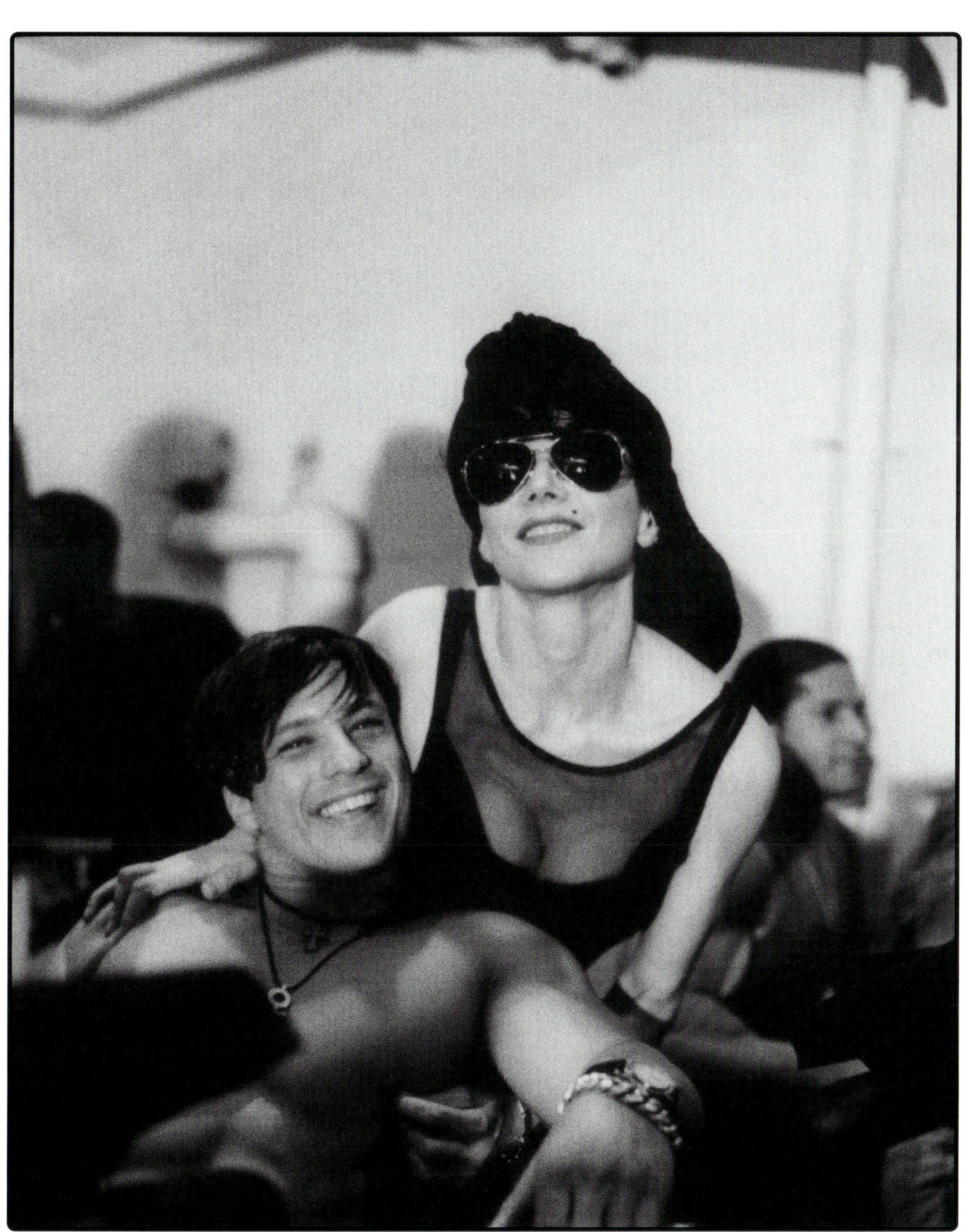

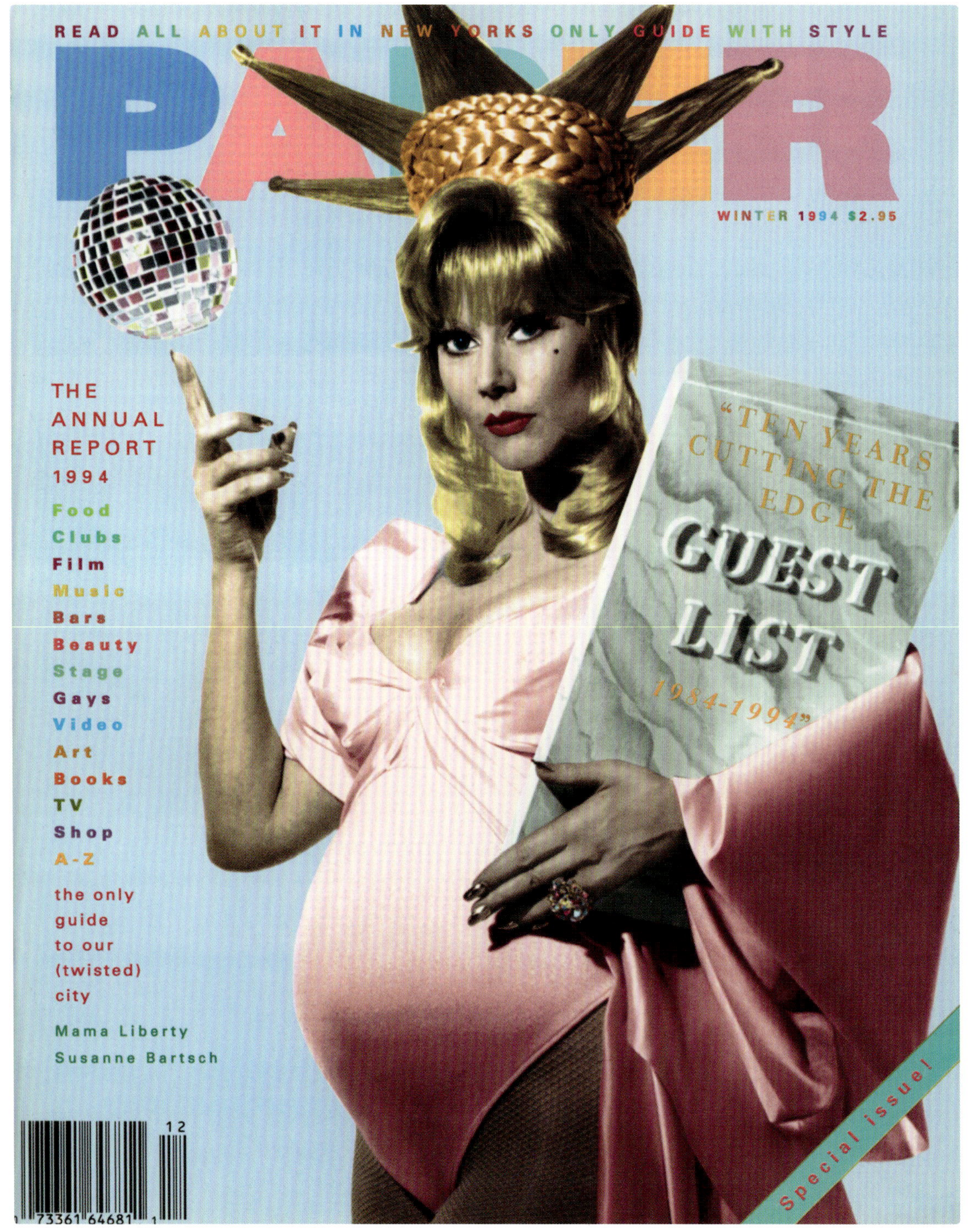

"A very pregnant Susanne Bartsch photographed as the Statue of Liberty." *Paper*, winter 1994. Photo by Mark Contratto, courtesy of *Paper* magazine.

Facing, clockwise from top left: Susanne with baby Bailey at the opening of the Delano Hotel in Miami Beach, circa 1995. © Patrick McMullan.

Family time for Susanne with husband, David, and son, Bailey. Photo by Roxanne Lowit.

Baroness with Bailey on thousands of lollipops, the décor for a New Year's eve party at Delano Hotel in Miami Beach. Courtesy of Susanne Bartsh.

Susanne with her son Bailey at her Delano Hotel suite, Miami Beach, 1997. Courtesy of Susanne Bartsch.

Family outing with Bailey and Schnauzie, 2000. © Patrick McMullan

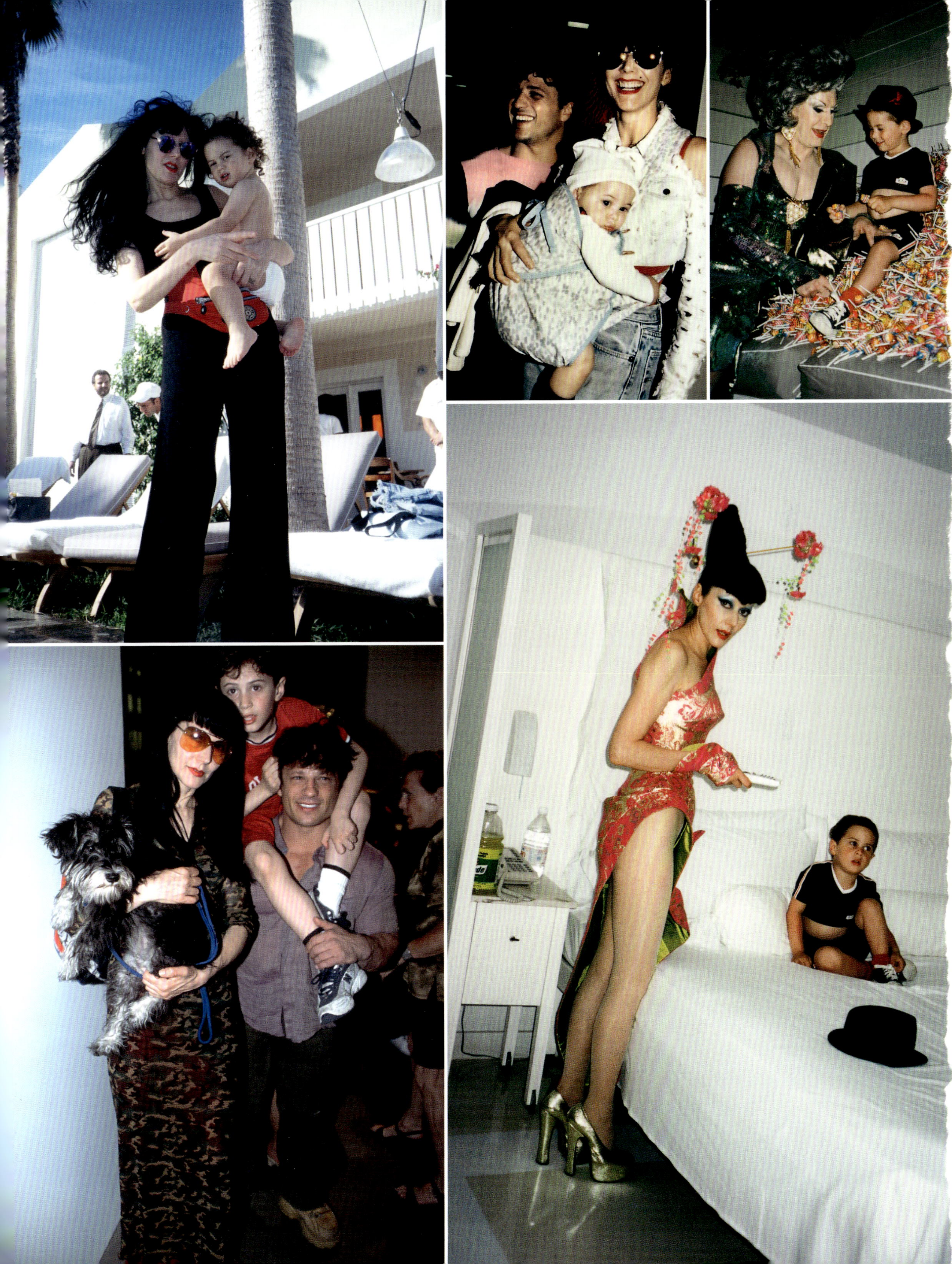

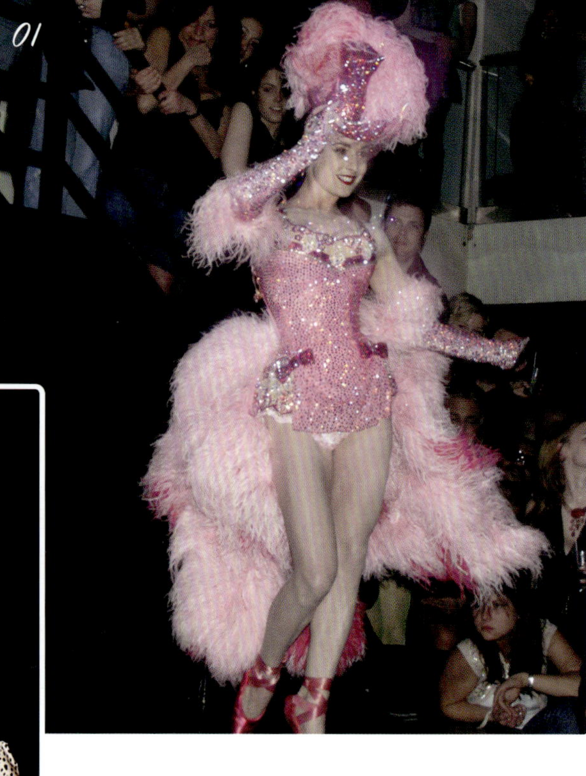

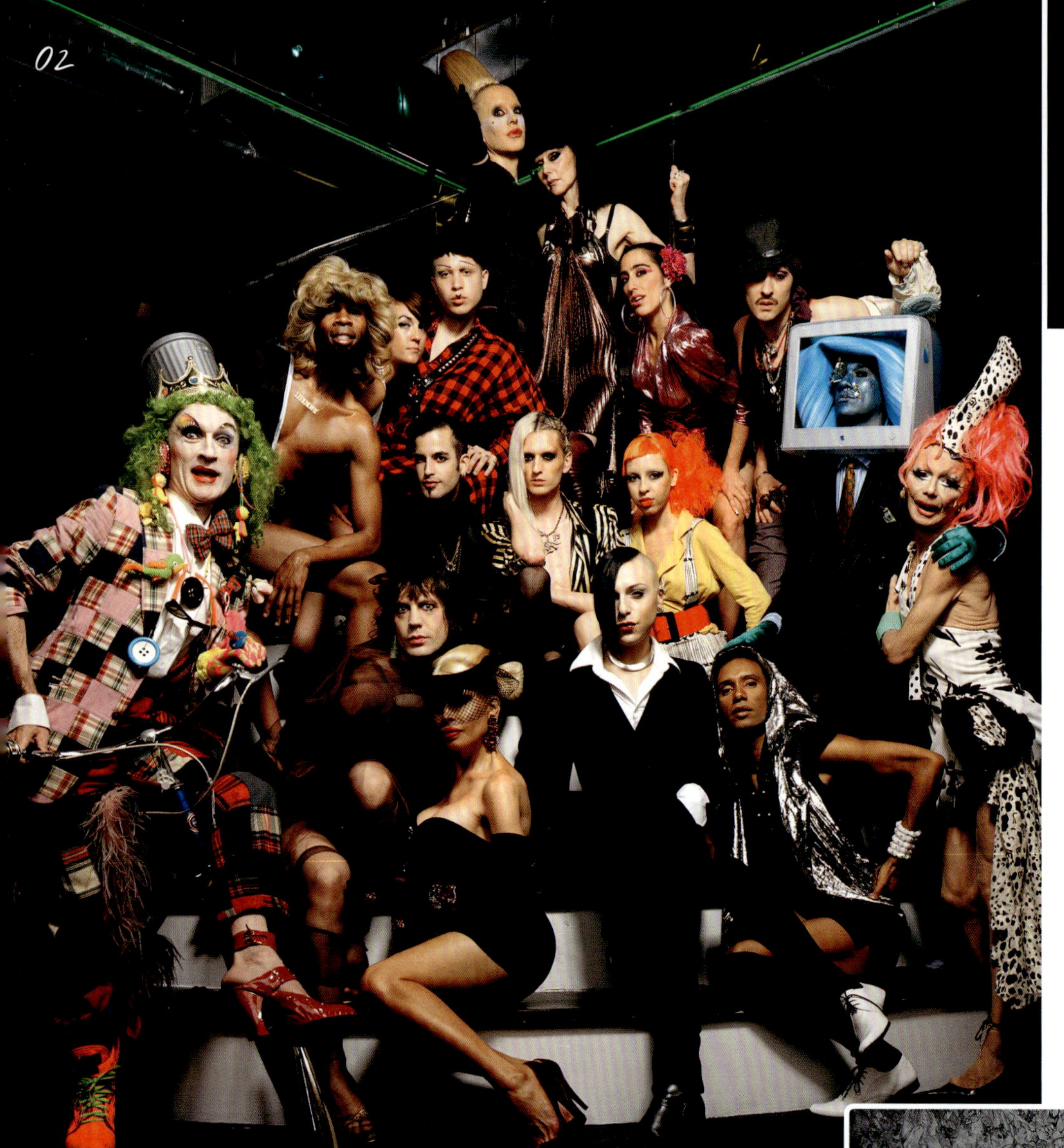

1 Special performance by Dita Von Teese at Happy Valley, New York City, 2006. Photo © Tina Paul, 2006. All Rights Reserved.

2 Susanne's comeback in night life, the Happy Valley party. From top, left to right: Kenny Kenny, Susanne Bartsch, Andre J, Chase Elder, Neon Music, Ladyfag, Jolo Americano, Gazelle, Lavinia Coop, Magal, Tre Knight, Raquel Reed, Flawless Mother Sabrina, Brandon Olson, Amanda Lepore, Moondust, Paul Alexander. Happy Valley, New York, 2006. Photo by Jesse Chehak.

3 Susanne in a Zaldy outfit, with Riccardo Tisci at Vandam Sunday party, 2012. Photo by Marco Ovando.

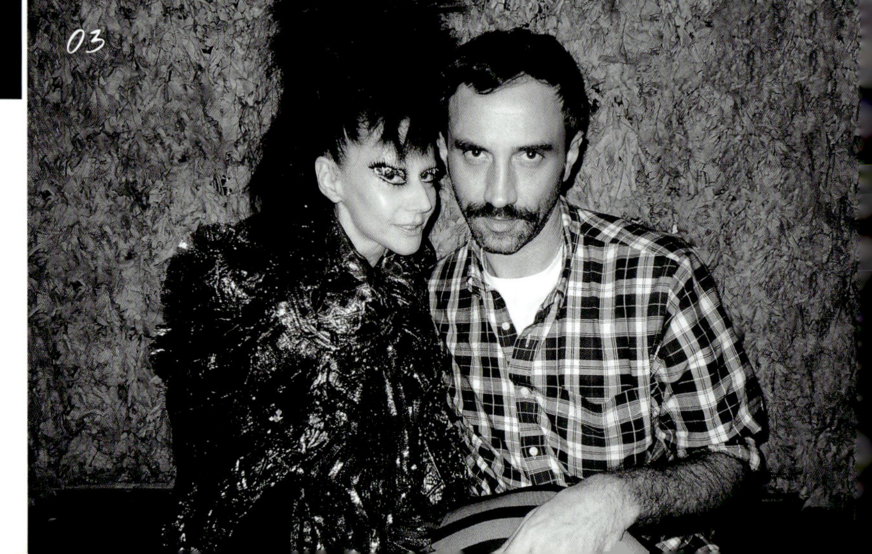

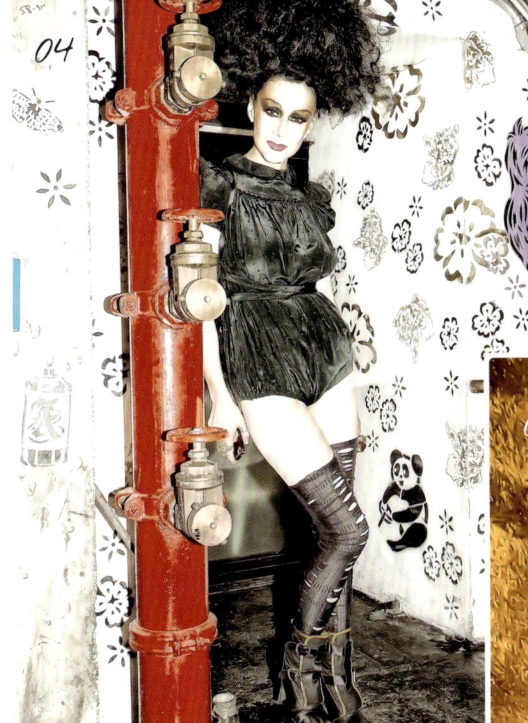

4 Susanne at *On Top* at the Standard Hotel. Photo by Robin Souma.

5 Susanne at a Swiss dance event at the Tribeca Grand Hotel, January 2015. Photo by Robin Souma.

6 Susanne hosting Valentine's party at Capitale with Patricia Field, 2011. Susanne's look by Chris March. Photo by Robin Souma.

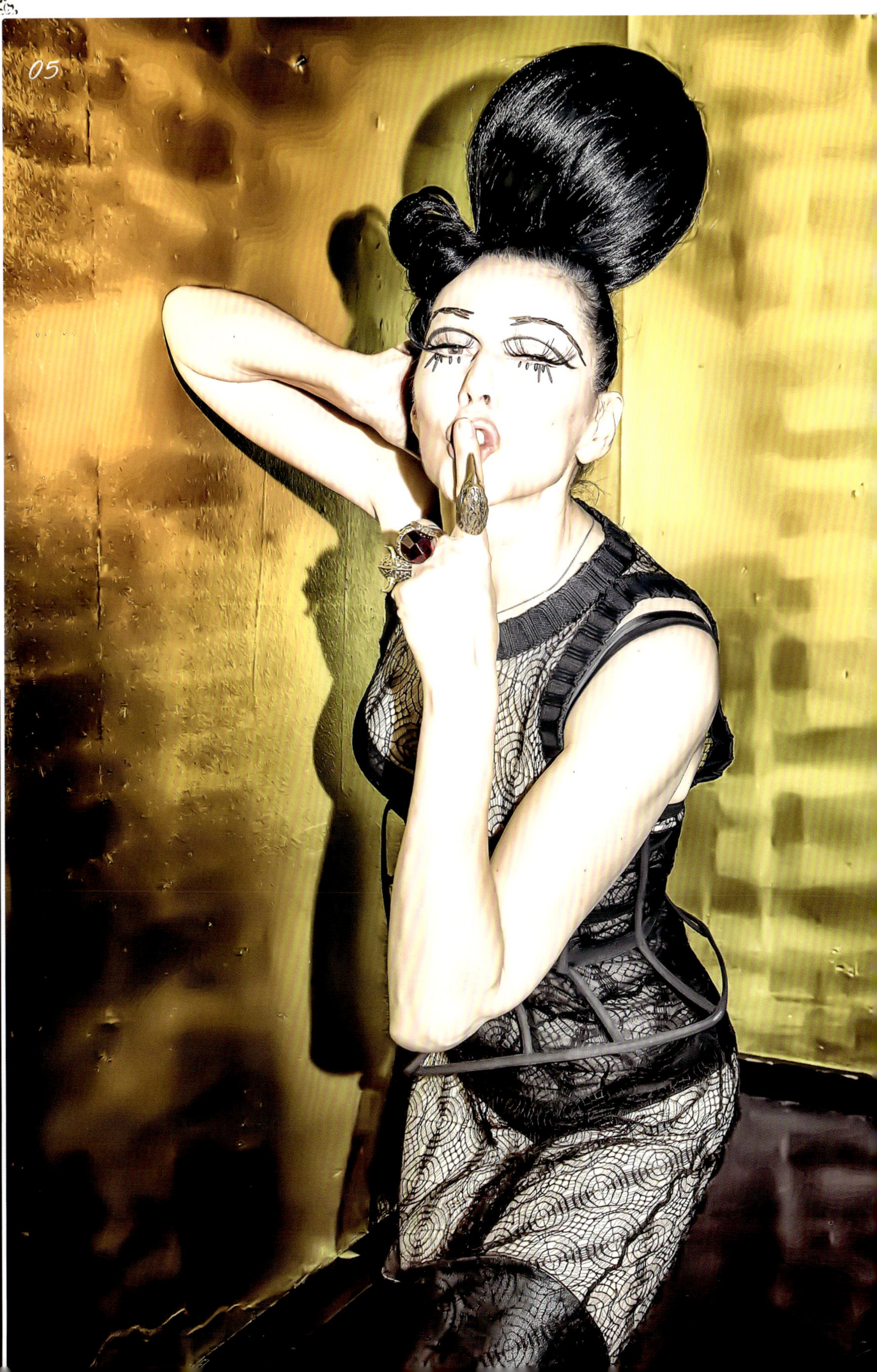

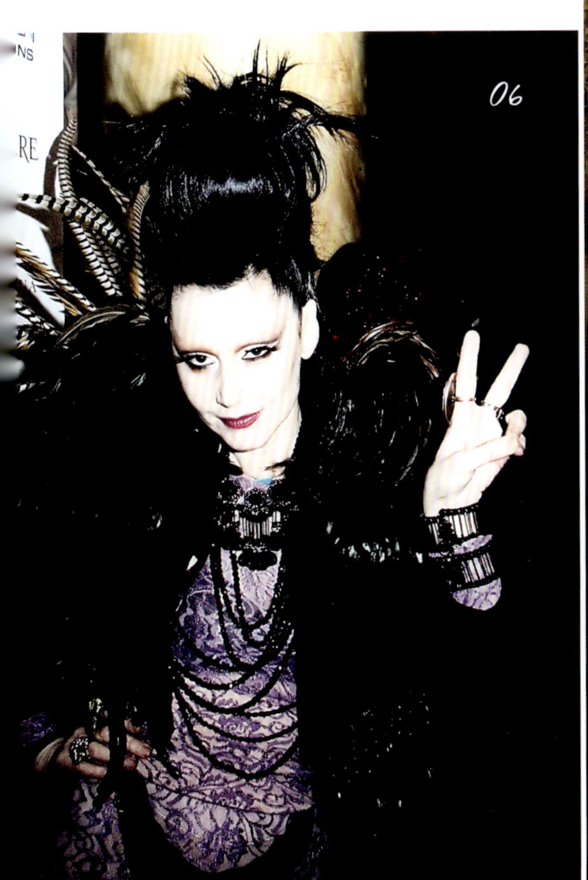

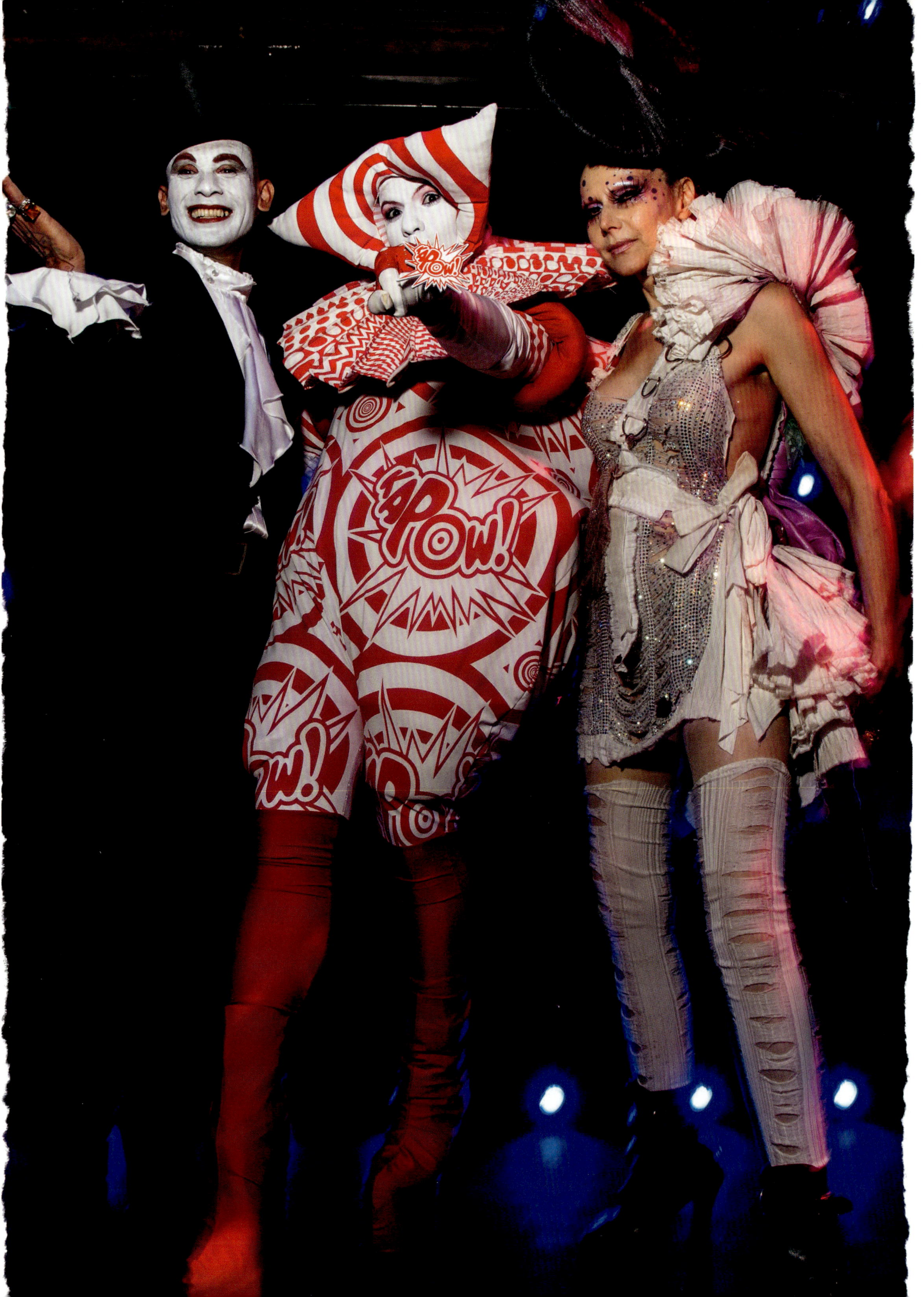
POW!
POW!
POW!

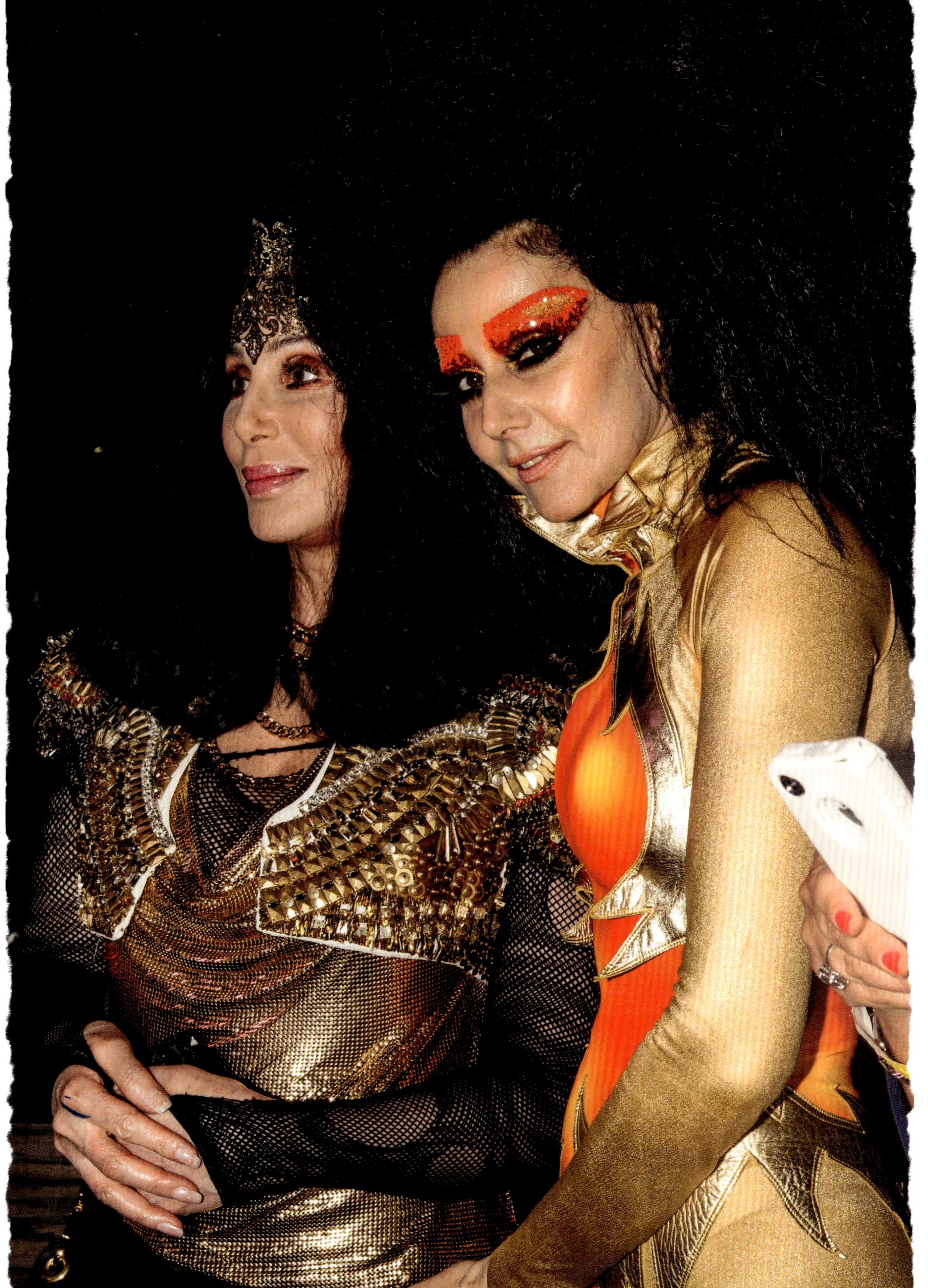

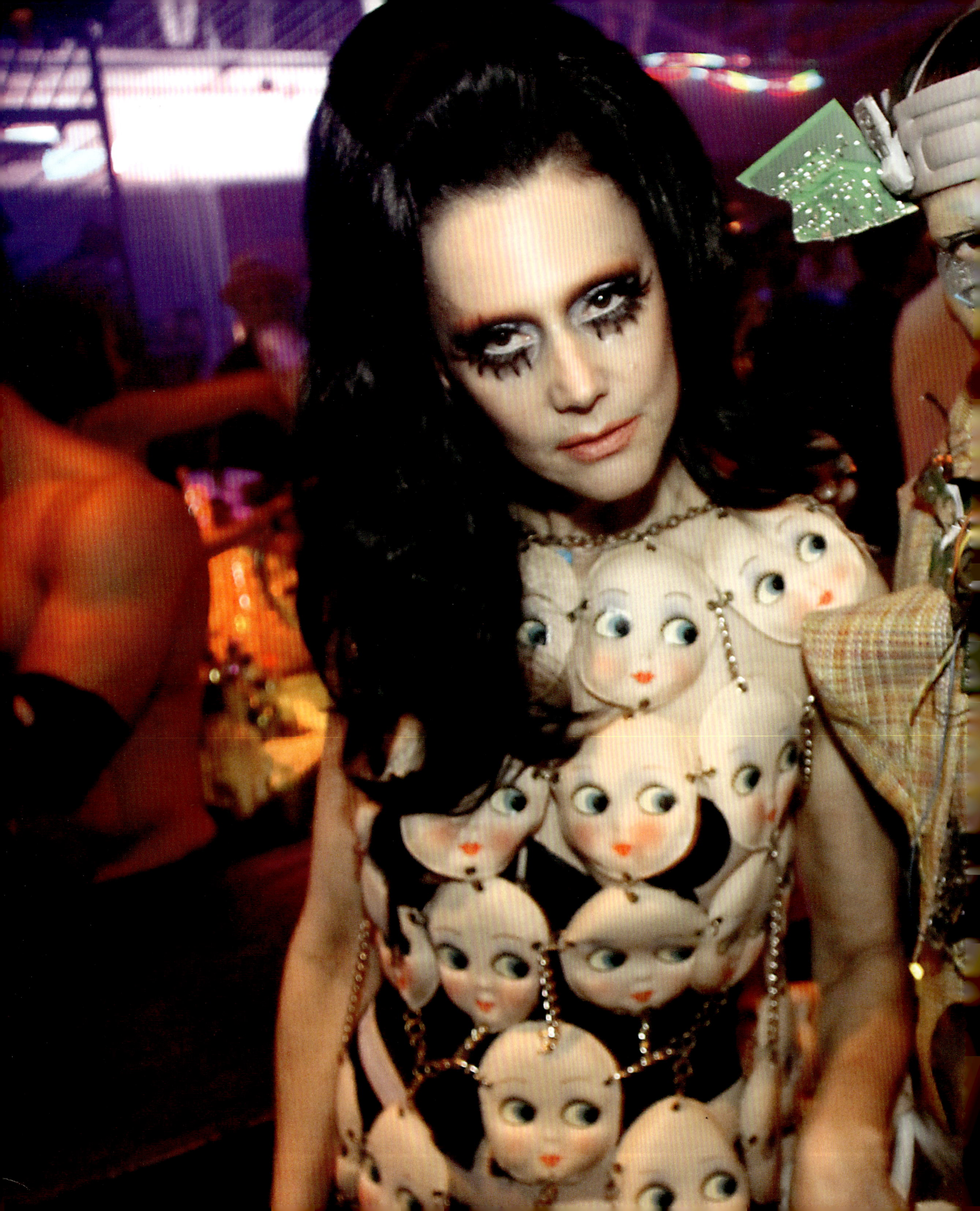

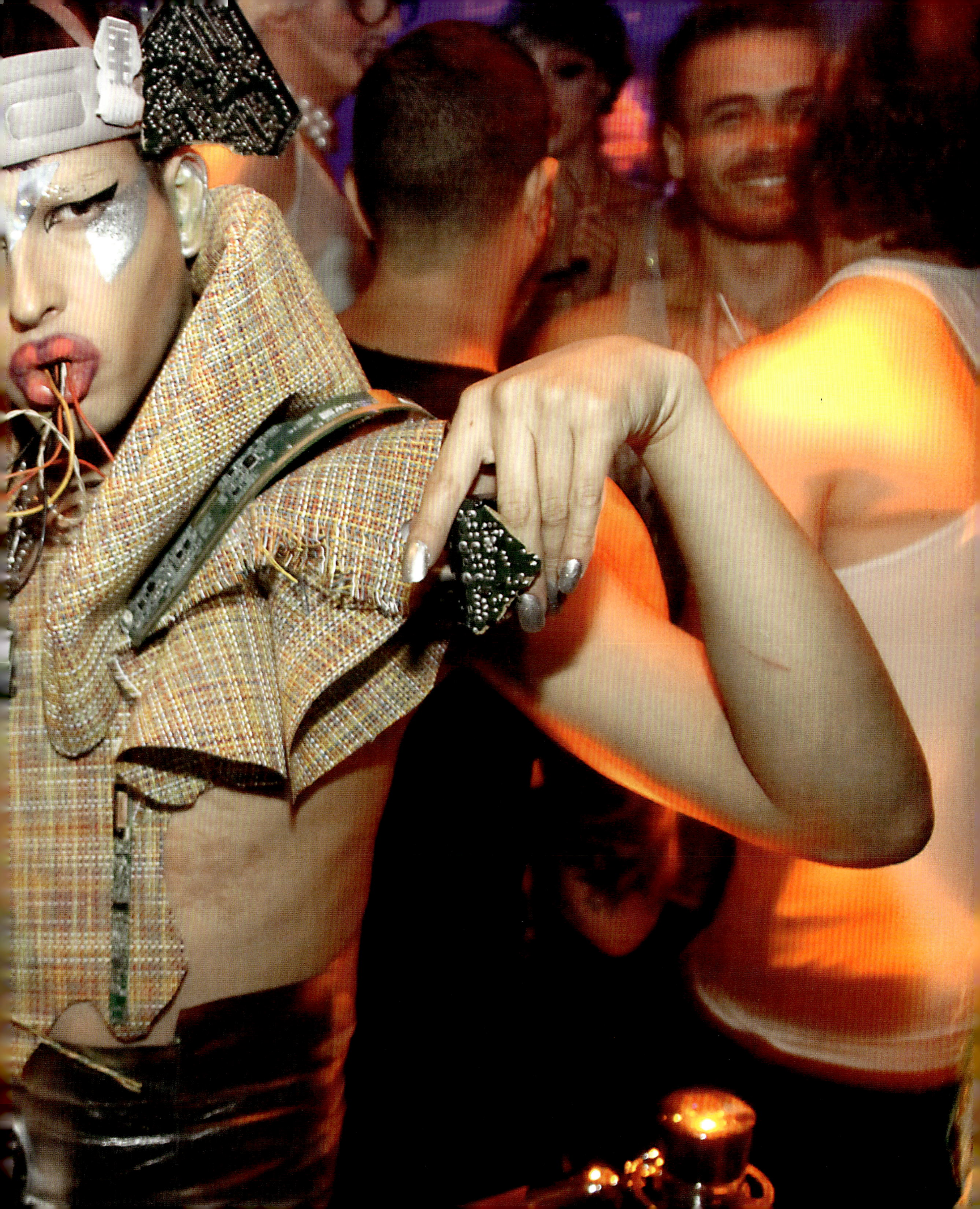

Page 92: Susanne in a Zaldy dress, with Muffinhead (center) at *Catwalk*, 2013. Photo by Mark Williams.

Page 93: Susanne at her *Catwalk* party with Cher, outfit by Mathu and Zaldy, 2013. Portrait by Rico & Michael.

Pages 94–5: Susanne with Gage of the Boone in vintage Mr. Pearl at Marquee, 2013. Photo © Wilson Models.

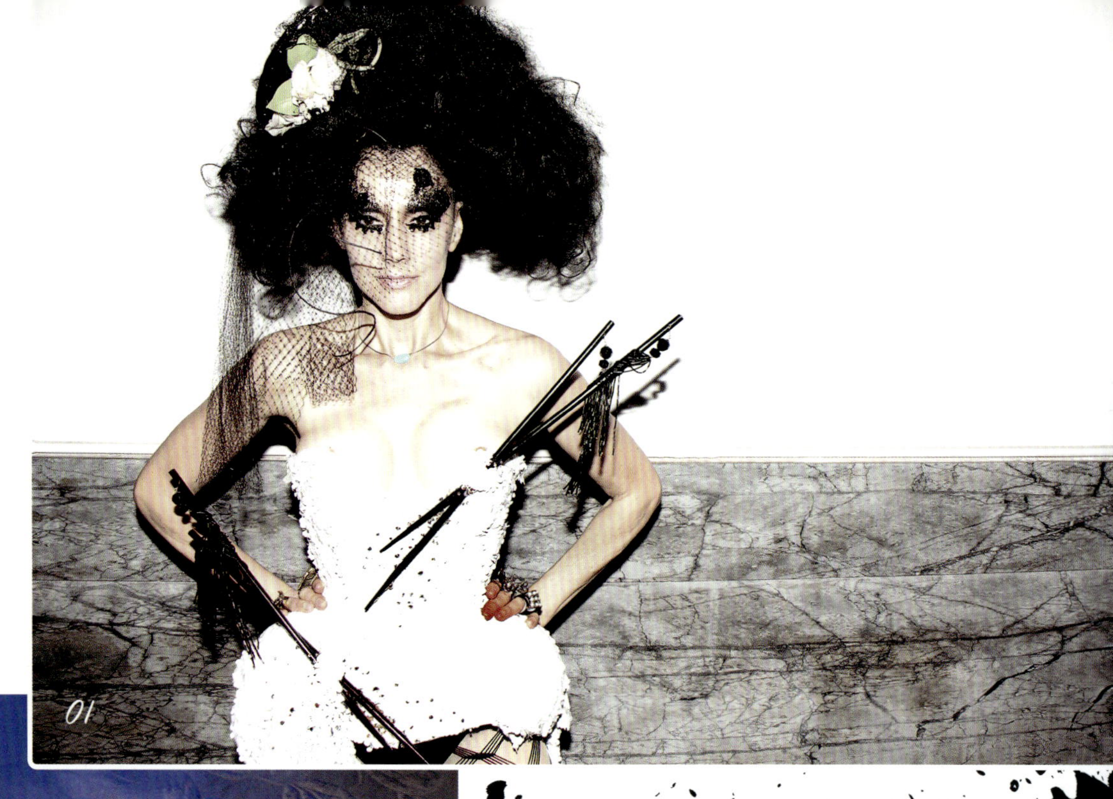

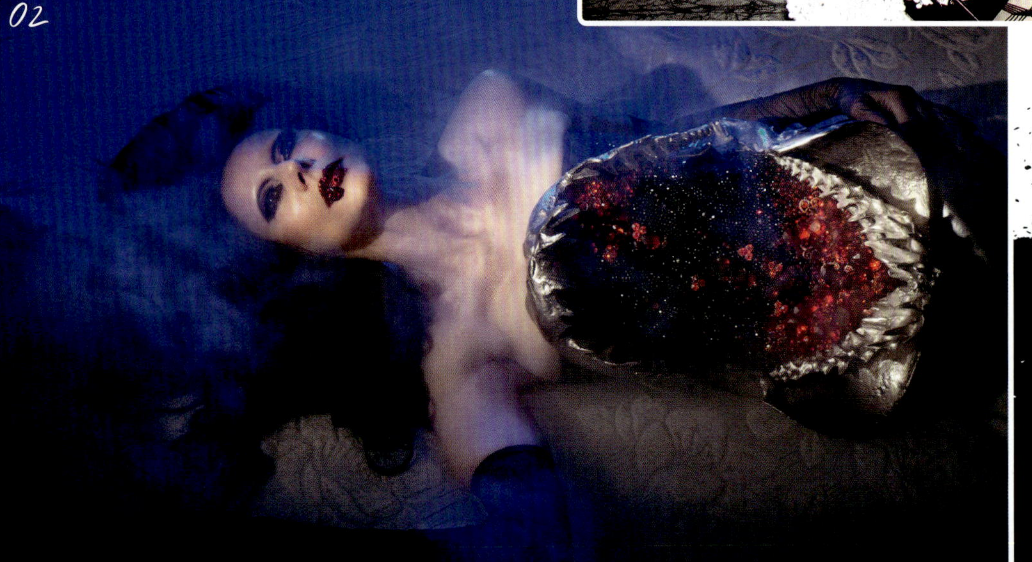

1 Susanne in the Chelsea Hotel Lobby, wearing corset by The Blonds, 2012. Photo by Marco Ovando.

2 *Annabelle* magazine, photoshoot, Zurich, 2013. Portrait by Rico & Michael.

3 Invitation for *On Top*, at the Standard Hotel, 2014. Photo by Robin Souma.

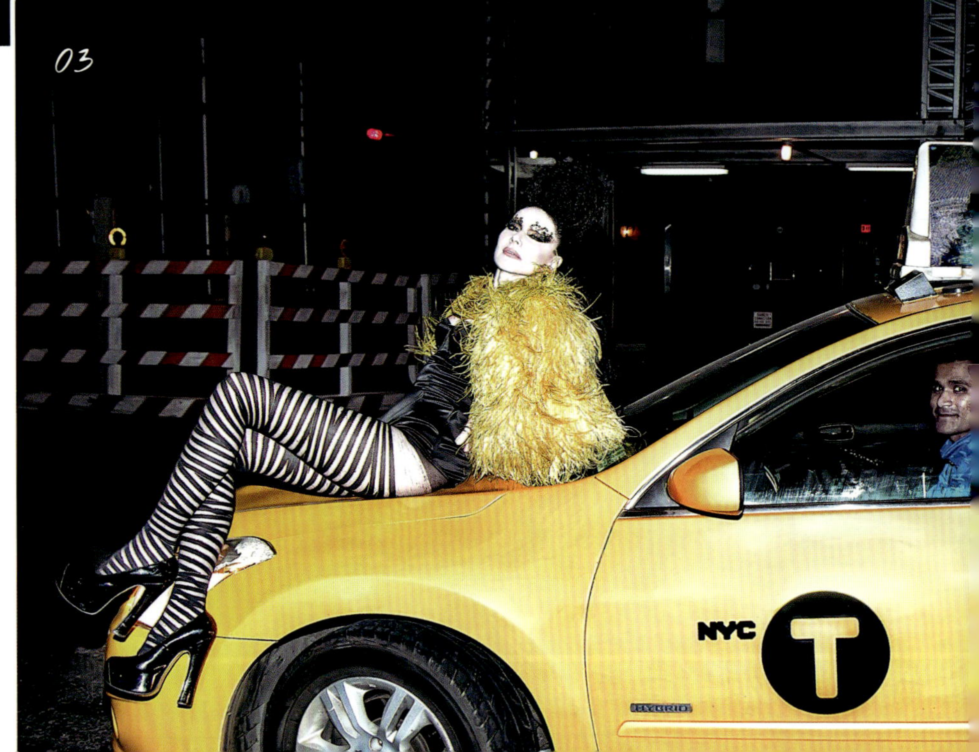

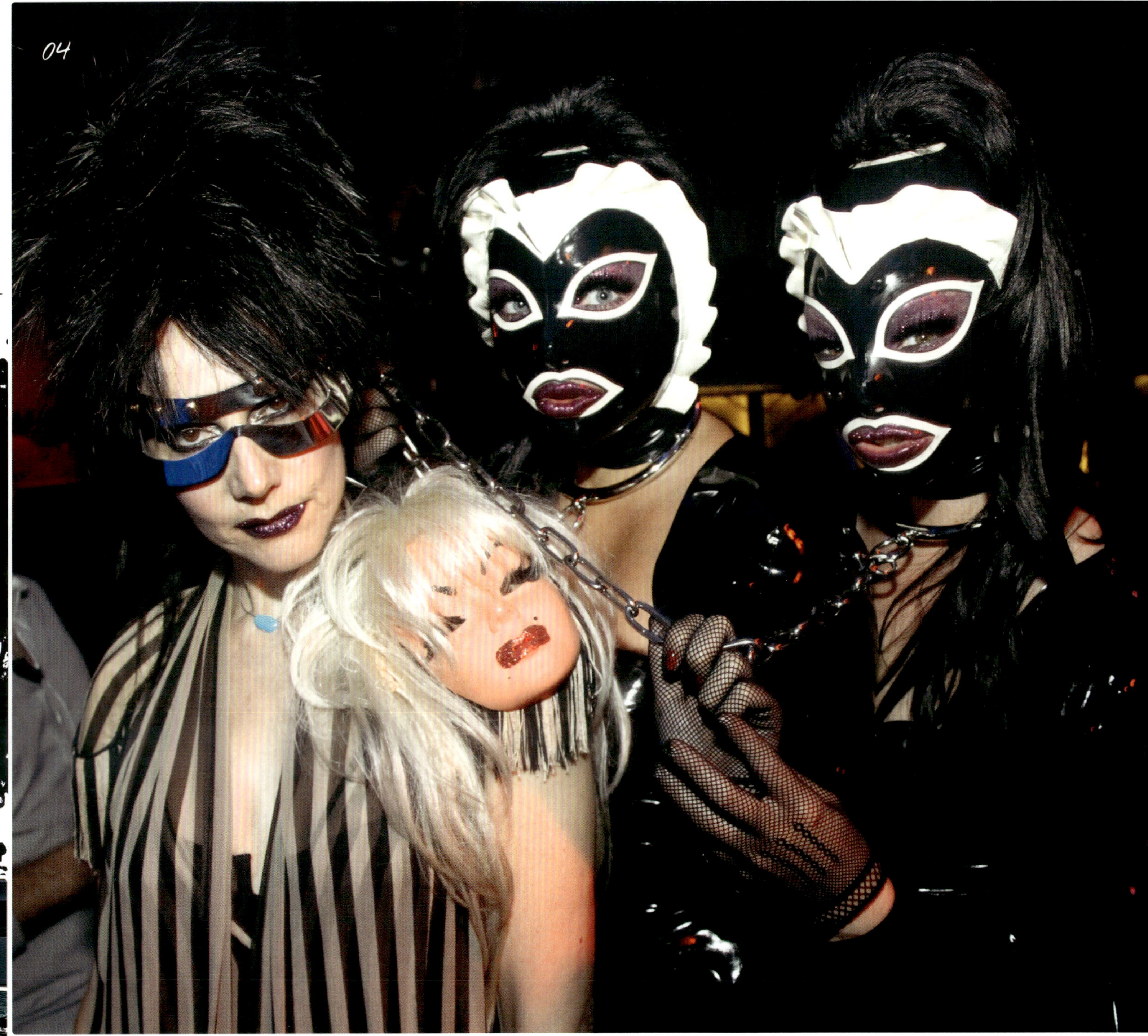

4 Susanne with the Daughters of
Devotion at Marquee, 2013.
Photo © Wilsonmodels.

Following spread: The Catwalk crew
at Marquee, 2013. Photo by Jason
Akira Somma.

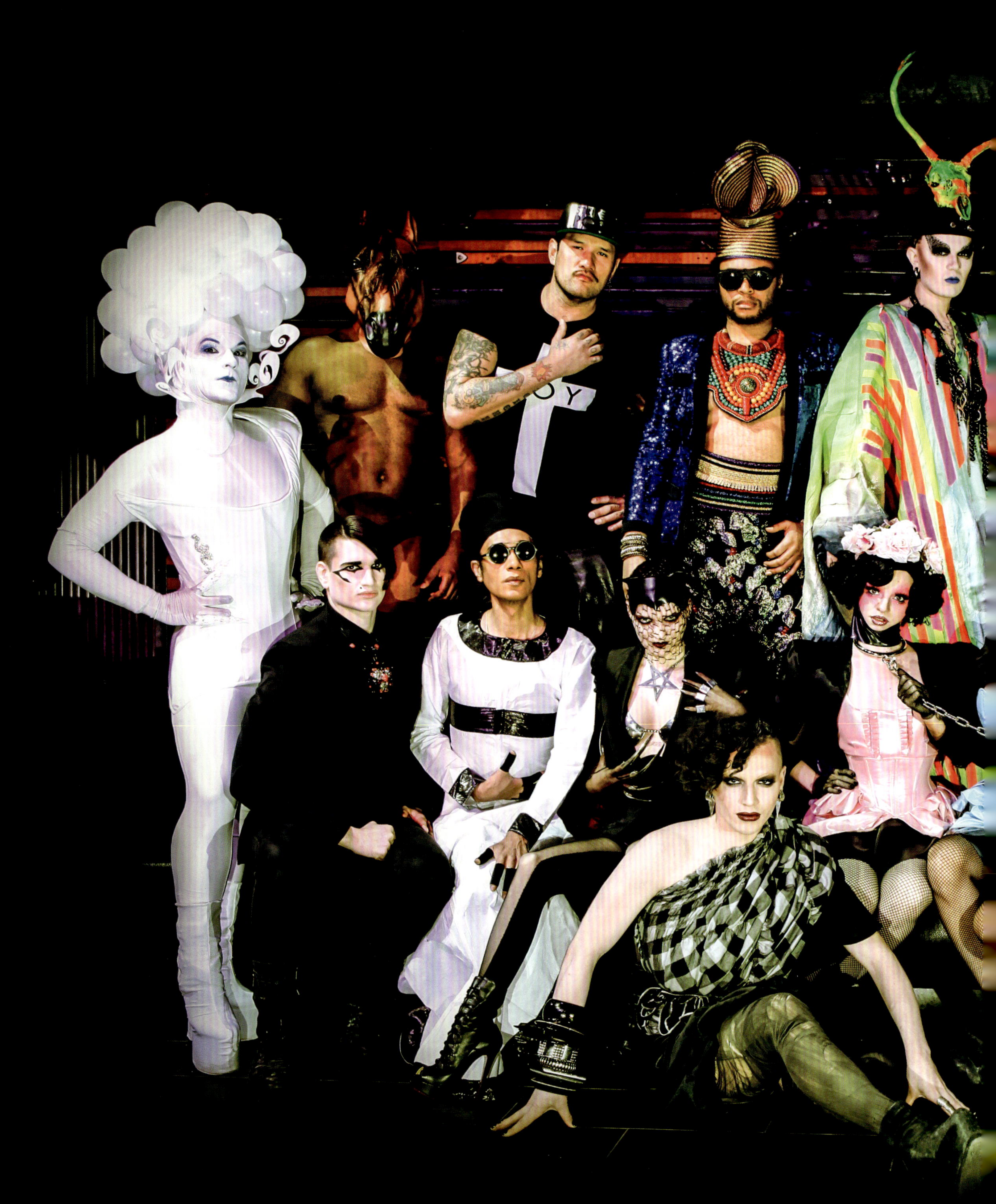

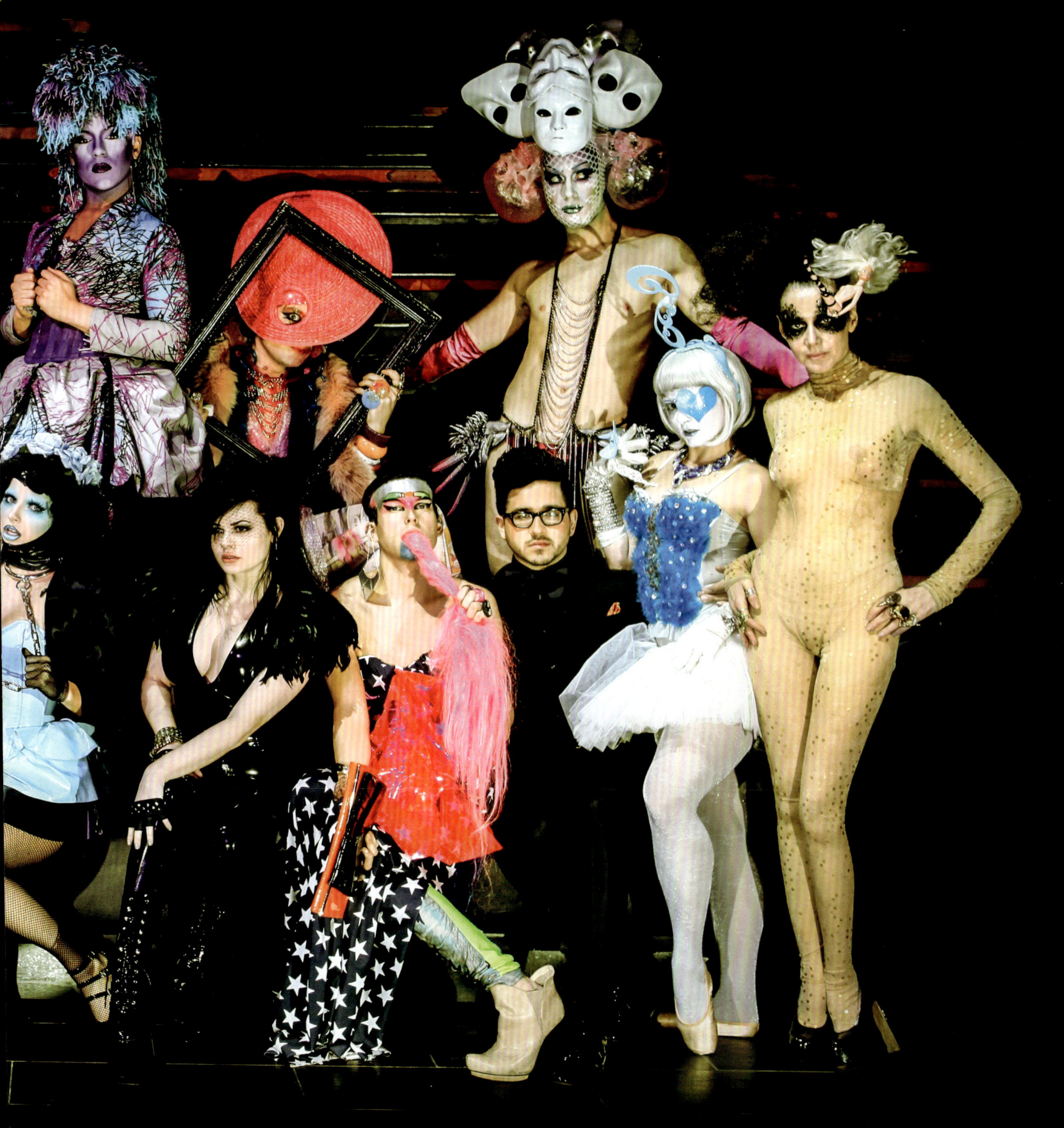

Salon at Soho Grand, 2014

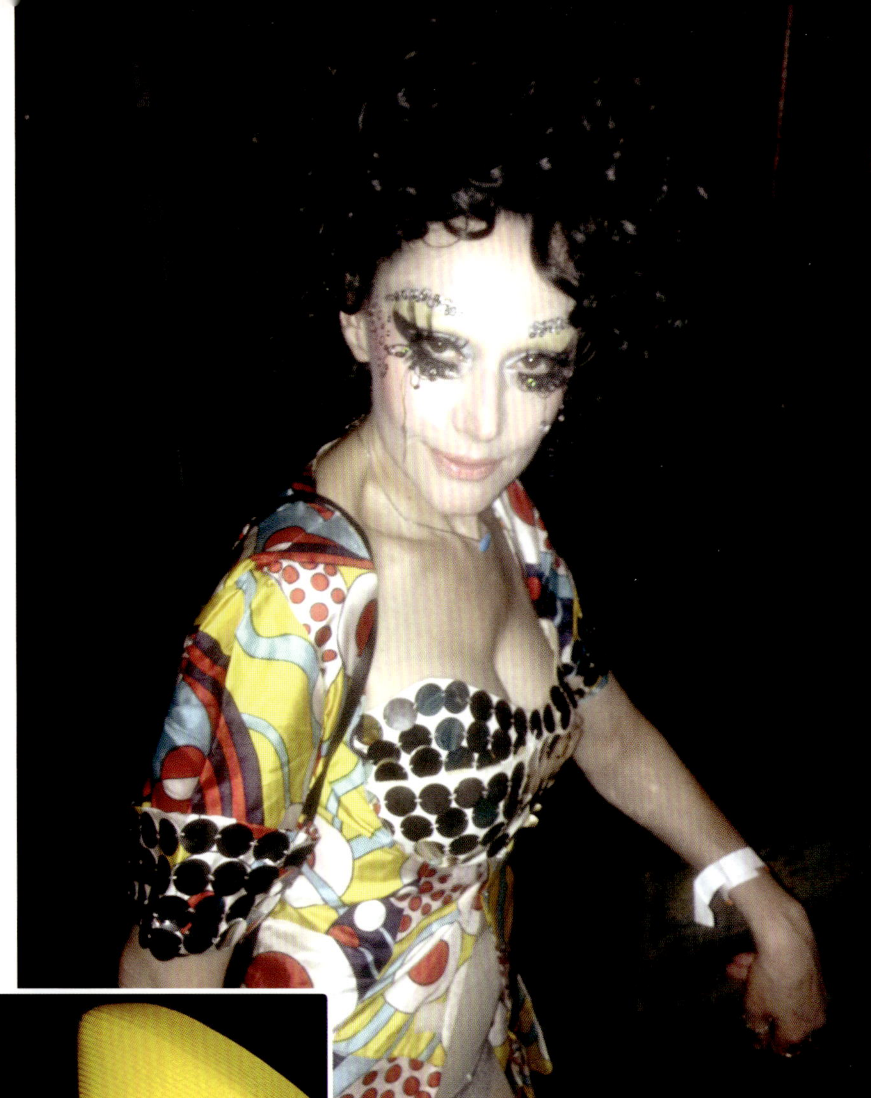

Right: Susanne wearing a
Rachel Auburn dress at Salon,
Soho Grand, 2014.
Photo by Mao Padilha.

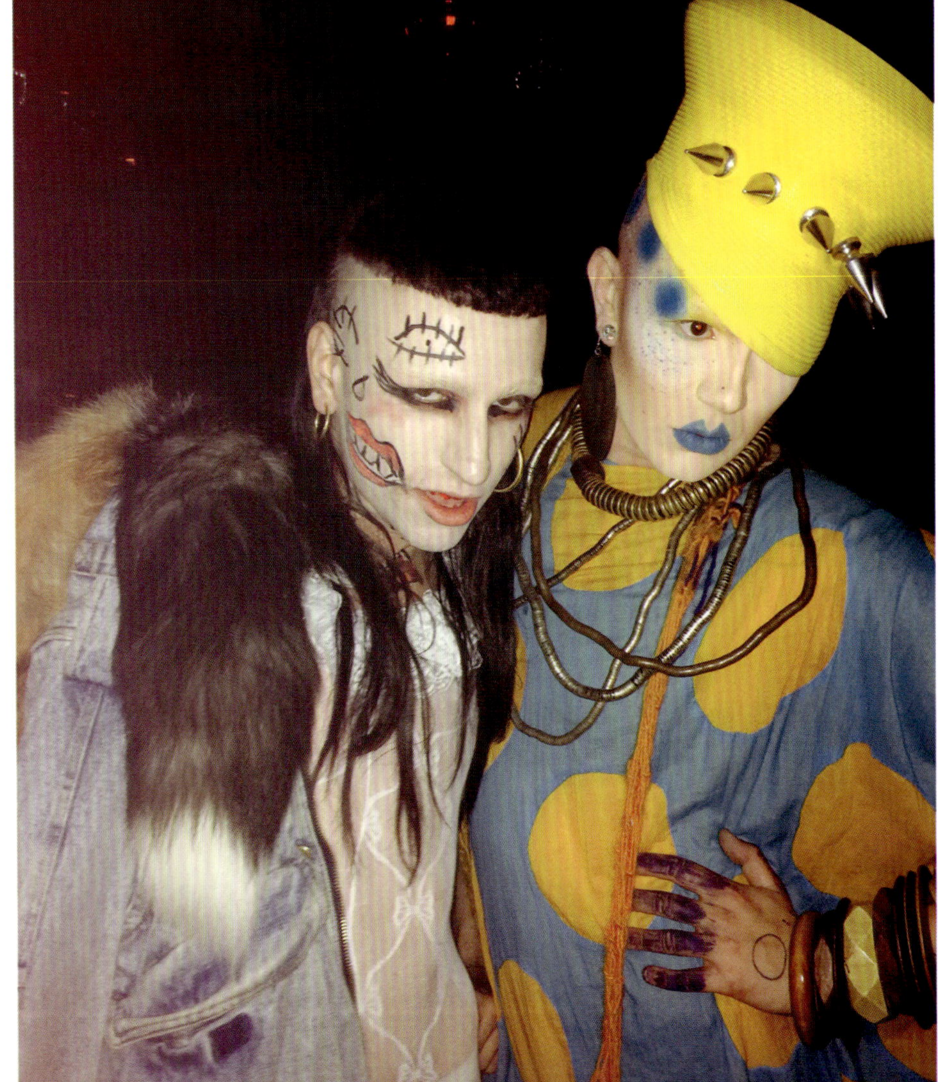

Left: Andy Bradin of Disco
Smack with Onehalf Nelson at
On Top, Summer 2014.
Courtesy of Susanne Bartsch.

Facing: Susanne in a Zaldy
outfit with Brandon Olson, 2013.
Photo by Mark Williams.

On Top, Summer 2014

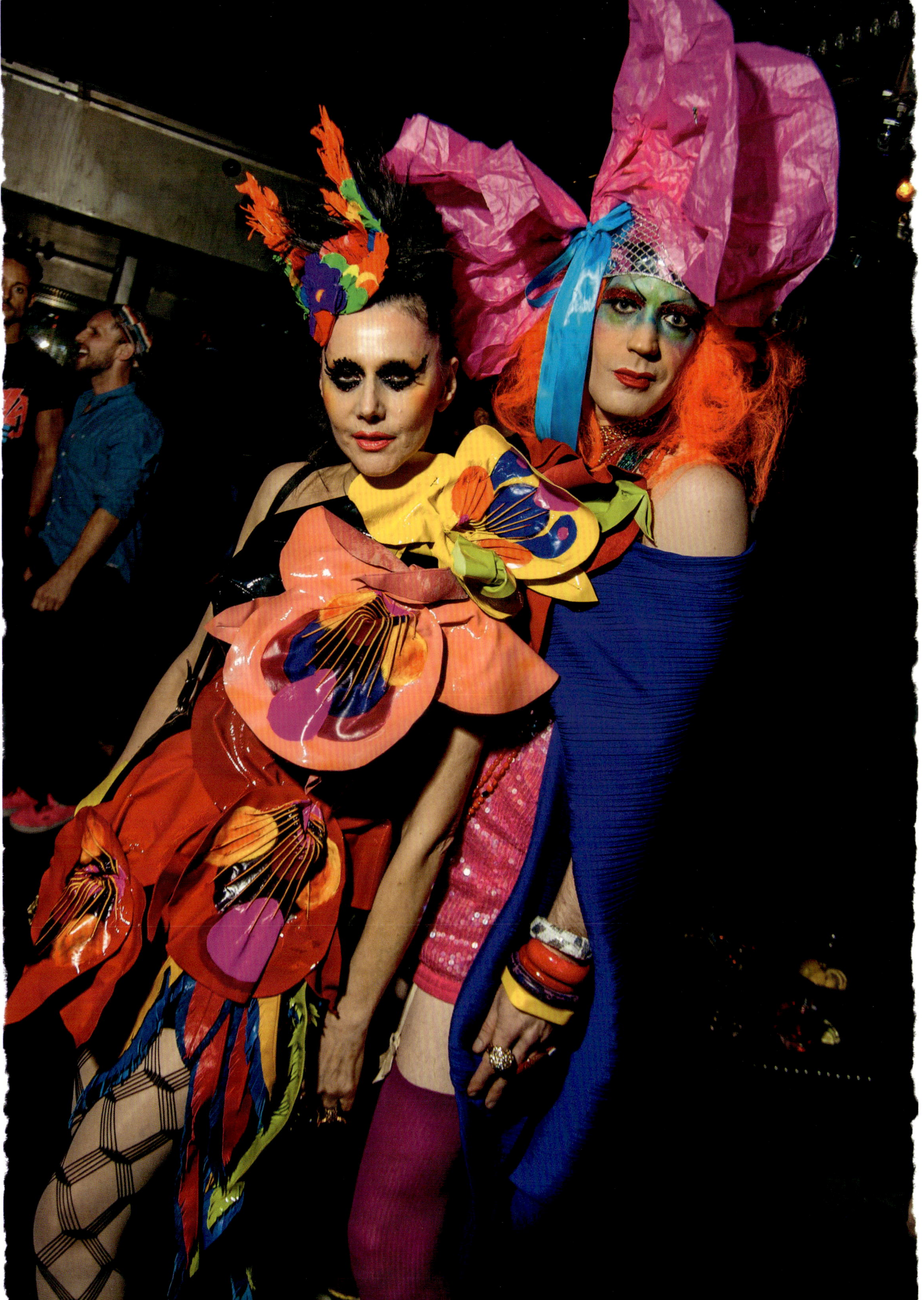

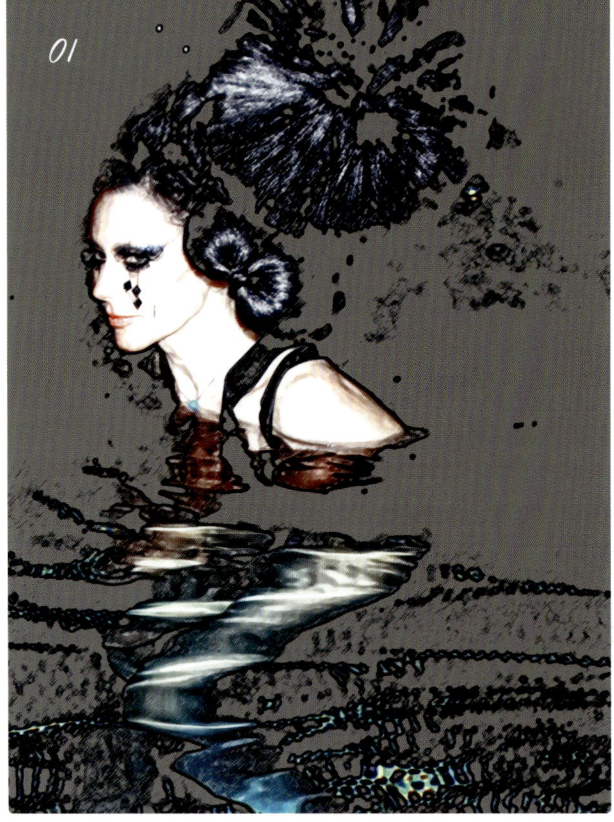

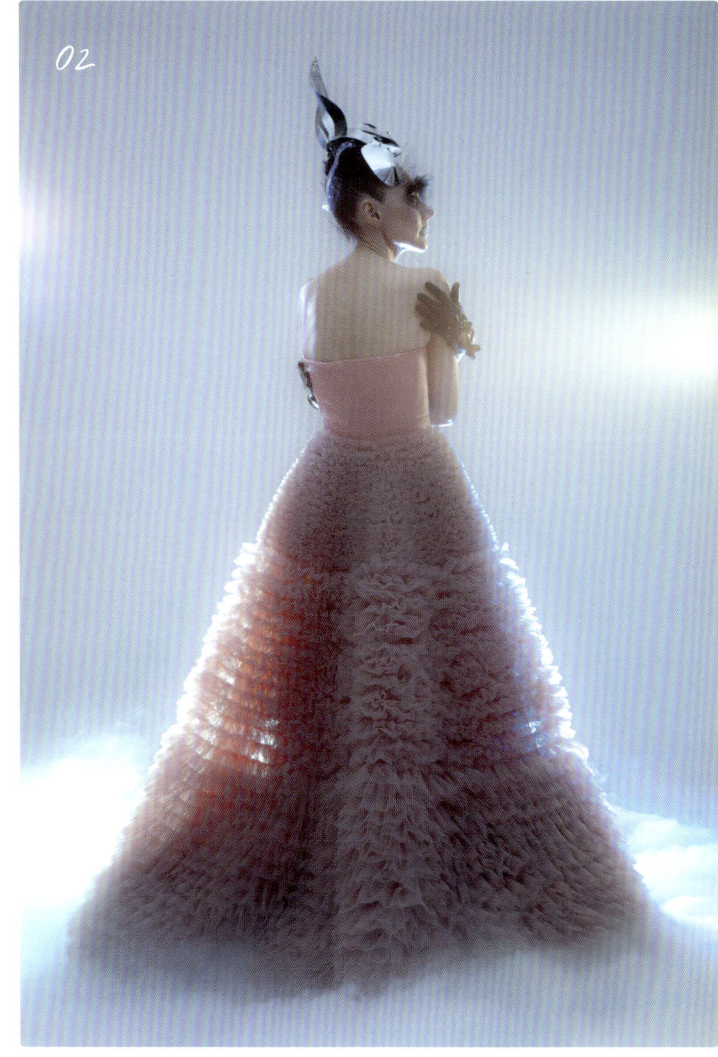

1 Invitation for On Top summer party at the Standard Hotel, 2000s. Photo by Robin Souma.

2 *Annabelle* magazine photoshoot, Zurich, 2013. Portrait by Rico & Michael.

3 Susanne with François Sagat at the Bloody Mary Halloween party, New York City, October 2010. Photo by Ves Pitts.

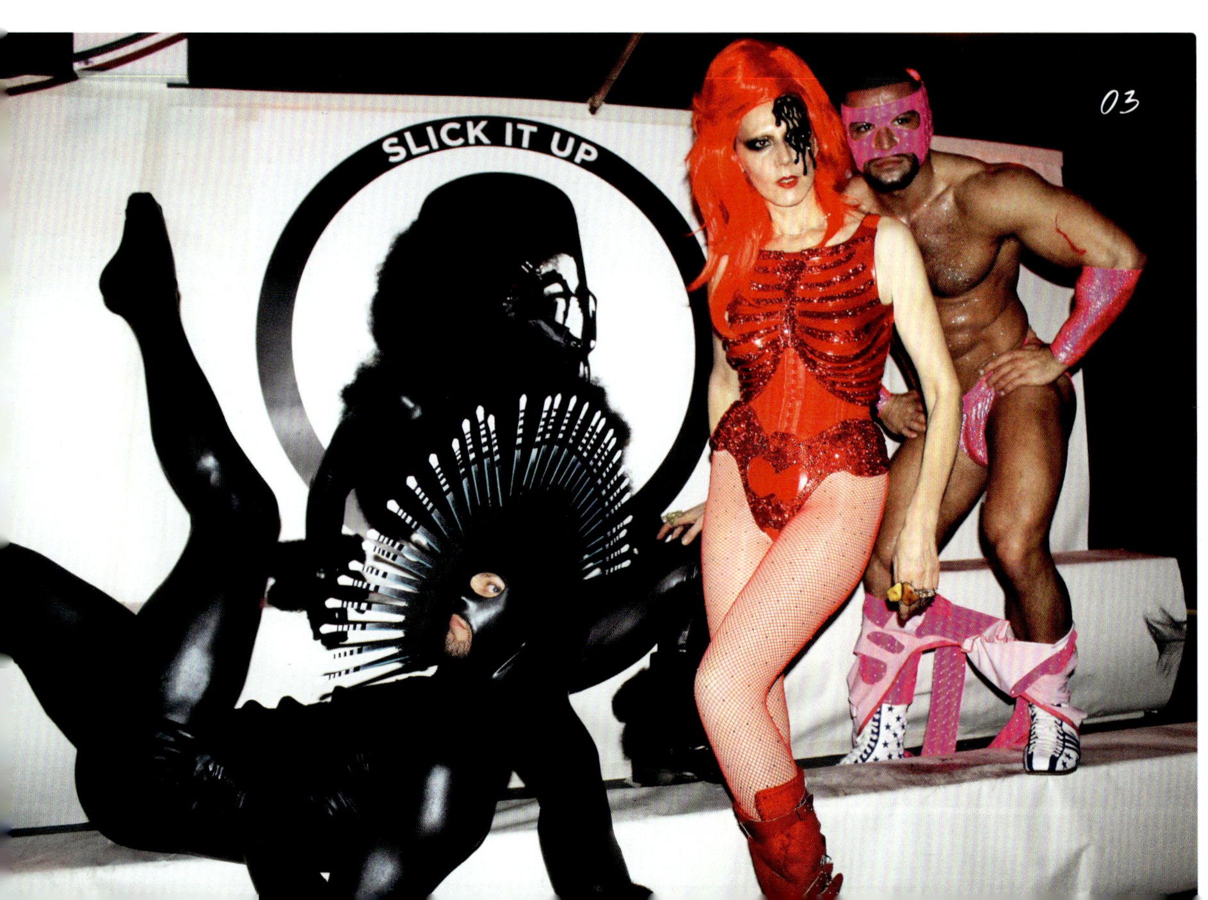

Page 104: Susanne at Catwalk, 2013. Dress by Zaldy. Photo by Mark Williams.

Page 105: Susanne at Catwalk, held weekly on Thursdays at Marquee, 2013. Photo by Mark Williams.

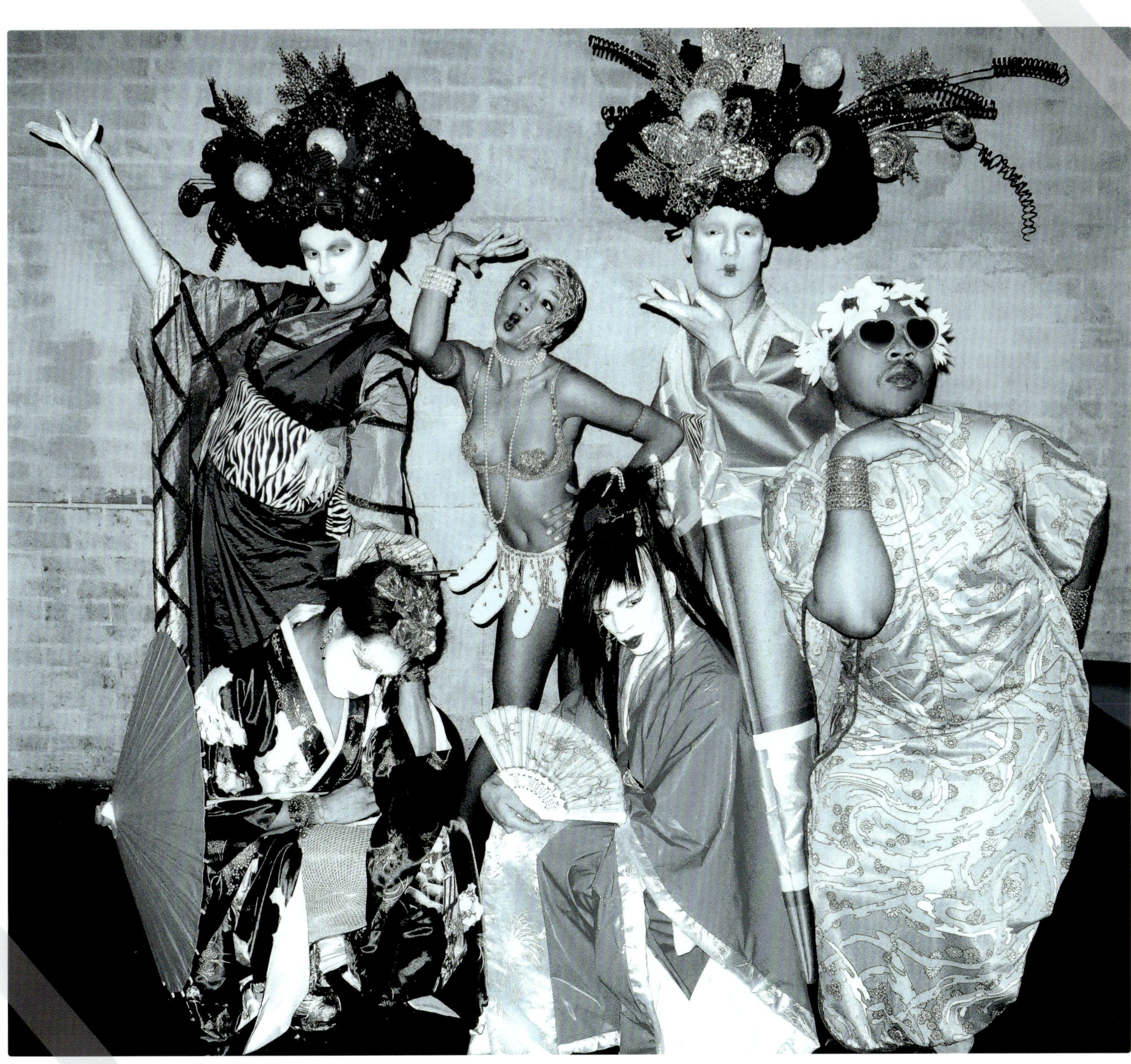

Buddhakan Halloween, Onehalf
Nelson, Erickatoure Aviance,
and a Bevy of Labeijas, 2013.
Photo by Citizen Chris.

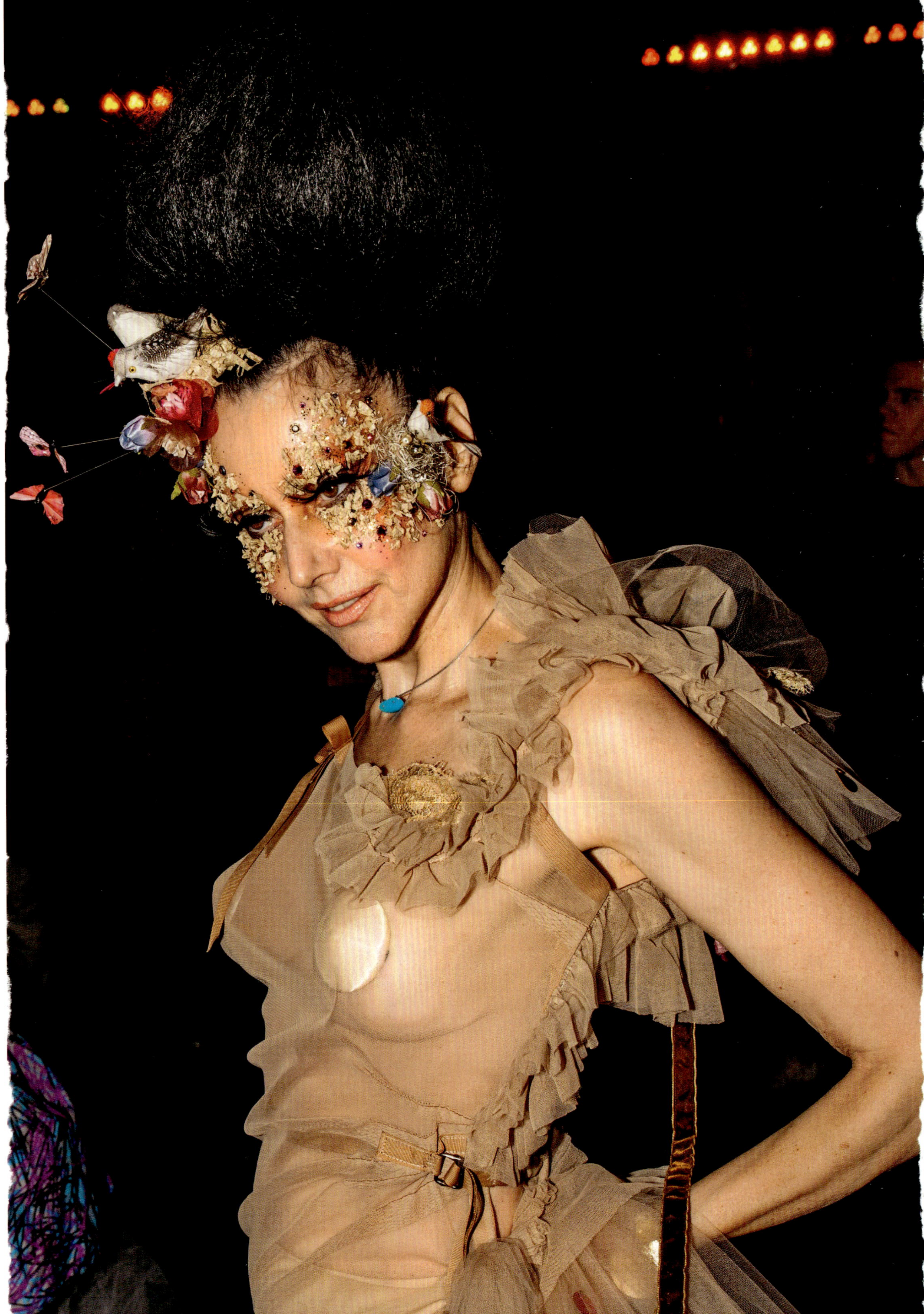

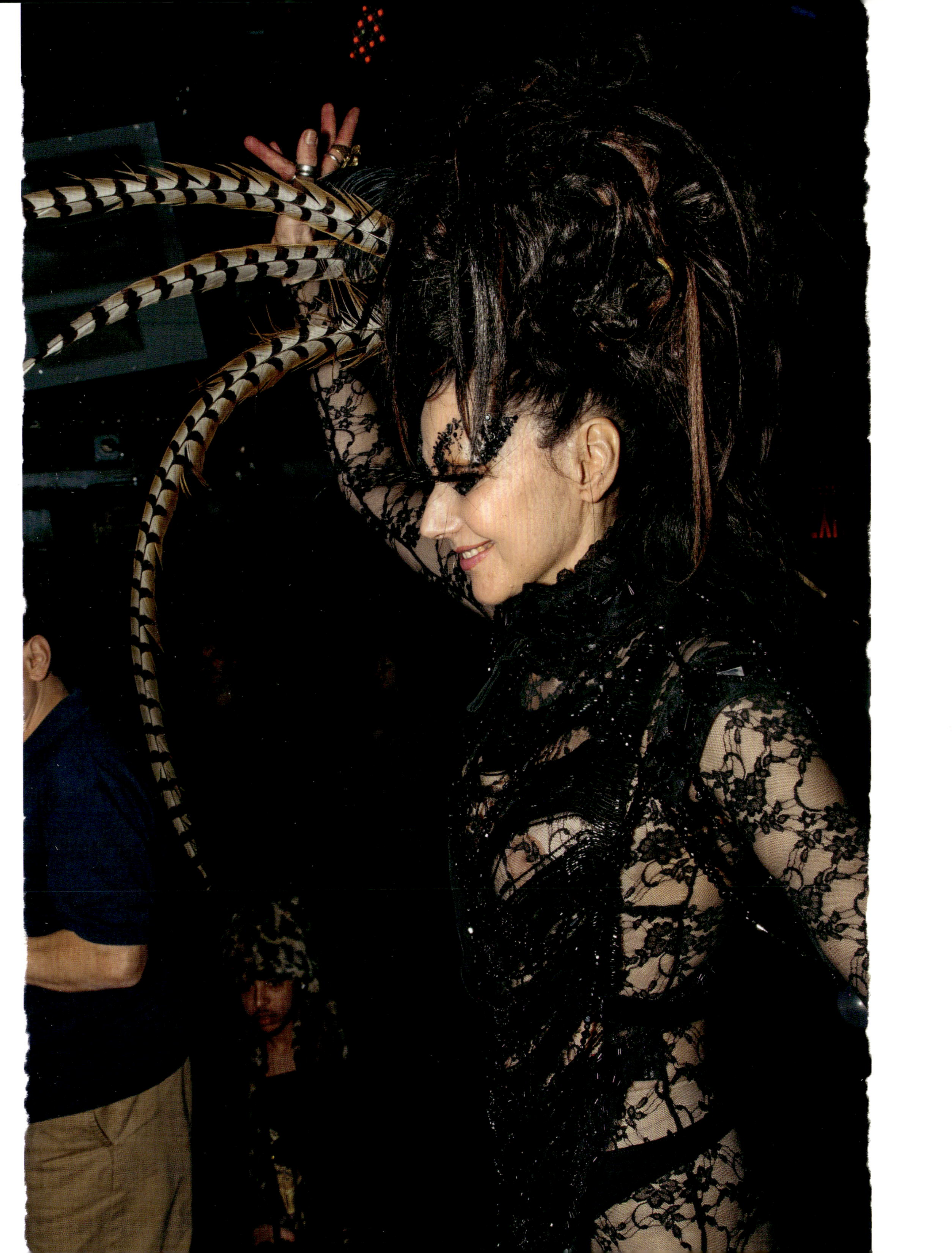

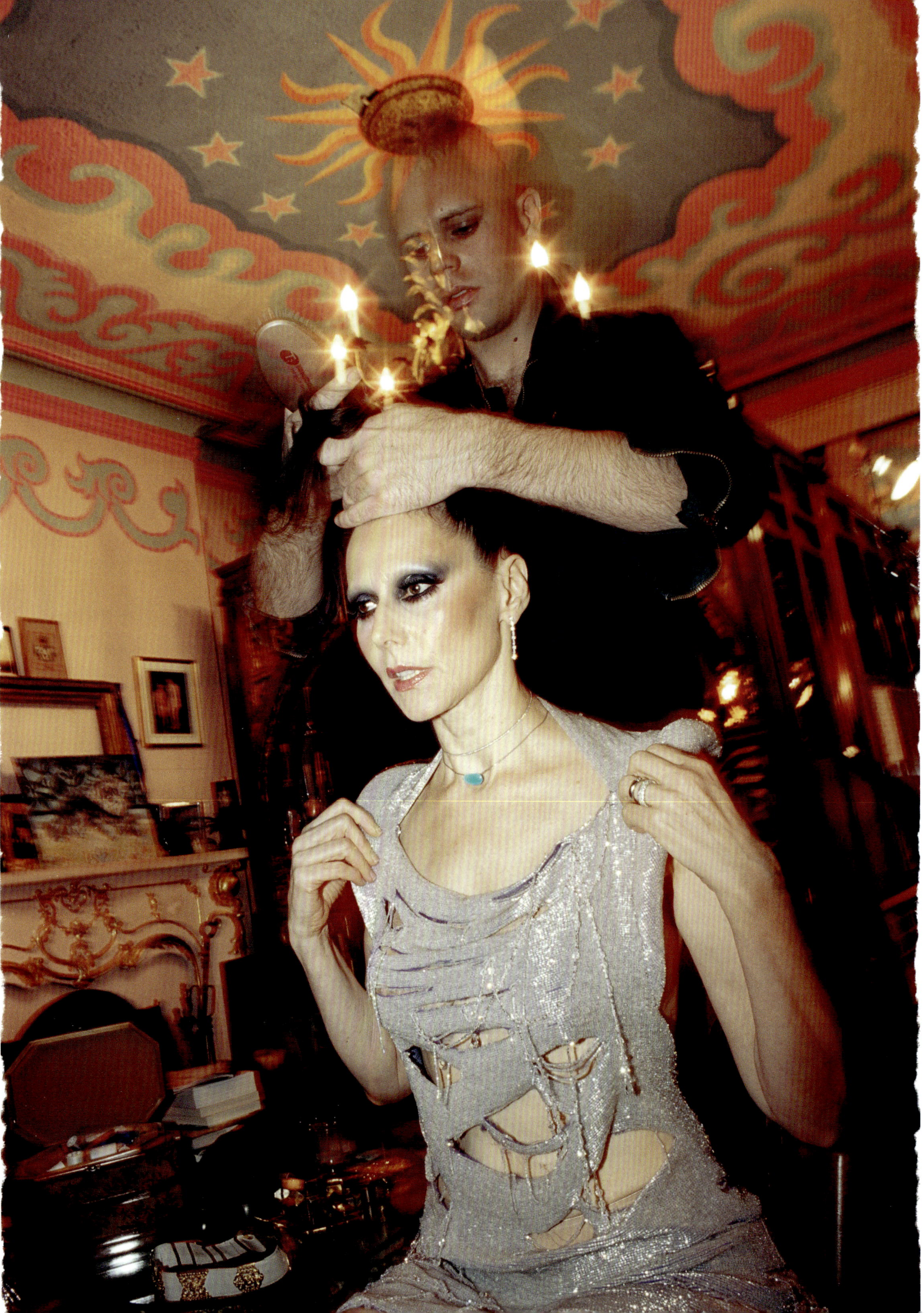

You Can Meet on the Internet

After a brief time-out to take care of the baby, Bartsch was back, staging parties and events in cities throughout the U.S., Europe, and Asia. Of course, the club scene has changed greatly since the late twentieth century. Back then, "it was all happening at the club," says Ronnie Newhouse. "It was a laboratory for music and art and fashion, all incubating in the same place. You tried things out in the clubs. Now you have the Internet. Clubs were like the Facebook of the time – a community of like-minded people meeting together."[83] The designer Andre Walker agrees: "Club culture was the social media of the time . . . That was the way we communicated. Susanne was one of the first merchants, instigators, and curators of the whole movement. Club culture was like the underbelly of fashion."[84]

"You don't have to go out anymore, you can meet on the Internet," admits Bartsch. New York City has also cracked down on nightlife, and designers increasingly get inspiration second-hand, including images from the Internet. But, as Andre Walker says, "Clubs are still important, like books are still important."[85]

Bartsch's Tuesday-night events at the Happy Valley nightclub were welcomed by many people who missed dressing up and going out, having authentic real-life experiences and a place to socialize with friends. Happy Valley was designed by Jeremy Scott, now the designer for Moschino. A few years later, Catwalk at Marquee became another nightlife fashion event. "With Susanne, it's an immersive experience," says Jed Root, the president of the artist management agency Jed Root, Inc. "Catwalk nights at Marquis had art happenings, live installations, a studio for photo shoots."[86]

"Nightlife at its best can be really high fashion, not just a kid in a garbage bag or a girl from New Jersey in a tight dress," says Mickey Boardman of *Paper* magazine.[87] "Susanne proves that style is a personal thing, not a trend thing." Bartsch has continued to promote upcoming designers like The Blonds, who have created extraordinary looks like her Shark corset. "And she's not scared to wear these crazy heels to dance on a bar," observes Theodora Sopko.[88]

As Michael Musto, puts it: "Even when things have gotten so oppressive, Susanne has relentlessly continued her conga-line through the wee hours, welcoming gays, straights, drag queens, people from across the spectrum to join in a euphoric – and totally legal – experience. She's like a sprite from Mars – surreal, gamine, enchanting, edgy. And as she's dancing on the bar, welcoming everyone, she's also being very savvy about all the details, because she realizes that it's a business – an artistic, creative business."[89]

"Susanne is so iconic in New York," says Marc Balet. "She stays the same – and the kids grow up around her. People come to New York wanting to be in the

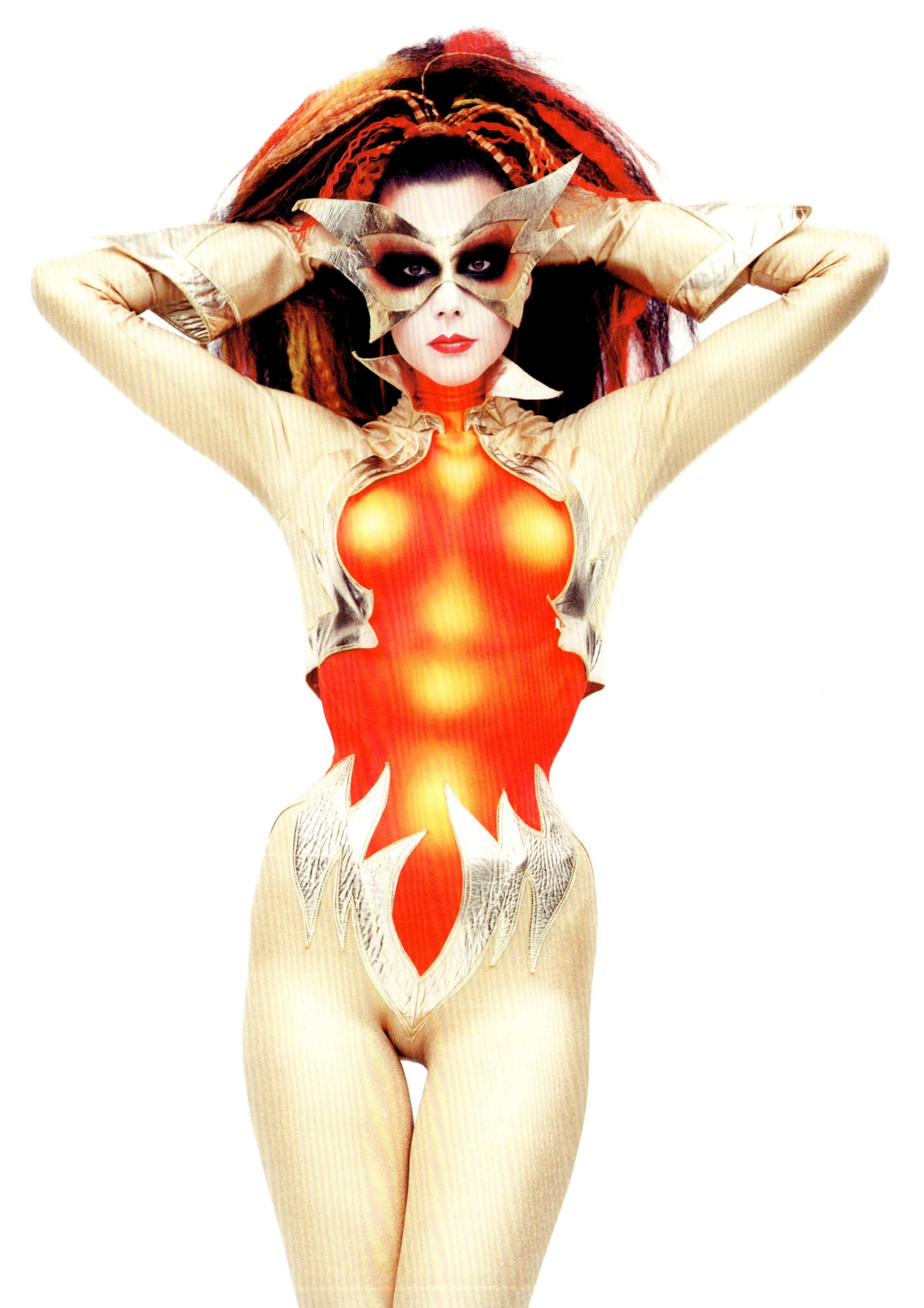

underground (if you can still call it that) and she's like Auntie Mame in Chelsea! She's authentic and that's more meaningful than ever."[90] According to the *New York Times* in July 2013, Bartsch's "empire" continues to flourish and remain relevant, "particularly among scene seekers too green to know her history. Wherever Ms. Bartsch goes, the demimonde seems to follow, as if summoned by the bat of her curlicued fake eyelashes."[91]

Her Own Creation

"Susanne is her own creation," says James Gager, the senior vice president and creative director for MAC Cosmetics. "MAC has done a number of master classes with Susanne to show what goes into her looks. It's creating a persona. It's very liberating. You can play another role. I'm always amazed by what she's done, particularly with her eyelashes. Her focus is always around her eyes, not so much eye shadow as eyeliner and eye lashes and jewels around her eyes. She has worked with people to fabricate eyelashes that are totally beyond fashion. She's made them out of feathers, curled paper. They are almost Calder-like mobiles on her eyelids, mini eye sculptures."[92]

"Make-up is one of Susanne's real contributions to fashion," says Roger Padhila. "Talk about coloring outside the lines! Her eyelashes go into her hair . . ."[93] The makeup artist Kabuki says, "I made her up a couple of times – it was like old Hollywood glamour, but without being nostalgic. Make-up can be glam or kooky, there are clowns and fashion plates. For Susanne, make-up is just another medium of design – it's almost limitless."[94]

Bartsch herself says, "The make-up is as important as the outfit – it's theater. I can't imagine dressing up without make-up. I get inspired to do make-up from travel, art, and other people." She describes a particular off-center make-up look as "like a Picasso." She loves collaborating with different make-up artists: "He wanted chains, I said 'No! I prefer gold leaf' or I say 'Black' and he gets a great idea and then I push him, I say, 'We have to be edgy.' I also love masks. Style is how you feel in the look."

Hair and wigs have also played an important part in Bartsch's looks. "She has a big collection of wigs and hats," says Theodora Sopko. "When she does a lot, most of her time goes into the headpiece and she just slips into her dress." Some of her wigs have been blonde, but most are black, like her own hair. As recently as 2015, Stephen Jones designed a hat called "The Love Ball," "inspired by Susanne's hairdo, but made of black turkey feathers."[95]

Danilo has worked closely with Bartsch to create various hairstyles, of which the most famous is the "Babe." "The Babe is dark with a supernatural quality and an abundance of hair," he says. "There's always height and glam. But I'm a couture kind of guy and the gown or the theme of the event will influence the hairstyle I do."[96]

Below: Susanne wearing a ring by
Joji Kojima, summer 2013.
Photographer Andrea Barbiroli.

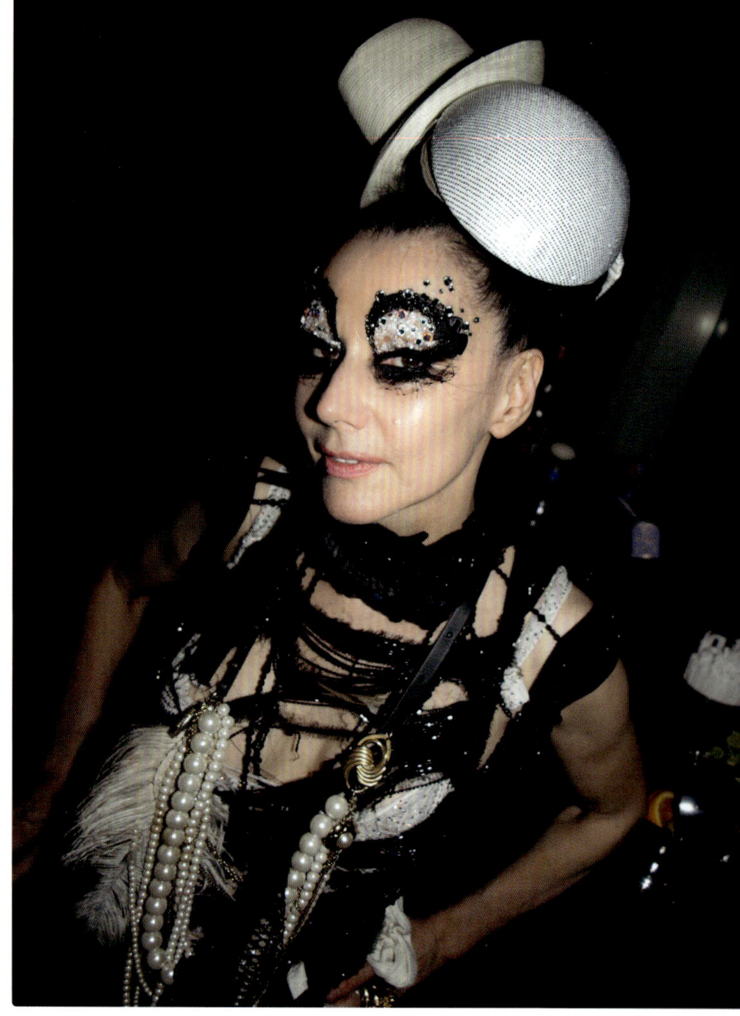

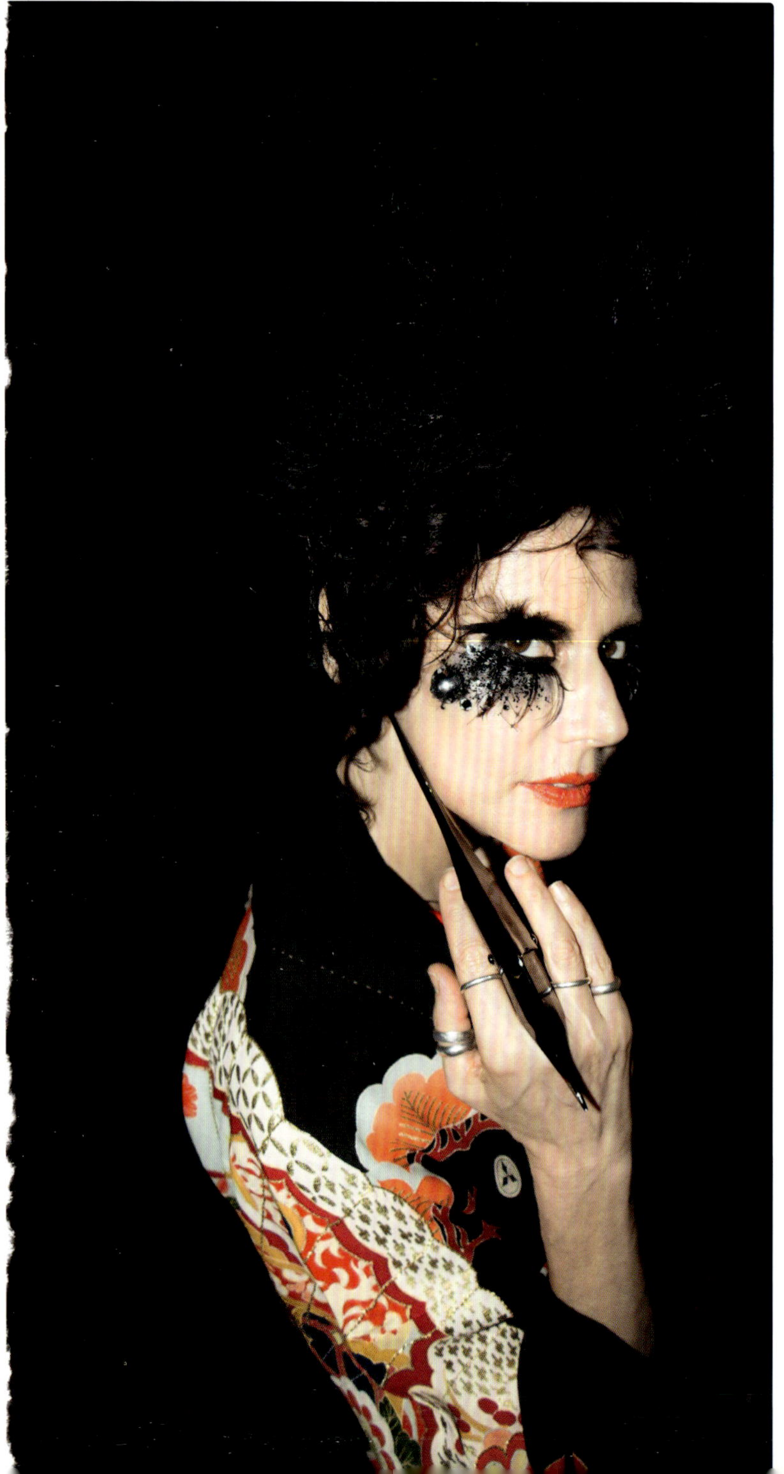

Above: "Tuesday, two hats, two
parties: Over the top at Susanne
Bartsch's party On Top," c. 2012.
Photo by Andrea Barbiroli.

Facing: "Going Glitter Goth in
Jean Paul Gaultier," Summer 2013.
Photo by Andrea Barbiroli.

Ring by Joji Kojima

Following pages: *Annabelle*
magazine photoshoot, Zurich, 2013.
Portrait by Rico & Michael.

"Going Glitter Goth in Jean-Paul Gaultier"

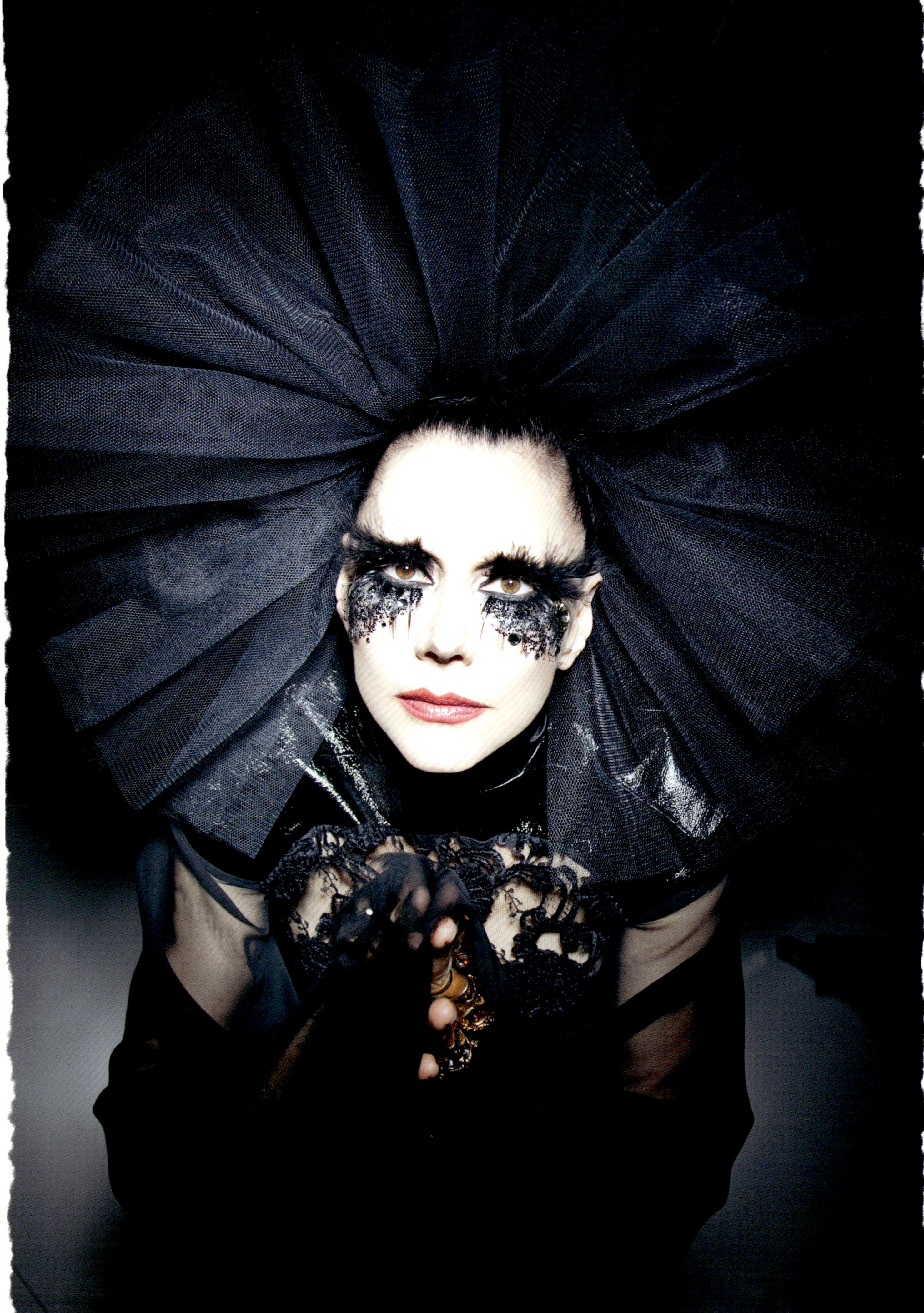

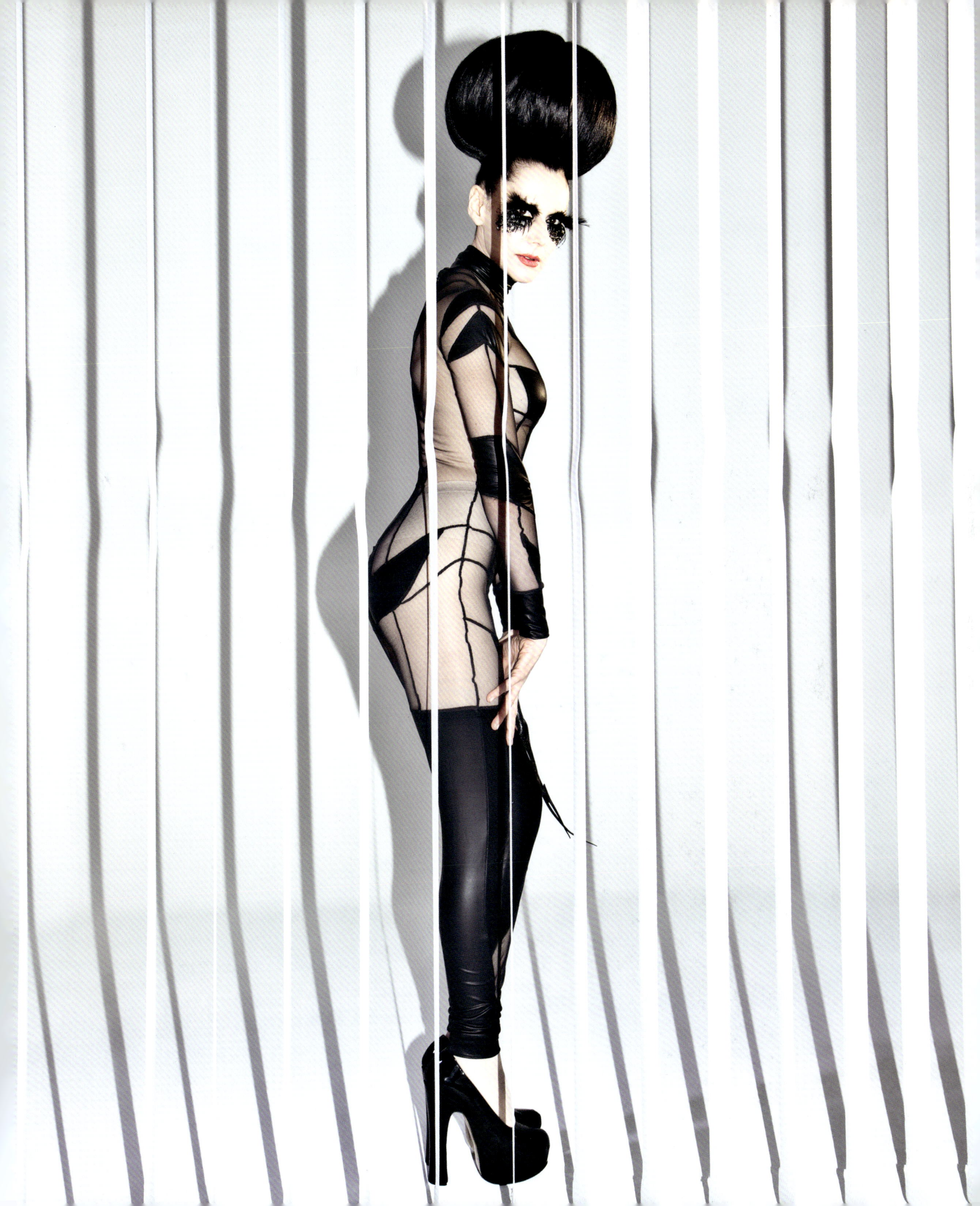

Right: Candid shot, photoshoot
for Webster Hall invitation,
grand opening, October 1992.
Photo by Mathu Andersen

Below: Susanne Bartsch on set
with Mathu Andersen,
New York City, *German Vogue*,
1992. Photo by Arthur Elgort.

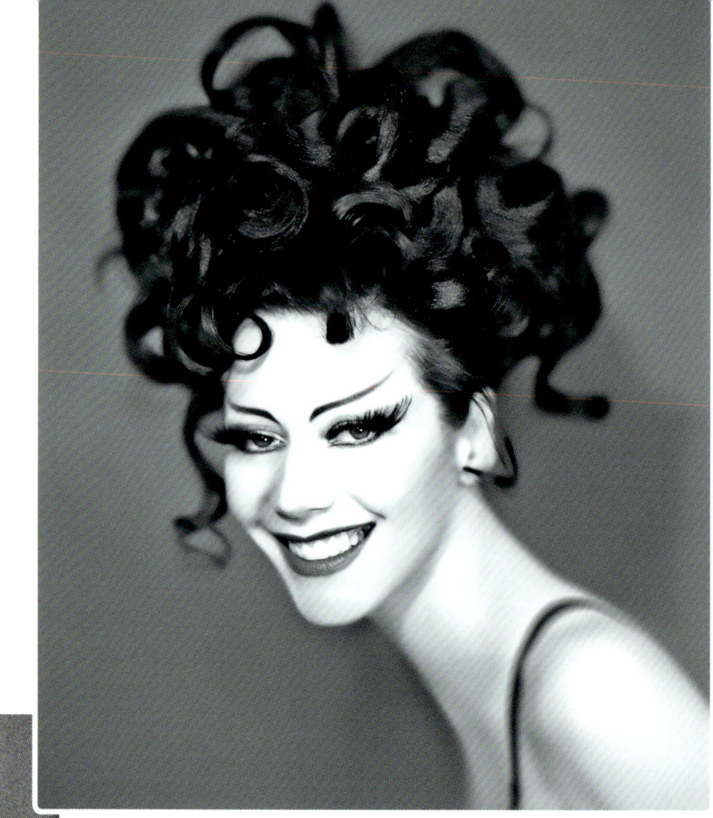

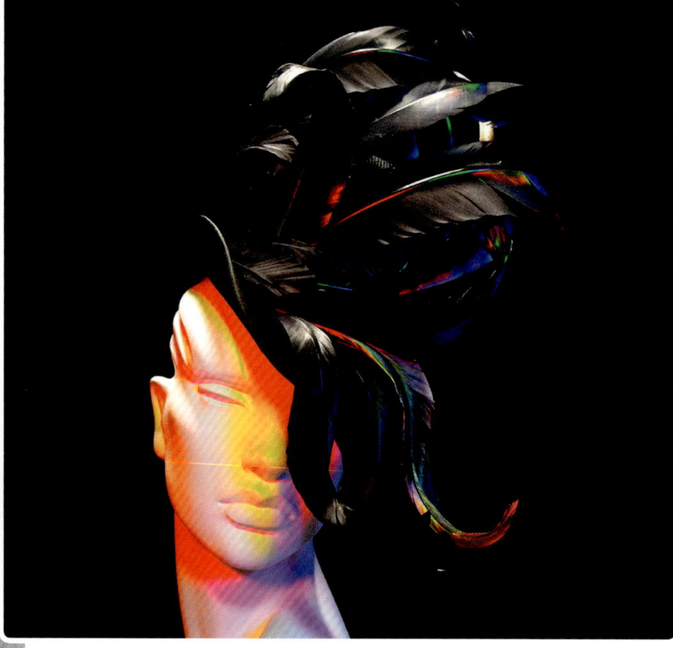

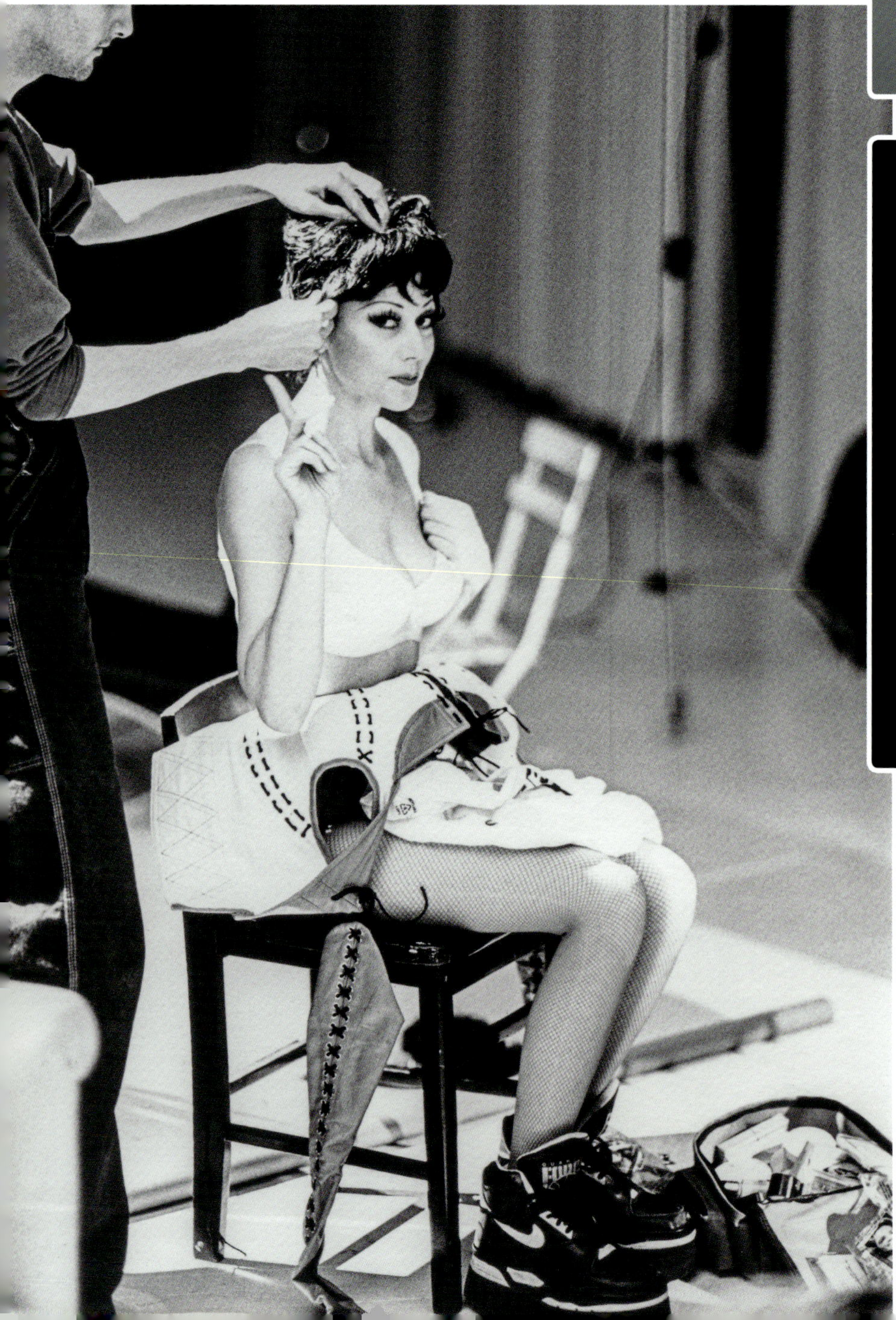

Above: Stephen Jones Millinery,
Loveball hat, inspired by
Susanne Bartsch's hairstyles,
Hot House collection,
Spring/Summer 2015.
Photo by Peter Ashworth.

Facing: "Ripping her to Shreds."
Dress by Jean Paul Gaultier.
Jewelry by Gabriel Shuldiner.
Photo by Santiago Felipe.

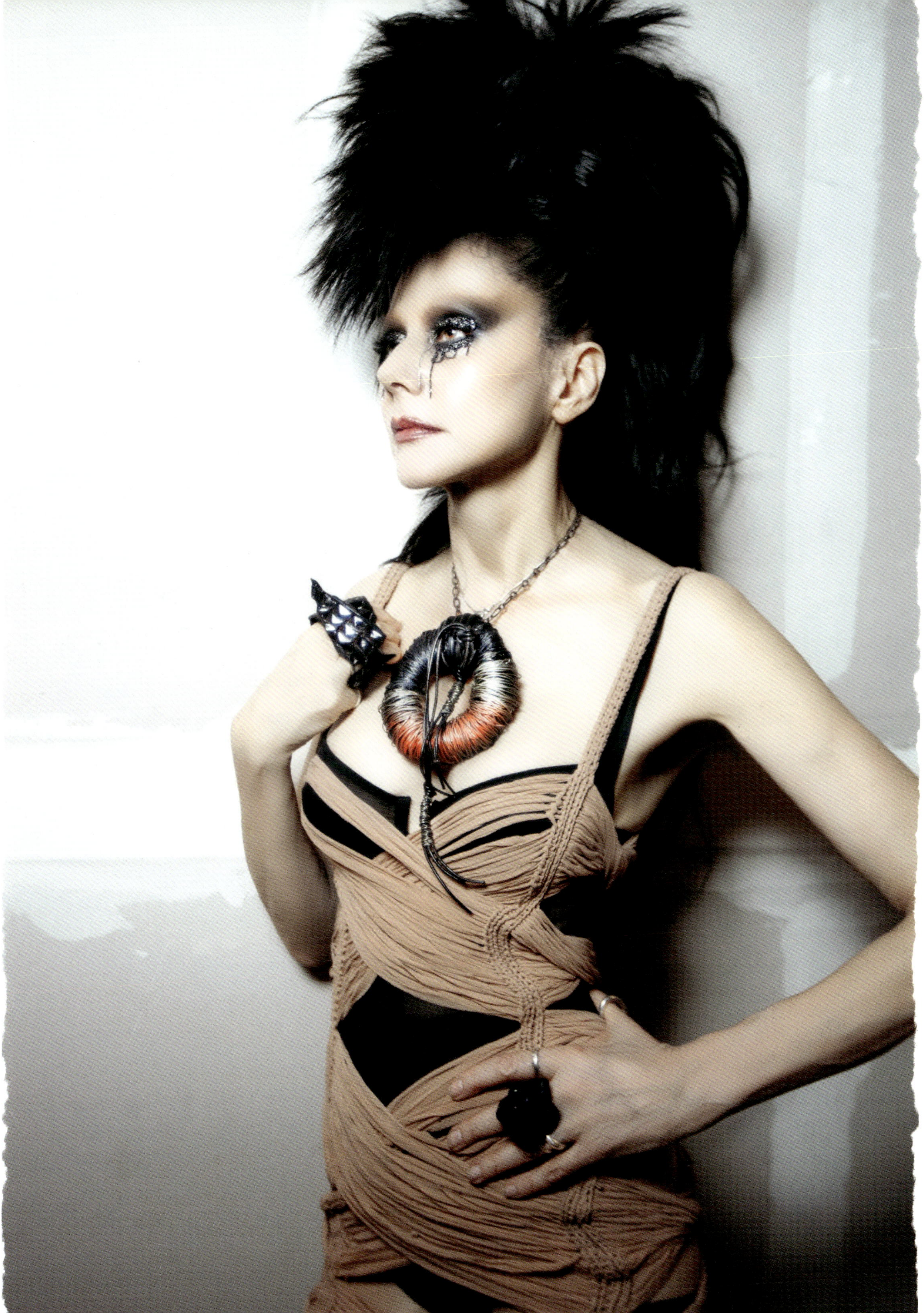

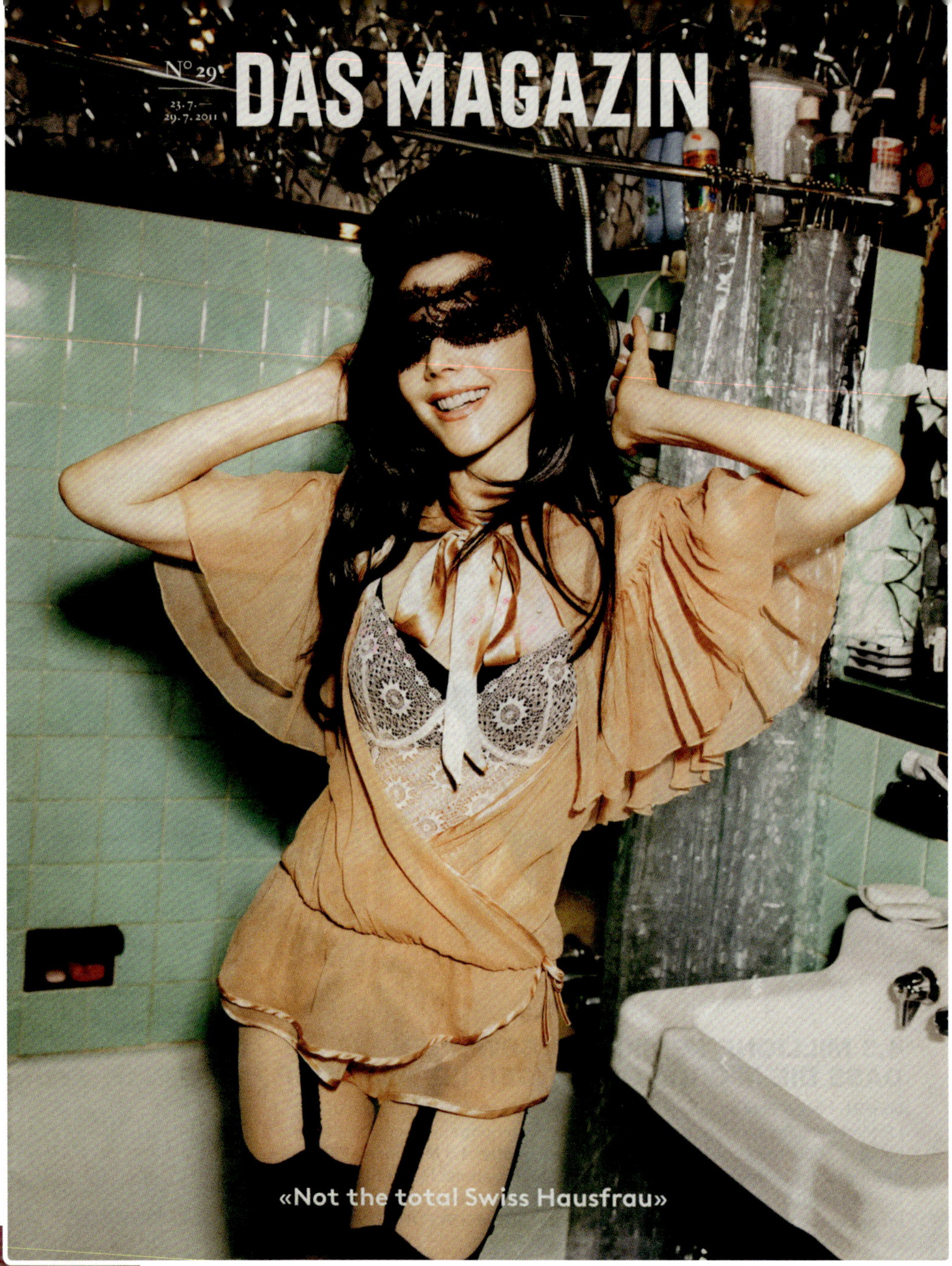

Right: Susanne is the cover girl in Kiki de Montparnasse, *Das Magazin*, No. 29, 2011. Photo by Ben Watts.

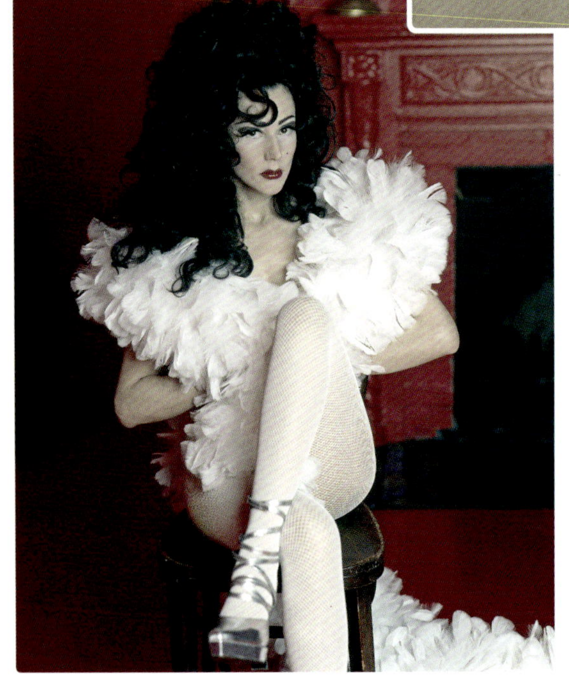

Left: Susanne at the Chelsea Hotel. © Michael James O'Brien.

Facing: Susanne in her apartment being a Chelsea Girl, late 2000s. Mark C. O'Flaherty.

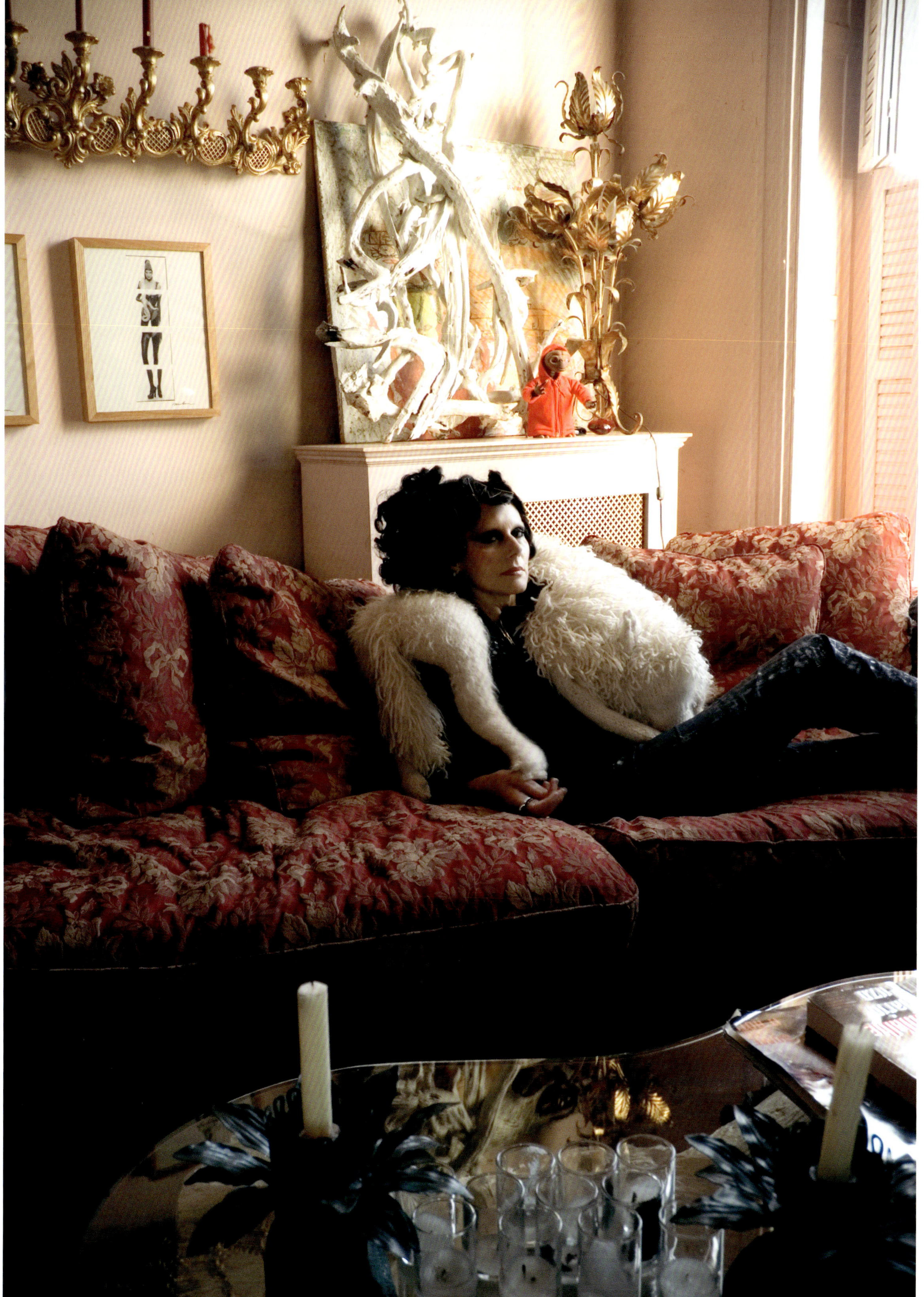

The Chelsea Hotel, Bartsch's home since she arrived in New York in 1981, has been the famous home of innumerable bohemians and artists. Almost all of them have left, but she remains in an apartment that expresses her personality and is a creative center in its own right. With lipstick red walls, huge graffiti like paintings, Chinese "opium" beds, and a wealth of odd accessories from Mexican masks to a giant Buddha – and lots of clothes.

"Susanne is an extraordinary person," says André Balazs, at whose hotels Bartsch has created events and parties. "She is the personification of a very liberating and empowering frame of mind. The spaces she creates are *psychic* spaces that encourage people to be themselves. The creative heart of New York owes a lot to Susanne."[97] "I've known Susanne since she came to America . . . she is a true original and marches to her own drumbeat. It is impossible to categorize her or put what she does in a nice, neat, box. I was always impressed with how daring and original she has been. I've collaborated with her on special events at my hotels and throughout the years and they were all one of a kind extravaganzas," explains Ian Schrager[98].

Art and Fashion

Bartsch is today exploring new venues beyond the club scene. "Lately, she's branched out, embracing multiple disciplines, such as fashion and art, to make nightlife a multi-media experience," says Michael Musto.[99] "I've started doing art and fashion installations," says Bartsch. One project took place during New York Fashion Week in September 2014. *Art-à-Porter* took place over five evenings on a walkway between Forty-second and Forty-third Street and in a Bank of America lobby. Thanks to support from Chashama, a non-for-profit group of theaters, galleries, and studios, "There were people doing installations, performance art, and art on the wall." Bartsch recalls: "One night there was a surrealist dinner with all these creatures, the next night a dance performance. Steven Klein played his unseen videos in Times Square."

Bartsch has also partnered with the Museum of Modern Art PS1 in Queens. Angela Golding, its director of development, describes Bartsch as "really an artist" and "such a strong, smart woman."[100] "We planned a Halloween Parade with artists on floats," says Bartsch, "but due to budget and time constraints, we ended up doing a Hallowen ball at PS1 and then we paraded over to a warehouse nearby for an after party. I want to do a surrealist ball." Bartsch has also begun organizing another monthly event, Kunst, in a club in Brooklyn, "with installations and lots of video art." Another special event, Shhh!, takes place four times a year in different spaces and encompasses installation art and performers.

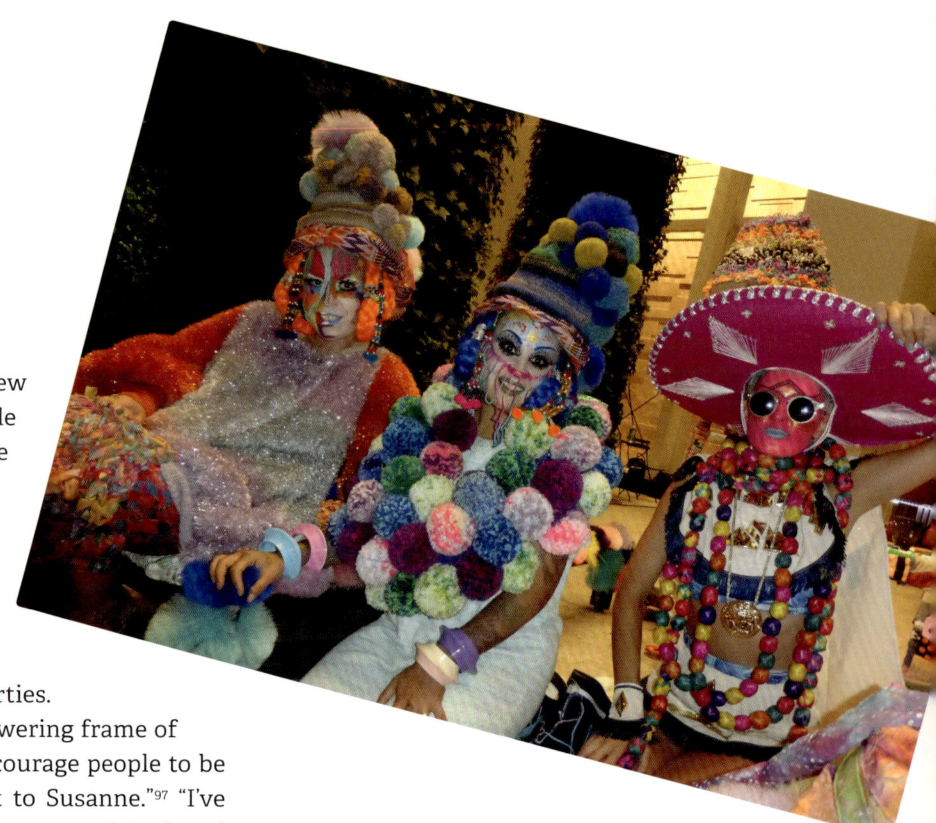

Above: "HuggyBears" (Rachel, Jeanise, and Gaffy) at *bARTsch: Inspiration Art-à-Porter* installation, for New York Fashion Week, September 2014. Photo © Tina Paul, 2014. All Rights Reserved.

Facing top: Adam VanBuren, Kiss, and Rachel Singer at the *SHHH!* event at the Gramercy Theater, New York City, January 2015. Photo by Citizen Chris.

Facing bottom: Susanne's *Botanicult* party at Gilded Lily, Fall 2014. From left to right: Gage of the Boone, Merrie Cherry, Amber Valentine, Onehalf Nelson, Horrorchata, and Brandon Olson. Photo by Robin Souma.

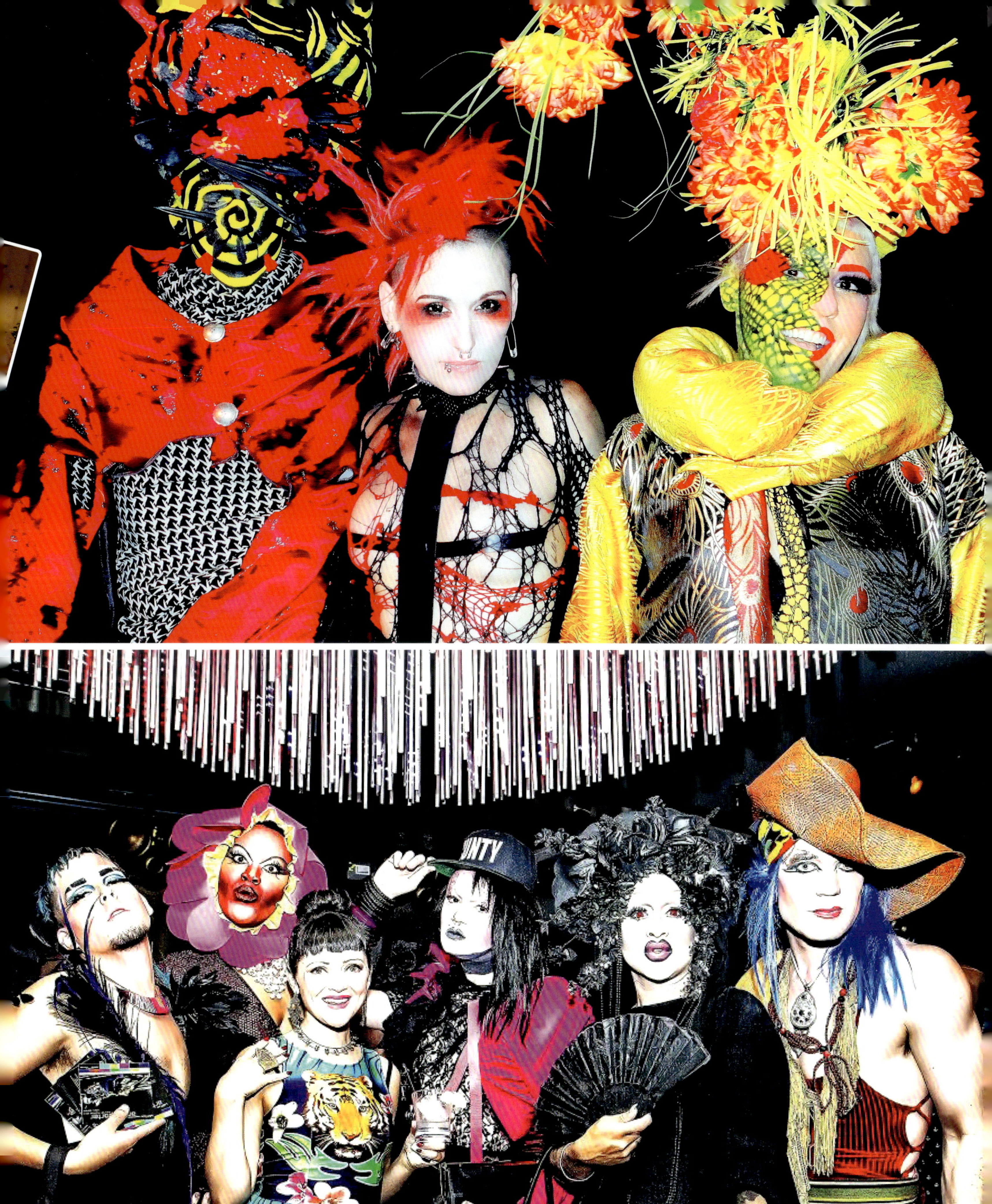

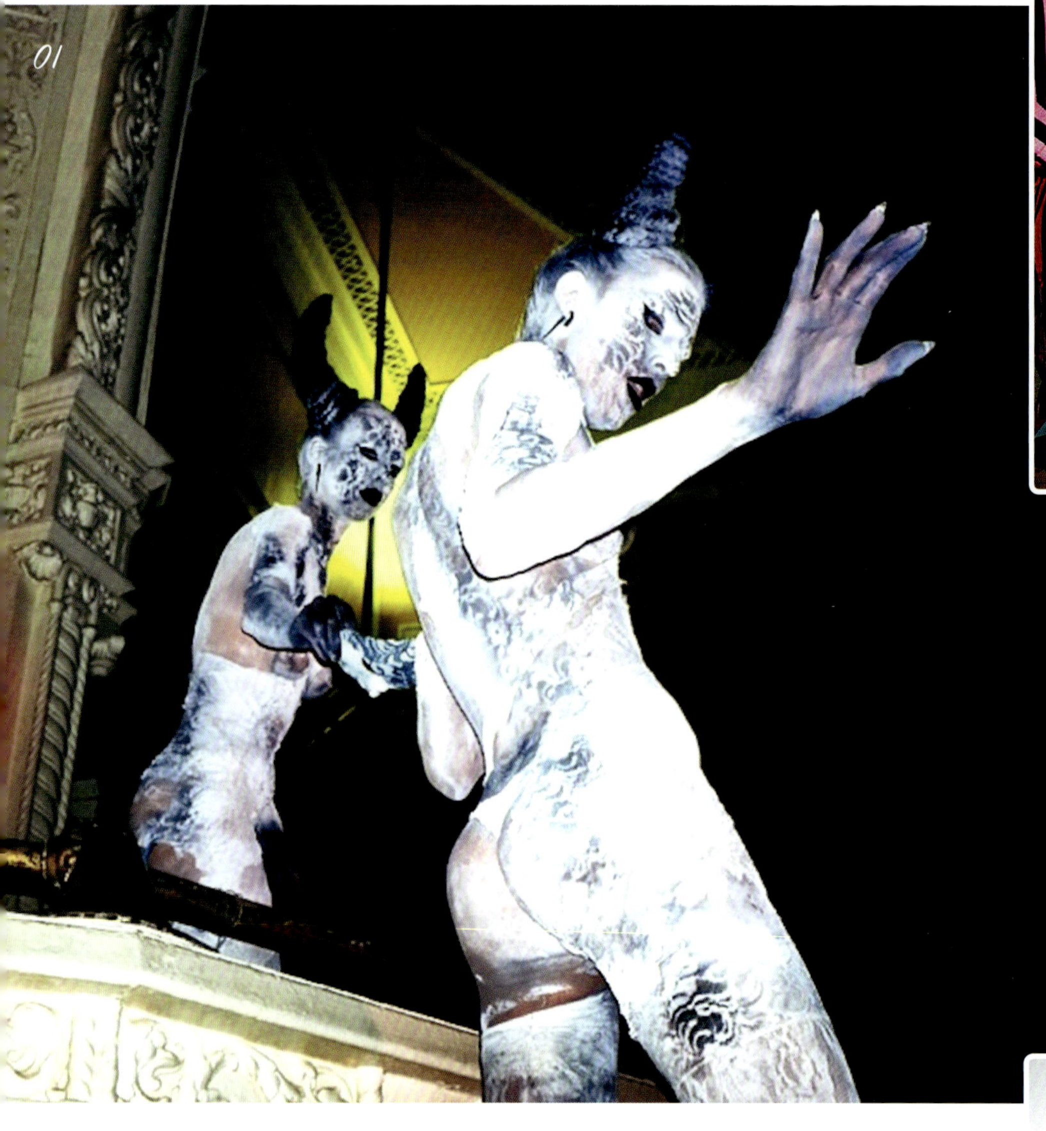

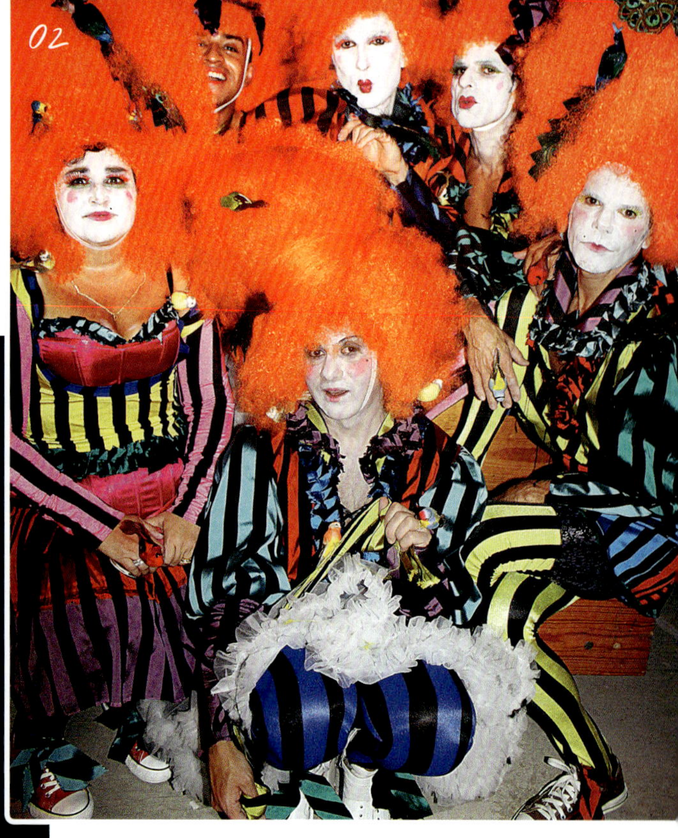

1 Jessica Love and Dylan Monroe at the Liberty Theatre in 2014. Photo by Gerry Visco.

2 Stephen Knoll and friends at Susanne's Bloody Mary Halloween party, NYC, October 2010. Photo by Ves Pitts.

3 Domonique Echeverria at Susanne's Botanicult party at Gilded Lily, fall 2014. Photo by Laura Weyl, courtesy of Susanne Bartsch.

4 Susanne at her Kunst opening party wearing Zaldy, Brooklyn, March 2013. Photo by Rebecca Smeyne.

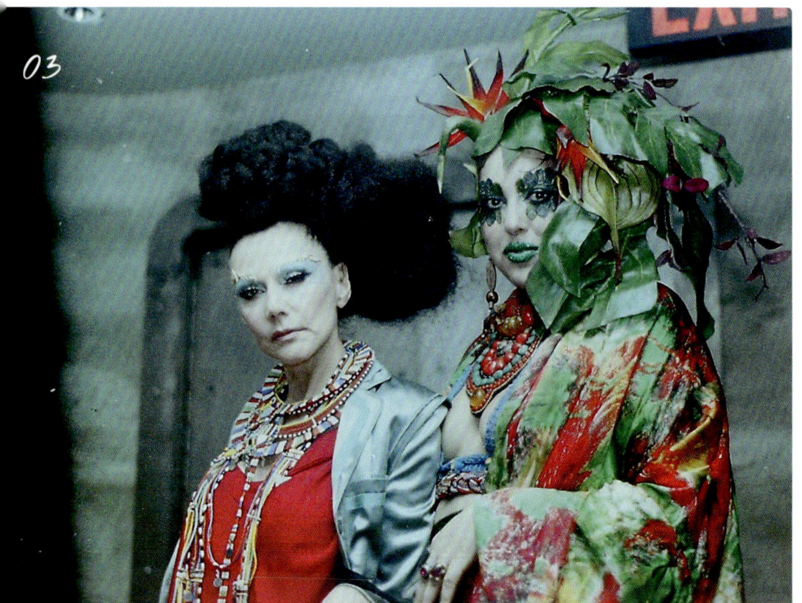

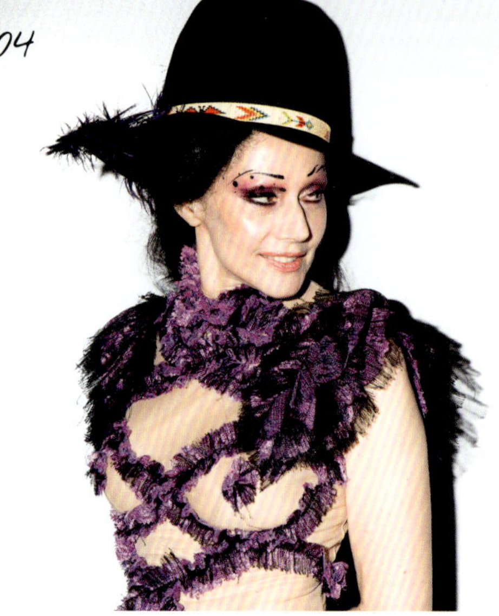

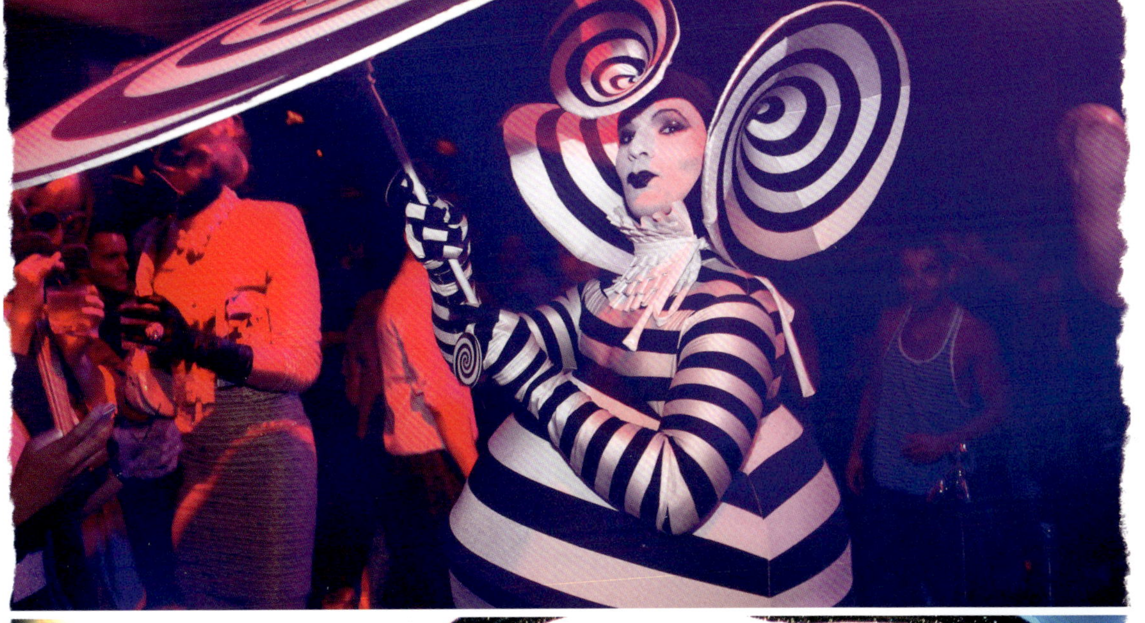

Top: Muffinhead at Catwalk, 2013. Photo by Brandon Voss.

Center: Hector House of Hallucination at Susanne's Bloody Mary Halloween party, October 2010. Photo by Ves Pitts.

Bottom: Erickatoure Aviance and Gage of the Boone on stage at Susanne's Kunst party, Brooklyn 2014. Photo by Ves Pitts.

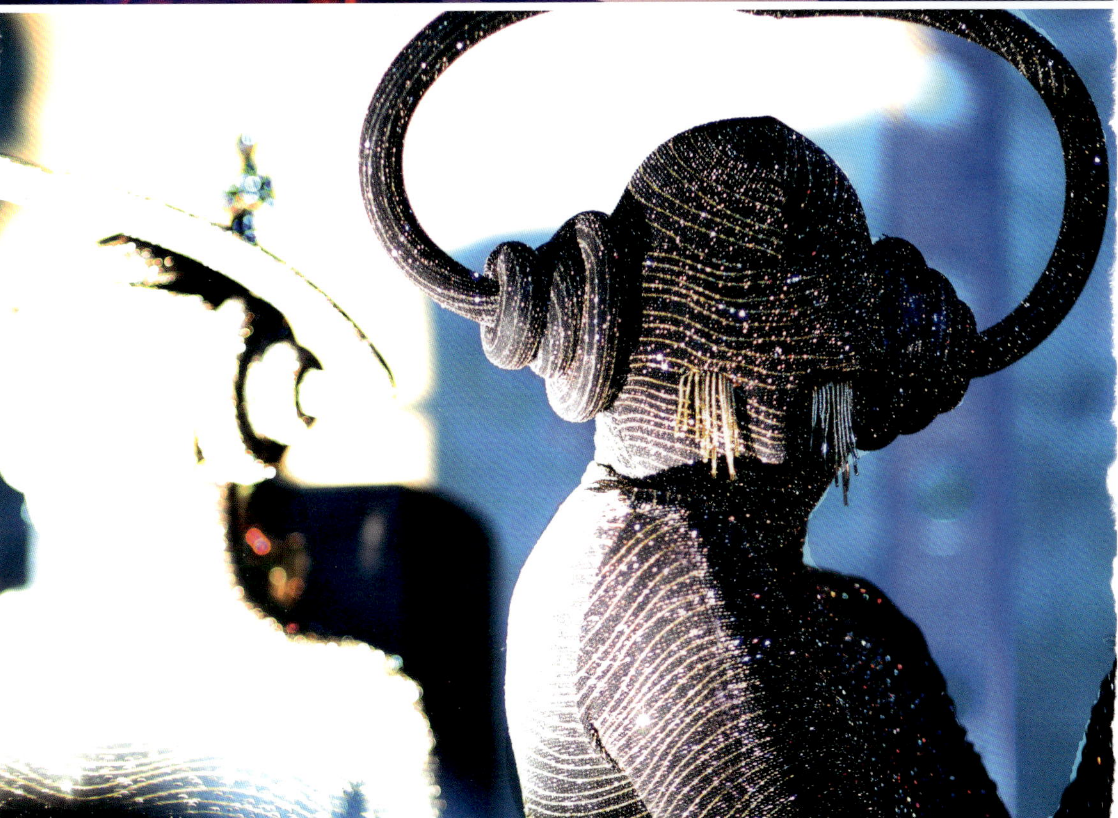

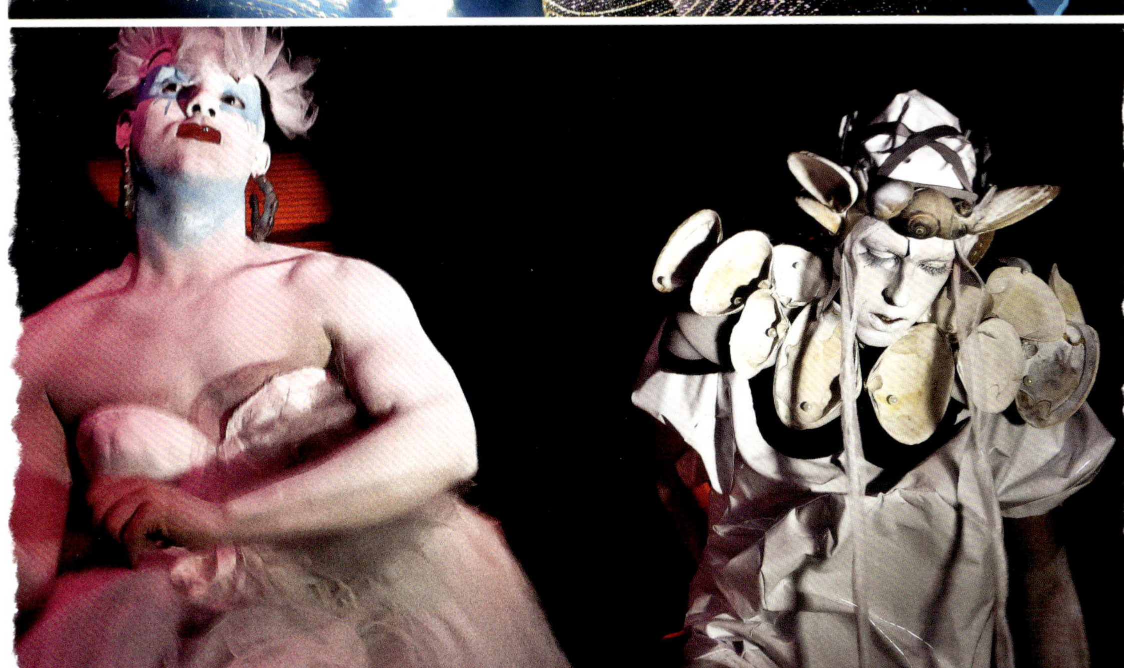

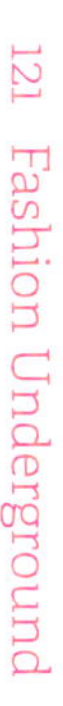

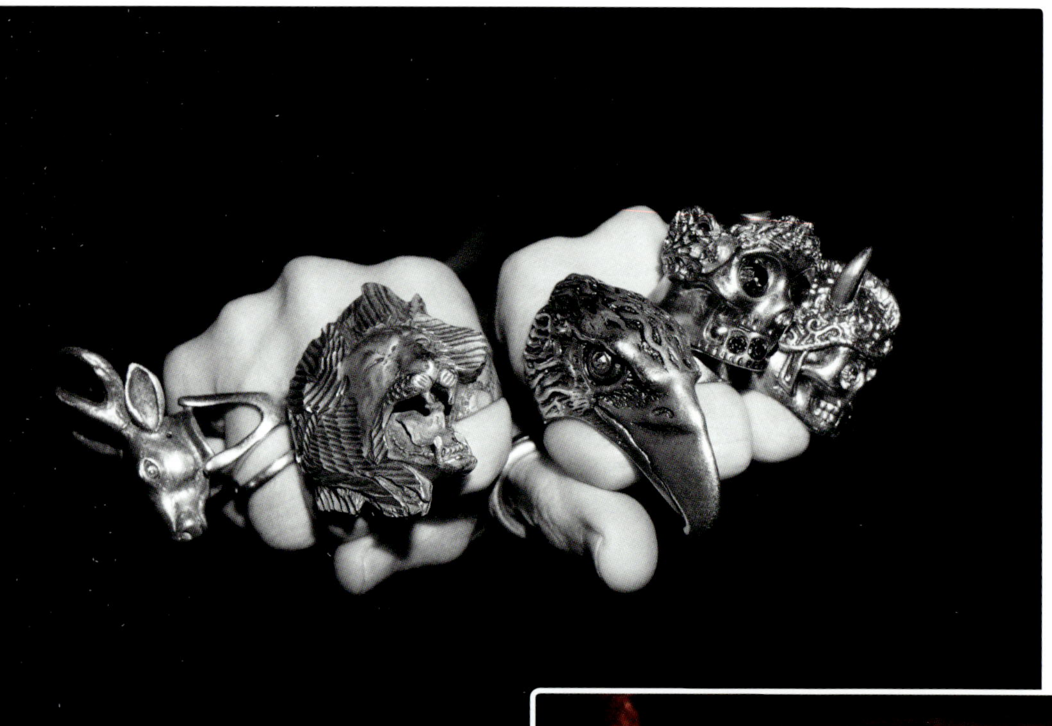

Left: Susanne Bartsch's animal
rings at the Gilded Lily,
New York, 2014.
Photo by Olivier Zahm.

Facing: Susanne in her favorite
contemporary look. Bodysuit by
The Blonds. Blonds fashion
show, February 2015.
Photo by Roxanne Lowit.

Right: *Annabelle* magazine
photoshoot, Zurich, 2013.
Portrait by Rico & Michael.

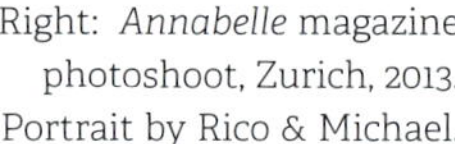

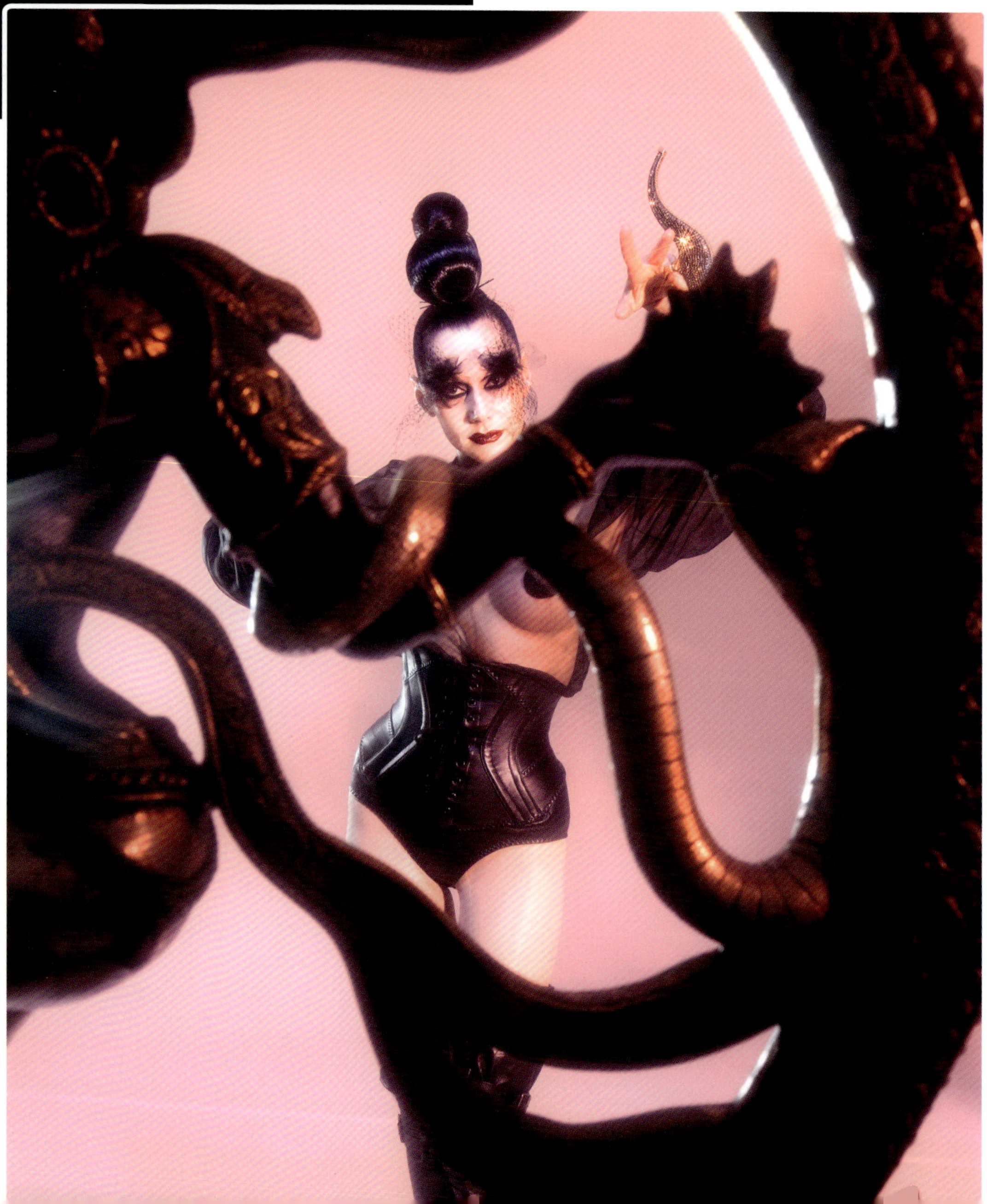

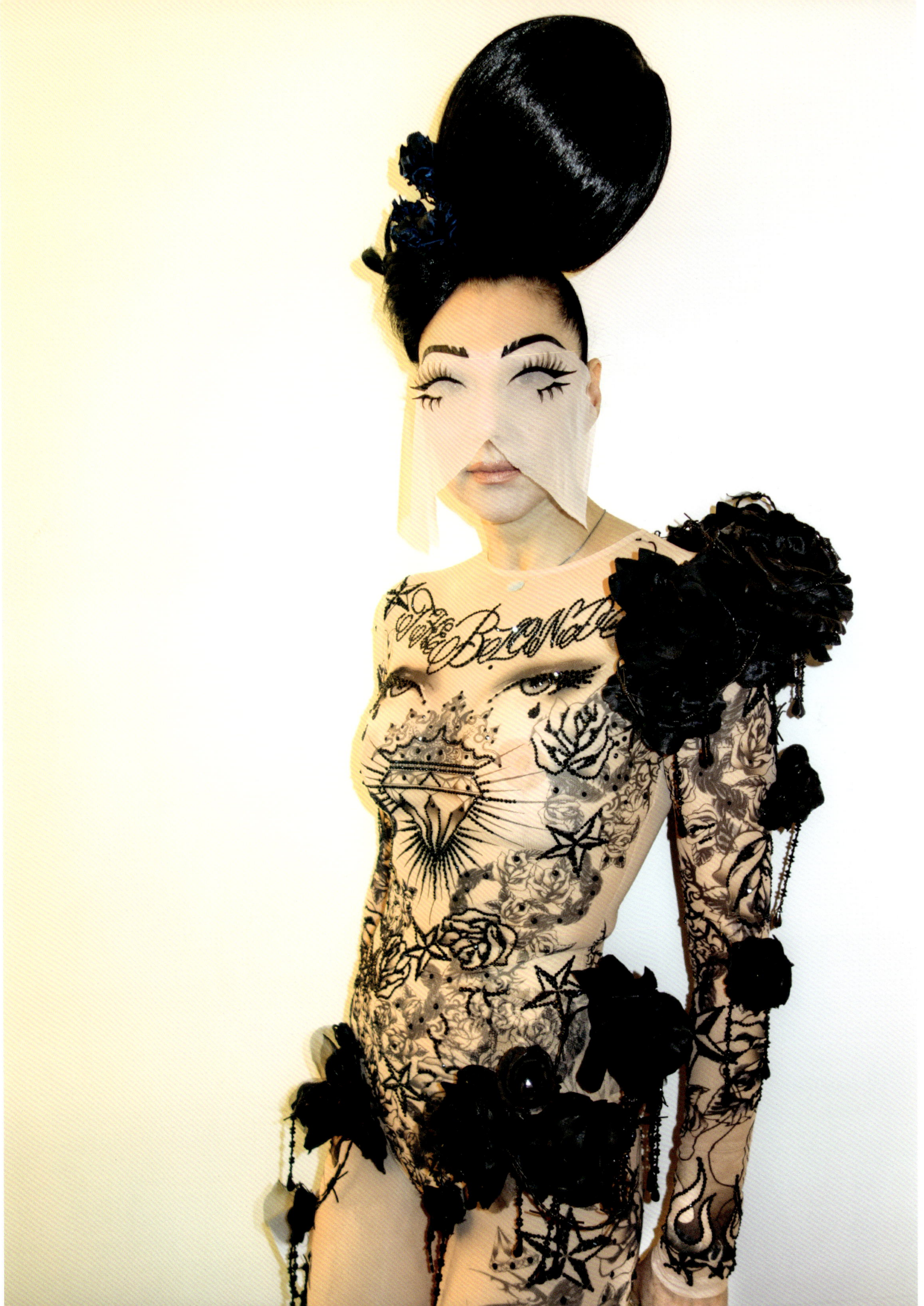

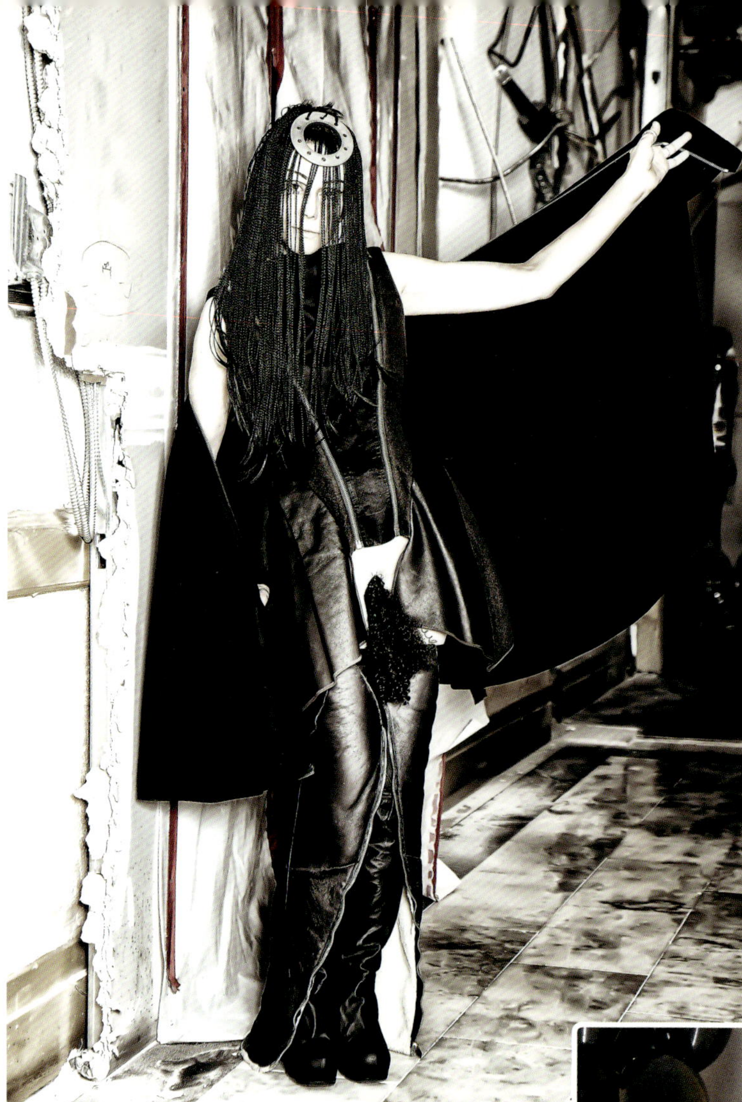

Left: Susanne styles a look
by Rick Owens, 2015.
Photo by Robin Souma.

Facing top: Kunst opening
invitation. Susanne's crew on a
subway platform. From far left
to right: Jordan Hall, Matt
Whipple, Kareem, Jordan Hall,
Susanne Bartsch, Odder P Elliot,
Brandon Olson, Ryan Burke,
Gage of the Boon. Front row
(left to right): Jordon, Heidi, and
Domonique. February 2013.
Photo by Rebecca Smeyne.

Facing bottom: Susanne
wearing Rachel Auburn at her
party at the Liberty Theatre
in Times Square, 2014.
Photo by Robin Souma.

Right: Susanne with Shayne
Oliver of Hood By Air,
Nicopanda Presentation at
Studio Formichetti, February
2015. Photo by Susanne Bartsch.

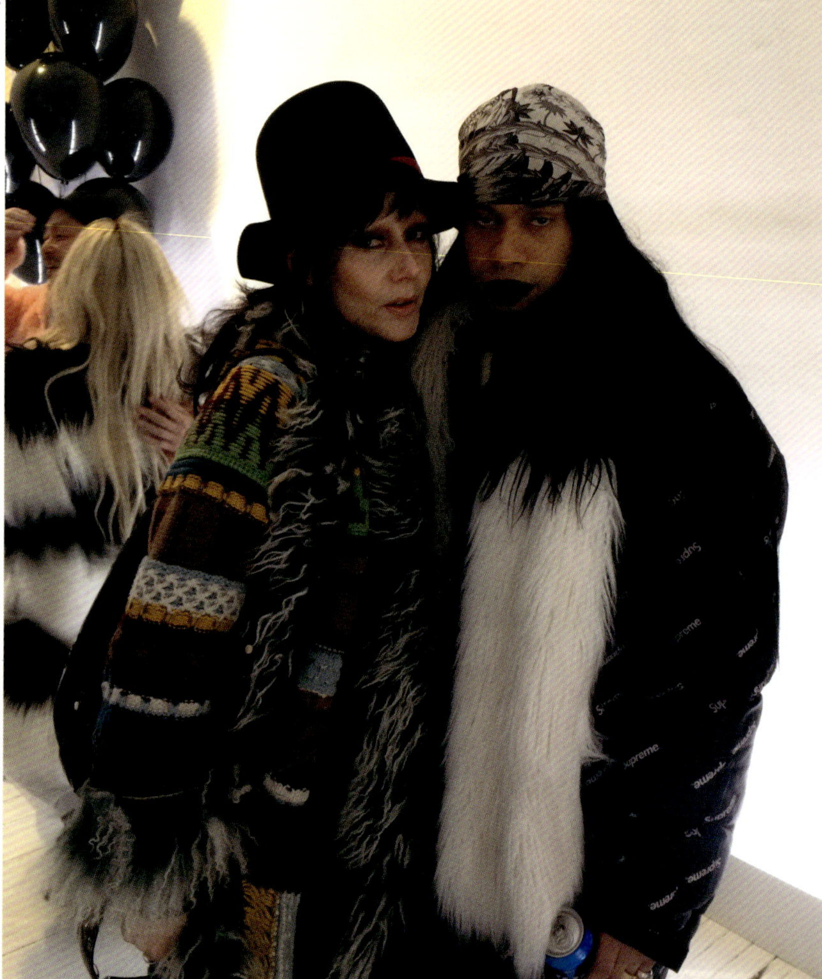

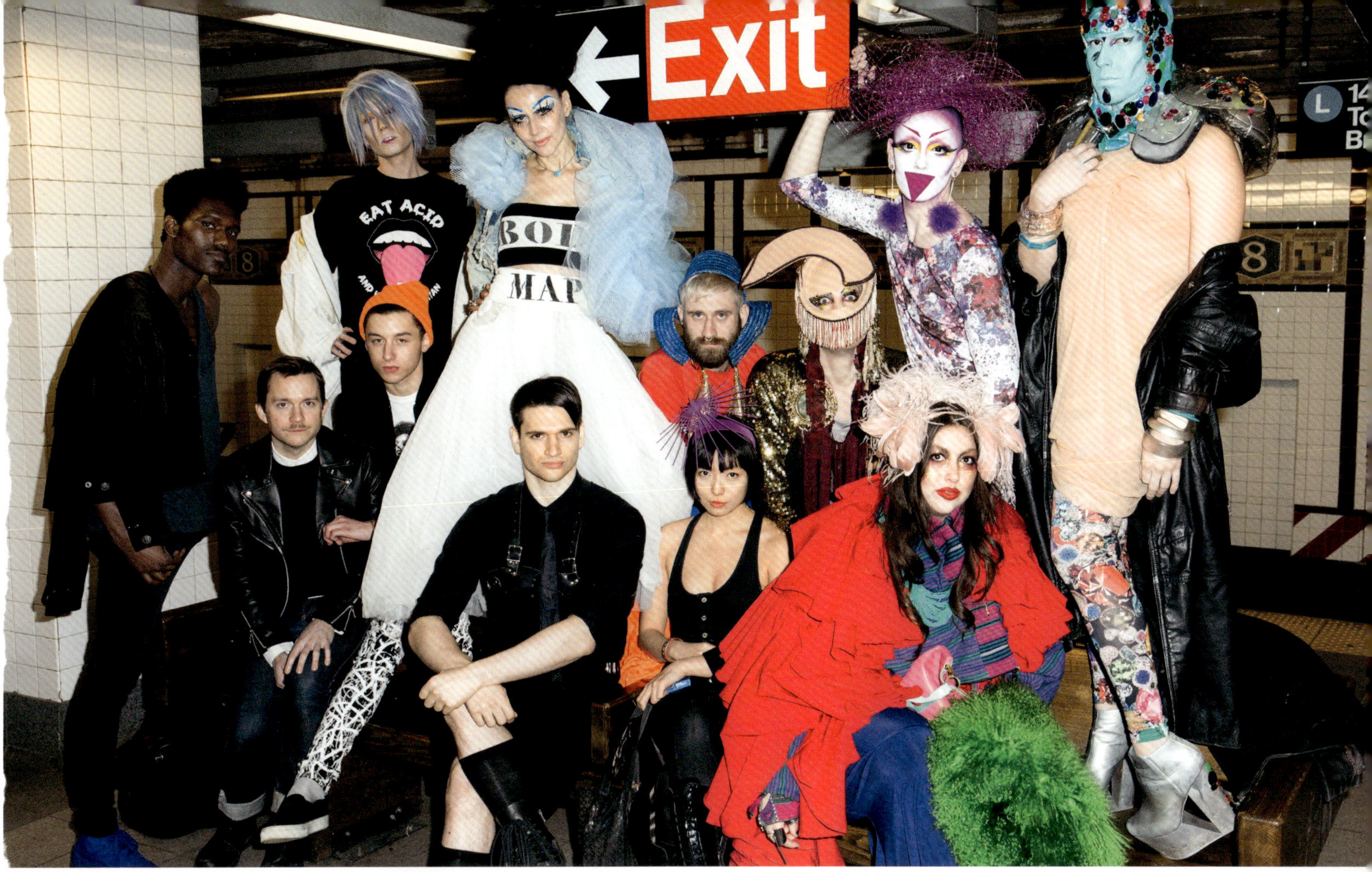

Exit
EAT ACID

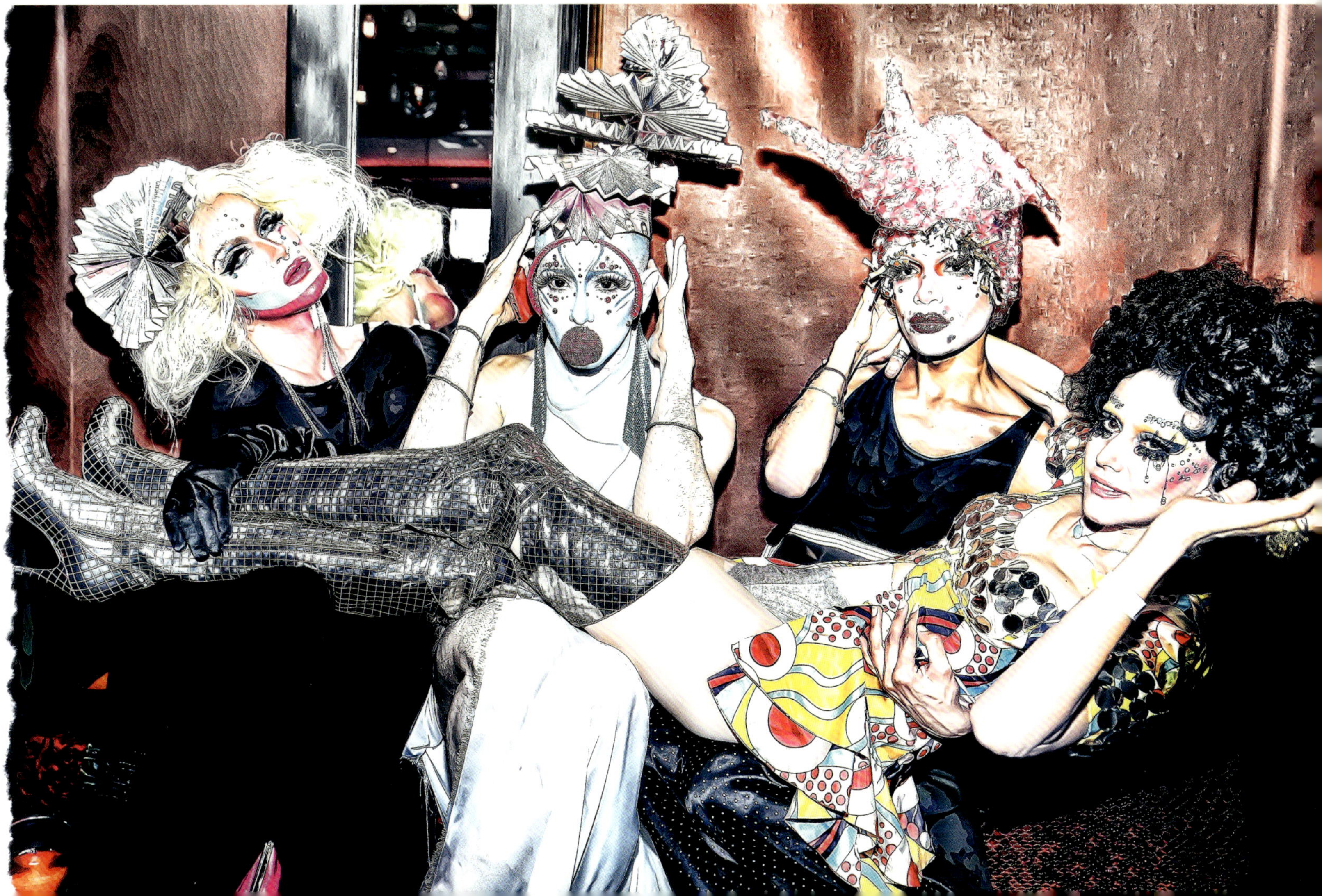

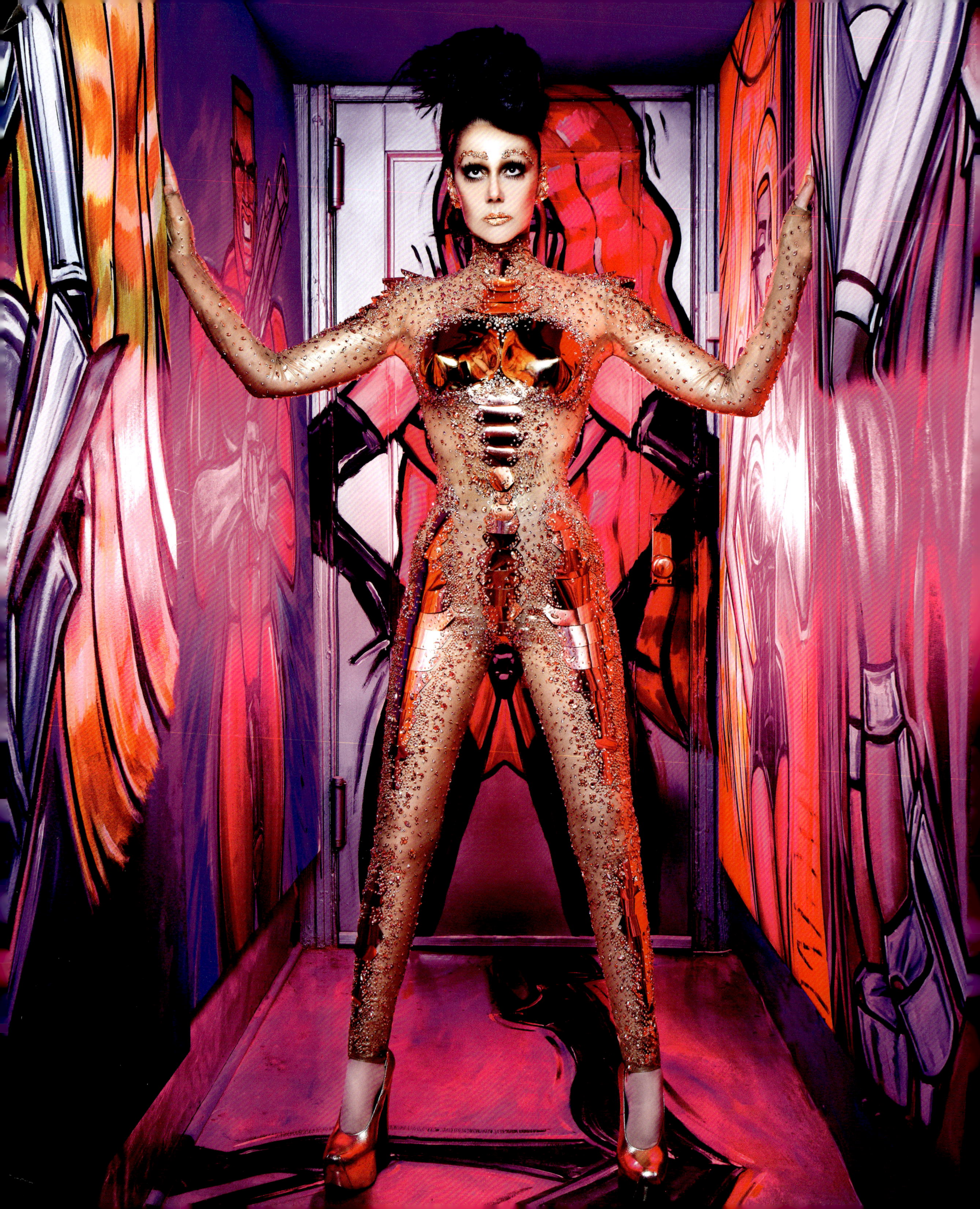

"The art thing is where I'm going," says Bartsch. "Doing parties that bring people together is important to me, but I prefer to do special events now. MAC [Cosmetics] wants me to curate an art event involving body art. It's really been art all along, but now I want to put it in a new context." "Susanne is a good-time girl, but she's also a performance artist," says Michael Leva, "and she's encouraged the other artists around her."[101]

"Susanne Bartsch has impeccable avant-garde taste and never ceases to amaze," says the photographer Stephen Klein. "She accepts people for what they are, and endorses the unique individual."[102] "The people she works with create a type of art," says the designer Waleed Khairzada. "They're using the body as a vessel for self-expression. As a young, gay kid transplanted from Afghanistan and studying at the Fashion Institute of Technology in New York City, Susanne gave me the freedom to be myself, to break boundaries of gender, class, and race. She created an ecosystem that was an incubator for fashion experimentation. It's not just that she's done great parties; she's created a kind of tribe. Fashion today is at a crossroads, very commercial and with technology providing so much access to visual information. How much more relevant is it to go back to Do-It-Yourself and just use your imagination? The world doesn't know the impact Susanne has had on fashion people, artists, and musicians because of her fascination with transformation and sartorial self-creation."[103]

"Susanne is a goddess-type of woman with her own unique style. The fashion world needs this," says Mauricio Padilha.[104] "There are certain people, like Leigh Bowery and Susanne Bartsch, who make fashion and make-up an art form – performance art," says his brother Roger. "If you look at old photos, you see how many of Susanne's looks have trickled down to performers like Rihanna, who wears the kind of insane, bejeweled corsetry that Susanne wore at the Copa. Susanne doesn't just wear fashion, she lives it. She's an editorial come to life, all these fantasies that fashion photographs present – she *is* the woman in the Helmut Newton photo. She's what fashion is about – it's not just about looking great, it's about living a dream."[105]

Notes

1   Susanne Bartsch, interview with author, January 7, 2015. Unless otherwise noted, all quotations from Bartsch are from author interviews conducted between January 5 and March 26, 2015
2   Smith Galtney, "A Night Out with Susanne Bartsch," *New York Times* (April 28, 2002), H4
3   Mickey Boardman, interview with author, February 27, 2015
4   Mihaly Csikszentmihalyi, *Creativity: Flow and the Psychology of Discovery and Invention* (New York: Harper Perennial, 2013), 1

5   See Richard Caves, *Creative Industries: Contracts Between Art and Commerce* (Cambridge: Harvard University Press, 2000); Barbara Townley, Nic Beech, Alan McKinley, and Gail Fairhurst (eds) "Managing in the Creative Industries: Managing the Motley Crew," *Human Relations*, vol. 62(7), 2009: 939–62

6   Ulf Larrson, ed., *Cultures of Creativity: The Centennial Exhibition of the Nobel Prize* (Canton: Science History Publications, 2001), 163

7   Zaldy, interview with author, February 24, 2014

8   Ibid.

9   Mathu Andersen, interview with author, February 10, 2015

10   Sarah Thornton, *Club Cultures: Music, Media and Subcultural Capital* (Cambridge: Polity Press, 1995), 3

11   Ibid., 10–11

12   Czikszentmihalyi, *Creativity*, 8–9

13   Ibid., 9

14   Hamish Bowles, interview with author, February 4, 2015

15   Richie Rich, interview with author, February 6, 2015

16   Stephen Jones, interview with author, February 5, 2015

17   Robert Forrest, interview with author, February 4, 2015

18   Michael Costiff, interview with author, March 13, 2015

19   Simon Doonan, interview with author, February 11, 2015

20   David Johnson, "Spandau Ballet, the Blitz Kids and the birth of the New Romantics." TheGuardian.com/music/2009/oct/04/Spandau-ballet-new-romantics, 28

21   Wendy Dagworthy quoted in Sonnet Stanfill, "Introduction," *80s Fashion: From Club to Catwalk* (London: V&A Publishing, 2013), 9

22   Hamish Bowles, interview with author, February 4, 2015

23   John Duka, "The Latest from London Arrives in SoHo (Ours)," *New York Times* (August 25, 1981), B13

24   Ronnie Cooke-Newhouse, interview with author, February 2, 2015

25   Piers Atkinson, interview with author, March 18, 2015

26   Andre Walker, interview with author, January 30, 2015

27   Rachel Auburn, interview with author, March 19, 2015

28   Greg Davis, interview with author, March 24, 2015

29   Quoted in Liz Smith, "What a Scream in New York," *Standard* (April 26, 1983), 18

30   Ronnie Cooke-Newhouse, "Bartschroom Tile," *Details* (June 1985), 116

31   "Between the Lines," *Daily News Record* (May 29, 1985) (Clipping)

32   Maria Cornejo, interview with author, February 23, 2015

33   Ruth La Ferla, "SoHo: Selling Tomorrow's Classics", *Women's Wear Daily*, vol. 150 (August 2, 1985), S56(2)

34   Michael Leva, interview with author, January 15, 2015

35   Leigh Bowery interview with David Yarritu, *Paper* (November 1987)

36   Oggy Yordanov, *New Club Kids* (Munich, London, New York: Prestel, 2011), unpaginated

37   RuPaul, correspondence with author, March 5, 2015

38   Quoted in Simon Doonan, *Wacky Chicks: Life Lessons from Fearlessly Inappropriate and Fabulously Eccentric Women* (New York: Simon & Schuster, 2003), 71

39   Joey Arias, interview with author, February 2, 2015

40   Patricia Field, interview with author, March 18, 2015

41   Joey Arias, interview with author, February 2, 2015

42   Scott Ewalt, interview with author, February 3, 2015

43   Susanne Bartsch, email message to author including correspondence from Sister Dimension, April 1, 2015

44   Michael Musto, interview with author, February 3, 2015

45   Susanne Bartsch, interview with author, January 5, 2015

46   Simon Doonan, interview with author, February 11, 2015

47   Scott Ewalt, interview with author, February 3, 2015

48   Michael Leva, interview with author, January 15, 2015

49   Robert Forrest, interview with author, February 4, 2015

50   Scott Ewalt, interview with author, February 3, 2015

51   Marc Jacobs, quoted in Holly Brubach, "In Fashion: The Life of the Party," *New Yorker* (March 4, 1991), 84

52   Kabuki, interview with author, March 13, 2015

53 Richie Rich, interview with author, February 6, 2015
54 John Bartlett, correspondence with author, March 4, 2015
55 Simon Doonan, interview with author, February 11, 2015
56 Doonan, *Wacky Chicks*, 67
57 Marc Balet, interview with author, February 2, 2015
58 Simon Doonan, interview with author, February 11, 2015
59 Ibid.
60 Scott Ewalt, interview with author, February 3, 2015
61 Danilo, interview with author, March 26, 2015
62 Joey Arias, interview with author, February 2, 2015
63 Kim Hastreiter, interview with author, February 24, 2015
64 Simon Doonan, interview with author, February 11, 2015
65 Ibid.
66 Kim Hastreiter, interview with author, February 24, 2015
67 Diane Pernet, interview with author, February 4, 2015
68 Theodora Sopko, interview with author, April 1, 2015
69 Patrick McMullan, interview with author, March 16, 2015
70 David Barton, interview with author, February 6, 2015
71 Danilo Dixon, interview with author, March 25, 2015
72 Mauricio Padilha, interview with author, March 17, 2015
73 Roger Padilha, interview with author, February 27, 2015
74 Abel Villareal, interview with author, February 26, 2015
75 Joey Arias, interview with author, February 2, 2015
76 Michael Leva, interview with author, January 15, 2015
77 Scott Ewalt, interview with author, February 3, 2015
78 Roger Padilha, interview with author, February 27, 2015
79 David Barton, interview with author, February 6, 2015
80 Roxanne Lowit, interview with author, February 26, 2015
81 Lynn Yaeger, interview with author, February 25, 2015
82 Paula Greif, interview with author, February 5, 2015
83 Ronnie Newhouse, interview with author, February 2, 2015
84 Andre Walker, interview with author, January 30, 2015
85   Ibid.
86 Jed Root, interview with author, March 31, 2015
87 Mickey Boardman, interview with author, February 27, 2015
88 Theodora Sopko, interview with author, April 1, 2015
89 Michael Musto, interview with author, February 3, 2015
90 Marc Balet, interview with author, February 2, 2015
91 Michael Shulman, "Not Going Gentle Into That Good Night,"
    New York Times (July 11, 2013) E1
92 James Gager, interview with author, March 2, 2015
93 Roger Padilha, interview with author, February 27, 2015
94 Kabuki Starshine, interview with author, March 13, 2015
95 Stephen Jones, interview with author, February 5, 2015
96 Danilo Dixon, interview with author, March 25, 2015
97 André Balazs, interview with author, March 31, 2015
98 Ian Schrager, email correspondence with author, May 10, 2015
99 Michael Musto, interview with author, February 3, 2015
100 Angela Golding, interview with author, February 23, 2015
101 Michael Leva, interview with author, January 15, 2015
102 Stephen Klein, email correspondence with author, May 1, 2015
103 Waleed Khairzada, interview with author, March 25, 2015
104 Mauricio Padilha, interview with author, March 17, 2015
105 Roger Padilha, interview with author, February 27, 2015

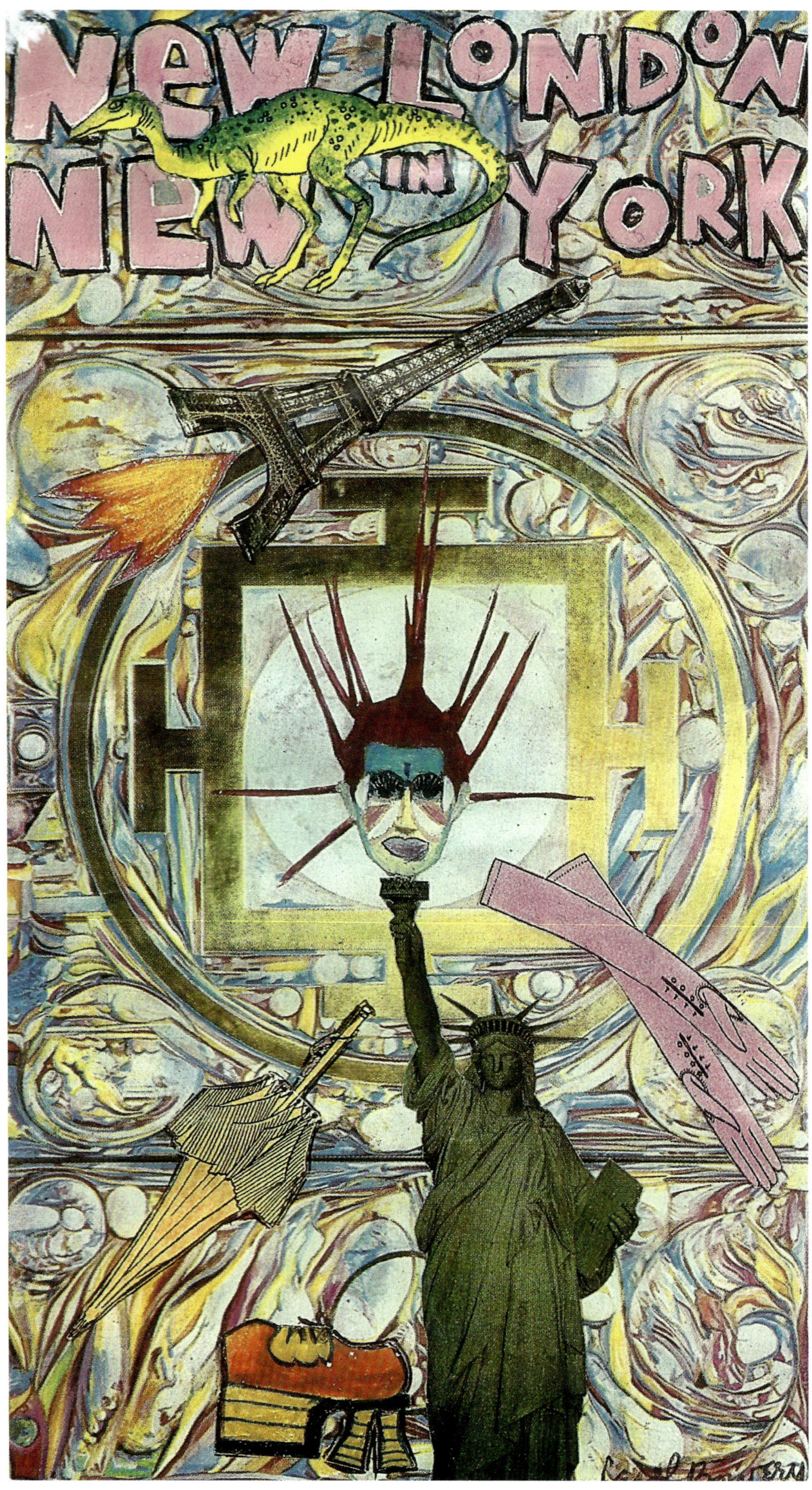
NEW LONDON
NEW IN YORK

Subcultural Capitals
London and New York City
By Melissa Marra

From the 1980s to the 1990s, fashion became increasingly integral to the nightlife and club cultures of London and New York City, just as club culture had a reciprocal impact on fashion during these decades. During the early years of the 1980s, London's provocative club culture transformed the city into a fertile ground for burgeoning fashion trends. In the foreword to her book, *80s Fashion: From Club to Catwalk*, Sonnet Stanfill (also the curator of the exhibition that the book accompanied at the Victoria and Albert Museum) writes, "This complex, vibrant, London scene is what really sparked young designers' imaginations."[2] Themed club nights, such as Blitz, established venues for dressing up that served to promote the glamorous aesthetic of the New Romantics subculture. Young men and women expressed their creativity through dress and pushed the boundaries of gender to their limits. "If clothing was our most immediate form of expression, then the club was where we exhibited it," noted Chris Sullivan, who ran the London club Wag.[3] By 1985, clubs like Leigh Bowery's Taboo were celebrating extreme dressing by creating an atmosphere entirely devoid of inhibitions.

On the other side of the Atlantic, Area, a New York City nightclub known for reinventing itself thematically every six weeks, was combining installation art, fashion, music, and performance in a "petri dish for creative activity."[4] Other club nights like Savage, hosted by Susanne Bartsch, attracted a motley assortment of city personalities who were explicitly directed to dress up and "make a statement with themselves."[5] In short, as Bartsch explains, "The nightclub was geared to [be] able to feature looks."[6] By the 1990s, clubs all across New York City were employing thousands of artists, designers, actors, and musicians, and these "were equipped with budgets and spaces to utilize for their creative projects, whether they be performances, fashion shows, or visual art exhibitions."[7]

"The only rule about dressing up to go out at night is that there isn't one. The wilder the style, the more fun you have."[1]

Invitation for the last "New London in New York" fashion show, designed by Leigh Bowery, 1984. Courtesy Susanne Bartsch.

Atmospheres such as these fostered an outside-the-box ideology that brought together a clientele enamored with sartorial grandeur, and provided, in turn, an endless source of inspiration for the designers, artists, and creative personalities who were attracted to them.

Referring to the London club scene of the 1980s, the designer Stevie Stewart has noted that "each group of people whether they were fashion designers, musicians or dancers, filmmakers or whatever, living together, going out together, and at the same clubs [. . .] had a passion for creating something new [. . .] that was almost infectious."[8] With respect to fashion specifically, the *Village Voice* journalist Frank Owen writes that "nightclubs are meant to function as laboratories of style where new trends and modes of being are spearheaded."[9] In fact, the work of many designers, including John Galliano, Stephen Jones, Alexander McQueen, Thierry Mugler, Vivienne Westwood, Jeremy Scott, and Anna Sui, and labels such as BodyMap and Heatherette were nurtured by the dynamic club culture of London and New York during the 1980s and 1990s, which often inspired the creation of clothing that was well beyond the norm.

Both London and New York cultivated club scenes that fed the appetites of creative types and provided an outlet for unbridled sartorial expression. The overarching theme that runs through club culture, and what it shares with fashion, is the notion of dressing up and creating looks. It is within this context that club culture provides a fertile source for what the sociologist Sarah Thornton calls "subcultural capital."[10] By exploring nightclubs as a space where music, fashion, and art merge in a cultural exchange, this essay will look at the reciprocal relationship between club culture and fashion, and the ways in which their subcultural capital is defined and created.

London: Blitz and the Birth of the New Romantics

Early in the 1980s, London's club scene gave rise to the highly influential subculture of the New Romantics, which would inspire a host of fashion personalities. Themed club nights such as Blitz in Covent Garden were instrumental in promoting the New Romantics' dressed-up aesthetic both domestically and overseas. But what precipitated this new wave of eccentrically dressed British youth? According to Ted Pollhemus, the author of *Street Style*, the movement emerged among a select crowd comprised of those who had grown disillusioned with punk. As he explains it:

> Since the earliest days of punk there had always existed within its ranks an energetic little clique of self-proclaimed Posers who took more interest in dressing up and clubbing than in formulating ideology of anarchic revolution. Invariably showing up in the most inventive creations, the key members of this group – people like Phillip Sallon, George O'Dowd, Steve Strange and Steve

Sullivan had been well received at Louise's (the lesbian club in Soho which had doubled as a Punk meeting place). But as punk tended more and more towards a stereotyped uniformity and as the 'Hard Punks' [. . .] turned their backs on fancy dress, these exquisite posers were increasingly left out in the cold.[11]

In 1978, key members of this group – Rusty Egan, Steve Strange, and Chris Sullivan – organized a weekly event titled "Bowie Night," at the Soho club Billy's.[12] "Drawing influence from the singer David Bowie, glam rock, and the new electronic music of bands such as Kraftwerk, the event encouraged a dress-up escapist fantasy,"[13] within which patrons could experiment sartorially, interacting with others who shared similar tastes in music and fashion. "They'd call us 'poofs' because we weren't dressed in a normal way," recalls Egan. "Hence why we formed the club. It was for those ex-punks who liked Lou Reed, Bowie, and Iggy."[14]

This nascent club scene was characterized by a sardonic rebelliousness exemplified by dressing up in the midst of an economic recession. As Egan professed, "You could dress up and be more than what Britain had to offer you."[15] The photographer Graham Smith further explains, "It was about rebellion, creativity, originality and being yourself outside normal and straight society."[16] The sociologist Sarah Thornton has observed that club cultures are in essence "taste cultures,"[17] facilitating the congregation of people with like mindsets, for example musical, sartorial, or sexual, and thereby housing *ad hoc* communities.[18] Thornton notes that for the majority of club-goers, the mainstream culture is the entity opposed to theirs and against which they define themselves. This, in turn, has led to the formation of new aesthetics and judgements of value.[19]

Teenagers and twenty-somethings, many of whom were enrolled in nearby art schools, donned amalgams of theatrical costume and re-rendered thrift clothes, intent on glamorizing their lives. Their looks were not only hybrids of historical references (medieval, nineteenth century, old Hollywood, and so on) but were also "experimental in terms of gender definition."[20] "Billy's was the birth of the London club scene and people expressing themselves through their clothes, hair and makeup [. . .] There weren't really any rules, apart from push your look as far as you can. Invent yourself. Entertain," recalls Nicola Tyson, at the time an eighteen-year-old student at Chelsea School of Art.[21]

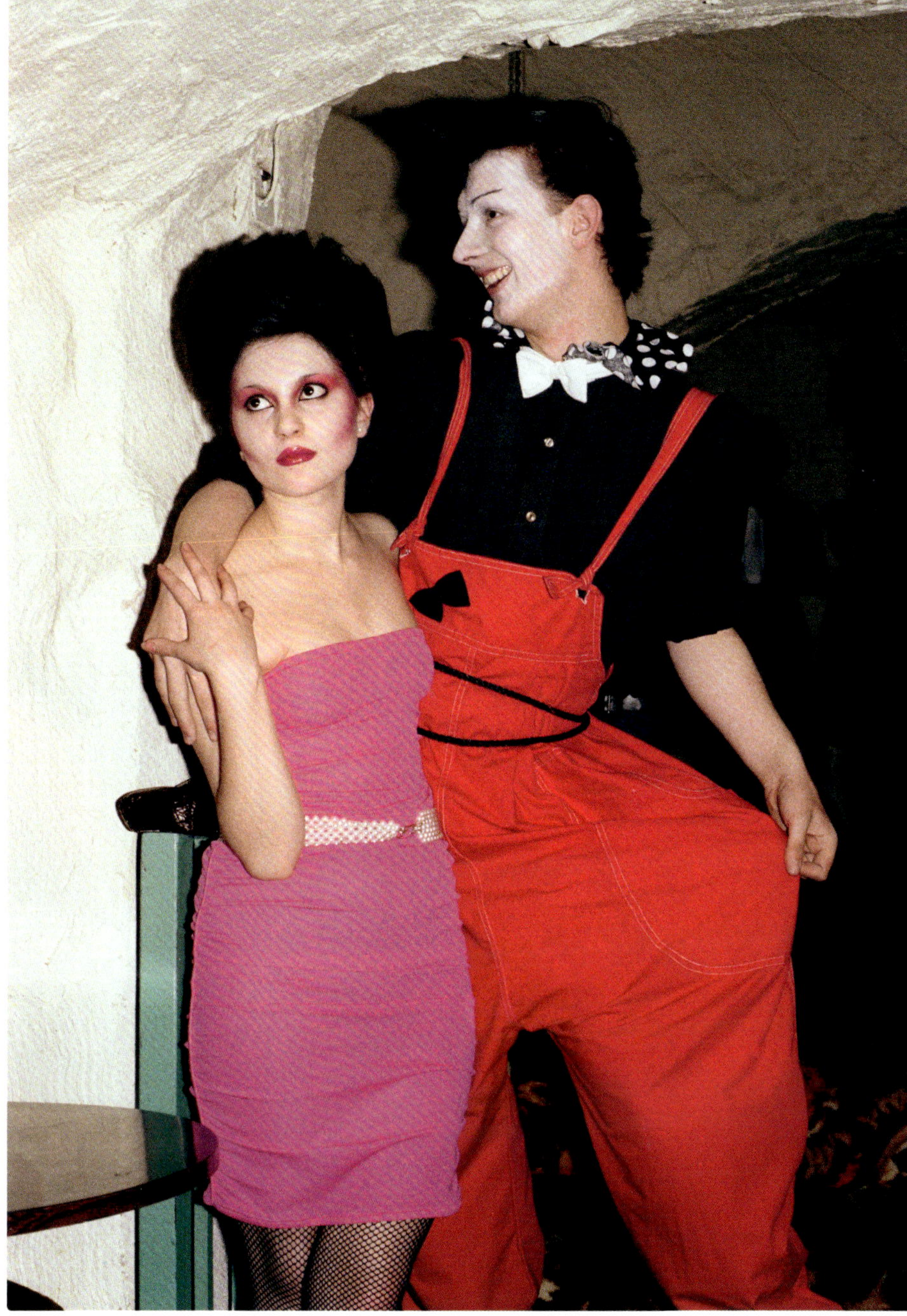

Julia Fodor (DJ Princess Julia) and George O'Dowd (Boy George) at Billy's, 1978. Photo by Nicola Tyson, © The Artist, courtesy Sadie Coles HQ, London.

Ultimately, Bowie Night grew too big for the confines of Billy's, and in 1979 Egan and Strange moved their brainchild to Blitz, a wine bar near Covent Garden. "There might have only been 200 of us but we were ready to take on the world,"[22] Strange recalled proudly. At Blitz, fashion and music merged to form the eccentric aesthetic that would dominate London's club culture for the next decade. While it served as a venue for new music, it was its eccentrically dressed clientele that gave Blitz its notoriety. "I ran a very tight shop […] I wanted creative-minded pioneers there who looked like a walking piece of art," Strange professed.[23] His rigorous Studio-54-esque door policy was about "showing your creative side, and about showing that you'd taken time and effort in what you had created."[24] The fashion historian Caroline Evans notes the significance of this precedence in club culture: "The high maintenance sartorial criteria of Blitz changed daily and was predicated on the notion of the self as a work of art, something that was continually rescripted within the club culture of the early eighties."[25]

The milliner Stephen Jones affirms, "The Blitz ruled people's lives […] inspired absolute devotion of the kind previously reserved for a pop idol. I'd find people at the Blitz who were possible only in my imagination. But they were real."[26] Expounding on this notion, the former Bananarama band member and Blitz club-goer Siobhan Fahey states, "We'd spend the whole week preparing our outfits for the club. We'd buy fabrics, customize our leather jackets […] find old military things and throw them together in a mix of Glam, military and strangeness." 27 Initially termed "Blitz Kids" or "Cult with no Name," this new generation of club-goers eventually garnered the moniker "New Romantics" from the media, and many of the most assiduous were music, art and/or fashion students from nearby colleges. In a departure from its predecessors, Blitz did not cater to celebrity clientele, and this was made infamously clear the night Strange denied Mick Jagger entrance for being too "rock and roll." Instead, many of its scene's stand-outs became celebrities in their own right. Boy George, for example, who served as a coat-check *girl*, was one of Blitz's most high profile habitués. "He was like the Pied Piper, 50 kids would follow him around. He was a real star," recalled Rusty Egan.[28]

"The Blitz meant a lot to me because there was so much creativity collected under one roof," Strange would later recall. "Not only bands like Spandau Ballet and Visage, but young designers,

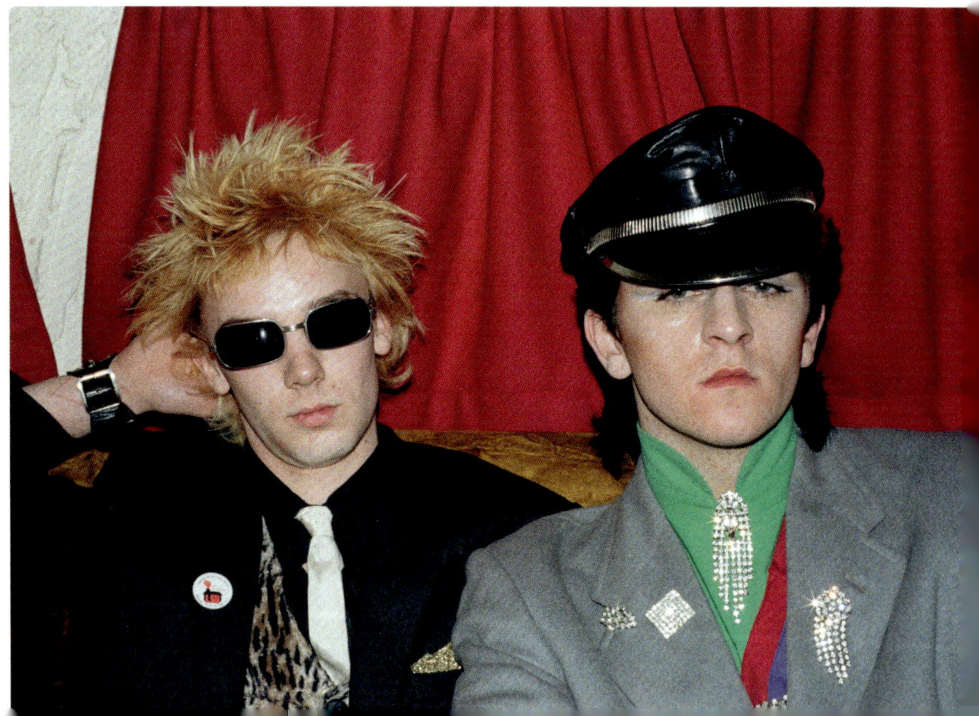

Unknown person (L) and Steve Strange (R) at Billy's, 1978. Photo by Nicola Tyson, © The Artist, courtesy Sadie Coles HQ, London.

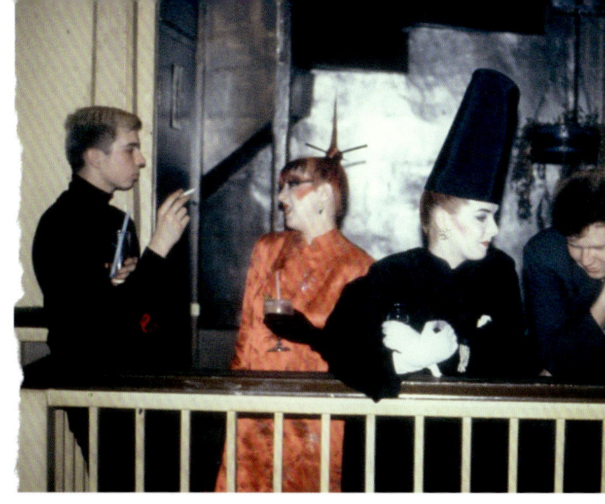

photographers – even milliners. It was like a burst of energy at a time when the London scene seemed so stagnant."[29] Among its weekly attendees were the designers Rachel Auburn, Sue Clowes, John Galliano, Stephen Jones, and Melissa Caplan – all of whom were influenced by this vibrant club scene, ultimately forging links between fashion, club culture, and music. Stephen Jones has asserted that "meeting people like George O'Dowd and Judith Frankland who lived their fashion, I learned more in one year at the Blitz than my three years at Saint Martins."[30] Galliano, who continued to be a "club daemon" well into the 1980s and 1990s would later observe, "The club scene fed me. Being with other creative people like Boy George was a crucial experience for me."[31]

Inspired by the French Revolution, Galliano's 1984 degree collection for Central Saint Martins titled *Les Incroyables*, presented a flair for theatricality, historicizing, and androgyny characteristic of the New Romantics style. Featuring markedly oversized shirts in white organdy, brocade vests with old coin buttons, and raj-style pants, it was immediately purchased by Joan Burstien and displayed during Fashion Week in the windows of the forward-thinking boutique Browns. In her book *Fashion at the Edge: Spectacle, Modernity, and Deathliness*, Caroline Evans notes, "This bricoleur's aesthetic that characterized British club and subcultures in this period also provided a model of the design process for designers like John Paul Gaultier in Paris and Westwood and Galliano in London, and goes some way to explaining their own versions of cut-and-mix in the 1980s."[32] This hybridization of past epochs, the tendency to "[pillage] history like an image bank," would characterize Galliano's designs into the 1990s.[33] Galliano's ascent in the echelons of the fashion world ultimately distanced him from club and street fashions, but his penchant for spectacle derives from his formative years as an active participant in London's club culture. In fact, in his Spring/Summer 2003 collection Galliano referenced directly club personalities such as the performer Leigh Bowery and the artist Trojan, who had inspired his early career.

London's exploding club culture was also influential in the work of Vivienne Westwood and Malcolm McLaren, designers whose previous creations had been inspired by elements of rebellion in British youth culture. Westwood and McLaren were in tune with the connection between London's new music and the innovative fashion trends emerging from its club culture. In 1980, the designers changed the name of their London store from "Seditionaries" to "World's End," making inventive reinterpretations of historical dress a hallmark of the World's End style.[34] Their clothes, which emphasized layering, drapery, and androgyny, were, in turn, favored by the image-conscious New Romantics.

Pirates (Autumn/Winter 1982), Westwood and McLaren's first runway collection, was staged in March 1981, and featured an imaginative assortment of eighteenth-century-inspired pirate clothes including white frilly blouses, styl-

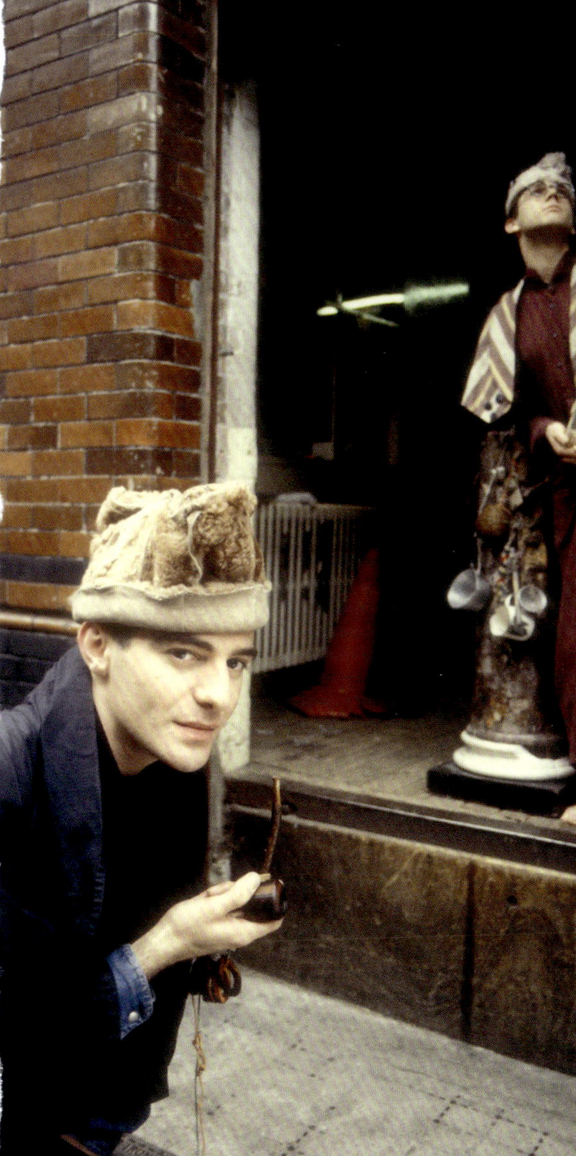

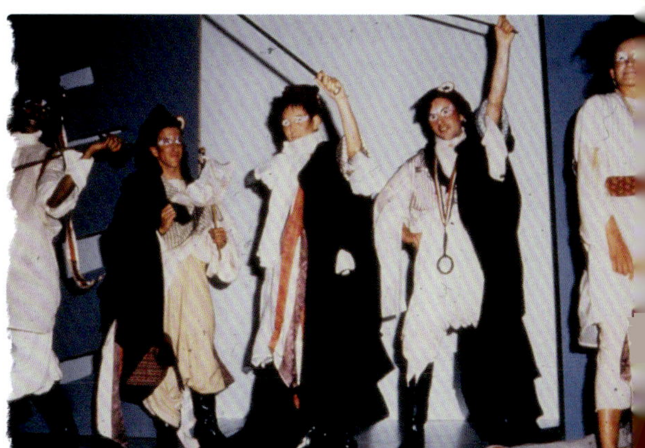

ized pirate hats, and waistcoats with historical detailing. McLaren, who incidentally, also managed a number of British bands, dressed his musicians in Westwood's designs, and in so doing created an entire ideology around the World's End shop.[35] Clothes from their *Pirates* collection, were worn by emerging musicians such as Adam and the Ants and Bow Wow Wow, and were eventually showcased in Adam Ant's video for "Stand and Deliver." In 1982, hoping to increase album sales for his own band, Visage, Steve Strange also exploited the growing connection between fashion, music, and club culture, orchestrating a fashion show of young London designers in Paris. Strange showcased the work of six designers integral to the band's image including Melissa Kaplan, Joseph Linard, and Stephen Jones, and titled his show *The Best of British Fashion*.[36]

The World's End collections that followed – *Savage* (Spring/Summer 1982), *Buffalo* (Autumn/Winter 1982), and *Hobo-Punkature* (Spring/Summer 1983) – were all characterized by a distressed aesthetic of mismatched elements, "presented in a seemingly thrown together-mix of historic and multicultural influences."[37] *Witches* (Autumn/Winter 1983), Westwood and McLaren's final collaboration, featured a mixture of street- and sportswear, that included graphics by the New York graffiti artist Keith Haring, who was himself a prominent figure in New York's club scene. These early collections are now widely credited with bringing London's club culture and street fashion scene to international prominence.

"In a way, I think my life was more influenced by club life than fashion design," remarked Stephen Jones.[38] Jones opened his first hat salon in 1980, in the basement of the store PX in Covent Garden. PX was *the* flagship store for New Romantics wares and Jones began receiving commissions from pop groups like Visage, Spandau Ballet, and Culture Club almost immediately. Diana, Princess of Wales and Isabella Blow were both regular customers at Jones's shop. In 1983, he was featured in the Culture Club video for their song 'Do You Really Want to Hurt Me,' wearing a fez and a vintage zoot suit.[39] This look provided John Paul Gaultier with the inspiration for his *The Return of Prints* collection, and led the "king of Paris fashion" to commission Jones to design hats for his next collection.[40] Since then, Jones has worked with a number of the world's top designers including

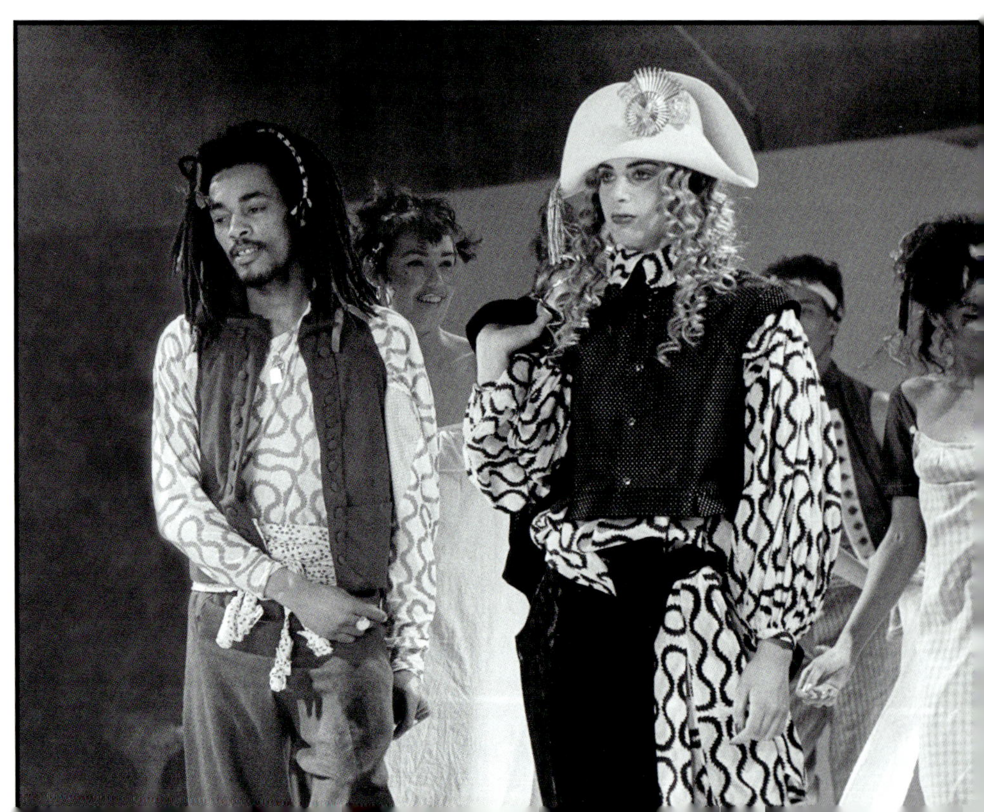

Vivienne Westwood, World's End
Fashion Show at Olympia,
London, October 23, 1981.
Photo © David Corio /PYMCA.

Azzedine Alaïa, Claude Montana, and Thierry Mugler. However, his collaborations with his fellow clubber John Galliano for Christian Dior are among his most notable.

Leigh Bowery, Taboo, and the New Glitterati

Blitz served to inspire a host of other regular club nights, including Taboo and Kinky Gerlinky, which attracted a clientele of fashionable club personalities such as the DJ Princess Julia, Trojan, and Leigh Bowery and were hugely inspirational to the designers who frequented them.[41] Bowery in particular would become one of London's most prominent nightlife figures, with his outrageous style garnering him a reputation as "London's most flamboyant after dark celebrity."[42] His sartorial leanings were clearly born of club culture, and he reveled in the spectacle of fashion, elevating dressing up to an art form. Bowery experimented with "gender bending" – a prominent theme in 1980s fashion – and manipulated clothing to create physical exaggerations, while referencing world cultures and the fashions of earlier decades. His methodical use of theatrical make-up, body paint, jewelry, and hats allowed him to transform his appearance in its entirety with each new look. However, Bowery's personality belied a serious interest in the history of fashion: his private library held a myriad of books about designers; the couturiers Cristóbal Balenciaga and Christian Dior in particular.[43] This was further exemplified by his desire to understand corsets, purchasing them second-hand with the corsetiere Mr. Pearl. Together they took the garments apart to study their construction.[44]

Born in Australia, Leigh Bowery studied fashion for two years before becoming disillusioned with the restrictions of formal training. Inspired by the New Romantics, he emigrated to London and immersed himself in its club scene, befriending the designer Rachel Auburn after meeting her at Kensington Market. As the nightlife legend Kenny Kenny recalls:

> I went to London and got involved with Rachel Auburn, who had a fashion line with Leigh Bowery. I don't think Leigh did the line for very long – probably months rather than years. But Rachel continued and he designed with Rachel, even though his name wasn't on the label. He was very involved with her and he was also running the club Taboo, and she was the DJ.[45]

Bowery and Auburn became close friends, collaborators, and regulars in the underground club scene alongside other visionaries such as the designer Judy

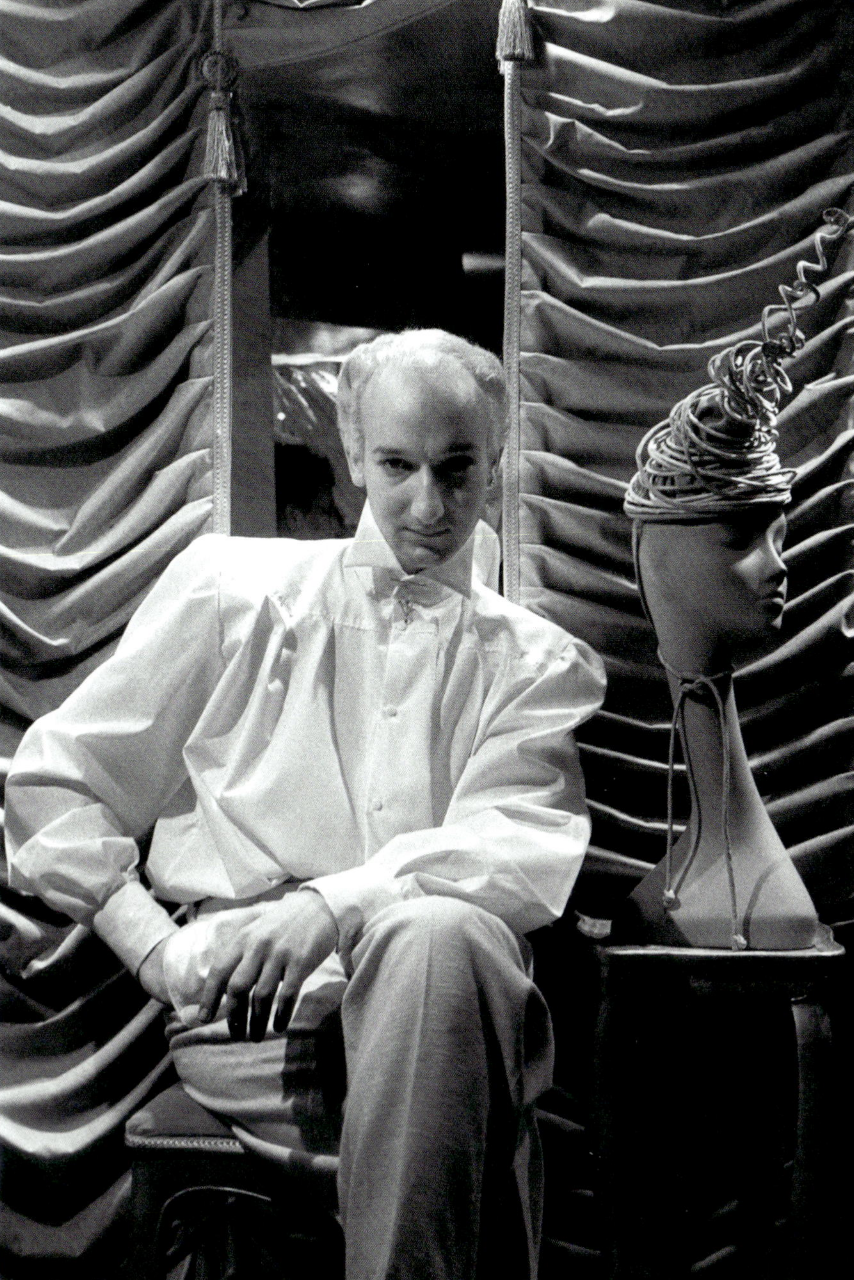

Stephen Jones in his first shop in the basement of PX on Endell St., Covent Garden, London, 1980. Photo © Graham Smith/ PYMCA.

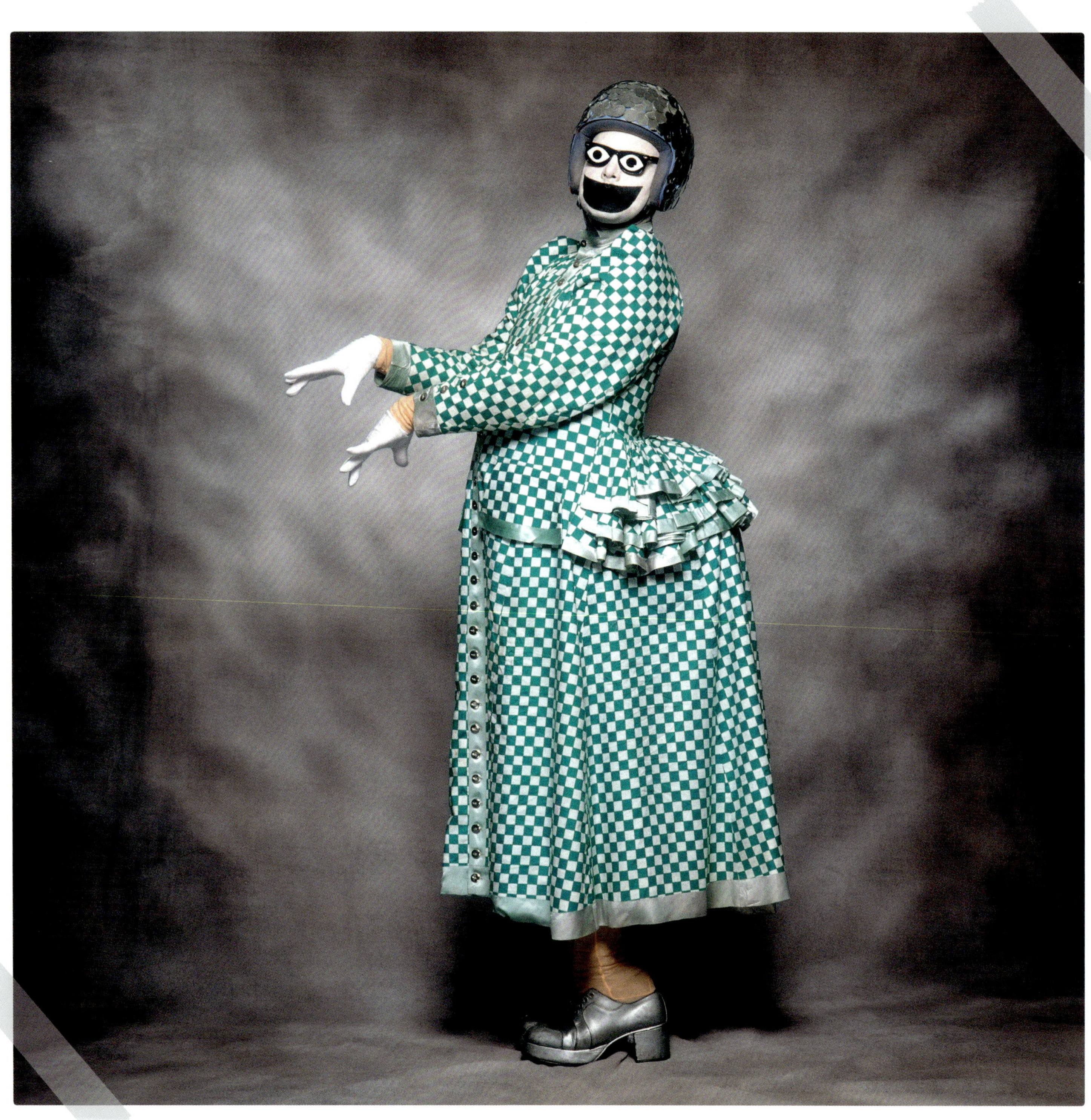

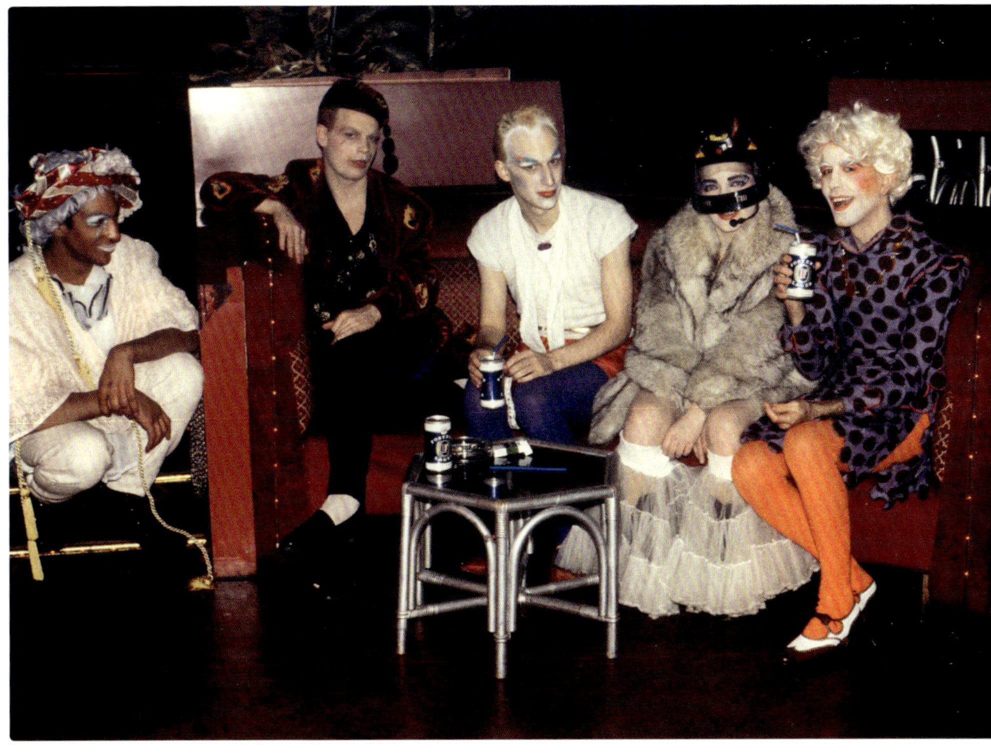

Above: Clubbers at Leigh Bowery's club night Taboo, London, 1986. Photo © Hartnett/PYMCA.

Below: The fashion designer and DJ Rachel Auburn at Taboo, London, 1985. Photo © Hartnett/PYMCA.

Facing: Leigh Bowery. Photo by Fergus Greer.

Blame, Trojan, and the designer/photographer Michael Costiff.[46] Bowery and Trojan, in particular, attained celebrity status with their flamboyant looks, which included flowing satin robes, velour tunic tops, striped tights, lycra pants, leatherette military hats, and an abundance of glittering gems.[47] "It's not a Glam-Rock parody," asserted Bowery in a 1984 *The Face* magazine article. "I'm just trying to make a bold statement through clothes and color. We have had enough of 'Hard Times' and saleable things. It's only a small scene at the moment but other designers like Westwood and BodyMap are picking up on it. I'm certain my look will really catch on."[48]

In January 1985, Bowery launched his own weekly club event, rakishly named "Taboo," because as he professed "there's nothing you can't do there."[49] Taboo and its crowd of radicals exalted the androgyny pervading the New Romantics scene. According to Boy George, "the Taboo scene was a kind of [a] deconstructed version of the New Romantics."[50] The club's mantra of "dress as though your life depends on it, or don't bother,"[51] promoted an exaggerated fashion aesthetic, and above all else, individual expression. For Bowery, Taboo was a reflection of his clothes and attitudes.[52] It provided Bowery himself with a venue to experiment freely with his performance art and showcase his extraordinary style, which was becoming increasingly provocative. "[Leigh] had created [. . .] an over the top, camp, dandy, surrealist persona and people were wearing frilly clothes and platforms and mixing everything up. It was definitely very new and very bold and I think that was extremely formative for me," admitted Kenny Kenny.[53]

Taboo featured its own set of "Warholian" superstars: Trojan, Rachel Auburn, the dancer Michael Clark, the BodyMap designers David Holah and Stevie Stewart, and the filmmaker John Maybury.[54] As Stewart recounts, "It was Taboo every Thursday night [. . .] It was the eighties and all the different fields of music, film, theatre, and dance were working together. There were interconnections being made between different worlds."[55] For her part, Auburn used the club to showcase her designs as soon as they were produced. In fact, the same year that Taboo opened, Bowery and Auburn opened a stall together in Kensington Market, calling it "Spend, Spend, Spend."[56] Stephen Jones, who met Galliano through his Taboo associates, and later introduced designer Claude Montana to the club remembers, "[Leigh] was fierce [. . .] he wore things like a German World War II helmet with polka dots and a polka dot outfit and a polka

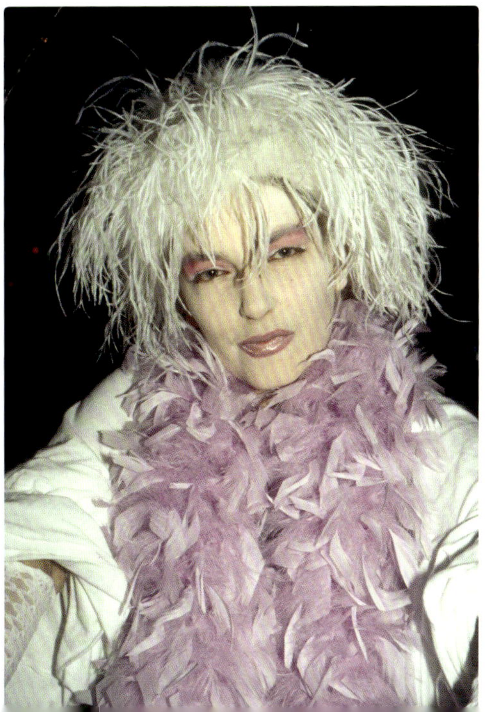

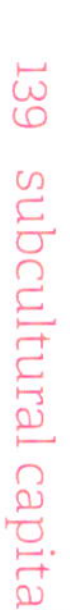

dot face – genius! [. . .] We always thought that the New York clubs were much more crazy, but actually Leigh made Taboo the most extravagant of them all."[57]

Taboo was forced to close its doors in 1986 after only eighteen months, following accounts of excessive drug use at the club,[58] but in its short existence it turned Bowery into a cult figure.[59] As Stephen Jones attested, "there was drug taking in the club scene, but it wasn't like you had to take drugs to be a part of the group. Really our drug was fashion."[60] While Bowery strove to be unique in his fashion extremism, ironically his influence would impact the likes of John Galliano, Alexander McQueen, Vivienne Westwood, and the fashion photographer David LaChapelle. Ultimately, it redefined nightlife in both London and New York City.

Founded by Michael and Gerlinde Costiff late in the 1980s, Kinky Gerlinky was one of Taboo's more outrageous successors. Described as "a wild, dressed-up-to-the-max, polysexual event,"[61] the atmosphere at Kinky Gerlinky lacked the implicit pretension of nights at the Blitz. This was enhanced by "dazzling stage shows" that drew their inspiration from the Rio Carnival or New York Vogueing Balls,[62] and the club's patrons were an eclectic mix of drag queens, Club Kids, muscle boys, fashion designers, models, and visual artists.[63] The latter were inspired by the parties of Susanne Bartsch, a London transplant who moved to New York City in 1981. Bartsch had been active in the London club scene in its early years, during which she befriended the Costiffs. By 1986, she had begun hosting club nights in New York City at venues such as Savage, and later at the Bentley Hotel and Copacanana. Bartsch attracted acclaim for her ability to draw together both downtown and uptown personalities, and this is what she considered to be her contribution to New York nightlife. As the *New Yorker* magazine explained, Bartsch "took all these people out of their various corners – the drag queens out of the gay bars, the musclemen out of the gyms, the strippers out of the sex joints – and brought them into her club."[64]

New London Goes to New York

By the early years of the 1980s Bartsch had opened a small clothing boutique in New York City, and via the underground club scene, she was introduced to Rachel Auburn and Leigh Bowery. "I would miss the incredible looks that were happening [in London] more and more. Every week there everyone

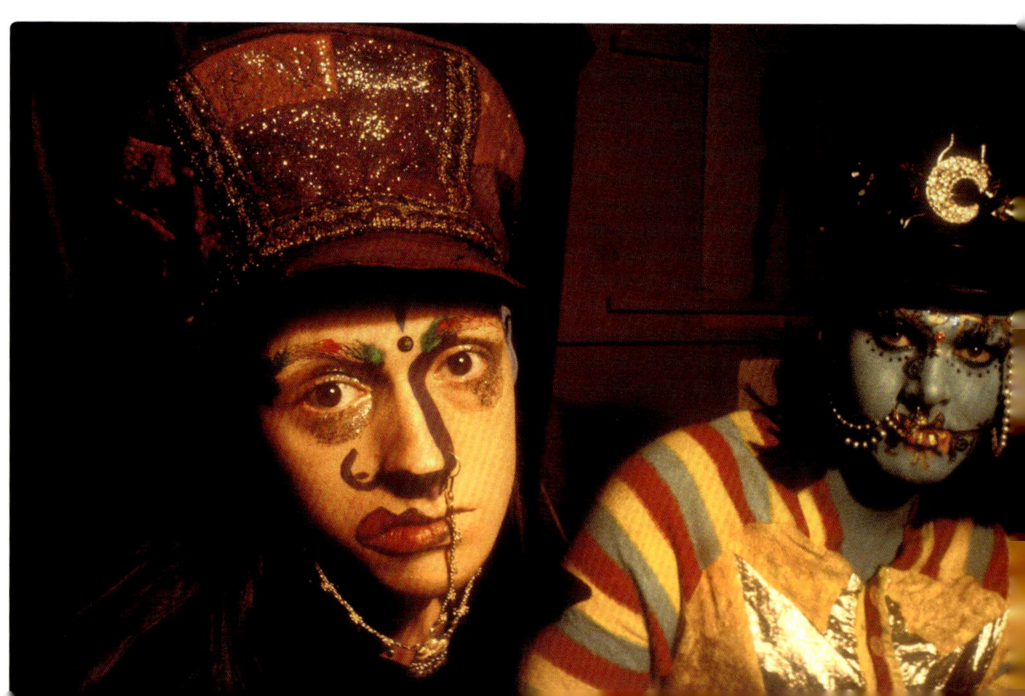

Trojan (L) and Leigh Bowery (R).
Photographed in the Art room
at Diorama, London, 1983.
Photo © Hartnett/ PYMCA.

had a completely new look. I missed that; nobody was dressing up here," Bartsch bemoaned.[65] "So I had this thought: *why not import what I missed?*"[66] So, she travelled between New York and London, serving as a kind of liaison and sourcing clothes from up-and-coming designers such as John Galliano, Stephen Jones, Leigh Bowery, and Mr. Pearl. "A lot of them were in college or behind-the-scenes," Bartsch explained.[67]

To further promote British talent, Bartsch recruited twenty young designers (many just out of college) including Leigh Bowery, Rachel Auburn, BodyMap, Sue Clowes (who outfitted Boy George), John Richmond, and Stephen Jones, to participate in a New York fashion show she herself organized. Titled 'New London in New York,' this show was presented at the Roxy Roller Rink on April 22, 1983, and showcased a number of designers whose work Bartsch often featured in her store. This event, with its sets by Michael Costiff and invitations designed by Leigh Bowery, proved an extravaganza of British ingenuity. "The show was amazing,"[68] Bartsch declared. "I had a line around the block with a huge attendance and that was the first time I knew I liked to bring people together and have a spectacle. It was really magical to see everybody."[69] 'New London Goes to New York' garnered such acclaim that New York department stores like Bloomingdales and Macy's placed orders for collections, including Bowery and Auburn's patchwork garments.[70] After staging three additional shows at the New York nightclub the Limelight, Bartsch was even invited to present the show in Tokyo in 1984.

BodyMap

One of the more commercially successful labels to emerge from London's club circuit was BodyMap. Its founders, David Holah and Stevie Stewart, met on their first day as fashion students at Middlesex Polytechnic. Initially designing clothes to wear clubbing, the pair used the nightclub arena to socialize and share ideas with other creative types such as Michael Clarke, John Maybury, and Boy George. "In the early eighties the fashion scene was completely mixed in with all the other media," Stewart explained.[71] By the time they graduated in 1982, Holah and Stewart were noted as rising talents both within club circles and among fashion insiders, and their graduation collection was purchased for Brown's by the boutique's far-sighted buyer, Robert Forrest.[72]

BodyMap was highly innovative in its approach to pattern making, garment construction, and in its use of modern materials such as lycra.[73] Its distinctive aesthetic was characterized by layers of form-fitting garments featuring bold geometric prints created by the textile artist Hilde Smith, which were rendered in cotton knits such as jersey and sweatshirt materials. "We invented our own style and way of dressing, layering big shapes [. . .] over proportioned tops, over figure hugging bottom silhouettes and the graphic prints changed the look of

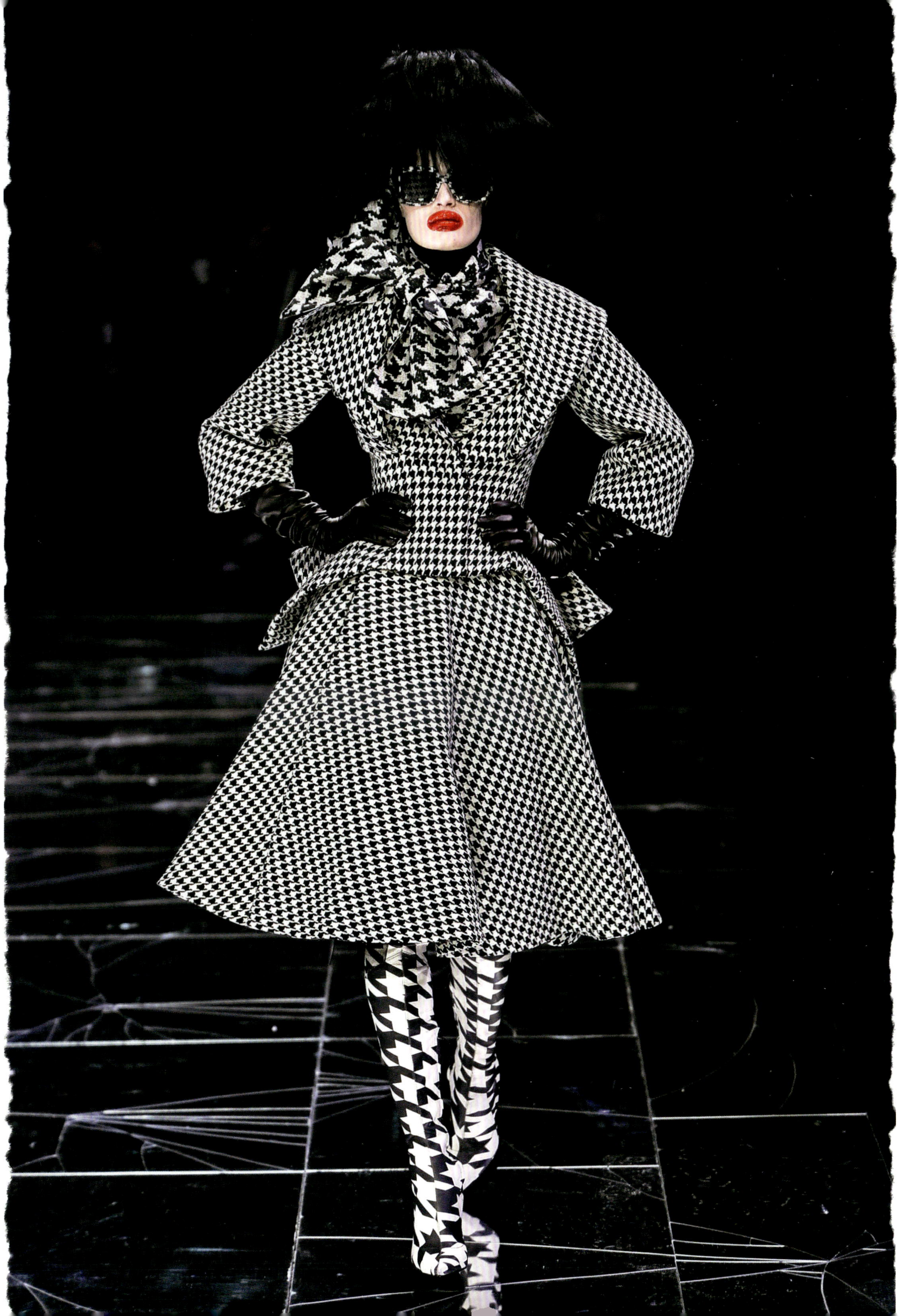

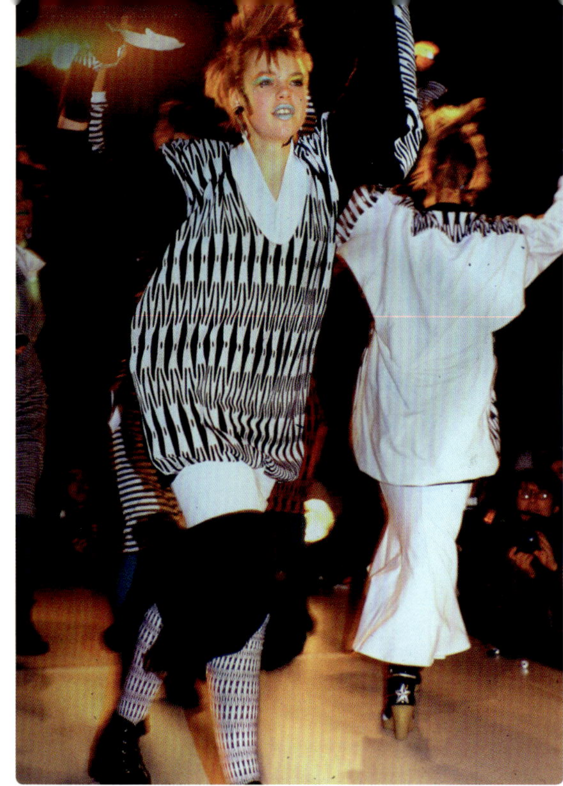

BodyMap, *The Cat in the Hat Takes a Rumble with the Techno Fish* collection, Autumn/Winter 1984. Bloomsbury Publishing, Photo by Niall McInerney

fashion and the way people were dressing in the 80's" Holah asserted.[74] The pair's first collection, *Cat in the Hat takes a Rumble with the Techno Fish*, which was presented at London Fashion Week in 1984, was inspired by the illustrations of Dr. Seuss – it featured elements such as whimsical hats and black-and-white stripes –and the Francis Ford Coppola film *Rumble Fish*. *Rumble Fish* was shot in black-and-white except for a scene in a pet store aquarium with the "fighting fish" in primary colors.[75] The show, described by the *New York Times* as "as bizarre as any rock star's video,"[76] proved quite successful, resulting in £500,000 in orders.[77]

Often reminiscent of performance art, BodyMap's catwalk presentations paid tribute to the label's club-culture origins by featuring appearances by Boy George, Leigh Bowery, and Michael Clark, along with cross-dressing models, all in choreographed routines with risqué wardrobe changes. "Our fashion shows were the hottest ticket in town," Holah affirmed. "They were spectacular and unique, they were like art performances." BodyMap routinely turned to the club scene to form imaginative collaborations. Michael Clark, for instance, choreographed a number of their fashion shows, and Holah and Stewart reciprocated by designing costumes for Clark's dance company. BodyMap's "in house" photo shoots, moreover, were shot by emerging photographers such as Mario Testino and David LaChapelle.[78] Despite BodyMap's meteoric rise, the high demand for their clothes together with the designers' lack of commercial experience and unsuccessful attempts to curtail "knock-off" designs, ultimately led to the label folding in the early years of the 1990s. Nevertheless, BodyMap remains a cult favorite among fashion insiders today.

NEW YORK CITY

Resurrecting New York Nightlife

In the year 1987, the *New York Times* observed, "Every few seasons a new club seems to take the spotlight, reflecting the mood of the times with a *modis vivendi* that is fresh and original."[79] During the 1980s, a number of New York City's clubs, including Mudd, Club 57, Pyramid, and Area, consciously catered to an art-fashion-performance crowd thus attracting "cool, creative people who looked great."[80] Area, in particular, brought installation and performance art into the nightclub setting.[81] It explicitly encouraged its patrons' participation, eliminating any distinction between performer and audience.[82] Meanwhile, the mega-club Palladium was forging its own connections between the art world and nightlife by commissioning works by the likes of Keith Haring and Jean-Michel Basquiat to serve as the club's decor. As the Palladium's co-owner Steve Rubell once proclaimed, "Artists [were] the new stars of the eighties."[83]

By the end of the 1980s, an economic crash and the AIDS epidemic – the "ghost that passed through New York nightlife" – ushered in a new wave of conservatism that stifled a once vibrant nightlife community. So palpable was this effect that the *Village Voice* columnist Michael Musto was inspired to write an article in April 1987 entitled "The Death of Downtown: Who took the Life out of Nightlife?" However, this ominous declaration proved somewhat premature, as in the 1990s New York City began experiencing the rebirth of its nightlife, and once more a cross-pollination between nightclubs, fashion, art, and music. With many of the city's mega clubs shuttered by the previous decade's economic downturn,[84] a radically different club scene emerged and with it a fresh troupe of night denizens. "The stock market collapse of October 19, 1987 was followed by a recovery [. . .] it was just when the mood seemed glummest that surfaces began to glitter," wrote Anthony Haden-Guest, the author of *The Last Party: Studio 54, Disco, and the Culture of the Night*.[85]

Susanne Bartsch was integral to New York's nightlife renaissance. In 1987 she began hosting weekly parties at the nightclub Savage. By transporting British underground fashion to New York, Bartsch also provided a unique link between the club cultures of London and New York. The atmosphere at Savage was reminiscent of "the best mixed gay clubs of the early 80s in London [. . .] but spiced with that uniquely New York attitude," according to *i-D* magazine.[86] Inspired by Taboo in London, Savage was one of the first New York clubs to introduce cross-dressing to the club mainstream. In 1991, the writer Molly Parkin told the *Independent*, "[Bartsch] did it first with those young British designers she exported to New York in the early Eighties [. . .] So, to take the best of London's club life – like hosting one-night-a-week events in otherwise untrendy clubs with lots of interesting looking people wandering around – that was a very astute, logical, progression."[87]

Bartsch started her parties at Savage during a time when New York nightlife was literally destitute. The impact of AIDS during this time can hardly be overstated: it claimed the lives of many of the city's free spirits, quelling the abandon that had fueled nightlife for over a decade. By filling her clubs with a mélange of drag queens, performance artists, and go-go dancers, she encouraged an atmosphere of "flesh and fantasy,"[88] and created a space free of inhibitions for the patrons. "The place is suffused with sex," reported *New York* magazine. "Everyone says no one is having it, because they are all too afraid of AIDS. Still you can feel it in the air."[89]

For Bartsch, dressing up is about enjoyment and making a visual statement. Championing complete creative freedom, she set the sartorial tone at her events by making herself the focal point, or as *Paper* magazine described, "The eye of the hurricane and a whirling dervish constantly inventing her own looks and do's."[90] Her parties resembled a fashion parade where those seeking their fix of the New York underground scene could project their personalities through stylistic dress. A year after Savage opened, Bartsch's parties moved to the club

Susanne with Julio Quinones at Area, New York City, c. 1985. Susanne is wearing an ensemble by Elmaz Huseyin. Photo by Roxanne Lowit.

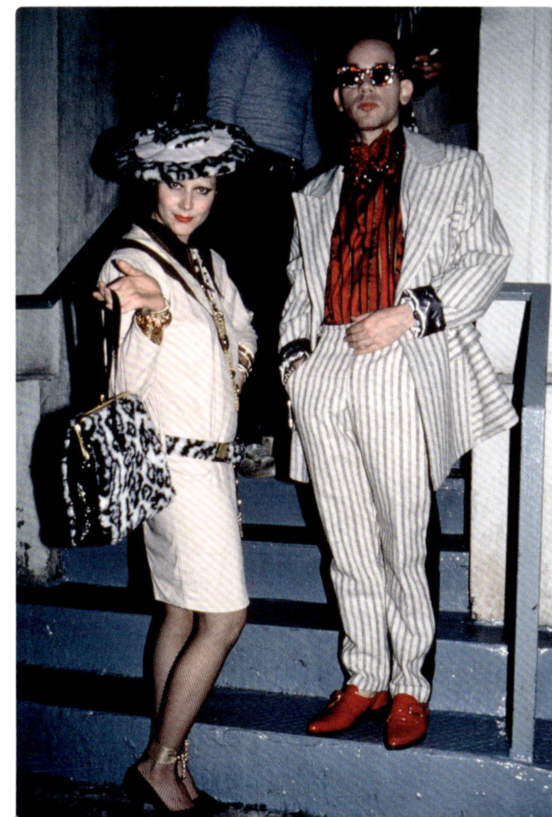

Bentley's, and in 1988 she began hosting a monthly party at the uptown club Copacabana, where tellingly, "ideas and true style rule[d] over designer labels." Her Copacabana parties were in the vain of a Mardi Gras, and these invariably attracted a large fashion contingent that included John Paul Gaultier, Donna Karan, Calvin Klein, Thierry Mugler, Claude Montana, and Stephen Sprouse, as well as fashion photographers such as Stephen Meisel and Mario Testino. "I think the ingredient that made it all take off was my being in the fashion business. People always associate me with dressing up, and whenever I had done something it was always new. So before I even opened the door there was an energy and excitement," Bartsch explained.[91]

Fashion was integral to creating the visual experience at Copacabana as well. The Paris-based hairstylist Karim Mitha agreed that "These parties are [...] useful for anyone in fashion. Everyone has complete creative freedom. Here, there are no boundaries."[92] Bartsch's blend of escapist fantasy and fashion would influence designers such as Thierry Mugler, whose own penchant for spectacle was evident in his theatrical runway presentations: Mugler was an active figure in New York's club scene befriended Bartsch and attended many of her parties during the 1990s. In 1992, *Women's Wear Daily* reported that "[Mugler] is also devoted to club-hopping. Like Jean Paul Gaultier, he draws much of his fashion inspiration from denizens of the night."[93] In fact, Mugler featured Lady Miss Kier and Dmitry of the American house/club music group Deee-Lite in his Spring 1992 runway presentation.[94]

The Nightclub, Fashion, and Art

By the 1990s, the cross-pollination taking place between the worlds of nightclubs, fashion, art, and music was in full swing, and according to Patrick McMullan, a photo-documentarian who has traced the evolution of New York nightlife since the mid-1980s, there were "usually a number of style movements going on simultaneously."[95] The reopening of clubs ushered a sociocultural pluralism represented by a motley crew of personalities who elicited – nay craved – attention with their personal styles and thus drew attention in turn to the New York club scene. "This was still before [the Mayor Rudy] Giuliani took over. There was still a wild abandon

Facing: Susanne and her crew at Copacabana, New York City, 1990. Photo by Tina Paul © 1990. All Rights reserved.

Below: Miss Guy and Perfidia striking a pose at Bentley's, New York City, 1988. Photo by © Tina Paul 1988 All Rights Reserved.

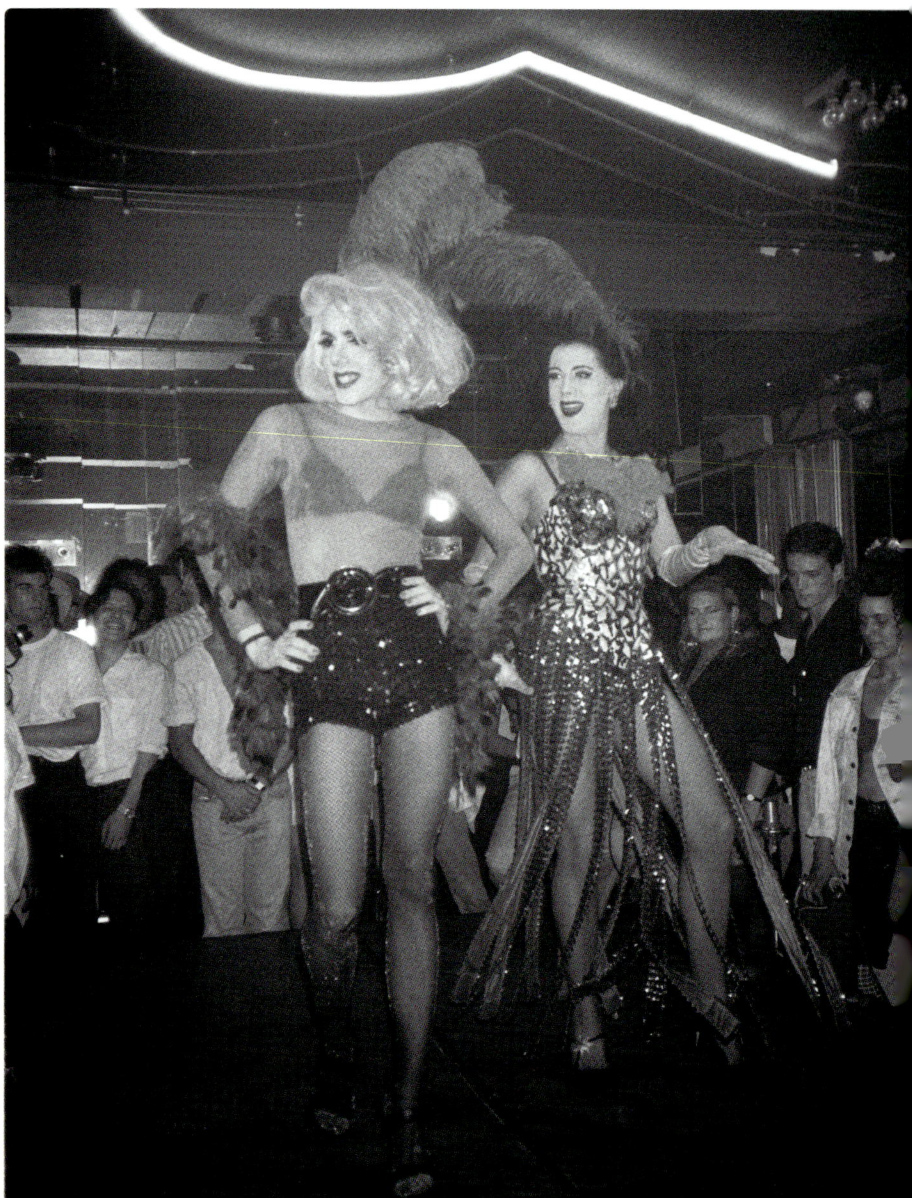

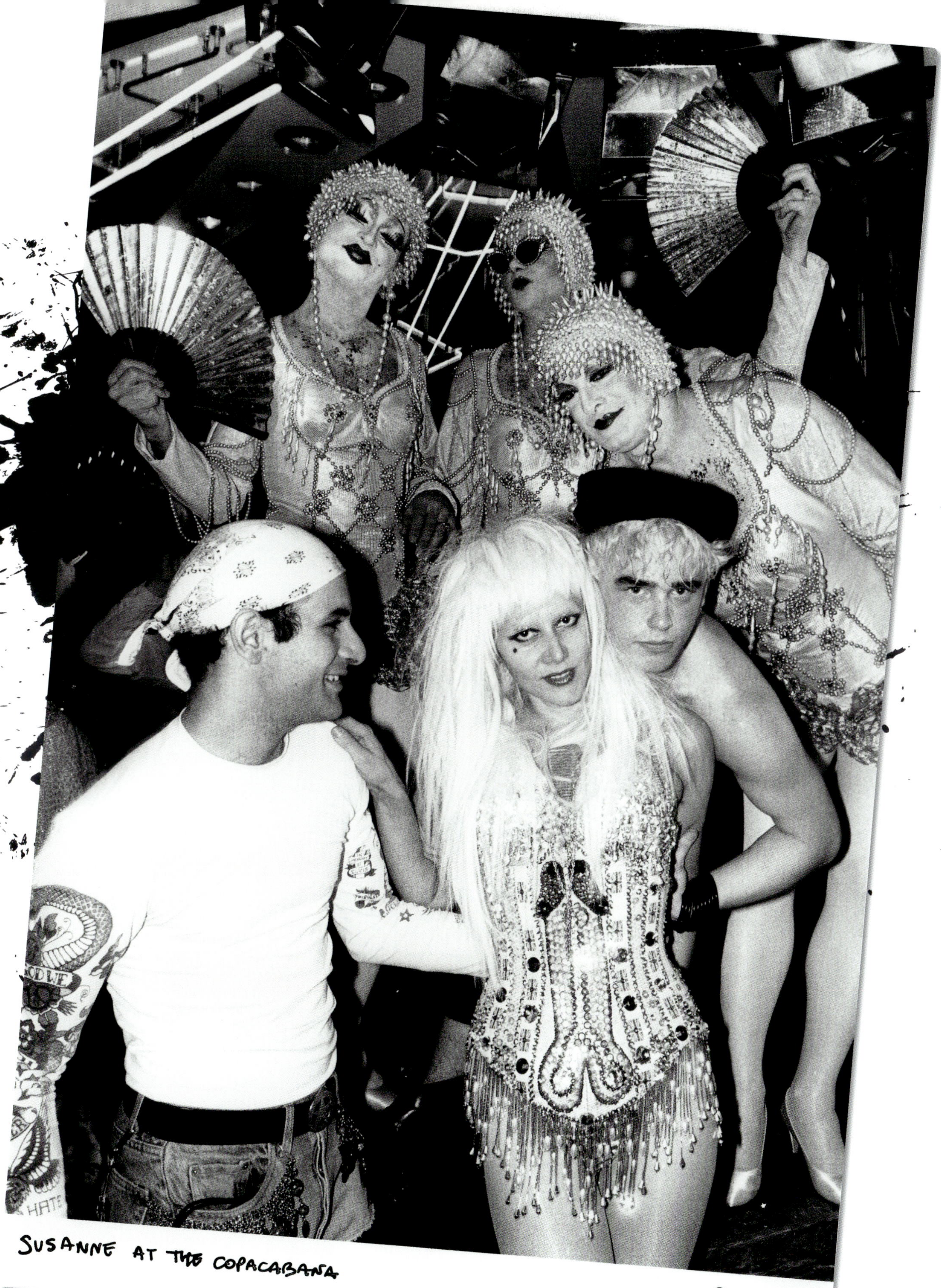

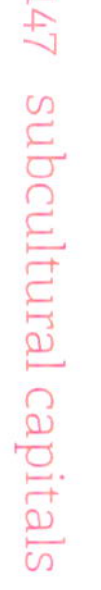

SUSANNE AT THE COPACABANA

in New York. There were a lot of eccentrically dressed people," attested the former Club Kid Ernie Glam. "Promoters would encourage that. They'd shower the eccentric people with free drinks or free admission to create a circus environment in the club that would be enjoyed by the other patrons."[96]

Betsey Johnson, Stephen Sprouse, Andre Walker, John Paul Gaultier, Thierry Mugler, and a host of other designers were not merely influenced by the atmosphere pervading New York clubs, they used these as spaces to promote their designs, sometimes holding fashion shows in them. Club U.S.A. even featured a V.I.P. room designed by Thierry Mugler himself. Moreover, stores like Patricia Field's eponymous downtown boutique provided settings for something akin to a rite of passage, as many of New York's "Club Kids" were at one time or another employed there.[97] Niche stores also arose: Liquid Sky, for example, sold ready-to-wear geared specifically towards rave and club culture.

Drag and Fashion

Over the course of a few years, drag would evolve from an underground phenomenon into a mainstream art form.[98] During the 1990s, New York's vibrant drag community became an indispensable component of the city's club culture. "Drag expanded to the entire nightlife scene; all of the clubs were clamoring for drag queen hostesses, go-go dancers, door people, etc.," recalls the drag celebrity Linda Simpson. "When RuPaul hit it big in 1992 with her song 'Supermodel,' it triggered an incredible amount of pop culture attention for the entire downtown drag scene. Every magazine and television talk show was heralding this new 'trend.'"[99] According to Michael Musto, "America was ready for it, the gay culture had come to the forefront, directly as a result of AIDS. It came to fruition in about 1990."[100]

The art of drag was cultivated in East Village establishments such as the Pyramid, a cornerstone of the city's underground art and performance scene. "The Pyramid queens expanded the parameters of what you could do in drag," explained the performer Lady Bunny.[101] They made it more about an art form – using costume and make-up to create evenings of "glamorous comedic theatre."[102] When Leigh Bowery was asked what he found most intriguing about New York's club scene he cited the Pyramid's uniqueness, stating, "What I love [. . .] about New York is the sort of thing that's happening at the Pyramid [. . .] people like Sister Dimension, Hapi Phace, Tabboo!, and Lady Bunny, who's a genius. All these people whose starting point is drag but then they take it someplace else, making it more modern and exciting. There is nothing like that in London."[103] The Pyramid served to cultivate the talents of RuPaul, who was drawn to the club when he first arrived in New York in 1984. Although the Pyramid was essentially a gay bar, the crowds it attracted were surprisingly diverse. "In reality, the Pyramid was not about being gay," RuPaul explained. "It was about being different and exploring differences, mixing and matching and not having to be the same person every night."[104]

Drag and the fashion world share an affinity for glamour and transformation, and New York's nightlife atmosphere served as the ideal context for a reciprocal exchange to occur. Drag certainly employed fashion and make-up to create looks or even personalities, but fashion designers, too, drew from elements of the drag culture in exploring and/or subverting gender boundaries in their creations. They found inspiration in the sartorial personas of performers such as Ru Paul's "slutty-cupcake," Lady Bunny's "frumpy southern belle," and Hapi's "bad acid-trip housewife."[105] The New York club icon Kenny Kenny was greatly influenced by the Pyramid, which, as he recalled "was full of avant garde artists like Happy Face, Tabboo!, Sister Dimension [. . .] running a club where you would get every fashion person in the world in there but also the most eccentric queens doing the most eccentric performances."[106] In a revolutionizing event, RuPaul became the face of MAC cosmetics' Viva Glam campaign in 1994, through which he helped raise millions of dollars to combat the AIDS epidemic.

According to Patrick McMullan, nightlife pioneers such as Susanne Bartsch and Dianne Brill, were hugely influential to drag performers and fashion designers alike: "Drag queens took a lot of inspiration from [Diane Brill], I think she even influenced Ru Paul. Jean Paul Gaultier and Thierry Mugler used Diane in their shows in Paris; years later Versace showed some elements as well with his Jayne Mansfield-meets-Wonder-Woman looks," he recounts.[107] Conversely, drag was co-opted by Bartsch to become an integral component in her events and even in her personal style. Observing the "throngs of drag queens in the audience" at a Thierry Mugler show, Amy M. Spindler, the style editor of the *New York Times Magazine* wrote, "Theirs is a magnified devotion to fashion's most alluring extremes. That is why they have always been fans of Mr. Mugler who appreciated their obsession."[108] Mugler, in fact, began using drag queens and transsexuals as runway models – Connie Flemming, known as "Connie Girl," appeared in his Spring/Summer 1992 fashion show – thus presenting gender itself as a kind of drag act.[109] Mugler also played with gender when he recruited Zaldy Goco and Kabuki Starshine – prominent figures in New York's club scene – to model as women in his runway presentations. "What I was saying in my choice of models is that in this game of femininity if you choose to play it [. . .] No one wants to be

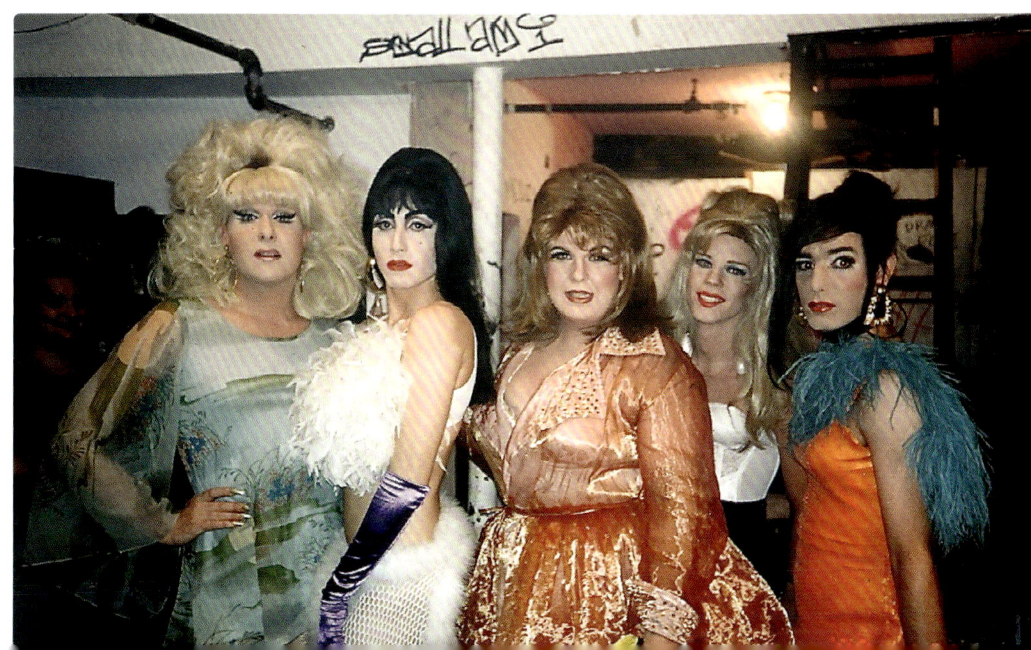

Lady Miss Bunny, Mistress Formika, Sweetie, Anna Conda, and Tabboo! at the Pyramid Club, New York City, August 1992. Photo by Linda Simpson/ Drag Explosion.

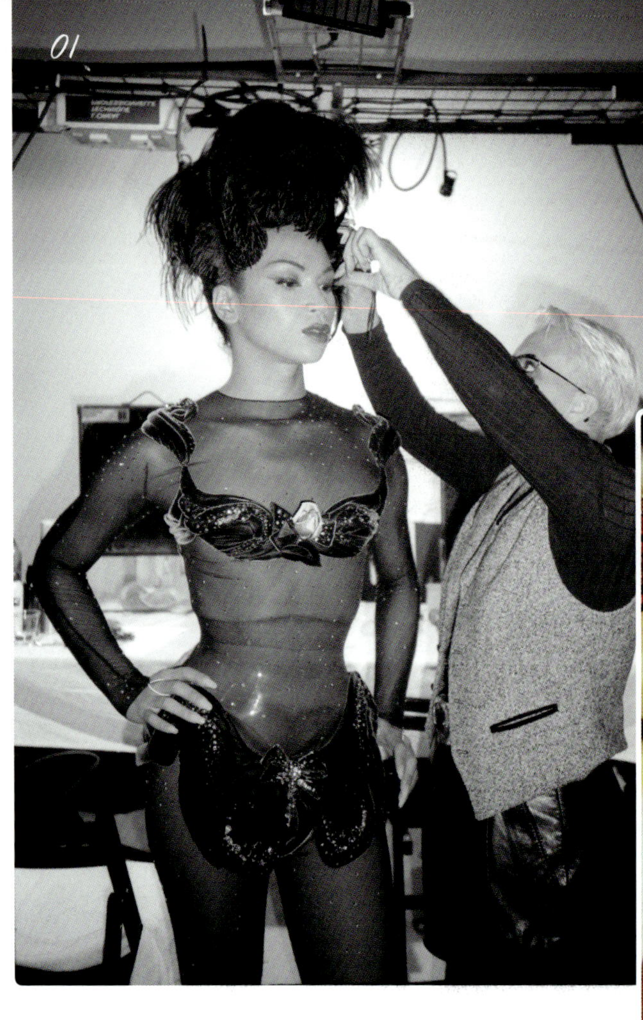

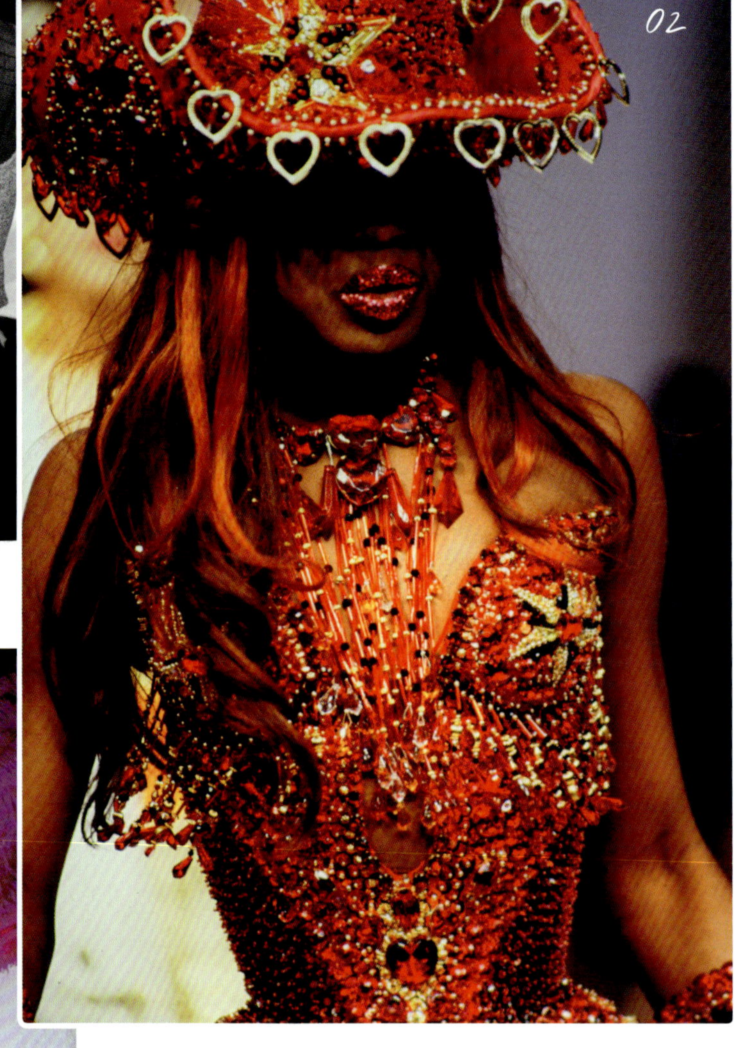

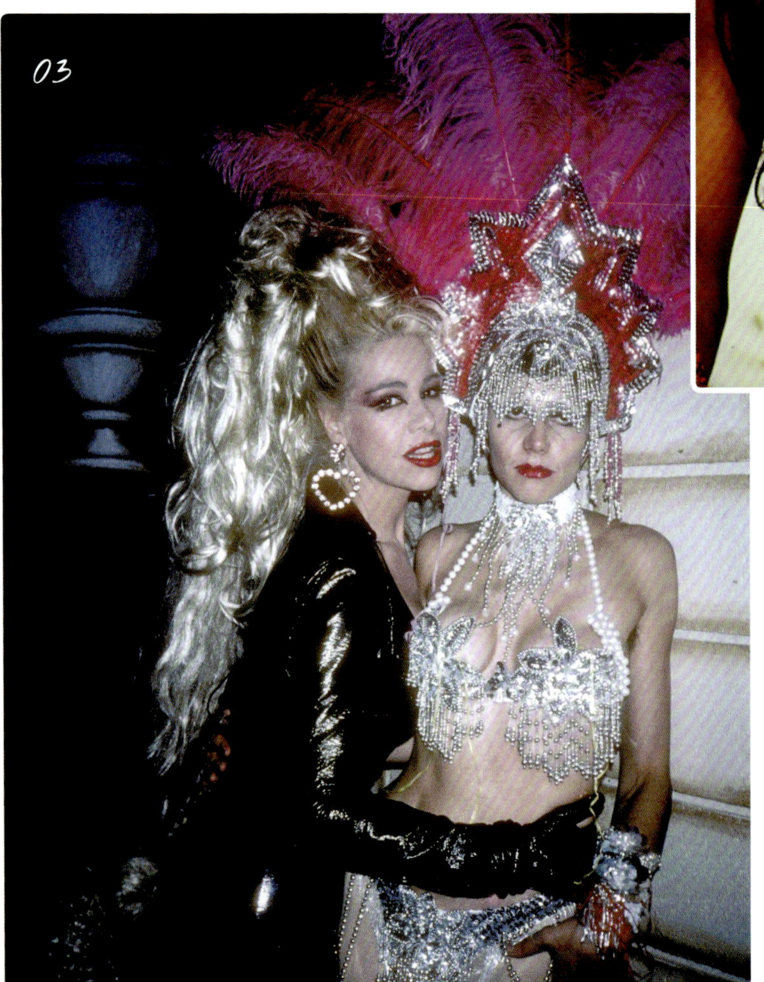

1 Zaldy Goco backstage at the
Thierry Mugler fashion show
in Paris, March 1995.
Photo by Tim Palen.

2 Connie Girl modeling for
Thierry Mugler, Spring/Summer
1992, Bloomsbury Publishing,
Photo by Niall McInerney.

3 Diane Brill (L) and Susanne (R)
at the Roxy Halloween party,
New York City, c. 1990.
Photo © Patrick McMullan.

more feminine than a transsexual," he once stated.[110] Ironically, by 1995 many active in New York's downtown culture bemoaned that drag now assumed such a prominent position in the mainstream. "Drag was once on the level of avant-garde fashion expressionism," explained Simon Doonan, fashion commentator and creative ambassador for Barneys New York . "We've reached a point where the whole idea of avante-garde doesn't resonate the way that it did."[111]

In Harlem, the phenomenon of "voguing" was also strengthening the relationship between fashion and club culture. The "dress-to-impress" aesthetic characteristic of voguing balls fostered an atmosphere where gay and transgender African Americans and Latinos could live out their fashion fantasies, emulating those featured in the pages of *Vogue* in competitions to be crowned the most "real." In the program notes for "An Evening Devoted to House Music and Voguing," which was hosted by the Latino cultural museum in Manhattan El Museo del Barrio in 1989, voguing is summarized as:

> an underground form of club entertainment which appropriates and subverts the images of fashion and music prevalent in mainstream culture. Voguing, which is manifested in competition between alternative social clubs who take their names from Paris fashion design houses, is an imitation of fashion shows performed by men who strive for best form, movement, and appearance. The standards for these competitions come from the fashion dictates and model's poses featured in *Vogue* magazine.[112]

In balls that took place first in Harlem, then throughout the city, participants with the most stylish walk, dance, and face were awarded trophies or other prizes and, perhaps more importantly, bragging rights.[113]

Susanne Bartsch, who had been going to the Harlem balls in the mid-1980s, was among the first to bring voguing into the mainstream, after noting that garments "grifted" from her boutique in SoHo were appearing on the vogue ball stage.[114] "I was blown away by the way this extremely socially and economically challenged community overcame their obstacles," said Bartsch. "They transformed potential roadblocks into brilliant creativity, art, beauty, and success."[115] Inspired by the voguer Willi Ninja, she organized the Love Ball in May 1989, an event that brought together the fashion industry elite to raise funds for the Design Industry Foundation Fighting AIDS (DIFFA). Modeled after vogue balls, the event was judged by fashion designers such as Carolina Herrera, Donna Karan, and Thierry Mugler. The Love Ball was "the biggest public display of 'voguing,'" according to the *New York Times*, incorporating "all the elements that make New York City night life remarkable."[116] The event raised $400,000 for AIDS research in a single night, and brought drag-ball culture into the mainstream.

The angular body movements and extreme body poses characteristic of vogueing would ultimately catch the attention of designers such as John Paul Gaultier and Thierry Mugler, who soon began featuring voguers in their own

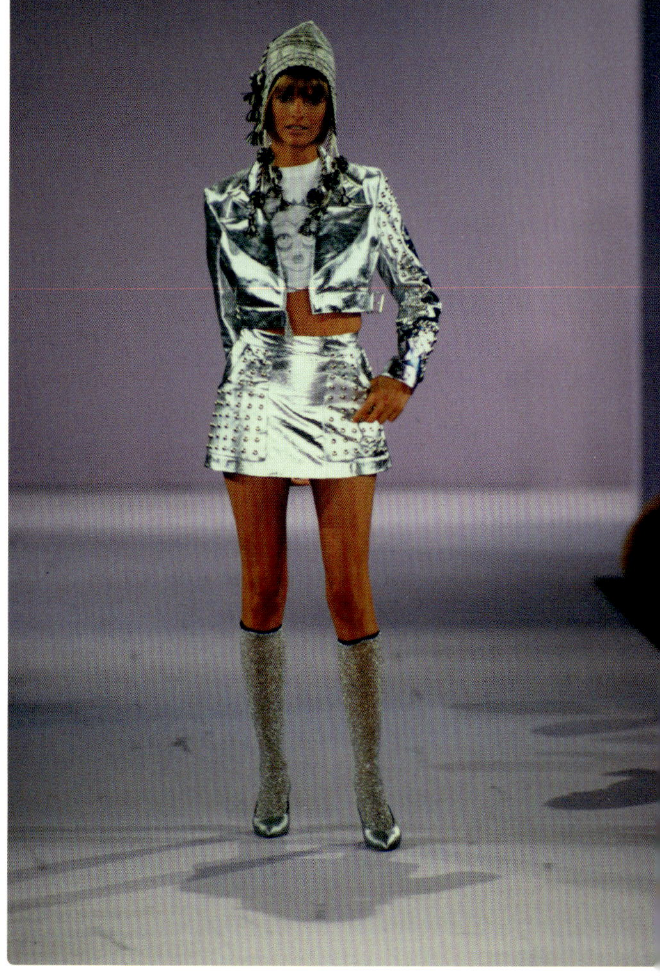

runway shows;[117] Thierry Mugler, ended his Fall/Winter 1989 show with the voguers Willi Ninja and Adrian Magnifique.[118] The following year, Madonna, who had been in attendance at Bartsch's Love Ball, released her hit song 'Vogue,' with a music video that starred Willi Ninja along with fellow voguers Jose and Luis Xtravaganza. Also in 1990, voguing was formally introduced to the public at large in Jennie Livingston's award-winning documentary *Paris is Burning*.

The Club Kids

The "Club Kids" were a group of decadent pseudo-celebrities who shocked the public-at-large with their outrageous looks and anything-goes mentality. They sought to break all the rules of convention by delving into fashion extremism and exhibitionism with inventive costumes specially created for each night out. The Club Kid scene began to take shape sometime late in the 1980s and into the 1990s, initially as a mere stylistic phenomenon defined by youths dressing in cutting-edge designer labels such as Stephen Sprouse, John Paul Gaultier, and Thierry Mugler.[119] However, this soon progressed to encompass looks showcasing creativity and provocation, via the subversion of gender stereotypes, for example, and the creation of style mash-ups, such as "Futuristic Geisha Gangsters."[120]

According to Frank Owen, "the original" Club Kid look came into being at the club Red Zone. Dressed like "pure pop products," these early Club Kids donned hats made out of Oreo boxes, dresses made out of Tide detergent containers, shirts fashioned from saran wrap and jewelry made from Fruit Loops, in a satire of "contemporary commodity fetishism."[121] However, it was their looks evoking imagery of babies and little children, with which they became most closely associated.[122] Carrying pacifiers and dressed in diapers, rompers, and babydoll dresses the Club Kids established a puerile sartorial style that celebrated, youth and a devil-may-care attitude. James St. James, one of the original Club Kids, recalls:

> The first generation of Club Kids was a little rough – mostly just kids in Halloween costumes. It evolved quickly, though. With each progressive wave of kids, it became more streamlined. As the '80s segued into the '90s and we migrated from the Tunnel to Red Zone to Mars, everything got sleeker, harder and shinier. The innovations were self-referencing, and the looks built on themselves rather than culling from past scenes. [123]

In common with past trends, however, the club not only served as a style laboratory, but also as a showcase wherein they paraded their extreme looks to gain recognition, or notoriety.

Above: Ana Sui, Spring 1994 collection. Bloomsbury Publishing, Photo by Niall McInerney.

Below: Sacred Boy, Keda, and Martin X at an outlaw fashion show on the #1 train at the Franklin Street station, c. 1993. Photo by Ernie Glam.

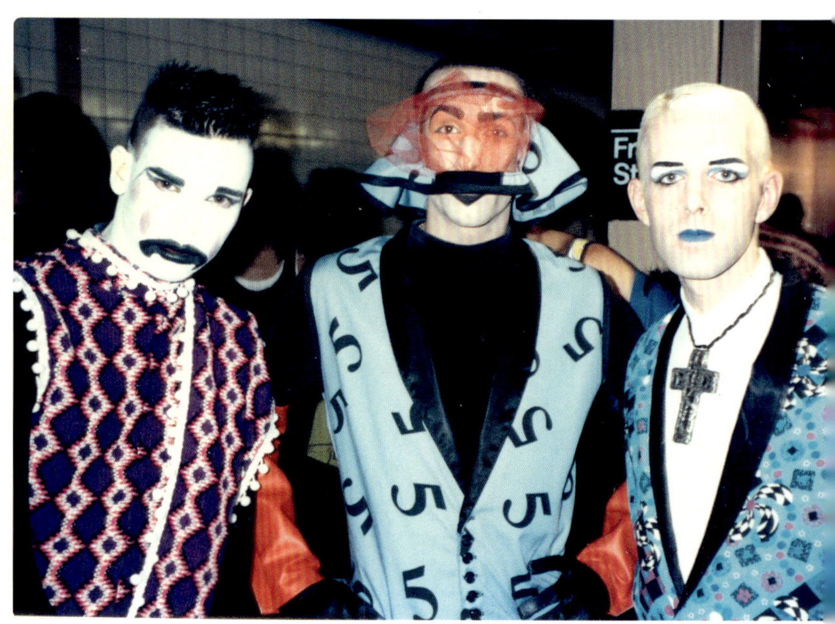

The Club Kids were successful in creating a movement with a clearly defined aesthetic: gender was fluid, everything was D.I.Y., and tapping into your inner "fabulosity" was paramount. "[The Club Kids] reinvented the do-it-yourself spirit of punk rock and incorporated sci-fi and the circus to create a scene that seemed new and exciting," recalled Ernie Glam. [124] Elaborating further, Michael Musto wrote, "To me it was a blending of Japanese anime, fractured fairytale Mother Goose chic gone amok, apocalyptic chic, and a heavy influence of British outrageous performance art in the person of Leigh Bowery."[125] In an interview with Boy George for *Interview* magazine, the DJ and record producer Mark Ronson noted that "Leigh and the whole Taboo culture had a big influence on New York, specifically what was to become the club-kid scene."[126] Indeed, Bowery was a great inspiration to the Club Kids. "Leigh was the club-kid God," extolled James St. James. "He was the one who outdid everybody."[127]

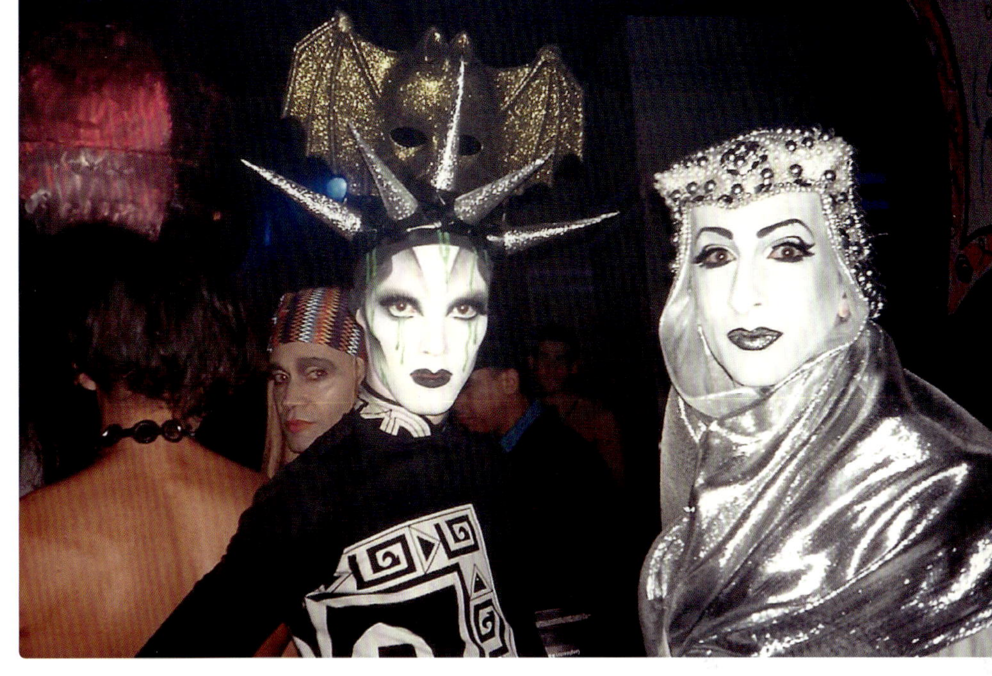
The Club Kids Kabuki (L) and Keda (R) at the Limelight, NYC, 1993. Photo by Linda Simpson/ Drag Explosion.

An emphasis on youth and childlike aesthetics permeated the Club Kid scene, expressed sartorially in by the use of tiaras, schoolgirl uniforms, baby doll dresses, and lunchboxes. However, as they dressed to outdo one another, more and more outré styles would emerge. Looks became extreme, often bordering on the grotesque, making use of facial piercings and extreme make-up. Ultimately, looks inspired by "S&M [. . .] or cyberpunk with some kind of lunchbox or kooky backpack and platform shoes," were all de rigueur.[128]

With appearances on national television programs such as *The Joan Rivers Show*, *Geraldo*, and *The Phil Donahue Show*, the Club Kids created an impromptu youth movement, becoming celebrities at both local and national levels. In the manner of drag, they constructed unique identities through their selection of clothes and application of make-up. In fact, they were creating a community for those who, by the standards of mainstream convention, had been made to feel like misfits. Youths from diverse localities throughout the United States sought out and converged on New York City's club scene, finding an outlet for creative expression. Annual style summits were organized to promote the movement, featuring fashion shows and style competitions that drew promoters, DJs, and of course, Club Kids from all over America.

The Club Kids heralded numerous fashion trends and fueled diverse fads relating to body piercings, lunchboxes, eccentrically colored hair, cyber punk, extreme platform sneakers, and baby doll dresses, to name a few. *New York* magazine's Spring fashion issue of 1994 remarked, "the ubiquitous ersatz-schoolgirl look expresses and extends the enduring fascination with all things youthful."[129] The issue featured a fashion editorial addressing the cyberpunk aesthetic, depicting models with facial piercings who were dressed in silver metallic garments by designers such as Anna Sui and Todd Oldham. That same year John Paul Gaultier, Donna Karan, Helmut Lang, Jil Sander, Stephen Sprouse, and Xuly-Bet all showed collections evidencing an edgy cyber-punk/club-kid influence.[130] During a 1993 television segment presenting Club Kids, the television personality Phil Donahue remarked "many of these outrageous fashion styles *do* make their way to the rack at [J.C.] Penny's."[131]

In 1995 a *New York Times* article observed that "a commercial art form like fashion almost immediately takes on those forms that have a degree of transgression or shock about them."[132] Certainly, Calvin Klein exploited the subcultural capital of New York's club scene. In the now-infamous advertisement campaign for his "CK One" fragrance of the 1990s, Klein employed as models a group of pierced, half-clothed young men and women, and invited buyers to put on the unisex scent to become "initiated into that exalted clan, even if your parents won't allow you a nose ring."[133] He also drew more overt connections to New York's club culture when he recruited the Club Kid Jenny Dembrow for his Spring 1995 Calvin Klein Jeans advertisement.

Rampant drug abuse by some of the more prominent Club Kids and their attendant legal troubles ultimately spelled the end for the 1990s club scene. However, some creative talents persevered and their art continued to be recognized by the fashion and music world. Kabuki Starshine, for example, known for his outlandish costumes and make-up, gained employment as a make-up artist for pop stars such as Lady Gaga, Madonna, Gwen Stefani, Katy Perry, and Michael Jackson.[134] The first-wave Club Kid Zaldy Goco, who studied at the Fashion Institute of Technology, went from nightlife denizen to Paris fashion model, and eventually established a career as a fashion and costume designer for the upper echelons of pop music.[135] Zaldy and his then-boyfriend Mathu Andersen had initially caught the eye of Susanne Bartsch, who asked them to design costumes for her. After working with Donna Karan at Bartsch's Love Ball, they were hired by her, later designing costumes for RuPaul and creating imagery for the make-up brand Shiseido.[136]

In 1999, along with his business partner Travis Rains, the former Club Kid Richie Rich created the label Heatherette. Featuring youthful clothing, it used the concept of fun as a marketable commodity and harkened back to the Club Kid ethos by "bring[ing] out the pop star in everybody."[137] The pair met while Rich was serving as Susanne Bartsch's assistant, and shortly thereafter began designing bright, glittery pieces together that attracted the attention of the likes of Gwen Stefani and Foxy Brown. "The clothes were attention getting and fun," recalls Amanda Lepore, Heatherette's transgender muse and a fixture in New York's club scene. "They had a distinct look, which at that time – everyone wanted it. David [LaChapelle] was using it. All the celebrities wanted it. It was in demand."[138]

"A commercial art form like fashion almost immediately takes on those forms that have a degree of transgression or shock about them."

1 Joey Arias (L) and the Club Kid Richie Rich (R) at Susanne's Dewar's Prom Night Party at Chelsea Piers, New York City, 1994. Photo by © Tina Paul 1994. All Rights Reserved.

2 The Club Kids Zaldy Goco and Mathu Andersen at Susanne's party at Copacabana, New York City, 1991. Photo by © Tina Paul 1991. All Rights Reserved.

3 James St. James working the door at a nightclub in Times Square, 1990. Photo by Alexis DiBiasio.

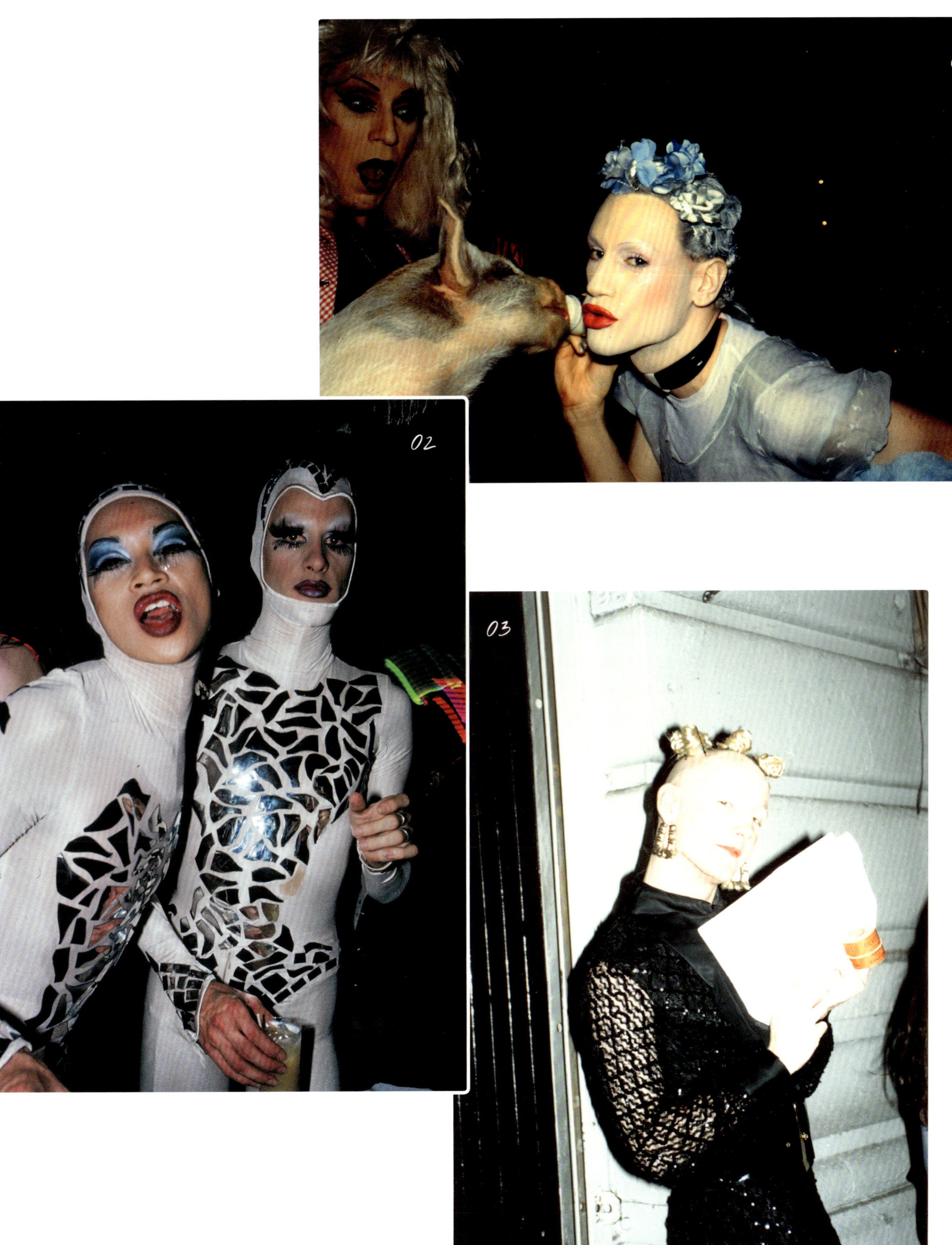
01
02
03

Right: Heatherette,
Spring 2004 collection.
Photo by Maria Chandoha
Valentino/MCV Photo.

Below: Moschino,
Fall 2014 collection.
Photo by Maria Chandoha
Valentino/MCV Photo.

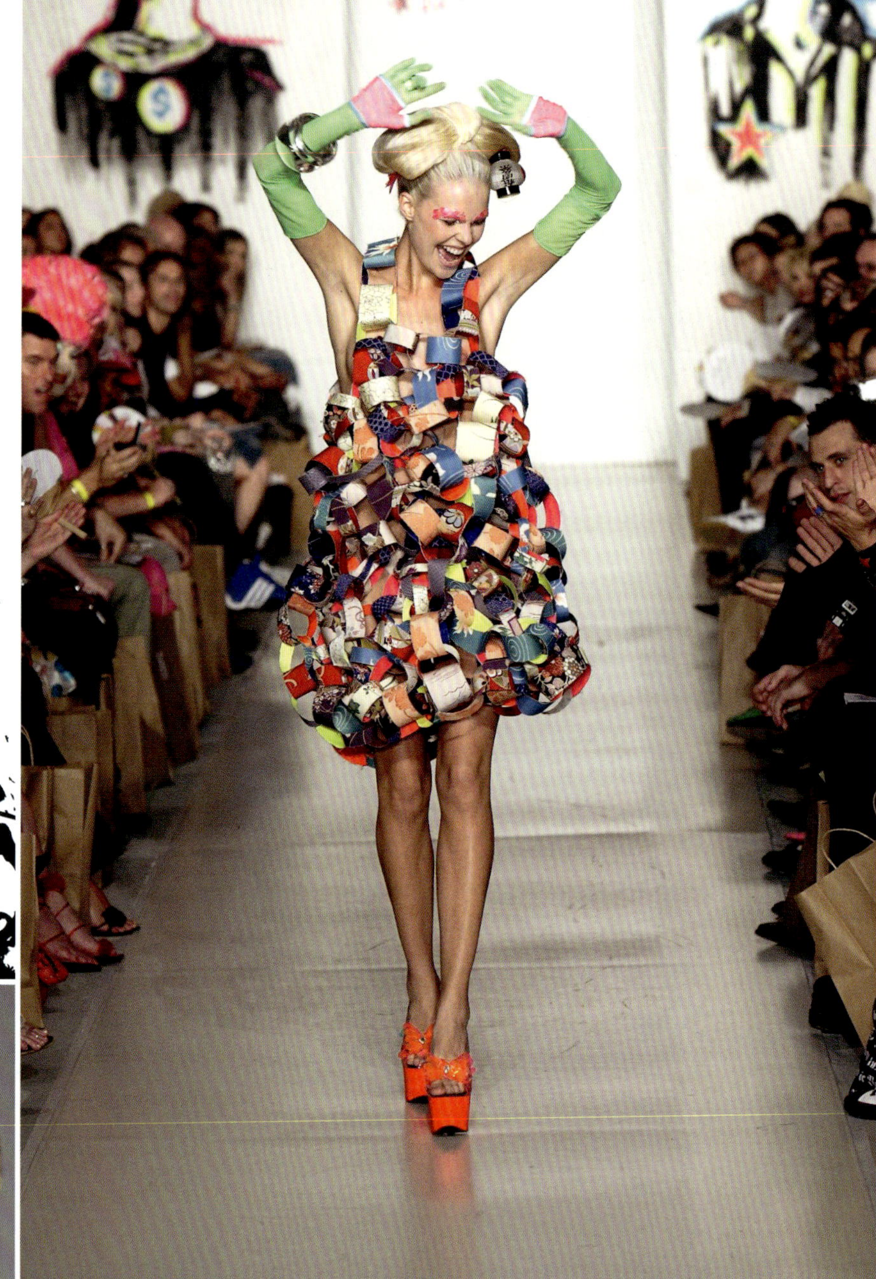

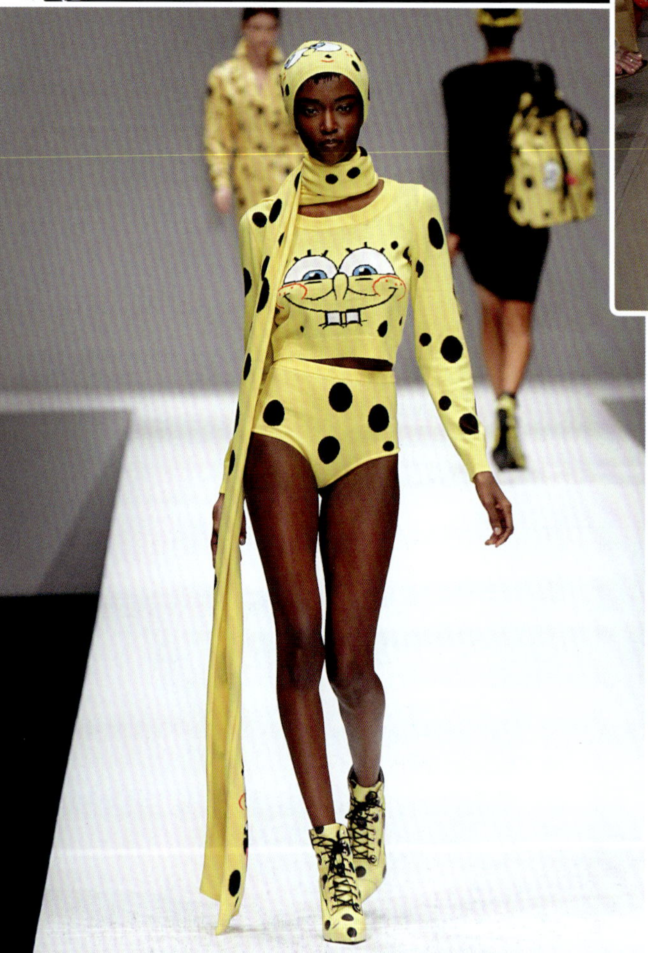

Facing top: Richie Rich and
Traver Rains, the founding
designers of Heatherette, with
Naomi Campbell. Heatherette,
Spring/Summer 2005 collection.
Photo by Maria Chandoha
Valentino/MCV Photo.

Facing bottom: Jeremy Scott
with Miley Cyrus at the finale of
his Spring 2015 fashion show.
Photo by Maria Chandoha
Valentino/MCV Photo.

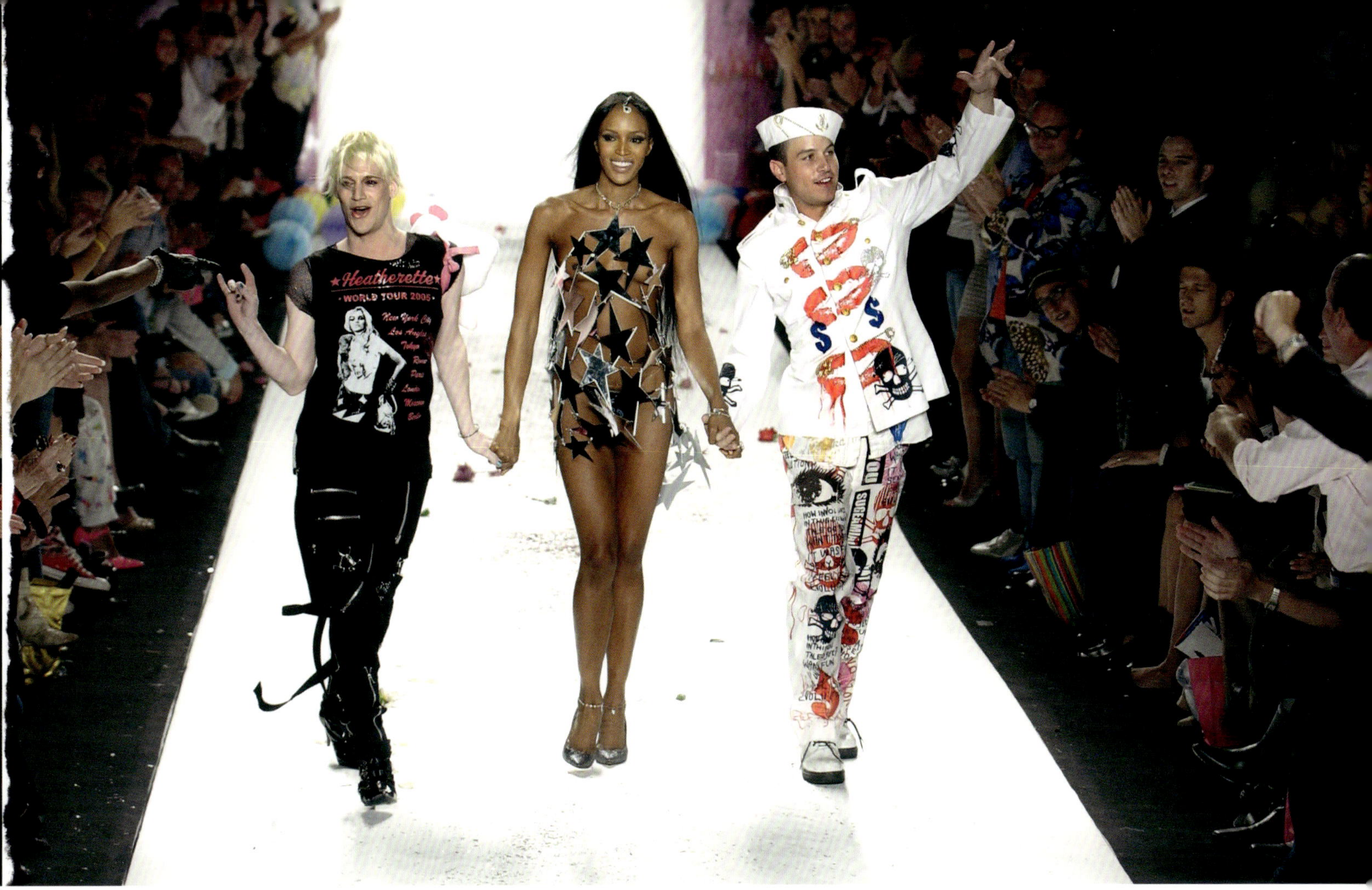

Heatherette
WORLD TOUR 2005

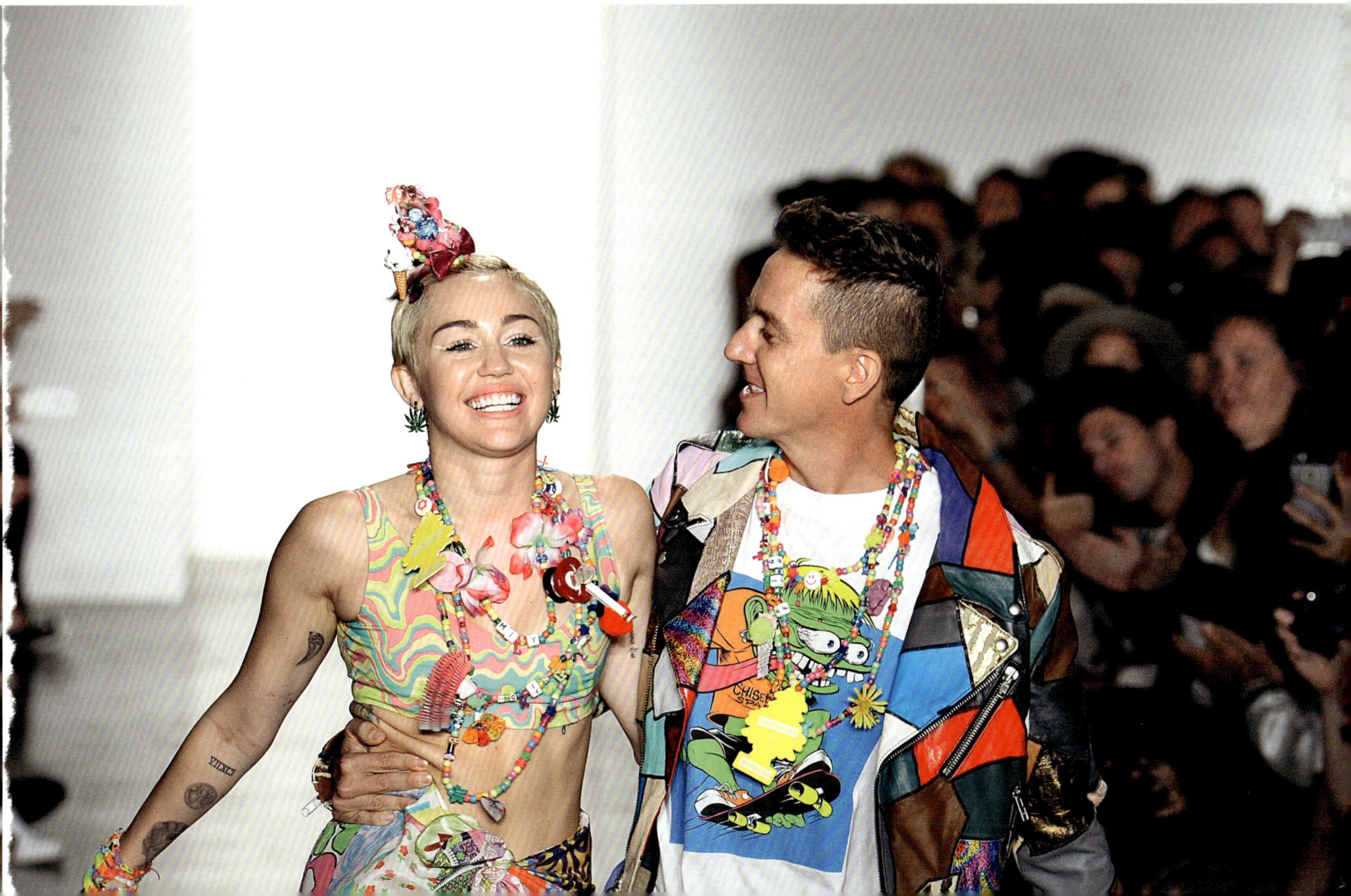

Heatherette was inadvertently "discovered" by the style guru Patricia Field, whose store manager spotted Richie Rich wearing a custom leather top during a night out at the club. Field ordered twenty of those tops for her store.[139] Her downtown boutique provided a unique intersection of club culture and fashion, and she often recruited talent directly from New York's nightlife community. Rich and Travis's collaborations with David LaChapelle, whom Rich had befriended thorough the club circuit, cemented the label's success. Heatherette's fashion shows were camp presentations with eccentric titles like 'Star-Spangled Smiles' and 'When Will I Be Famous: From Kyoto With Love.' These often featured runway appearances by "celebutants," such as Paris Hilton and Anna Nicole Smith (the term was coined by *Newsweek* to describe the Club Kid James St. James).

Club culture also informed the work of the designer Jeremy Scott who, as a Pratt fashion student, had immersed himself in New York's club scene. "I used to create on myself, create with my look and my persona," he has said.[140] He found his muse in Jenny Dembrow, whom he outfitted for her nightly debuts at clubs like Limelight. "These weren't glue-gunned pieces he threw glitter on," says Dembrow, who has saved many of the creations. "They were beautifully constructed."[141] Dembrow also served as a model in Scotts's graduation show, the latter inspired by the Chernobyl disaster: the all-white collection depicted futuristic Russian peasants in plastic vinyl, platform sandals, and ski masks. "I was bald and had no eyebrows," Dembrow recalls. "I wore a white quilted vinyl skin-tight hazmat suit and face mask."[142] "I also wore a sheer floor-length gown with corseted boning."[143] Scott who had grown up admiring the designs of John Paul Gaultier as well as the art of Andy Warhol has produced collections that subvert the norm and parody consumer culture. His recent collections for the Italian fashion house Moschino, where he is creative director, have referenced McDonald's (Fall 2014), SpongeBob SquarePants (Fall 2014), and Barbie (Spring 2015). Today, his designs for both his namesake label and for Moschino, embrace pop culture, and regularly recall the youthful spirit and enthusiasm of the 1990s club culture that nurtured his creativity.

A Runway for the Strange and Extraordinary

Although the heyday of 1980s and 1990s club culture has passed, its influence on fashion still persists. Designers such as Walter Van Beirendonk and Bernard Willhem, for example, have produced collections with decidedly Club Kid vibes. Gaultier referenced eighties club culture in his Spring 2013 collection, which paid homage to the sartorial style of Boy George. And music artists like Lady Gaga and Niki Minaj affirm the club-culture ethos of spectacle, self-expression and creativity. "Lady Gaga kind of brought a nouveau club kid style to the world," remarked Michael Musto.[144]

Susanne with Erickatoure Aviance, 2013. Susanne is wearing a bodysuit by Zaldy and teddy bear coat by Jeremy Scott. Photo by Mark Williams.

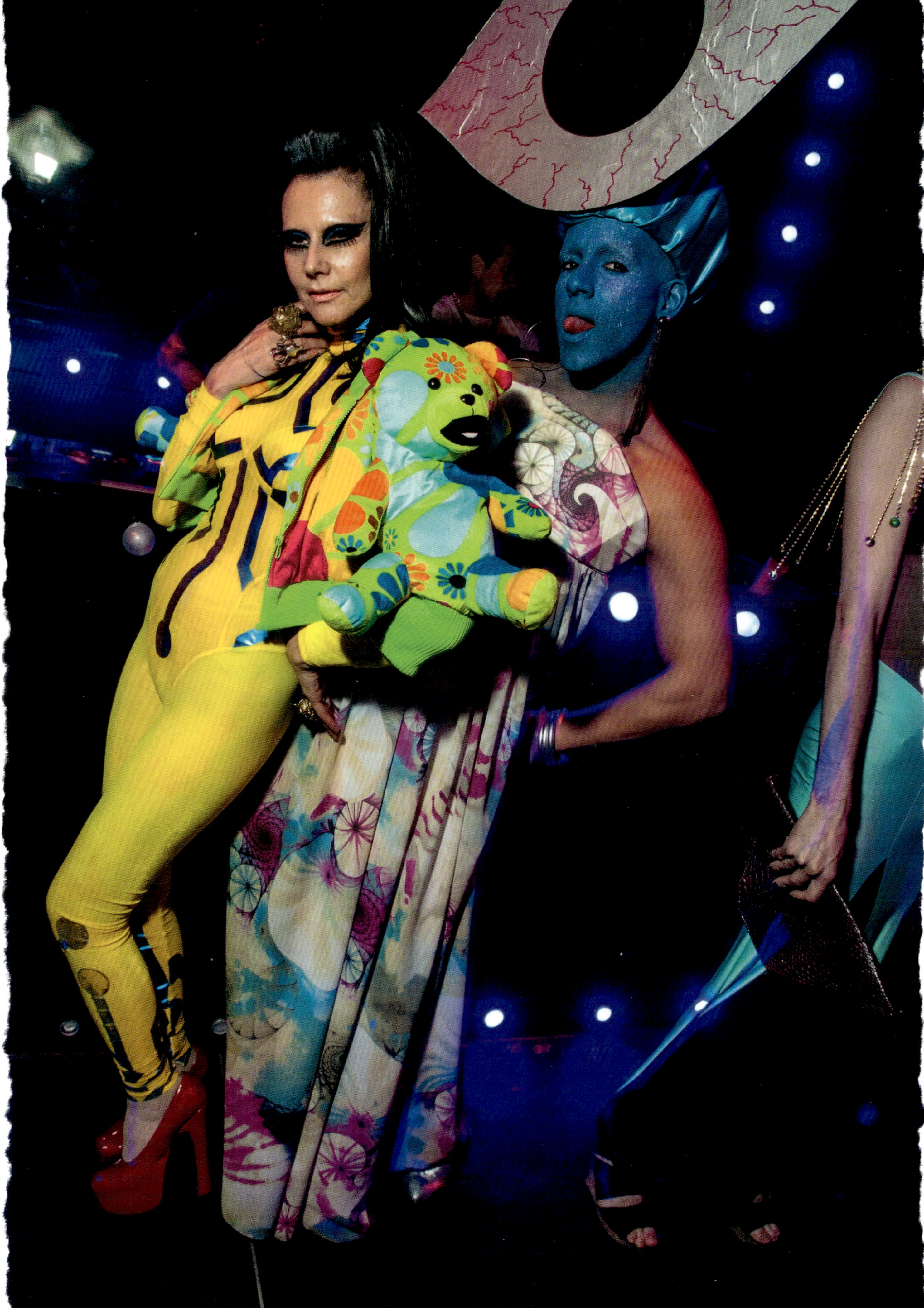

In 2010, the *New York Times* wrote, "the last year saw rumblings of a return of club-kid finery and the kinds of madcap outfits that were a mainstay of the 1980s and early 1990s nightclub scene."[145] There is still a burgeoning nightlife scene cultivated by impresarios such as Susanne Bartsch, who provide a space for creativity to flourish. Bartsch's latest projects have begun to bring the sartorial art of the night world out of the clubs and into art galleries.

Today there are still those who continue to illuminate parties with their looks and dress – and designers who continue to be inspired by them. The fashion designer and nightlife personality Dominique Echeverria has said, "I [look] at nightlife as an opportunity to showcase my work. 99 percent of the time everything I wear is something I dreamt up and made – headdresses and all. It's a good way to force me to come up with new work [. . .] I push myself to not only come up with new costumes, but completely different aesthetics too [. . .] The club is a runway for the strange and extraordinary."[146]

Notes

1   Kim Hastrieter and David Hershkovits, eds, *20 Years of Style: The World According to* Paper (New York: Harper Collins, 2004), 59

2   Sonnet Stanfill, *80s Fashion: From Club to Catwalk* (London: V&A Publishing, 2013), 7

3   Shaun Cole, "New Styles New Sounds: Clubbing, Music and Fashion in 1980s London," in Stanfill, *80s Fashion*, 33

4   "Have you Seen Satan? The Conservative Cabal has Managed to Make Nightlife Exciting Again," *Paper* (November 1990), 12

5   Holly Brubach, "In Fashion: The Life of the Party," *New Yorker* (March 4, 1991), 83

6   Ibid.

7   Walt Cassidy, interview with author, March 6, 2015

8   Stevie Stewart quoted in Cole, "New Styles New Sounds," in Stanfill, *80s Fashion*, 36

9   Frank Owen, *Clubland: The Fabulous Rise and Murderous Fall of Club Culture* (New York: Broadway Books, 2004), 313

10 Sarah Thornton, *Club Cultures: Music, Media and Subcultural Capital* (Cambridge: Polity Press, 1995), 11–12

11 Ted Pollhemus, *Street Style: From Sidewalk to Catwalk* (New York: Thames & Hudson, 1994), 95

12 Ibid.

13 Shaun Cole, *Don We Now Our Gay Apparel* (Lon-don: Bloomsbury, 2000), 157

14 Rusty Egan quoted in Priya Elan, "It's Blitz: The Birth of the New Romantics," *Guardian* (May 14, 2010). http://www.theguardian.com/music/2010/may/15/blitz-boy-george-steve-strange-visage

15 Ibid.

16 Graham Smith quoted in "We can be Heroes – A New Collection by Graham Smith," Photographic Youth Music Culture Archive (P.Y.M.C.A.), (May 6, 2012) last accessed, February 19, 2015. https://pymca.wordpress.com/2012/05/16/we-can-be-heroes-a-new-collection-by-graham-smith/

17 Thornton, *Club Cultures*, 3

18 Ibid., 3, 22

19   Ibid., 4–5

20   Polhemus, *Street Style*, 95

21   Tim Lewis, "'The Birth of the London Club Scene': Bowie Nights at Billy's Club," *Guardian* (January 25, 2013). Last accessed February 12, 2015. http://www.theguardian.com/music/gallery/2013/jan/25 bowie-nights-billys-club-pictures

22   Steve Strange quoted in David Johnson, "What Other People Say: David Johnson," *The Blitz Club* website. Last accessed February 5, 2015. http://www.theblitzclub.com/about-dj.php

23   Steve Strange quoted in Elan, "It's Blitz," *Guardian* (May 14, 2010). Last accessed February 14, 2015. http://www.theguardian.com/music/2010/may/15/blitz-boy-george-steve-strange-visage

24   Mark Savage, "Steve Strange: The Custodian of New Romantic Pop," *BBC News* website (February 13, 2015). Last accessed February 17, 2015. http://www.bbc.com/news/entertainment-arts-31452452

25   Caroline Evans, *Fashion at the Edge: Spectacle, Modernity, and Deathliness* (New Haven and London: Yale University Press, 2003), 143

26   Quoted in David Johnson, "Spandau Ballet, the Blitz Kids and the Birth of the New Romantics," *Guardian* (October 3, 2009). Last accessed February 8, 2015. http://www.theguardian.com/music/2009/oct/04/spandau-ballet-new-romantics

27   Siobhan Fahey quoted in Elan, "It's Blitz," *Guardian* (May 14, 2010). Last accessed February 14, 2015. http://www.theguardian.com/music/2010/may/15/blitz-boy-george-steve-strange-visage

28   Rusty Egan quoted in Ibid.

29   "What I Did at the Blitz," excerpt from *Record Mirror* (December 1983). *The Blitz Kids* website. Last accessed January 24, 2015. http://www.theblitzkids.com/site_archive/sharahmakeup/blitzheroes.html

30   Lauren Milligan, "We Can Be Heroes," *Vogue* (Dec-ember 15, 2011). http://www.vogue.co.uk/news/2011/12/14/we-can-be-heroes-new-book-london-clubland

31   Robert O'Byrne, *Style City: How London Became a Fashion Capital* (London: Frances Lincoln Limited, 2009), 82

32   Caroline Evans, *Fashion at the Edge*, 25

33   Caroline Evans, "Cultural Capital: 1976–2000," in *The London Look: Fashion from Street to Catwalk*, Christopher Breward, Edwina Ehrman, and Caroline Evans (New Haven and London: Yale University Press, 2004), 143

34   "Vivienne Westwood: 1980-1989," online exhibition, The Musuem at FIT. Last accessed May 18, 2015. http://sites.fitnyc.edu/depts/museum/Vivienne_Westwood/exhibit_all.html

35   Kathleen Beckett, "Fashion: A New Groove," *Vogue* (September 1, 1985), 478

36   "1982, Strange Takes Fashion to the French" *Shapers of the 80s* website. Last accessed February 16, 2015. http://shapersofthe80s.com/blitz-kids/strange-takes-fashion-to-the-french/

37   Cole, "New Styles New Sounds," in Stanfill, *80s Fashion*, 39

38   Dean Mayo Davies, "Stephen Jones," *Dazed & Confused* (2013). Last accessed April 5, 2015. http://www.dazeddigital.com/fashion/article/15636/1/stephen-jones

39   Stephen Jones quoted in Thierry-Maxime Loriot ed., *The Fashion World of John Paul Gaultier: From the Sidewalk to the Catwalk* (New York: Abrams, 2011), 333

40   Ibid.

41   Lauren Cochrane, "1980s Throwback: Clubland's Charming Impact on Fashion Examined at V&A," *Guardian* (July 8, 2013). Last accessed February 5, 2014..http://www.theguardian.com/artanddesign/2013/jul/08/1980s-club-to-catwalk-vanda-fashion

42   Lesley White, "The New Glitterati," *The Face*, Issue 485 (April 1984), 56

43   Robyn Healy, "Taboo or Not Taboo: The Fashions of Leigh Bowery," *Art Journal of the National Gallery of Victoria*, Edition 42 (2002) National Gallery of Victoria (Australia) Last accessed February 18, 2015. https://www.ngv.vic.gov.au/essay/taboo-or-not-taboo-the-fashions-of-leigh-bowery/

44   Ibid.

45   James Michael Nichols, "After Dark: Meet Kenny Kenny, Visual Poet and Nightlife Icon," *Huffington Post* (August 31, 2014). Last accessed March 31, 2015. http://www.huffingtonpost.com/2014/08/31/kenny-kenny-after-dark_n_5742624.html

46   Isabella Burley, "Cult VIP: Rachel Auburn," *Dazed & Confused* (February 2013). http://www.dazed-digital.com/fashion/article/15548/1/cult-vip-rachel-auburn

47   White, "The New Glitterati," *The Face*, Issue 485 (April 1984), 57

48   Ibid.

49   Sue Tilley, *Leigh Bowery: The Life and Times of an Icon* (London: Hodder & Stoughton, 1997), 57

50   Mark Ronson, "Taboo"*Interview*, (website post, date n/a. Last accessed February 18, 2015. http://www.interviewmagazine.com/culture/taboo/#

51   Sue Tilley, *Leigh Bowery: The Life and Times of an Icon* (London: Hodder & Stoughton, 1997), 53

52   Ibid., 57

53   Nichols, "After Dark: Meet Kenny Kenny"

54   Phillip Hoare, "Obituaries: Leigh Bowery," *Independent* (January 5, 1995). Last accessed February 15, 2015. http://www.independent.co.uk/news/people/obituaries-leigh-bowery-1566637.html

55   O'Byrne, *Style City*, 87

56   Burley, "Cult VIP: Rachel Auburn," *Dazed & Confused* (February 2013).

57   Stephen Jones quoted in Christine Whitney, "The Original Club Kids," *Harper's Bazaar* (May 31, 2013). Last accessed February 8 2014. http://www.harpersbazaar.com/culture/features/a978/stephen-jones-london-club-scene-0613/

58   Tilley, 60

59   Ronson, "Taboo

60   Whitney, "The Original Club Kids"

61   James Anderson, "Kinky Gerlinky," in Michael Costiff, *Michael and Gerlinde's World* (London: Slow Lorus Publishing, 2012), 294

62   Ibid.

63   Ibid.

64   Brubach, "In Fashion: The Life of the Party," 83

65   James Michael Nichols, "After Dark: Meet Susanne Bartsch, Party Curator and Nightlife Legend," *Huffington Post* (November 30, 2014). Last accessed December 3, 2014. https://docs.google.com/a/fitnyc.edu/document/d/1ESbOPSzJej0dE00-E1jmSaGKumUsXxeQi8H6CCHg9TM/edit#heading=h.t8xvropb5qwu

66   Ibid.

67   Ibid.

68   Ibid.

69   Nick Vogelson, "Susanne Bartsch Talks with Joey Arias about Resurrecting Nightlife Countless Times Over," *Document* (September 29, 2014). Last accessed March 6, 2015. http://documentjournal.com/article/susanne-bartsch-joey-arias

70   Burley, "Cult VIP: Rachel Auburn," *Dazed & Confused* (February 2013)

71   "The Legend of Leigh Bowery," directed by Charles Atlas, YouTube video, 1:22:36, posted by "Patricia Field," July 28, 2014, https://www.youtube.com/watch?v=0VQVhkDDf14

72   O'Byrne, *Style City*, 87

73   O'Byrne, *Style City*, 90

74   "BodyMap Interview with David Holah," *Fashion Fox(July 10, 2013)*. Last accessed March 14, 2015. http://www.fashionfox.co.uk/2013/07/10/bodymap-interview-with-david-holah/460

75   "BodyMap – Shaping the 1980s / Personalities / People / V&A Channel." Vam.ac.uk. Last accessed May 13, 2015. http://www.vam.ac.uk/channel/people/personalities/bodymap/

76   Bernadine Morris, "A New Vitality Marks Openings in London," *New York Times* (16 October, 1984)

77   O'Byrne, *Style City*, 90

78   "BodyMap – Shaping the 1980s / Personalities / People / V&A Channel," Vam.ac.uk

79   Lisa W. Foderaro, "Giltz, Funk, and Victoriana Enliven New York's Discos," *New York Times* (March 27, 1987), C1

80   Hastrieter and Hershkovits, 12

81   Glen O'Brien, "Foreward," in Eric and Jennifer Goode, *Area: 1983–1987* (New York: Abrams, 2013), 8–9

82   Ibid.

83   Steve Rubell quoted in Anthony Haden-Guest, *The Last Party: Studio 54, Disco, and the Culture of the Night* (New York: It Books, 1997), 268

84   Jordan T. Teicher, "New York's Fabulous 1980s and '90s Club Scene," *Slate* (March 13, 2014). http://www.slate.com/blogs/behold/2014/03/13/alexis_di_biasio_photographs_1980s_and_90s_new_york_club_culture_in_the.html

85   Haden-Guest, *The Last Party*, 353

86   Jezz Harkin and Tracey Wingrove, "Queen of Clubs," *i-D* (March 1991), p. n/a

87   Lisa Armstrong, "The First Lady of the Love Ball," *Independent* (22 May, 1991), 16

88   Eugene J. Patron, "Susanne Bartsch, Queen of the night," *M* (September 1989), 240

89   "Savage," *New York Magazine* (April 18, 1988), 53

90   David Yarritu, "Queen of Clubs," *Paper* (November 1988), 23–4

91   Quoted in Patron, 240

92   Roger Tredre, "Beautiful People's Fashion statement," *Independent* (20 March, 1991), p. n/a

93   Amy M. Spindler, "Monsieur Mugler," *Women's Wear Daily* (July 22, 1992), 4–5

94   http://www.dailymotion.com/video/xs2dyr_thierry-mugler-spring-summer-1992_creation

95   Patrick McMullan, "Nightlife: They Come Out at Night and Sparkle," in *20 Years of Style*, ed. Hastrieter and Hershkovits, 56

96   Teicher, "New York's Fabulous 1980s and '90s Club Scene"

97   Walt Cassidy, interview with author, March 6, 2015

98   James Michael Nichols, "After Dark: Linda Simpson, Drag Queen Celebrity and Nightlife Personality," *Huffington Post* (July 12, 2014). Last accessed February 12, 2015. http://www.huffingtonpost.com/2014/07/12/linda-simpson-after-dark_n_5578487.html

99   Ibid.

100 Michael Musto quoted in Haden-Guest, *The Last Party*, 353–4

101 James Michael Nichols, "After Dark: Meet Lady Bunny, Drag Icon and Wigstock Founder," *Huffington Post* (July 12, 2014). Last accessed February 13, 2015. http://www.huffingtonpost.com/2014/10/05/lady-bunny-after-dark_n_5932236.html

102 Ibid.

103 Leigh Bowery interview with David Yarritu, *Paper* (November 1987), p. n/a

104 RuPaul, "Drag, You Better Work!" in *20 Years of Style*, ed. Hastrieter and Hershkovits, 24

105 Fenton Bailey, "Superdrag: Get into Drag and Save the World," *Paper* (May 1990), 15

106 Nicholas, "After Dark: Meet Kenny Kenny"

107 McMullan, "Nightlife," 56

108 Amy M. Spindler, "A Mature Mugler, Demeulemeester, and Lang," *New York Times Magazine* (March 18, 1995), 29.

109 Evans, *Fashion at the Edge*, 20.

110 Holly Brubach (moderator), "Whose Vision is it Anyway?" *New York Times* (July 17, 1994), SM46.

111 Amy M. Spindler, "The Cutting Edge: In Need of a Whetstone," *New York Times* (May 16, 1995), B9.

112 "Talk of the Town: Attitude," *New Yorker* (January 16, 1989), 26.

113 Julianne Escobedo Shepherd, "New York is Burning: *Vogue*'s Move from Ballroom to Limelight," *Red Bull Music Academy* magazine (May 23, 2013). Last accessed March 28, 2015. http://www.redbullmusicacademy.com/magazine/new-york-is-burning

114 Ibid.

115 Ibid.

116 Woody Hochswender, "Vogueing Against AIDS: A Quest for 'Overness,'" *New York Times* (May 12, 1989), B1

117 Lola Ogunnaike, "Willi Ninja, 45, Self-created Star who Made Vogueing into an Art," *New York Times* (September 6, 2006), D8

118 *Project X*, Issue 9, 28; and Woody Hochswender, "Thierry Mugler: Nuts, Bolts, and Sequins," *New York Times* (March 18, 1989) 32

119 Haden-Guest, *The Last Party*, 319

120 James St. James, *Party Monster: A Fabulous but True Tale of Murder in Clubland* (New York: Simon & Schuster, 2003), 75

121 Owen, *Clubland*, p. 130.

122 Ibid., p. 130-131

123 Nichols, "After Dark: Meet James St. James"

124 Mhairi Graham, "Ernie Glam on the Fabulosity of Club Kids," *AnOther* (September 4, 2013). Last accessed February 24, 2015. http://www.anothermag.com/art-photography/2982/ernie-glam-on-the-fabulosity-of-club-kids

125 Marissa G. Muller, Michael Musto on the Prevailing Influence of Club Kid Fashion," *Fader* (May 2, 2014). Last accessed April 3, 2015. http://www.thefader.com/2014/05/02/michael-musto-on-the-prevailing-influence-of-club-kid-fashion

126 Mark Ronson, "Culture: Taboo," *Interview*. Last accessed May 18, 2015. http://www.interviewmagazine.com/culture/taboo/

127 Haden-Guest, *The Last Party*, 358

128 Graham, "Ernie Glam"

129 "The Age of Innocents," *New York* magazine (February 28, 1994), 62, 104–8

130 Janet Siroto, "Vogue's View: Future Chic," *Vogue* (March 1994), 164, 172, 178

131 Phil Donahue quoted in "New York Club Kids on Phil Donahue talkshow, 1993" YouTube video, 44:45, posted by "Theflush" (January 5, 2014), https://www.youtube.com/watch?v=llnSZqNGJtk

132 Amy M. Spindler, "The Cutting Edge," B9

133 Mary Tannen, "Under the Influence," *New York Times* (July 14, 1996), SM37

134 http://www.kabukimagic.com/biography.php. Last accessed April 4, 2015

135 William van Meter, "Another Life in the Many Lives of Zaldy: Zaldy, Onetime Club Kid, Model and Costumer to Pop Stars, Returns to Fashion Week," *New York Times* (September 7, 2014), ST18

136 S. M., "Mathu & Zaldy," *Project X*, First Anniversary Issue, No. 22, 43

137 Lawrence Ferber, "Heatherette: Pop Fashion Divas Richie Rich and Traver Rains," *Passport*. Last accessed March 9, 2015. http://www.passportmagazine.com/businessclass/Heatherette.php

138 Maggie Dolan,"Catching Up With Past Nightlife Award Winners: Heatherette," *Paper* (October 15, 2013). Last accessed May 18, 2015.

139 Ferber, "Heatherette: Pop Fashion Divas . . . "

140 Alicia Drake, "The Talented Mr. Scott," *W* (October 2010), 301

141 Wiliam van Meter, "Jeremy Scott, Fashion's Last Rebel," *New York Times* (December 1, 2011), E1

142 Ben Reardin, "We Love You Jeremy Scott!"*i-D*. The Ice Cream Issue, No. 278 (July 2007). Last accessed April 3, 2015. https://i-d.vice.com/en_au/article/we-love-you-jeremy-scott-aunz-translation

143 Meter, "Jeremy Scott "

144 Muller, "Michael Musto on the Prevailing Influence of Club Kid Fashion" *Fader* (May 2, 2014)

145 David Colman, "Going Gaga," *New York Times* (February 25, 2010), E1

146 James Michael Nichols, "After Dark: Domonique Echeverria, Fashion Designer and Nightlife Personality," *Huffington Post* (August 3, 2014). Last accessed April 3, 2015 http://www.huffingtonpost.com/2014/08/03/domonique-echeverria-after-dark_n_5641976.html

"1982, Strange Takes Fashion to the French," *Shapers of the 80s* website, Shapersofthe80s.com (date unknown)

Armstrong, Lisa. "The First Lady of the Love Ball," *Independent* (22 May, 1991)

Bailey, Fenton. "Superdrag: Get into Drag and Save the World," *Paper* (May 1990)

Beckett, Kathleen. "Fashion: A New Groove," *Vogue* (September 1, 1985)

"Between the Lines," *Daily News Record* (May 29, 1985)

Breward, Christopher, Edwina Ehrman, and Caroline Evans, *The London Look: Fashion from Street to Catwalk,* (New Haven and London: Yale University Press, 2004)

"BodyMap Interview with David Holah," *Fashion Fox* (July 10, 2013)

"BodyMap – Shaping the 1980s / Personalities / People / V&A Channel," Vam.ac.uk

Bowery, Leigh. Interview with David Yarritu, *Paper* (November 1987)

Brubach, Holly. "In Fashion: The Life of the Party," *New Yorker* (March 4, 1991)

—, "Whose Vision is it Anyway?" *New York Times* (July 17, 1994)

Burley, Isabella. "Cult VIP: Rachel Auburn," *Dazed & Confused* (February 2013)

Caves, Richard. *Creative Industries: Contracts Between Art and Commerce* (Cambridge: Harvard University Press, 2000)

Cochrane, Lauren. "1980s Throwback: Clubland's Charming Impact on Fashion Examined at V&A," *Guardian* website (July 8, 2013)

Cole, Shaun. *Don We Now Our Gay Apparel* (London: Bloomsbury, 2000)

Colman, David. "Going Gaga," *New York Times* (February 25, 2010)

Cooke-Newhouse, Ronnie. "Bartschroom Tile," *Details* (June 1985)

Costiff, Michael. *Michael and Gerlinde's World* (London: Slow Lorus Publishing, 2012)

Csikszentmihalyi, Mihaly. *Creativity: Flow and the Psychology of Discovery and Invention* (New York: Harper Perennial, 2013)

Doonan, Simon. *Wacky Chicks: Life Lessons from Fearlessly Inappropriate and Fabulously Eccentric Women* (New York: Simon & Schuster, 2003)

Drake, Alicia. "The Talented Mr. Scott," *W* (October 2010)

Duka, John. "The Latest From London Arrives in SoHo (Ours)," *New York Times* (August 25, 1981)

Elan, Priya. "It's Blitz: Birth of the New Romantics," *Guardian* (May 14, 2010)

Evans, Caroline. *Fashion at the Edge: Spectacle, Modernity, and Deathliness* (New Haven and London: Yale University Press, 2003)

Ferber, Lawrence "Heatherette: Pop Fashion Divas Richie rich and Traver Rains," *Passport* http://www.passportmagazine.com/businessclass/Heatherette.php?pagenum=1

Foderaro, Lisa W. "Giltz, Funk, and Victoriana Enliven New York's Discos," *New York Times* (March 27, 1987)

Galtney, Smith. "A Night Out with Susanne Bartsch," *New York Times* (April 28, 2002)

Goode, Eric and Jennifer. *Area: 1983–1987* (New York: Abrams, 2013)

Graham, Mhairi. "Ernie Glam on the Fabulosity of Club Kids," *AnOther* (September 4, 2013)

Hastrieter, Kim, and David Hershkovits (eds.), *20 Years of Style: The World According to Paper* (New York: Harper Collins, 2004)

Haden-Guest, Anthony. *The Last Party: Studio 54, Disco, and the Culture of the Night* (New York: It Books, 1997)

Harkin, Jezz, and Tracey Wingrove, "Queen of Clubs," *i-D* (March 1991)

"Have you Seen Satan? The Conservative Cabal has Managed to Make Nightlife Exciting Again," *Paper* (November 1990)

Healy, Robyn. "Taboo or Not Taboo: The Fashions of Leigh Bowery," *Art Journal of the National Gallery of Victoria,* Edition 42 (2002) National Gallery of Victoria, Australia

Hoare, Phillip. "Obituaries: Leigh Bowery," *Independent* (January 5, 1995)

Hochswender, Woody. "Vogueing Against AIDS: A Quest for 'Overness,'" *New York Times* (May 12, 1989)

—, "Thierry Mugler: Nuts, Bolts, and Sequins," *New York Times* (March 18, 1989)

Johnson, David. "Spandau Ballet, the Blitz Kids and the Birth of the New Romantics," *Guardian* (October 4, 2009)

—, "What Other People Say: David Johnson," *The Blitz Club* website (date unknown)

kabukimagic.com/biography.php

Larrson, Ulf (ed.), *Cultures of Creativity: The Centennial Exhibition of the Nobel Prize* (Canton: Science History Publications, 2001)

Lewis, Tim. "'The Birth of the London Club Scene': Bowie Nights at Billy's Club," *Guardian* (January 25, 2013)

Loriot, Thierry-Maxime (ed.), *The Fashion World of John Paul Gaultier: From the Sidewalk to the Catwalk* (New York: Abrams, 2011)

M., S. "Mathu & Zaldy," *Project X,* First Anniversary Issue, No. 22 (date unknown)

Mayo Davies, Dean. "Stephen Jones," *Dazed & Confused* (2013)

Meter, William van. "Another Life in the Many Lives of Zaldy: Zaldy, Onetime Club Kid, Model and Costumer to Pop Stars, Returns to Fashion Week," *New York Times* (September 7, 2014)

—, "Jeremy Scott, Fashion's Last Rebel," *New York Times* (December 1, 2011)

Milligan, Lauren. "We Can Be Heroes," *Vogue* (December 15, 2011)

Morris, Bernadine. "A New Vitality Marks Openings in London," *New York Times* (16 October, 1984)

Muller, Marissa G. "Michael Musto on the Prevailing Influence of Club Kid Fashion," *Fader* (May 2, 2014)

Nichols, James Michael. "After Dark: Meet Kenny Kenny, Visual Poet and Nightlife Icon," *Huffington Post* (August 31, 2014)

O'Byrne, Robert. *Style City: How London Became a Fashion Capital* (London: Frances Lincoln Limited, 2009)

Ogunnaike, Lola. "Willi Ninja, 45, Self-created Star who Made Vogueing into an Art," *New York Times* (September 6, 2006)

Owen, Frank. *Clubland: The Fabulous Rise and Murderous Fall of Club Culture* (New York: Broadway Books, 2004)

Patron, Eugene J. "Susanne Bartsch, Queen of the night," *M* (September 1989)

Pollhemus, Ted. *Street Style: From Sidewalk to Catwalk* (New York: Thames & Hudson, 1994)

Project X, Issue 9

Reardin, Ben. "We Love You Jeremy Scott!"*i-D.* The Ice Cream Issue, No. 278 (July 2007)

Ronson, Mark. "Taboo," *Interview,* (date unknown)

"Savage," *New York Magazine* (April 18, 1988)

Savage, Mark. "Steve Strange: The Custodian of New Romantic Pop," *BBC News* website (February 13, 2015)

Shepherd, Julianne Escobedo. "New York is Burning: *Vogue*'s Move from Ballroom to Limelight," *Red Bull Music Academy* magazine (May 23, 2013)

Siroto, Janet. "Vogue's View: Future Chic," *Vogue* (March 1994)

Smith, Liz. "What a Scream in New York," *Standard* (April 26, 1983)

Spindler, Amy M. "Monsieur Mugler," *Women's Wear Daily* (July 22, 1992)

—, "A Mature Mugler, Demeulemeester, and Lang," *New York Times Magazine* (March 18, 1995)

—, "The Cutting Edge: In Need of a Whetstone," *New York Times* (May 16, 1995)

St. James, James. *Party Monster: A Fabulous but True Tale of Murder in Clubland* (New York: Simon & Schuster, 2003)

Stanfill, Sonnet. *80s Fashion: From Club to Catwalk* (London: V&A Publishing, 2013)

"Talk of the Town: Attitude," *New Yorker* (January 16, 1989)

Tannen, Mary. "Under the Influence," *New York Times* (July 14, 1996)

Teicher, Jordan T. "New York's Fabulous 1980s and '90s Club Scene," *Slate* (March 13, 2014)

Thornton, Sarah. *Club Cultures: Music, Media and Subcultural Capital* (Cambridge: Polity Press, 1995)

Tilley, Sue. *Leigh Bowery: The Life and Times of an Icon* (London: Hodder & Stoughton, 1997)

Townley, Barbara, Nic Beech, Alan McKinley, and Gail Fairhurst (eds.) "Managing in the Creative Industries: Managing the Motley Crew," *Human Relations*, vol. 62(7) (2009)

Tredre, Roger. "Beautiful People's Fashion statement," *Independent* (20 March, 1991)

Vogelson, Nick. "Susanne Bartsch Talks with Joey Arias about Resurrecting Nightlife Countless Times Over," *Document* (September 29, 2014)

"We can be Heroes – A New Collection by Graham Smith," Photographic Youth Music Culture Archive (P.Y.M.C.A.) (May 16, 2012)

"What I did at the Blitz," excerpt from *Record Mirror* (December 1983). *The Blitz Kids* website (date unknown)

White, Lesley. "The New Glitterati," *The Face*, Issue 485 (April 1984)

Whitney, Christine. "The Original Club Kids," *Harper's Bazaar* (May 31, 2013)

Yarritu, David. "Queen of Clubs," *Paper* (November 1988)

Yordanov, Oggy. *New Club Kids* (Munich, London, New York: Prestel, 2011)

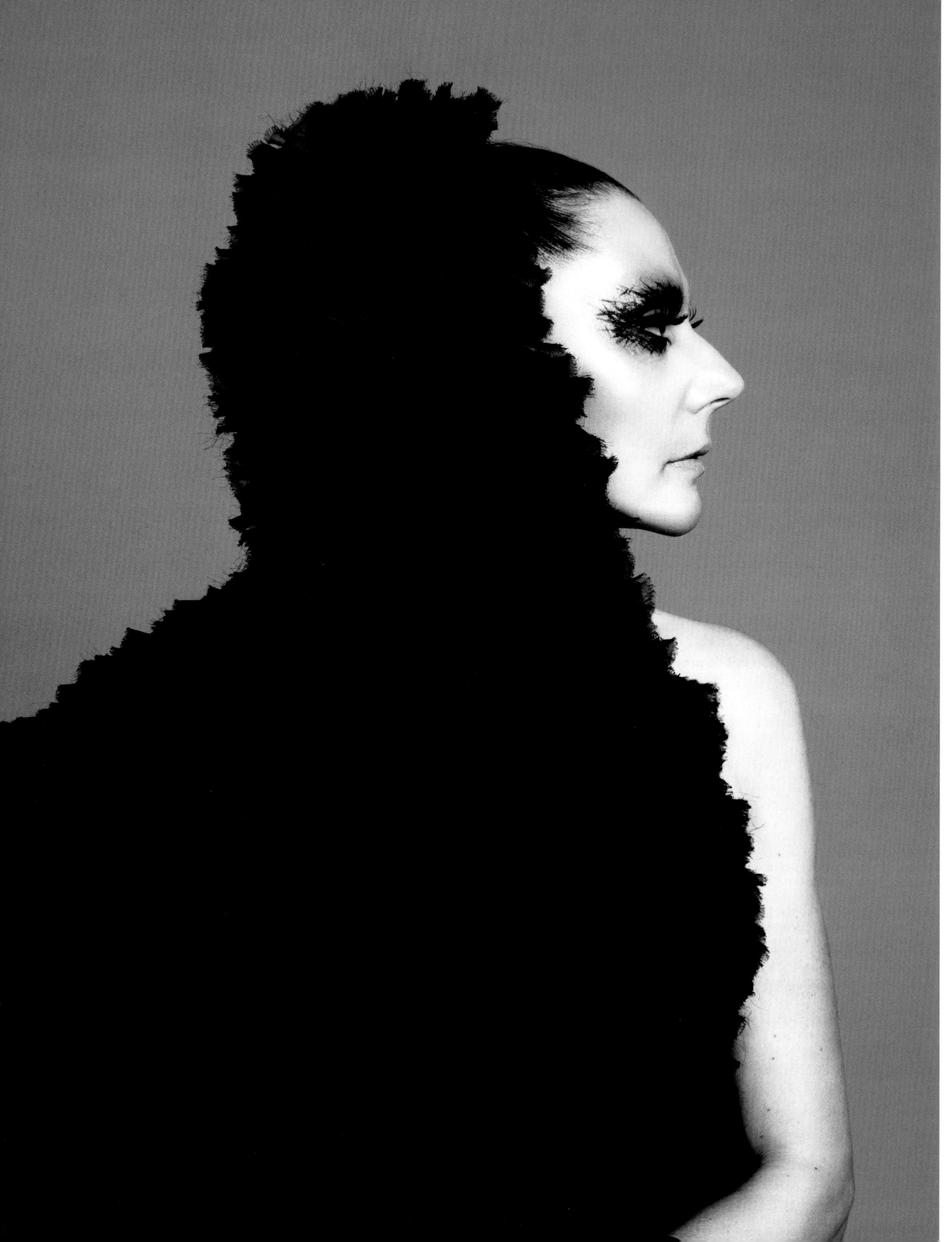

Acknowledgments

Many people helped to make this book possible. It was a pleasure working with Susanne Bartsch and Waleed Khairzada, our collaborators on this project. The exhibition, book, and related public programs have been made possible thanks to The Couture Council of The Museum at FIT and MAC Cosmetics, with additional support provided by the Standard Hotel. As always we wish to thank Dr. Joyce F. Brown, the president of the Fashion Institute of Technology, as well as our FIT colleagues, Shari Prussin, Loretta Lawrence Keane, Cheryl Fein, Carol Levin, Alexandra Mann, Robert Ferguson, Dirrane Cove, Stephen Tuttle, and Rina Grassotti.

Thanks also to our colleagues at the Museum at FIT who contributed their time and efforts to this book, especially Eileen Costa, museum photographer; Julian Clark, publications coordinator; Vanessa Vasquez, assistant to the director; Nateer Cirino and Theresa Reniere, administrative assistants. Because this book accompanies an exhibition, we would also like to extend our thanks to Patricia Mears, deputy director; Fred Dennis, senior curator of costume; Ann Coppinger and the conservation team, Marjorie Jonas and Nicole Bloomfield; Thomas Synnamon, installation specialist; Sonia Dingilian and the registrarial department, Jill Hemingway, Laura Gawron and Lynn Weidner; Michael Goitia and the exhibitions team, Boris Chesakov, Gabrielle Lauricella, and Gail Bowden; Tanya Melendez, curator of education and public programs; Faith Cooper, education assistant; Tamsen Young, digital media and strategic initiatives manager; Mindy Meissen, assistant museum media coordinator; the curatorial team, Colleen Hill, Ariel Elia, Emma McClendon, Ellen Shanley, Elizabeth Way; and Lynn Sallaberry, administrative secretary. Thanks also to Julie Marinet, education intern, as well as to Laura Donovan and Blaze Javier Mandela.

Our sincere thanks also go out to Kim Ackert, exhibitions designer, and Matthias Kern, graphic designer for the exhibition. Special thanks to Thierry-

Susanne Bartsch for *Annabelle* magazine, Zurich, Switzerland, December 2012.
Photo by Paola Kudacki.

Maxime Loriot for his contributions to the exhibition design. Thanks also to Will Automagic, Johnny Dynell, Alan Mace/Sister Dimension, Michael Magnan, Severino Panzetta (Horsemeat Disco), and Amber Valentine for the music in the exhibition. Thanks to Leo Herrera, Adriana Kaegi, Anton Perich, and Jeff Schwartz (Primalux) for their work on the video that accompanies the exhibition.

We extend our gratitude to everyone who participated in interviews and shared their insight and experiences with us for this project: Mathu Andersen, Piers Atkinson, Joey Arias, Rachel Auburn, Marc Balet, André Balazs, David Barton, Mickey Boardman, Hamish Bowles, Walt Cassidy, Maria Cornejo, Michael Costiff, Greg Davis, Danilo, Simon Doonan, Scott Ewalt, Patricia Field, Robert Forrest, James Gager, Zaldy Goco, Angela Golding, Paula Greif, Kim Hastreiter, Stephen Jones, Waleed Khairzada, Steven Klein, Michael Leva, Roxanne Lowit, Patrick McMullan, Michael Musto, Ronnie Newhouse, Tim Palen, Ru Paul, Diane Pernet, Mao Padilha, Roger Padilha, Richie Rich, Jed Root, Ian Schrager, Kabuki Starshine, Abel Villarreal, Andre Walker, and Lynn Yaeger.

We are grateful to the photographers and artists whose work is featured in this book, especially Mathu Andersen, Amy Arbus, Josef Astor, Andrea Barbiroli, Emily Berl, Lukas Beyeler, David LaChapelle, Jesse Chehak, Citizen Chris, David Corio, Oliver Correa, Michael Costiff, Bill Cunningham, Wouter Deruytter, Alexis Di Biasio, Simon Doonan, Driu Crilly & Tiago Martel, Jeff Eason, Todd Eberle, Arthur Elgort, Scott Ewalt, Santiago Felipe, Lisa Fiel, Jesse Frohman, Fergus Greer, Ernie Glam, Michel Haddi, Hartnett, Steven Klein, Paola Kudacki, Roxanne Lowit, Patrick Mettraux, Niall McInerney, Patrick McMullan, Steven Menendez, Jeff Mermelstein, Rob Moritz, Françoise Nars, Michael James O'Brien, Mark C. O'Flaherty, Marco Ovando, Mao Padilha, Tim Palen, Tina Paul, Ves Pitts, Ted Polhemus, Len Prince, Albert Sanchez, Rico & Michael, Norbert Schoerner, Linda Simpson/Drag Explosion, Rebecca Smeyne, Graham Smith, Jason Akira Somma, Robin Souma, John Swannell, Nicola Tyson, Maria Chandoha Valentino, Gerry Visco, Brandon Voss, Ben Watts, Bruce Weber, Laura Weyl, Mark Williams, Richie Williamson, and Olivier Zahm.

A special thanks to all those who took time to dig through their archives to source materials for our project.

We would like to thank all the designers who provided looks especially for this project: Piers Atkinson, Dsquared, Zaldy Goco, Heather Huey, Pam Hogg, Hood by Air, Stephen Jones, Norma Kamali, Manfred T. Mugler, Rick Owens, Gareth Pugh, Studio Formichetti, and The Blonds. Thank you to all the creatures for contributing looks to the exhibition: Ryan Burke and Dominique Echeverria, Gage of the Boone, Onehalf Nelson, Johanna Constantine, Muffinhead, and Adam VanBuren.

Thanks are owed also to the many individuals and institutions who provided assistance along the way, especially: Deney Adam; Adele Roostein Mannequins;

Vanessa Aviles; *Annabelle* magazine, especially Annette Keller; Antoine and Nicholas at Diktats Books; Art Department, especially Melody Brynner; Bailey Barton; Bloomsbury Publishing, especially Emily Ardizzone; Charley Brown; Condé Nast, especially Leigh Montville; Dayfornightoffice, especially Riyo Nemeth; Danilo; Keith Dunhill; Nicola Formichetti; Zoltan Gerliczki; Chris Gonzalez; Sara Gruenwald; Autumn Johnson; Kim Jones; Devin Kelly; Peter Koblish; LaChapelle studio, especially Kumi Tanimura and Ghretta Hynd; Marcus Leatherdale; Little Bear Inc., especially Hillery Estes and Matthew Richards; Michael Magnan; Raquel Martuscelli; MCV Studio, especially Nina Westervelt; Bob and Darlene Moritz; Manfred T. Mugler; NARS cosmetics, especially Yana Chernova; the *New York Times*, especially John Kurdewan; Linda Ogawa (INFAS); Shayne Oliver; Alicia Oliveri; Brandon Olson; Oribe; *Paper* magazine; Patrick Elziere of Gayvox.fr; Patrick McMullan Company, especially Ava Grumberg and Ashley Collins; Petzel Gallery, especially Andrew Black; Dustin Pittman; Mike Prieto; PYMCA, especially Jamie Brett; Kareem Rashid; Raechel Jae Rosen; Roxanne Lowit Studio, especially Shoko Takayasu; Aaron Sciandra; Horatio Silver; Stephen Jones Millinery, especially Annika Lievesley; Steven Klein Studio, especially Adam Sherman; Todd Eberle Studio, especially Vincent Munoz; and Brandon Voss.

And, last but not least, we would like to thank Gillian Malpass, our editor at Yale University Press, and our talented book designer, Paul Sloman.

If we have forgotten anyone or if despite our best efforts, we have not been able to trace all copyright holders, please inform us and we shall make corrections in the next edition of the book.

Valerie Steele and Melissa Marra

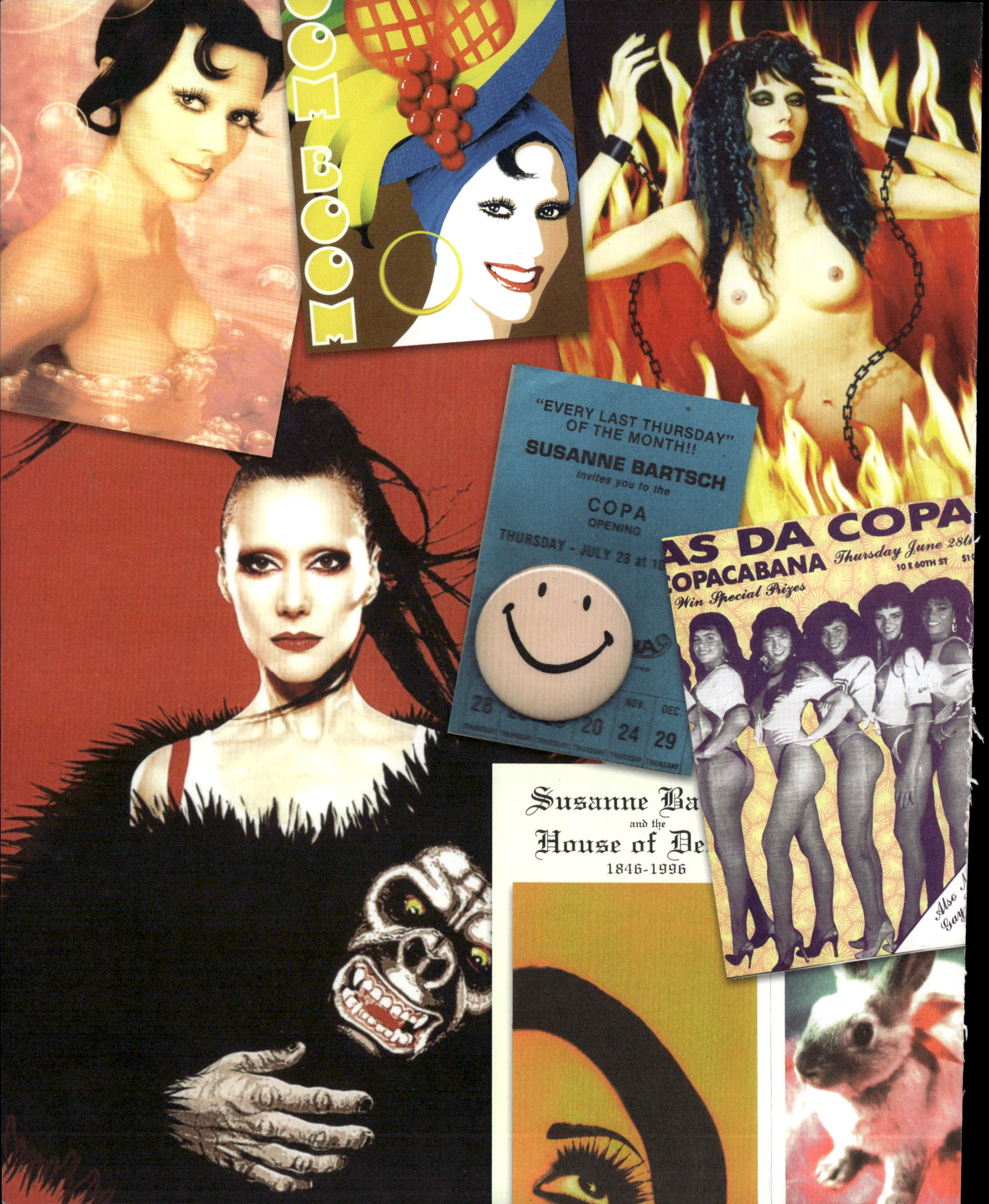
BOOM BOOM
"EVERY LAST THURSDAY"
OF THE MONTH!!
SUSANNE BARTSCH
invites you to the
COPA
OPENING
THURSDAY - JULY 28 at 10
28
NOV.
20
24
DEC.
29
AS DA COPA
COPACABANA
Win Special Prizes
Thursday June 28
10 E 60TH ST
$10
Susanne Ba
and the
House of De
1846-1996
Also
Gay